"1999 will see a stampede of small businesses to the Web, eager to profit from a niche in ecommerce. This Gold Rush mentality will lead to exorbitant prices for questionable services, extravagant promises, broken hopes and a fair amount of fraud. Too bad. As Peter Kent and Tara Calishain point out in this remarkably readable book, building a brand online is mainly a matter of investing a reasonable amount of time and effort. It doesn't have to take a huge budget. The authors take the reader through the ins and outs of all the various approaches—banner ads, reciprocal links, cross-promotion with print, etc.—and present a clear, balanced discussion that is completely free of jargon and hype. Any small business interested in the Web and any Web designer helping small business establish an online presence will find this book invaluable. Five stars."

Web d[...]

"As if *Poor Richard's Web Site* wasn't helpful enough [...] Calishain) has gone one better in *Poor Richard's Internet Marketing and Promotion.* These folks are human spiders; they've crawled into every corner of the 'net and spun their findings into a compact, immensely practical guide and source book. As the developer of *It's Your Move!*, and having just now finished phase one of my first Web site, this book fills me with confidence that I can engage in all of what it takes to bring value to many through the Internet, and reap value in return.

The genie of Peter Kent's and Tara Calishain's experience appears the moment you turn the first page. Their considerable knowledge and expertise are at my command. If one had to pay a consultant for this information the outlay would likely be as vast as the net itself. I cannot overstate the value and utility of this book."

—Bart Windrum
Developer of It's Your Move: http://softsmart.com/

"I found some good ideas in *Poor Richard's Internet Marketing and Promotions.* It also answered some questions I had about promoting our business on the Internet. As I go through the book for the second time, I will be extracting the sections that I need to accomplish our goals. This book is written at a level such that moderately skilled computer users should have no problem applying the information."

—Bob Fiddes, Yuma, Arizona

"Some of the best down-to-earth, commonsense advice that anyone could hope for on the topic of building and surviving on the Net. It was easy to read and flowed very nicely. I can't see anyone being disappointed after receiving and reading it. A great 'no hype' guide!"

—Big Al
Director, Online Success, Member Support Dept.
http://www.online-venture.com/

"Peter Kent again delivers! As with *Poor Richard's Web Site: Geek-Free Commonsense Advice on Building a Low-Cost Web Site,* Peter gives us an amazing amount of highly practical, timely, cost-effective and *in-depth* information and advice on a very broad subject in a highly-readable style and in *plain English.* Kudos to you, Peter!"

—Sylvia Willis
ELEKTRA-WORX: Promotion by Design

"Five stars! Excellent! This book is the perfect investment for anyone planning to market or promote on the Internet. Sure to be another best seller for Peter Kent, this is the only book on the subject that I would recommend."

—Sammi Karkkainen
WriteTech Communications, Astoria, Oregon

"This is an absolute marketing essential for any DIY webmaster responsible for getting a new site up for the first time. If you want your site to produce results, look no farther.

—Walter Strong
Halcyon Communications Group

"I have just finished reviewing a draft of the Peter Kent's new book *Poor Richard's Internet Marketing and Promotions* and I believe he has another winner. I trust he will continue the great work of offering advice and fresh material on this book as he did with the last one."

—Maurice Shuck
SilkenWeb

Press reviews of the first book in the *Poor Richard* series, *Poor Richard's Web Site: Geek-Free, Commonsense Advice on Building a Low-Cost Web Site ...*

"**Poor Richard's Good Advice.** With all great new things comes a proliferation of hucksters and snake-oil salesmen, and the Internet is no exception. The antidote to this swirl of confusion lies in Peter Kent's *Poor Richard's Web Site.* The analogy to Ben Franklin's volume is appropriate: the book is filled with the kind of straightforward information the Founding Father himself would have appreciated."

—Jennifer Buckendorff ⌂ **amazon**.com

"**Hot Site** ... Let [Peter Kent] provide what he calls "geek-free, commonsense advice" on building a low-cost site on the Web."

—*USA Today* Web site

"**Book of the Week**" *SmartBooks.com*

Poor Richard's Internet Marketing and Promotions

How to Promote Yourself, Your Business, Your Ideas Online

by
Peter Kent and Tara Calishain

TOP FLOOR PUBLISHING
http://TopFloor.com/

For my wife, Debbie.
—*Peter Kent*

This book is dedicated to my husband and my family.
—*Tara Calishain*

Acknowledgements

I'd like to thank everyone involved in creating this book. Tara Calishain, of course, who, with her background in public relations and Internet research, added a lot of information that I wasn't aware of. I'd also like to thank Phyllis Beaty, of Magnolia Studio, for her book design, layout, and project coordination; Tim Doyle, of Doyle Communications, for the cover design; Faithe Wempen for editing; David Wise for proofreading; and Elizabeth Cunningham for indexing.

I'd also like to thank all the people who read the book before publication. And a really special thanks to all the members of the press who reviewed the first in this series, *Poor Richard's Web Site*, and praised it so highly. It gave the series a fantastic launch, and allowed *Poor Richard's Internet Marketing and Promotions* to follow in the footsteps of a publishing success.

—*Peter Kent*

Peter Kent—Peter, thank you so much for letting me be a part of this book. I've wanted to write about this topic for a long time, and I'm thrilled you gave me the opportunity.

My husband—Living with a writer is not easy sometimes. Luckily I have the greatest spouse in the universe. My step-kids are pretty great, too—while they were visiting over the holidays, they had to put up with Tara-As-Typing-Zombie-On-Deadline.

My friends—Martha has helped me get more focus in my writing this year and has been a good friend. Thanks, Martha! Calvin helped me get some much-needed work done. Thanks, Calvin!

My family—Granny, Nora, Jay, Rachel, Gerd, Michael, Caroline, and everybody else in the supper bunch. I have a great family. Also a big thanks to my extended family up North—Irene, Becky, Bill, Art, Marie, Joy, June, Jim, Tina, and everyone else …

—*Tara Calishain*

About the Authors

Peter Kent is the author of 36 business and computer books. His work has appeared in a variety of publications, from the *Manchester Guardian* to *Internet World, Computerworld* to *Dr. Dobb's Journal.*

Also by Peter Kent

The CDnow Story: Rags to Riches on the Internet
     (Top Floor Publishing; with Jason Olim and Matthew Olim)
Poor Richard's Web Site: Geek-Free, Commonsense Advice on
     Building a Low-Cost Web Site (Top Floor Publishing)
Poor Richard's Internet Marketing and Promotions
     (Top Floor Publishing–February 1999)
The Complete Idiot's Guide to the Internet, 5th Edition (Que)
The Ten Minute Guide to the Internet (Que)
The Best Sex of Your Life (Barricade; with Dr. Jim White)
Discover Windows NT Workstation 4.0 (IDG)
Discover FrontPage 97 (IDG)
The Official Netscape JavaScript 1.2 Book (Ventana; with John Kent)
Using Netscape Communicator 4 (Que)
Making Money in Technical Writing (Macmillan/ARCO)
The Official Netscape JavaScript Programmer's Reference
     (Ventana; with Kent Multer)
Career Ideas for Kids Who Like Computers (Facts on File)

———————

Tara Calishain is the co-author of *Official Netscape Guide to Internet Research, 2nd Edition,* and has been the author or co-author of several other books. She's the owner of CopperSky Writing & Research.

Contents at a Glance

Table of Contents

PART II: WEB SITE REGISTRATIONS

PART V: OUTSIDE THE INTERNET

Introduction

We all know the Internet is paved with gold; we've heard that enough from the press over the last five years. "Just set up shop on the Internet, and you'll be inundated with orders. So you don't really need this book ..."

Of course reality is very different from the Internet hype we've been fed. You may have heard that a Web site is a billboard on the Information Superhighway; it's not. A Web site sits in the darkness of cyberspace, waiting for people to visit. Unlike a billboard, which is seen by anyone who glances up as they drive or walk by, a Web site is only seen if the viewer has *chosen* to see it. A conscious decision must be made. And the competition for attention is stiff, too. There are far more Web sites to choose from—many thousands of times more—than billboards lined along your daily drive to work or school.

So in the real cyberspace, as opposed to the media-created myth, the Internet most certainly is not paved with gold, or even with silver. That's the bad news. The good news is that you really can benefit from the Internet, either in a direct financial manner or a more indirect way. You've just got to work at it.

That's where this book comes in. Tara and I have been using the Internet for real. This isn't a book written by a writer who's been given an assignment. It's not a "find out as much about marketing and promotions on the Internet and write a book for us" sort of thing. We actually market and promote real products and services on the Internet.

Here's an example. I promoted the first book in this series—*Poor Richard's Web Site: Geek-Free Commonsense Advice on Building a Low-Cost Web Site*—on the Internet. Despite the fact that my publishing company, Top Floor Publishing, is a small company with very limited resources, that book became probably the most widely reviewed title in computer-book history. Top Floor Publishing grossed around $35,000 in Web site sales in the first 12 months of the book's life, and thousands of copies were sold through bookstores. Around 10,000 copies were sold in the first year, a decent number for any publisher, let alone one working on a shoestring budget. And at the time of writing sales of that book seem to be accelerating, as it becomes more well-known and appears in the press over and over again.

How was this publicity achieved? I used many of the techniques you'll learn about in this book to get *Poor Richard's Web Site* into the hands of journalists, to drive people to my Web site, and to sell the book at the site. But there's more. Tara Calishain has added many other things to the mix, little techniques that I was unaware of. Tara's specialty is research; she's written a book about Internet research (*Official Netscape Guide to Internet Research, 2nd Edition*, Netscape Press), and has worked in public relations (out in the "real world"). She has also used many of the techniques you'll find in this book to promote her work online.

In fact, one problem you may run into is that you'll find *too many* techniques in this book. I received an e-mail message the other day from an entrepreneur asking how he could "apply all of this dynamite information to two (as yet unpublished) Web sites, run one business, start the second, learn FrontPage while simultaneously designing both Web Sites, …" Good question. Sometimes you just have to pick and choose what you're going to do. You can't do everything, so you have to decide what you think might work for you. And don't imagine that everyone else out there on the Internet is working a 40-hour week. Someone once said that an entrepreneur is someone who works 18 hours a day for himself, so that he doesn't have to work 8 hours a day for someone else. The Internet is a new entrepreneurial arena; there are plenty of us working 18-hour days!

Read the entire book, and then pick and choose the techniques you want to use. But do *something*. If you're trying to promote a product, service, or idea on the Internet, you can't afford to just set up a Web site and wait for something to happen. You've got to *make it happen*, and this book will show you how.

—*Peter Kent*

PART I

PREPARATION

CHAPTER ONE

What Are You Promoting and Who Are You Targeting?

The first thing you need to do before beginning your marketing and promotion campaign is to decide exactly what you are promoting, what you want to achieve, and who you are targeting. Before we begin, though, we need to explain a little shortcut that we use throughout this book. We talk about how you can promote your *product* or *service,* but in fact you can use the techniques in this book to promote just about anything. You can promote a physical item you're selling, your political ideas, your religious beliefs, a charitable institution, a sports team, a hobby, a club or association ... just about anything you want to get into the public eye. The principles are the same. Perhaps most readers of this book have something to sell. But a great deal of activity on the Internet—possibly most, depending on how you measure it—is non-commercial. So those of you promoting something other than a product or service will, we hope, forgive us if we sound a little too commercial ... and should understand that these techniques can be used for many different purposes.

Let's begin, then. We'll start with three premises—let's call them *Poor Richard's Laws of Promotions*:

1. No one knows as much about you and your product or service as you do.
2. No one cares as much about you and your product or service as you do.
3. That's as it should be.

Whether you've got a million-dollar company or a dog-walking service (or even a million-dollar dog-walking service) no one's ever going to feel the drive and enthusiasm for your product or service that you do. Even if you hire someone to advertise and promote your company, you'll never be able to impart to them everything you know about your company or industry. Nor will you be able to infect anyone else with your enthusiasm. (Remember, every parent thinks his or her child is beautiful … but other people may have a quite different view!)

If you've picked up this book, it's quite possible that you're on your own and you need to do some online marketing and promotion. The above laws are good news for you! You've got the knowledge to effectively promote your product; now all you need are the tools. And here's a little more good news: the tools we're going to describe in this book, the various Internet systems and techniques, provide a very low-cost and effective way to promote your products and services. (We'll be looking at a few expensive tools, such as banner advertising, but it's quite possible to create a very effective Internet-promotion campaign without getting involved with those sorts of things.)

But maybe you're a little suspicious of this whole promotion and marketing thing. Who needs it, anyway?

WHY PROMOTE?

Long ago, when everyone lived within the confines of a small town, promotion wasn't an issue. If you ran the only grocery store, people *had* to buy their groceries from you. Hanging out your shingle pretty much ensured some business when you were the only game in town.

As cities got bigger, of course, more options became available. Suddenly grocers had to compete. But there was still a limit; people would drive only so far for groceries. Grocers for the most part had to be concerned with other grocery stores only within a limited area.

With the Internet, the limitation on geography is virtually eliminated—in some cases, at least. Perhaps not so much for grocery stores, but certainly for stores of other kinds. Customers can order from music and bookstores all over the world, for instance. Even before CDnow (http://www.cdnow.com/) opened a distribution center in Europe, for example, they were shipping 25 percent to 35 percent of their products outside the borders of the U.S. The process of freeing commerce from geography has just begun, but it's moving quickly. People will do more and more of their shopping—for goods and services—online.

From the marketing point of view, this is a double-edged sword. Yes, you may be able to sell your products on the other side of the world. But perhaps people on the other side of the world can now sell products in *your* neighborhood, too. Unless you're selling specialty items for left-handed yak herders whose favorite color is mauve (and perhaps not even then), you're not the only game in town! You've got the whole world, potentially, to compete with.

So this Internet thing is both good and bad news. We hear a lot about the good news, but don't underestimate the bad; online *sales* are cutting into real-world sales. Bookstores in Europe, for instance, are very concerned about the number of books being sold by Amazon.com.

Still, from the marketing and promotion point of view, it's pretty good news. You also have the whole world as potential customers. But in order to reach them you're going to have to market and promote your product or service. You're going to have to get the word out, rise above the crowd, shout above the storm, and all those other clichés.

You've probably heard the maxim that if you "build a better mousetrap, the world will beat a path to your door." Well … it's not true. It doesn't matter how good your product is; if nobody knows about it, nobody will buy it. This is not news to people who have been in sales, promotions, and marketing in the real world. Many people on the Internet don't understand this concept, though, for two main reasons:

1. Because it's relatively cheap and easy to set up a business on the Internet, many people who have never been in business before are setting up shop online. Many of these people don't understand very basic principles of sales and promotions.

2. The media has hyped the Internet terribly. You've probably heard that a Web site is like a billboard on the Information Superhighway. It's not. If it were true, all you'd need to do is set up a Web site and take orders. But a Web site sits in the darkness of cyberspace, seen by nobody … until you convince someone to visit your site.

Here's another reason to promote a product online. Promoting on the Internet really does work. But of course that's what this book is all about. You're going to discover *how* to make it work.

Now that you're converted (we hope), let's take a look at what promotion and marketing actually involve.

WHAT ARE PROMOTION AND MARKETING?

There's a little confusion about these two terms, *promotion* and *marketing*. So let's look at a couple of dictionary definitions. The term *marketing* has been used for more than 400 years. It's variously defined as the process of selling a product or service; as the process of promoting, selling, and distributing a product or service; and as the entire process of moving goods and services from a producer to a consumer. So *promotion* or *promotions* is a subset of marketing; it's the process of encouraging people to accept or buy your goods or services.

This book is titled *Poor Richard's Internet Marketing and Promotions* because the two processes are interlinked, because they overlap, and because in many people's minds they tend to mean much the same things. To make clear what this book covers, then, here's what we plan to explain in this book:

This book covers how to let people know about your products and services using newsletter ads, giving away products at other people's Web sites, reciprocal links, answering questions in discussion groups, free and paid banner ads, and other methods. It will teach you how to use a Web site to provide information and take sales—how to find a shopping-cart system, for instance, how to take orders, and even how to find a fulfillment company (a company that can ship your products for you). This book is an overview of the entire process of marketing and promotions.

PROMOTION AND MARKETING REQUIRE STEADY WORK

You have to promote and market over time because ...

- Getting an idea into people's minds and keeping it there takes a lot of time and effort. It's not something that's done once and "sticks;" you have to keep working at it. Call it "mindshare."

- More people get on the Internet every day. (The Internet population was at one point increasing exponentially and has only recently slowed.)

- More competition gets on the Internet every day (unless you're catering to those left-handed yak herders, of course).

- There is still time to brand yourself. Yes, everyone thinks of Amazon when it comes to buying books online—but who do they think of when shopping for a car? Looking for a real-estate service? Trying to buy videos online? When it comes to buying and selling, the Internet is still very young, and by marketing and promoting yourself you can establish your dominance in an unclaimed niche.

As you can see, there are several reasons to promote online, several ways to do it, and a strong impetus to continue your effort over time. But enough about the whys and wherefores of this book—let's talk about *you*.

YOUR WEB SITE AS A MARKETING AND PROMOTIONS CENTER

We believe that a Web site is a great way to start your marketing and promotions. Your Web site can be your center of operations, your headquarters.

It's possible to promote products and services without ever creating a Web site. Many consultants promote themselves in newsgroups and mailing-list discussion groups, for instance, a subject we discuss in Chapter 9. In the late eighties and early nineties, for example, Peter promoted his technical-writing services in CompuServe's discussion groups. At that time there was no Web, so having a Web site was not an option. Still, he was able to find literally tens of thousands of dollars in business by promoting his services online.

We really believe that these days, however, it makes sense to have a Web site, if only because Web sites are so cheap and easy to create. So we're working under the assumption that you will have a Web site, and that your Web site will be your center of operations. And indeed that's what most people do. If the Web had been available to Peter during his CompuServe-promotion days, he would have created a Web site to hold a resumé, samples of his work, a list of clients, and so on. However, most people don't think of their Web site as the center of their operations. Here's what most people do:

1. Set up a Web site.
2. Register the Web site with the search engines.
3. Wait for people to visit.

That's not making the Web site the *center* of operations. In this case the Web site is the entirety of the operations.

Here's what we think you should do:

1. Set up a Web site.
2. Register the Web site with the search engines.
3. Do lots and lots of other things to bring people to your site.

We'll be talking about #1 in Chapter 3. We'll be talking about #2 in Chapters 5 and 6. And as for #3, that's what the bulk of this book is all about.

In effect your Web site becomes an intermediate step. You go out and promote your Web site in order to bring people to the site, so that they will learn about your products and services and, we hope, buy something.

PROMOTING YOUR WEB SITE, PRODUCTS, AND SERVICES

There's a very important principle to consider here. Your Web site has to serve you, and it has to serve your visitors. If it doesn't serve you, it has no purpose, of course. But if it doesn't serve your visitors … you won't have any visitors.

If you use your Web site as an intermediate step—bringing people to the site to promote your products and services—then you have to think carefully about what you have to offer at your Web site. Just as there are good products and bad products to sell, there are good and bad Web sites to promote. When you are out there promoting your products and services directly, you should also consider what you are saying, and whether people are really likely to care. Let's look at the bad stuff first.

The Bad Stuff

Your Web Site as a Brochure

Let's get something clear. We have no objections to brochures as instruments of marketing; a photograph on slick paper really is worth a thousand words. However, sometimes you'll see someone who puts up a Web site that is, essentially, only a brochure. It has a price, and lots of marketing copy, and a couple of snazzy photographs. And they try to promote it. There's nothing to promote! Nobody cares about a Web site that's a brochure any more than they'd care about a plain old brochure. A Web site needs community, case histories, support, good ideas, examples, testimonials, or any of a dozen other elements in order to be attractive. It's not attractive just because it's got a cool photograph and features your price list.

There's an exception to this rule, though. It's what Peter calls the *resumé* or *business card* Web site. You direct people to the site to get information about you, your products, or your services. So people aren't just wandering around the Web looking for a type of product or service … they've already learned about you and want to know about *your* products and services. Here's how it works. You set up a simple Web site, perhaps just a single page. The purpose of the site is really to get people to call you; you include all your contact info—business name, phone number, e-mail address, and so on. Then you put the URL to your Web site wherever you can.

For instance, let's say you're a house painter. You put the URL on the sign that you post outside houses you're painting. Of course you want a distinctive URL, something like BostonPainters.com, PaintPaintPaint.com, WePaintQuick.com, or whatever. (By the way, all those URLs were available at the time of writing. With a little imagination, it's still possible to find a distinctive URL that will work on a sign.) You don't have to use a domain name that is the same as your company name—the important thing is to pick a memorable and descriptive domain name.

Now, as people drive by your sign, they'll see a phone number (you *do* put your phone number on your signs, don't you?) and a URL. They won't remember the phone number, but if they see the URL a few times, there's a good chance they'll remember it. They'll be able to reach your site; in effect, you passed out a business card, without either you or the recipient realizing it at the time. The URL can be displayed on everything—the side of your trucks and cars, the employees' uniforms, your windows ... anything you know people will see. People don't go online to look for a house painter, or a lawn service, or a plumber; they use the Yellow Pages. But if they've seen a memorable URL a few times, they'll remember it and may go to the business-card Web site.

Business-card Web sites can work well for delivery services, carpet-cleaning services, plumbers, house cleaners, kids cutting lawns, milk-delivery services, diaper services, window cleaners ... you get the idea.

Ancient Web Sites

You're just getting around to promoting a site that's so out of date it's got

Make Your URL Distinctive

Use this little trick to make your URL more distinctive when you use it in signs, brochures, business cards, e-mail, and so on. Uppercase some of the letters to make it easier to read.

Instead of writing paintpaintpaint.com *or* bostonpainters.com, *write* PaintPaintPaint.com *or* BostonPainters.com—*you see how it's easier to read that way?*

You don't really need the www. *bit at the front, either; at least you shouldn't have to include it, but this depends on how your Web site is set up. Make sure people can reach your site using* www.BostonPainters.com *or simply* BostonPainters.com. *(Don't fool around with the capitalization of the rest of the URL, the directory and file names—only the domain name can be modified.)*

Consider using colors where possible, too: in Web pages, brochures, business cards, and so on. By using different colors for each word in the URL, you make it easier still to read. Look at what the **Computer Literacy bookstore** *does with their URL (http://www.computerliteracy.com/). They make the word* computer *red and the word* literacy *black or blue. Sometimes they also make the* www. *and* .com *pieces gray to underplay those pieces (after all, you're trying to get people to remember the significant part of the URL, and the* www. *and* .com *pieces go without saying).*

dust bunnies in the source code? Don't bother. Do something, add something to the site, before you start talking about it. Ask yourself this: Is my Web site useful to people *today* (forget about how useful it *used* to be). If you have a plan to make it useful tomorrow, and keep it useful forever, you're ahead of the game.

Minor Details

If you're in charge of promotion for a publicly-held company, there are things you have to announce in the interest of disclosure. But even that has its limits. You don't need to trumpet the fact that you're now using Doodad 3.1 instead of Doodad 3.0 to maintain your Web site. Nobody except your maintenance people needs to know that you've upgraded to stain-free carpet. These may seem like silly examples to you, but you'd be amazed what people consider grounds for a press release!

When you spend a lot of time focusing on minor events, you're conditioning people to respond as if all your news is minor—and your major news loses a lot of its impact. Save your loudest voice for the biggest news and mention the minor stuff in passing, if at all.

Vaporware

If it hasn't happened yet, don't get noisy about it. If you've used computers for any length of time, you've probably heard of the term *vaporware*. Vaporware is software that's been announced (usually with much fanfare) but over time doesn't appear on the store shelves. It's delayed, and delayed, and delayed, and eventually it's quietly cancelled. This not only costs a company money, it costs credibility; anyone familiar with your company will look askance at future announcements.

Vaporware applies not only to products but also to services. If you're preparing to offer a three-leash dog-walking service, make sure you've got all the leashes ready and your license upgraded to triple-leashing; a delay could cause you trouble.

Lousy Products

There are many people searching for the pavements of gold on the Internet. The Internet hype has been so intense that people are desperate to get involved in some way. They're scared of "missing the boat." So what do they do? They run out and find a product—any product—and set up shop on the Internet.

Many of those products are trash. There's enough trash being sold on the Internet today to fill half the landfills in North America.

It really is possible to sell trash. You can promote the hell out of a product, and you'll sell some of it. But it's far better to have a *good* product, as we'll explain in a moment.

The Good Stuff

Okay, that's the bad stuff. In contrast there's really good stuff to market and promote.

Consistently Updated Resources

If you've put together a Web site containing a list of links that deals with your industry, product, or service, and you update it regularly (that is, check for new resources and remove old ones that no longer work), you're providing an invaluable service to the Internet community. Likewise, if you publish a listing of resources on paper, or in some other way publish a list that provides value, that's something worth promoting. If you have information of any kind that your target market will find useful, it's worth promoting. Here's an example. Visit one of Peter's sites at http://PoorRichard.com/freeinfo/special_reports.htm and you'll find a number of special reports, such as the *Shopping-Cart Software & Services Directory* and a report called *Places to Register Your Email Newsletter*.

Just this morning someone posted a message about this Web page to a discussion group about newsletter publishing:

> *This is a GREAT site!!! It will keep you busy for days with places to register your ezine and resources on promoting your ezine. There are a TON of links …*

Comments like this lead visitors to Peter's site … and some of them buy his books.

About the URLs

We're going to be mentioning a lot of URLs—Internet addresses—in this book. You can view a Web page containing all these address links at a Web site associated with this book: http://PoorRichard.com/promo/. Copy the page to your hard disk and then create a bookmark to the page stored on your hard disk, so it will be easily accessible.

Free Training and Support

You make WidgetWare, and on your Web site you have free training units that teach how to use WidgetWare in certain vertical markets, as well as a technical support site that helps beginners with frequent WidgetWare problems. If you're offline, you have a newsletter called *WidgetWare for the Bemused* that assists beginners with your product. You have an extensive faxback service and update your documentation regularly, sending out free updates as necessary. You're not only providing super customer service, but you've also got a great service to promote. Anything that falls in the line of free training and support—maybe it's a housecleaning service giving out a database of tips on cleaning household items, or a business realtor offering seminars on readying retail stores for hurricanes—is a good thing to promote.

Samples and Demonstrations

Samples are great. On the Internet, software is easily distributed as a sample or demonstration (often called Trialware). But there are other things you can provide as online samples, too—for example books, issues of newsletters, stock photography, and so on. If you cannot physically provide the sample online, you can provide an order form for a visitor to request one to be sent by mail. (Keep things in perspective—no one is going to get too excited about the ability to order a sample of dishwashing liquid online. However, if you've just completed a major upgrade to a $600 product, and you're making a free trial available online, you're going to attract some interest.)

Here's another real-life example. When Peter published *Poor Richard's Web Site: Geek-Free, Commonsense Advice on Building a Low-Cost Web Site,* he posted several sample chapters at his Web site (see http://PoorRichard.com/sample_ chapt/). Do these benefit him? Absolutely; people often buy the book after reading these chapters, and journalists often contact him for review copies.

Communities and Discussions

A well-moderated discussion is a beautiful thing. You may have noticed that in open forums like newsgroups and mailing-list discussion groups, chaos does occasionally reign in the form of inappropriate messages, fights (also called *flame wars*), new users asking the same question over and over again, and so on. Taking the time and trouble to create and moderate a discussion that answers questions about your product and industry, provides answers and support, and facilitates discussion among your customers will really pay off. You're getting ideas for your customers and content for your Web site, and prospects will see your community as a sign that you stand behind your product or service.

Good Products

When you're promoting a good product, here's what happens:

1. You convince people to buy the product.
2. They love the product, so …
3. They tell friends, family, and colleagues.
4. Their friends, family, and colleagues buy the product.

If you have a bad product, you miss out on steps 2, 3, and 4. The best product to promote is one that can promote itself. Then, in effect, what you are doing is priming the pump. Your initial promotional efforts are multiplied several times, perhaps many times, by the effects of steps 2, 3, and 4.

We've mentioned only a few examples here; we haven't mentioned things like announcing new products, new services, the appointment of new executives, and other things that traditionally call for marketing or promotion. If you're not sure whether the thing you want to promote is a good thing or a bad thing, look at it from your customers' viewpoint and ask yourself, "So what? Who cares? What's in it for me?" If the answer is, "I don't know what, not me, nothing much," you should think twice about promoting it. On the other hand, if you do have a good solid answer, make sure it's incorporated into your marketing and promotion materials.

Now that you have an idea of what makes a good (and bad) marketing or promotion push, you need to think about who needs to see the push.

WHAT DO YOU WANT TO HAPPEN?

If you're simply selling a product or service, this question might strike you as the king of no-brainers. You want people to go out and grab your product or sign up for your service, of course! However, if you're promoting a cause or you're trying to build recognition for your company, the question is not that easy to answer. There are a few ways it might be answered.

I want people to buy my product (join my cause, use my service, sample my new brand of cheese dip, etc.)

If you want people to buy your product, you'll need to concentrate on *visibility*—making sure people hear about your product or service—with a secondary focus on *credibility*—making sure that they hear, from a third party, that your product or service is good. Visibility can be obtained through both promotional and advertising efforts, while credibility can best be obtained through promotional efforts like reviews, newspaper articles, and case studies. Don't neglect credibility in your search for visibility, however; customers will have questions about your product that strong credibility will help answer.

I want to build recognition for my company, product, or service

If you want to build recognition, then it follows that you want to concentrate on visibility. To a much lesser extent, you want to build credibility. Recognition should not be the first and last goal of your campaign, however; you should aim for a critical mass of recognition (via visits to your Web sites, sales calls, orders, whatever) and then concentrate on another goal, such as sales. You can also use this goal to build recognition for individual happenings within the company—a product upgrade, a new service, or a significant shift in personnel.

I want to build credibility for my company, product, or service

This is the flip side of building visibility. Once a lot of people have heard about your product or service, you want to concentrate on giving them a good reason to buy, which calls for concentrating on credibility. Editorial coverage of your product or service is much more credible to a reader than an advertisement; you want to try to get *other* people to say nice things about your products and services. People do pay attention to ads, to some degree, but they don't necessarily trust them. They know the person paying for the ad is biased, after all. But if someone who isn't apparently linked with your company says good things, then that counts for a lot.

You can also combine these two goals into one, and build visibility and credibility at the same time. In this case, you'll want to split your resources between generating both visibility and credibility. (It should be noted that if you have a bad or marginal product, no amount of promotional effort is going to keep the truth from eventually coming out. We're assuming that you've got a good product that you're proud to sell.)

I want to diffuse a rival's efforts

Is a competitor promoting that they have better prices than you do? That the quality of their service is superior to yours? What you'll need to focus on depends on what claim you're trying to deflect. If they're saying you have a shoddy product, you want to build credibility. If they're trumpeting their service and you know yours is better, you want to concentrate on visibility. If they're merely making vague claims that their product is "the best around" or "the only service of its type" and you know that's not true, you want to concentrate on:

- Building visibility for you and your product (so the "only service of its type" claim is put to rest) and
- Building credibility (so the "best around" is at least put to a challenge.)

So think carefully about what you are trying to achieve. What do you have to promote or market? Is there something you can do to improve it before you begin your marketing or promotion campaign? What do you want to happen? Do you want people to rush out and buy your product? Do you want them to get a warm fuzzy feeling when they think of you? Do you want them to think of you immediately when the need arises for a certain service? Knowing the outcome you want will help you decide your program.

WHO ARE YOU AIMING AT?

Who are you aiming your promotion at? The short answer is, of course, customers. A longer answer will serve you better. Consider whether you are aiming at …

> **Consumers in general**—Do you have a product as ubiquitous as pencils that everyone needs to have, or is it at least fit for a large group of people? (We're not saying that there won't be some demographic group that's most appropriate for your product or service, just that it will be a large group or several groups.)
>
> **Businesses**—Is it more a business-to-business product or service, like a retail accounting form?
>
> **Vertical Markets**—Vertical markets are markets that are oriented to one particular specialty. For example, plastics manufacturing is a vertical market. Transportation engineering is a vertical market. Medical supply companies need to deal only with healthcare customers; therefore a press release to the Small Town Gazette isn't going to do much good. A press release to *Medical Supply Monthly* would be far more appropriate.
>
> **Very specific, smaller markets**—If your product or service deals with a particular niche—the disabled, a specific age group, or a specific locale (like a catering service)—then you need to focus very specifically on those people.

It may seem like those products and services related to consumers in general might have an advantage. After all, there are many more outlets available for their advertising, more places they can send press releases, etc.

But on the other hand, having so many outlets available tends to diffuse efforts. One can't contact every newspaper in the country to deliver a promotional pitch without expending a lot of time and money. In addition, when you try for coverage in those media outlets, you're competing with a lot of other products and services. If you're in a specialized niche, you have less competition, and fewer media outlets on which you can focus more attention.

Take a little time now and think about who your product is aimed at. In some cases, it'll be really obvious; in other cases, some thought will be necessary. Who are you selling your product or service to now? Who helps you develop it? What markets do you hope to expand into? What new products or services are you developing and what markets have you developed them for?

It's extremely important to decide whom you are trying to reach, or your efforts won't be concentrated in the best way possible. If you've got a product or service with a wide prospect base, take some time and think about how you can break down the prospects into different segments and focus on one segment at a time. For example, maybe you sell an educational toy. You could break your focus down into several segments:

- Teachers
- Child-development experts
- Parents
- Grandparents and other family members
- Professional caregivers

Breaking down your prospect base into segments like this will keep you from becoming overwhelmed when you're searching for your marketing and promotional targets. (We'll get into that in Chapter 4.)

But be creative when identifying these groups. For instance, when Peter was promoting the first book in the Poor Richard's series, *Poor Richard's Web Site*, he wanted to find periodicals to publish reviews of the book. He could have focused solely on the computer press—computer magazines, technology columnists in newspapers, computer papers, and so on. But he also realized that the book would be of interest to many people who might not consider themselves "geeks" or even particularly computer literate. After all, everyone these days seems to want to create a Web site. So he also approached the business press, and a variety of other niches. The book has been reviewed or mentioned in a wide range of periodicals, such as *The Philadelphia Inquirer*, *The New England Non-Profit Quarterly*, *Home Office Computing*, *Keyboard Magazine*, the *USA Today* Web site, *Marketing Technology*, and so on. (In fact, this may be the most widely reviewed computer book ever.)

When computer-book publishers send out review copies, they generally focus on the computer press. A computer subject should be reviewed in the computer press, right? But Peter thought about who he wanted to read the book, and why they would read it, and realized that he could reach these people through a wide variety of periodicals.

Tara did a similar thing with a book she co-authored, *Official Netscape Guide to Internet Research* (IDG). She approached editors at business publications, educational publications—any group that she felt would need to find information on the Web regularly. And it did pay off, as her book was reviewed in several business- and education-related publications.

To summarize, before you can promote a product or service you have to think about what it is you are trying to promote, who you are promoting it to, and what you want the outcome to be. This may sound obvious, but when you look at the way in which many companies promote themselves, their products, and their services, it's clear that they've spent little or no time thinking through this process. A few hours spent on this process early on will save you a great deal of time, money, and effort later.

Once you know what you want to do, it's time to prepare the tools and materials. Chapter 2 will show you what you need to get started.

ABOUT THE URLS

We've mentioned in this book literally hundreds of links to all sorts of useful resources that will help you in your marketing and promotions. To save typing all those links, we suggest you visit the Web site associated with this book (http://PoorRichard.com/promo/). You'll find a Web page with all the links sorted according to chapter and alphabetically within each chapter. You can save that page on your hard disk or simply bookmark the page; then you'll be able to go to the sites that we've mentioned in this book with a quick click.

We'll be checking those links periodically so that we can update them as they change—as any group of hundreds of Web links surely will over time. Also, let us quickly explain a simple trick for using links that appear to be broken—a handy little trick you can use whenever you're traveling around the World Wide Web. Let's say, for instance, that you see a URL like this (or a link containing this URL):

http://www.thisdomain.com/firstdirect/seconddirect/this.html

Now, you type this URL (or click on the link), and you get a browser error telling you that the requested item has not been found. What can you do? Well, if you typed the link, make sure you typed it correctly; in particular, make sure you used the correct file extension (.html and not .htm in this case). If you did type it correctly, or if you clicked on a link, then it may be that the file has been moved or deleted. What next? Do you just give up?

No, you can work your way up the directory path to see if you can find another Web page that might contain information that will help you find the page you're looking for. Remove the filename from the URL in the browser's Location bar and try again:

http://www.thisdomain.com/firstdirect/seconddirect/

Press Enter, and one of three things will happen. Your browser may display a document which is the default document for that directory, or it may display a listing showing all the files in that directory. You can then click on the different .htm and .html files shown in the directory to display them. Or it may display another error, telling you that nothing was found. If so, try moving up to the next directory. Type this:

http://www.thisdomain.com/firstdirect/

Again, you may see a Web page, a directory listing, or an error. If you see an error, move back to the next directory. In this example you'd type the following:

http://www.thisdomain.com/

Now you'll almost always find something, assuming the domain name is correct. You may find a page that indicates where you can find the information you want … or that the information is no longer present at that server. Using this technique, you can often find the information you need, even if it's been moved to a new location at the Web site.

CHAPTER TWO

What You Need Before You Start

There are a number of things you're going to need before you set to work. This book doesn't describe in detail the beginner's stuff—the basic things you need to know to work effectively on the Internet. We explain what to do once you understand all the basics. But we will at least explain the sort of background information and the tools that you need before you start.

Even if you already have Internet access and think you're ready to jump right in and get started, please don't skip this chapter. Many Internet users don't understand the relationship between their Internet service, their e-mail system and their Web site, for instance, and to work efficiently you must know how these three systems hook together. At least skim through and see what we have to say.

Later in the chapter we'll be looking at a number of tools that most people don't know about, yet which are very useful when promoting a product or service online. So, here's a quick rundown of what you need to effectively promote online. This is a basic list—the things a small business needs as a minimum to get started:

- A computer
- Hardware connecting the computer to the Internet
- Internet access through an Internet service provider
- A POP e-mail account
- Somewhere to put your Web site
- Basic Internet-access software
- Basic Internet knowledge
- Advanced research and marketing software
- Text-automation tools

- Offline browsers
- Web Page Archives
- Contact-management software
- Full-Blown Databases

We'll take a look at each of these things one by one.

YOUR COMPUTER

This almost goes without saying: you need a computer. Pretty much any recent PC or Mac computer—one that was built since, say, 1995—will work okay. Older computers may have problems; while you'll probably be able to get by with a 386 PC, for instance, you'll have trouble finding good software that will run well on a 286 PC.

PC owners are lucky in that they have a huge selection of software to choose from; if you own a Mac, you'll find that you can get hold of very good programs for some tasks, but may have a severely limited choice of software for other things. For instance, if you look at the list of search-engine registration software in Chapter 6, you'll see that there are loads of Windows programs ... but we've only managed to find one of these programs that runs on the Mac. In some cases there may be no Macintosh equivalents, either, so it's not merely a matter of picking another brand of software. (Please, don't write and complain that we're being unfair to Macs! We're not saying that Windows machines are better, just that there's more software available!)

You need a fast computer with lots of RAM (Random Access Memory). RAM is very cheap these days, so don't skimp. You could easily spend hours each day with multiple programs running—your browser, word processor, e-mail program, some kind of clipboard or text-automation program, a contact-management program, and so on. All this uses a lot of memory. Don't believe the nonsense about how Windows 95 or Windows 98 can run in 16MB of RAM; the simple truth is, it can't, even if you're only using one or two programs. Rather, it uses "virtual memory." That's a euphemism for storing information on your hard disk instead of in memory. Hard-disk space is much, much slower than RAM, so your computer will run much, much more slowly. Virtual memory made sense in the old days, when memory was expensive. These days memory's dirt cheap, so buy plenty; 64MB on a PC is not too much ... 128MB is better. In fact RAM is more important than processor speed. If you buy a new computer, for instance, it's far better to buy a 300 MHz Pentium II with 128MB of RAM than a 450 MHz Pentium with 32MB of RAM. (Better still is a 450

MHz Pentium with 128MB of RAM. You can never have too much RAM!) If you have just a little extra money when you come to choosing your computer, consider increasing the RAM before going for a faster processor.

CONNECTING YOUR COMPUTER TO THE INTERNET

The other piece of critical hardware is the line-access hardware. This could be one of these things:

- A modem
- A cable modem
- An ISDN terminal adapter (often known as an ISDN modem)
- A DSL (Digital Subscriber Line) service
- A Satellite connection
- Something horribly expensive and probably unnecessary (T1 and a routcr)

Modems

A modem is used to connect your computer to normal phone lines. It takes the signal from your computer, modulates it—that is, converts the digital computer data into analog phone data—then sends it across the phone lines to the computer you've connected to. When data is sent across the phone lines to your computer, the modem demodulates it—that is, converts it from analog to digital data—and sends it to your computer. The word *modem* is a contraction of *mo*dulate/*dem*odulate.

You can buy external modems—boxes that you connect to your computer's serial port—and internal modems—which are the same as external modems except the processor card is installed inside the computer. We recommend that you buy a 56K modem, that is, one that runs at a speed of 56kbps (bits per second, a measure of how fast the modem can send data). That rating is just theory, though; the modem will actually run more slowly than that (though still faster than other, slower-rated modems). 56K modems are reasonably cheap these days, and if you're working on a phone line you'll find the Internet frustratingly slow anyway … so you'll need to squeeze whatever speed you can out of it.

There's been a lot of confusion about 56K modems, because for two years there were two competing, and non-compatible, systems: 3Com/US Robotics' X2 system and Rockwell/Lucent's K56Flex. There is now a standard, though, known as V.90. In theory, then, all 56K modems should be able to operate with all others.

In practice, the modem you buy may not yet have the V.90 programming, though it's probably upgradeable. Also, many service providers have not yet converted to V.90; they may still be using one or another of the old methods.

If you buy a 56K modem, make sure that it's already V.90 compatible, or that it's going to be easy to upgrade it (the manufacturer may have placed upgrade software at their Web site). And make sure that you'll be able to use the modem with your Internet service provider.

If you'd like to find more information about the two main 56K manufacturers, check the **3Com/USRobotics** Web site (http://www.3com.com/ or http://www. 3com.com/56k/) and the **Rockwell** Web site (http://www.nb.rockwell.com/ K56flex/), where you'll also find lists of service providers using the respective modem standards.

By the way, if you're really short of money, it's perfectly possible to work on the Internet with a 28,800bps or 33,600bps modem. However, you wouldn't want to go much slower than that! 14,400bps modems are irritatingly slow, and anything below that feels positively glacial.

Cable Systems

You might also be able to connect to the Internet through your local cable-TV company. Call and ask—they may already have Internet service, but may not be promoting it very heavily because they know they don't have the staff or equipment to keep up with the demand if they advertised the service. It can take two or three installers several hours to get one of these things up and running ... if they're lucky. Cable-TV access has had some serious teething problems—remember, the cable companies were promising this service back in 1994. But it really wasn't until late in 1998 that they started to roll out cable access on a large scale.

Peter connects to the Internet through cable, and loves it. It's very fast, and really quite reliable—there have been a few periods during which it was close to unusable, but overall it's been more reliable than his other Internet access accounts. Cable access typically costs around $150 to install and $40 a month.

Cable speeds vary from system to system, somewhere between 200kbps and 2mbps (2000kbps). A few cable systems are only uni-directional; you have to use a phone line at the same time that you are connected through the cable modem. The data coming from the Internet flows along the cable, while information from your computer back to the Internet goes along the telephone line. The better systems are fully bi-directional—no need for a phone line.

For more information, see the **Cable Modem Resources on the Web** page at http://rpcp.mit.edu/~gingold/cable/, and **Yahoo!'s Cable Modems** page at http://

www.yahoo.com/Computers_and_Internet/Hardware/Peripherals/Cable_Modems/.
Or call your local cable company.

A quick warning about the cable companies' dirty little secret—security. Security on these cable systems is *very* bad. Every cable modem is connected to a local neighborhood network "node." For instance, you may have, say, 240 computers connected together in one neighborhood. If those individual computers are not configured properly, it may be possible for other people on the network to access data on the computers. Peter estimates that 10 percent or more of the computers in his neighborhood node are open to the outside—that is, anyone else can view the data on their hard disks! So make sure, if you get one of these systems, that you ask the installers exactly how to either disable file sharing, or at least password protect your data.

> ## View These Links Online
>
> *Remember, you can view a Web page containing these links at http://PoorRichard.com/promo/.*

ISDN

Another option available in many areas, though not all, is to install an ISDN (Integrated Services Digital Network) phone line. This is a digital phone line and can carry data much more quickly than an ordinary analog phone line; you can transmit and receive data at either 64kbps or 128kbps, depending on the type of line you select (yes, the faster line is more expensive). In the U.S., ISDN typically costs around $60 to install and $60 a month to run—more if you use it extensively, because there are per-minute charges—and that's if you can get it. (ISDN prices can vary greatly between regions, though—the installation price may be two or three times that, and in some cases you won't pay per-minute charges.) In many areas you'll find it impossible to obtain ISDN service at present. In fact the unofficial definition of ISDN is: It Still Doesn't Work. At least that's the U.S. definition; in some other parts of the world, ISDN is much more easily available.

You'll also have to pay more to get ISDN Internet access. That is, not only will you pay the phone company

> ## Internet Service Provider (ISP)
>
> *An Internet service provider (ISP) is a company that provides access to the Internet. Your computer connects to one of the company's computers, allowing your computer to communicate with the Internet. ISPs are also known as Internet Access Providers (IAP).*

$60 or more a month to use the line, but you'll also pay a special fee to the ISP. On top of that you'll pay around $250 to $300 for an ISDN terminal adapter. Though often called an ISDN modem, a terminal adapter doesn't actually modulate or demodulate.

You can find more information about ISDN at the **ISDN Info-Centre** (http://www.isdn.ocn.com/) or your local phone company's Web page. However, here's a warning. ISDN is not for the technically timid. It can be very difficult to install an

---

ISDN Hype

Sales people from ISDN-hardware companies often tout the phenomenal speeds possible through ISDN. If data is compressed, you can actually transmit at several times the 128kbps limit we've mentioned here. Don't be fooled, though. You almost certainly won't be able to go above 128kbps when connecting to the Internet, because most Internet service providers are not set up to compress data.

ISDN line and get it running properly, partly because the phone companies seem to be technically incompetent. Horror stories about ISDN abound. Peter had an ISDN line at one point, and dumped it because the phone company was unable to get it running properly and reliably. A friend recently installed an ISDN line and spent literally days trying to get it to run correctly.

DSL

The phone companies also have a system called DSL (Digital Subscriber Line). It may be available in your area, or perhaps not. But if it isn't, you may be lucky. Horror stories about DSL are almost as common as horror stories about ISDN.

DSL comes in various flavors: HDSL (High-Rate DSL), ADSL (Asymmetric DSL), RADSL (Rate Adaptive DSL), VDSL (Very High Data-Rate DSL), and so on. These lines will range in speed from 128kbps to 700kbps. Rates will probably range from $75 a month to $175 a month. You may be able to get a DSL line, and then find an ISP that you can dial into—but remember, the ISP will also charge more for this special access. Or your phone company may provide both the line and Internet access.

Peter recommends getting a cable system if possible over DSL or ISDN; he's had too many problems with the phone company, and heard too many complaints from others. Of course *your* phone company may be better!

Satellite Systems

If you can't get cable, DSL, or ISDN, you might try a satellite connection, using **DirecPC** from **Hughes Network Systems** (http://www.direcpc.com/). This is available in some areas of North America. It'll cost around $200 to $300 for the equipment, plus an installation fee, and you'll still need a modem connection across a phone line, too. It works like this: your software uses the modem connection to send information out onto the Internet. When you want to display a Web page, for instance, you click on a link in the Web browser, and a message is sent across the modem to the Web site. When the Web site sends the page back, it's grabbed by a computer at the DirecPC operations center, transmitted up into space, picked up by a satellite, and transmitted down to earth, where it's picked up by your satellite dish. Incoming data—the data coming from the satellite—moves at 400kbps; outgoing data (along the phone line) moves at normal modem speeds. You'll pay Hughes anywhere from $20 a month to $130 a month, plus hourly fees over a certain number of hours. For instance, the $130 plan gives you 200 free hours, and charges $1.99 an hour for additional hours.

T1s and Other Stuff

The phone company can provide you with other neat things—special phone lines with names such as 56K lines, T1 lines, fractional T1s, and T3s. These are generally quite expensive and complicated, and more than the average small business really needs.

Which Do You Pick?

What should you get? The cheapest and easiest thing is to buy a fast modem, and for most small companies this is fine. It's relatively cheap, and it will be easy to find an ISP that will work with you. Don't cheap out and buy a low-cost or slow modem, however. Get a high-quality, fast modem. It'll make a big difference. If you can get a cable modem, go for it! It's cheap, fast, and probably quite reliable. If you can't get cable access, you may want to try ISDN or DSL, but be prepared for headaches and make sure you are really tough on the phone company—make sure they live up to their promises. Or consider a satellite system, perhaps, rather than fool with the phone company.

Tara is very jealous of Peter's fast access, but she wants to point out that you can use the Internet efficiently using only a phone line. The trick is to make sure you take advantage of the Internet's "slow periods"—when not as many people are online. If you access the Internet at one o'clock in the morning, you'll find it a lot faster and easier to use than if you access it at 6 PM. She also recommends you avoid the Internet between 8 and 11 PM; in her experience this is when the Internet is slowest and least responsive.

INTERNET ACCESS

The next thing you need is a connection to the Internet. The Internet is a giant public network. In order to connect to it, you must connect to a computer that is already connected to the Internet. That's done through what's known as an *Internet service provider (ISP)*. There are more ISPs than you can shake a stick at, ranging from free systems providing very limited service to a few hundred people in a single community, to huge companies providing access to millions of people in several countries. In general, the free services won't be of use to you. The majority provide old-style command-line Internet access, and you require the newer graphical-user-interface type of access, what's known as *TCP/IP access*.

There are several different types of ISPs:

- True ISPs
- Online services
- Phone companies
- Cable-TV companies

True ISPs are companies that are primarily in the business of providing Internet access and associated services—Web-page design, Web-hosting, and so on. These companies range from small local companies with a few hundred subscribers, to national companies with hundreds of thousands of subscribers. If you already have some form of Internet access, you can track down service providers in your area using **Yahoo!'s Internet Access Provider's** page at http://www.yahoo.com/Business_and_Economy/Companies/Internet_Services/Access_Providers/ or **The List** at http://thelist.iworld.com/. You may be able to get to these pages from a computer at your local library, for instance.

Online services are companies such as CompuServe, America Online (AOL), Prodigy, Microsoft Network, and GEnie. These companies are like private clubs. They provide access to all sorts of services: thousands of discussion groups about almost any imaginable subject—chat rooms, news and weather information, and so on. If you want to access these services, you have to join the club. But they also provide Internet access. So if you're a member of the club, you can still get onto the Internet and use the World Wide Web, newsgroups, and other services.

Some phone companies also provide Internet access. Companies such as Sprint (Sprint Internet Passport), AT&T (AT&T WorldNet), and MCI (internetMCI) now provide low-cost Internet access throughout North America. Many local phone companies provide Internet access, too. However, the phone companies often "just don't get it," and although they understand how to connect everything together, they don't really understand what people want to do on the Internet. You'll often get better service from a true ISP than from one of the phone companies.

Finally, the cable-TV companies are the next big players in this arena, providing Internet access through the cables they've been using to provide TV shows.

Which of these should you use? Well, that depends partly on the type of access you want. If you want cable access—which is a really good choice, if you can get it—then you'll be going with a cable-TV company, of course.

Whatever you choose, we recommend that you have at least two ways to get onto the Internet, from two separate ISPs. For instance, Peter has access through cable TV, but he also has a CompuServe account. In his earlier, pre-cable days, he had several accounts—from Sprint, CompuServe, and EarthLink, for instance. He's considering getting rid of his CompuServe account, because the cable connection seems so reliable now. But when he was dependent on ISP connection through a phone line, he found he would often have to switch between accounts. Three different accounts, with three different services, ensured that he could always get online. It's possible to play this multi-account game for as little as $30 a month.

Not only does having two accounts allow you to get on at all times, but it increases your chances of getting to the Internet sites you want to visit. It's quite feasible for network problems to make it impossible for you to access a particular Web site through one Internet service provider, but possible through another service provider. Also, if you use one of the "private club" type access providers—like AOL or Compu-Serve—you are limited in some of your choices. For example, when you use AOL, you're pretty much stuck with AOL's mail program. You won't be able to use some of the e-mail programs we'll discuss later in the book. On the plus side, local dial-up numbers for AOL and similar services are available practically everywhere, so if you travel a lot it's easy to check your e-mail without incurring long-distance charges.

Unlimited Access?

Just because a service advertises that it provides unlimited Internet access for $19.95 a month, it doesn't mean it really does so. It may mean "$19.95 for as many hours as you're able to connect, if you can get past the busy signals, and if we don't drop you off the system." A year or two ago 20 state Attorneys General threatened to sue AOL for promising unlimited access but providing only busy signals.

We advise that you talk with other Internet users in your area, check ads in local papers and magazines, and try a few services to find a reliable one. We don't want to recommend any particular service nor denounce any particular service (well, except for the phone companies!). We've used many, and found that they all have their ups and downs—and none we've tried so far is completely reliable.

A POP E-MAIL ACCOUNT

You need an e-mail account, but you really need a POP e-mail account. POP means Post Office Protocol, and it's the standard e-mail system used on the Internet. While most true Internet service providers, the phone-company Internet service providers, and the cable companies will give you a POP account, it's important to understand that the online services generally do not. Rather, they have their own mail systems that were designed before Internet access was important, so they work in a very different manner. If you have an AOL account, for instance, you probably don't have a POP e-mail account. If you have a CompuServe account, you *can* have a POP account, but you have to sign up for it—it's not provided automatically.

Why do you need a POP account? Because it's so much more flexible than a non-POP account. Ideally you want your own domain name (which you'll learn all about in Chapter 3) and a POP account. For instance, Peter's domain name is topfloor.com. Because he has his own POP account and his own domain name, he can create as many e-mail addresses as he wants:

> pkent@topfloor.com,
> info@topfloor.com,
> sales@topfloor.com,
> ipn@topfloor.com,
> whateveriwant@topfloor.com.

Furthermore, with a POP e-mail account, you have your choice of e-mail programs. With an online

Filters Are Essential

If you're serious about promoting on the Internet, you'll be flooded with e-mail; at times you'll get scores, even hundreds of messages every day. So it's essential that you get to know your e-mail program's filtering system. You may want to use a special e-mail address while contacting people on the Web. Some mail programs allow you to use various From: addresses. Eudora and AK-Mail, for instance, let you set up separate "accounts," each account with a different e-mail address. So you could use different Reply To: addresses for different purposes. Of course in order to be able to use different addresses, you'll have to have your own domain name. We'll talk about this—and more detail about working with e-mail—in Chapter 16.

service's own proprietary system, you get whatever software they give you or, in some cases, you can choose from a limited selection. With POP, you have a huge choice, and some really good programs to work with.

For instance, you could pick a POP program that can filter messages (most can, these days). That is, it automatically sorts messages into separate folders. When you send a message a copy is placed in the appropriate folder, and when you receive a message it's automatically routed to the correct folder. This capability is really essential for anyone serious about doing business on the Internet.

You don't have to get your POP account at the same place you get your Internet access, though. If you wish, you can get a POP account from a completely different company. See, for instance, the **Yahoo! E-mail Providers** page (http://www.yahoo.com/ Business_and_Economy/Companies/ Internet_Services/Email_Providers/), where you'll find links to all sorts of e-mail services, and **Web-Quote Central** (http://www.centeroftheweb.com/ webquote/), which has lists of all sorts of Internet services, including e-mail providers.

So you can have an account with CompuServe or AOL, for instance, and still have a POP e-mail account somewhere else. How will you access your mail? You'll use CompuServe or AOL to connect to the Internet, then

Which Program?

Peter's currently using an e-mail program called **Eudora**, *which is very good. It's available in a freeware or commercial version for Windows and Macintosh—though in order to use filters you'll have to get the commercial version:* http://www.eudora. com/. *In the past he's used* **AK-Mail**, *which is also pretty good. It's a Windows 95/NT shareware program, and you can get it from* http://www.akmail.com/ *or from many shareware libraries. It has some filter features that Eudora doesn't have, but all in all Eudora is easier to use, and it seems likely that* **AK-Mail** *won't be developed any further. Another very highly rated program is* **Pegasus Mail** (http:// www.pegasus.usa.com/), *which is free and available for Windows 3.1 and Windows 95/NT. See also* **Yahoo!'s Electronic Mail** *page:* http://www.yahoo.com/Computers_ and_Internet/Software/Internet/ Electronic_Mail/.

start a POP e-mail program (such as Eudora, Netscape Messenger, Microsoft Outlook, AK-Mail, Pegasus, or one of many others). You'll then use this program to connect to your POP account, wherever on the Internet that happens to be, and grab your mail. In the same way that you can start a CompuServe or AOL connection, open a Web browser, and connect to a Web site, you can start a CompuServe or AOL connection, open a POP e-mail program, and connect to an e-mail account hosted on a computer out on the Internet.

When you get your POP account, make sure that you can have unlimited e-mail aliases within that POP account, that is, unlimited e-mail addresses that will be accepted by that account. Some services may set up the POP account to accept e-mail to only one address: pkent@topfloor.com, for instance. But you want to be able to accept e-mail addressed to various addresses—pkent@topfloor.com, info@topfloor.com, sales@topfloor.com, ipn@topfloor. com, whateveriwant@topfloor.com, and so on. So ensure that you're getting the right kind of account before you buy.

But before you run off and buy a POP account, read on. You'll be looking for a place to put your Web site, and most Web-hosting companies will give you a free POP account.

SOMEWHERE TO PUT YOUR WEB SITE

You also need somewhere to put your Web site. We'll go into this subject in detail in Chapter 3, but for the moment we want to clear up two misconceptions. The first is that when you get Internet access, you get a Web site with it. Some service providers don't give their members Web space, and even if a service provider does, the Web site probably won't be suitable as a business Web site. In Chapter 3 you'll learn about the services you need, and you may, in fact, find that your service provider can provide all the required Web services. You're more likely to discover, however, that your ISP cannot provide what you need, or will provide everything for an additional (exorbitant) fee.

The other misconception is that you have to have a Web site with the same company that you get Internet access from; in other words, that if your service provider doesn't provide Web space, you'll have to leave and find one that does. But Internet access and Web space are two completely different things. As with POP accounts, you can set up your Web site on any Web-hosting service anywhere in the world. You can then connect to your ISP, and connect to your Web site across the Internet.

HOW IT ALL HOOKS TOGETHER

So you need Internet access, a POP account, and a Web site. This confuses people. Aren't these all much the same thing; don't you get all three at once? No, and no. Let us just clarify how all these hook together.

Internet access merely allows your computer to communicate with the Internet—nothing more, nothing less. It's like your phone service; having your house connected to the phone system allows you to make calls across the system. It doesn't provide friends and a family for you to call; you have to provide them yourself.

Once you have Internet access, you can connect to computers all over the world. Those computers can provide some of the services you're going to need: your POP account and your Web site. You pay a fee to a company somewhere out there on the Internet, it sets up your POP account and provides space for your Web site, and away you go.

Your business may be in Vancouver, Canada. You may be using a large international ISP headquartered in, say, Washington, D.C., in the U.S. You may have your Web site on a computer sitting in London, England. And you may have a POP account in Dublin, Ireland. (Actually you'll generally have your Web site and POP account at the same place.)

Geographical location makes little difference, except that the ISP has to have a phone number in your area.

IAP, ISP, Hosting Companies

There's a lot of confusion about the term Internet Service Provider (ISP). The problem is that this term was in use long before hosting companies appeared on the scene; it used to mean a company providing access to the Internet. Yet these days many people use the term ISP to mean any company providing any service on the Internet—including hosting companies. Some people use the term to mean a company providing any Internet service other than Internet access (based on the theory that as there's another term for Internet-access businesses—Internet Access Providers (IAP)—that should "free up" the term ISP). If you want to refer to a Web-hosting company, be specific—don't use the term ISP or you're likely to confuse.

You can use services anywhere in the world. What's more important is how reliable those services are. Here's why it's important to look at these things as separate items. You want the best ISP, and the best hosting company (which will also provide you with a POP account). It's not always easy to find those things separately, so the chance of getting both together is pretty slim. And these companies may be good today, but bad tomorrow. You may have a great ISP now, but a few months from now it may be very hard to connect to them, so you'll have to find another ... there's no need to switch your Web host at the same time.

BASIC INTERNET-ACCESS SOFTWARE

Before you can do business on the Internet, you need the software that allows you to move around on the Internet. When you sign up with a service provider, that company will generally provide you with software to get started, though you may want to switch to better programs later. Here's what you need:

- Dial-up software
- An e-mail program
- A World Wide Web browser
- A newsreader
- An FTP program

Those are the basic tools you need, but we'll be adding things to that list as we go along. The dial-up software is the software required to make the connection to the Internet. There are loads of options, but generally an ISP will give you the software you need or tell you how to configure your operating system to make the connection. Windows 95, 98, and NT, for instance, come with built-in dial-up software.

You need an e-mail program to send and receive electronic mail. You need a Web browser in order to view pages on the World Wide Web. You need a newsreader to read newsgroup messages. And you need an FTP (File Transfer Protocol) program to upload files to your Web site.

Note that the two major Web browsers, Netscape Navigator and Microsoft Internet Explorer, come bundled with e-mail and newsreader programs. However, you may be better off working with another, more sophisticated program. The bundled programs are fine for getting started, and Outlook—which many people have available—has quite a few advanced tools. But still, you may need the tools provided by the specialized programs. Also, most Web browsers, including these two, can work with FTP to some degree. But you really need a true FTP program

FTP Programs

For Windows users, we'd suggest CuteFTP or WS_FTP, both of which you can find at various shareware libraries. For the Macintosh, Fetch is the most popular program, though there are a number of other FTP programs, including several new ones that are getting good reviews: NetFinder, NetBatch, Mirror, and Download Deputy. For a list of shareware libraries, see "Where Will You Get The Software?" later in this chapter.

to work with file transfers quickly and efficiently (which is important for maintaining a Web site).

Which browser should you get? There are literally scores of different browsers available, but only two are popular and only two are up-to-date: **Netscape Navigator** (http://www.netscape.com/) and **Microsoft Internet Explorer** (http://www.microsoft.com/ie/). We suggest you use one of these two—in fact, you'll probably be given one of these when you sign up for Internet service. Actually it's a good idea to have *both* of these on your system; when you create your Web site you want to make sure it looks good in both browsers.

If you're using an old computer, you might find that Netscape Navigator and Internet Explorer run somewhat sluggishly. Even on a 486, the most recent version of Navigator or IE can use up a lot of memory and processing power. You might want to try working with Opera, a "back to basics" browser available at http://www.operasoftware.com/. Opera's designers state that it'll work well even on a 386 with 8MB memory.

BASIC KNOWLEDGE

You're going to need two forms of basic knowledge. You'll need to understand how to work with your computer, and how to work with the Internet. You'll have to understand how to open compressed files that you've download from the Internet, how to work with your own computer's file-management system, how to move around on the World Wide Web, how to work with e-mail, and lots, lots more.

It's not the purpose of this book to explain these sorts of things. We've got plenty to do once you understand how to get around on the Internet. We suggest that, if you don't already understand the Internet, you read a few good books; you might start with Peter's *Complete Idiot's Guide to the Internet* (Que).

For now, though, in case you are just exploring the idea of setting up a Web site and need to understand some of the basic lingo, here's a mini-glossary with a few basic definitions:

The Internet—A giant computer network connecting millions of computers and millions of people around the world. This is a public network, though many of the computers connected to it are also part of smaller private networks.

The World Wide Web—Contrary to popular misconception, the World Wide Web is not a synonym for the Internet. The World Wide Web is a software system running across the Internet. The

Internet is the hardware; the Web is just one type of Internet software. You might think of the Internet as a huge highway system, and the Web as a trucking company moving things hither and thither across these roads. Other software systems include e-mail and FTP.

Web browser—This is a program that displays Web pages. If you want to "go onto the Web," "navigate the Web," "surf the Web," or whatever else you might call it, you need a Web browser.

Web server—This term can refer to a couple of things. It's often used to mean the software that manages one or more Web sites. When a Web browser wants to view a Web page, it sends a message to the Web server, which transmits the page back to the browser. The term also often refers to the whole kit and caboodle involved in this process—not just the Web server software but the computer on which the software is running too.

Web site—This term generally means a collection of associated Web pages: The Yahoo! Web site, The Library of Congress Web site, and so on. A single Web server may administer multiple Web sites— sometimes a few dozen, sometimes hundreds. One Web-hosting company's staff told us that its two servers had almost 1,000 Web sites. You will be creating your own Web site—your own collection of pages.

Web page—This is also known as a Web document. It's a single document stored at a Web site. A single Web browser window generally displays a single Web page at a time, though the window may be split into separate frames with a document in each frame. A Web page is stored in a single computer file, generally with the .htm or .html file extension. (You'll see other file extensions, generally when a page is created "on the fly" by a program.)

URL—A Web "address." It tells your Web browser exactly where to find a particular file. For instance, http://PoorRichard.com/freeinfo/ special_reports.htm means: Open the file named special_reports.htm, which is in the directory named freeinfo, at the host computer named PoorRichard.com. In some cases the URL doesn't include a filename, in which case the Web server will send the default file, probably a file named index.html.

Web host—If you don't have your own Web server (and you probably won't), you can find someone else to "host" your Web site for you. There are companies known as Web-hosting companies, or Web presence providers, which sell space on their Web servers. You'll learn about these companies in Chapter 3.

host computer—This simply means a computer connected to the Internet.

hypertext—A system by which electronically stored documents are linked together. The World Wide Web is the world's largest hypertext system, in which documents are viewed in Web browsers. Links are operated by pointing with the mouse at a picture or underlined text and clicking. Using a link loads the document referenced by the link.

Home page—This has two meanings. Originally it meant the page that a Web browser displays when you start the program or when you use the browser's Home command. Now it frequently means the main page at a Web site.

E-mail—This is short for electronic mail, a system in which messages can be sent across the Internet to an individual mailbox. Messages may take a few minutes to travel across the world or, when things are getting sluggish, a day or two.

FTP—File Transfer Protocol, one of the earliest software systems running on the Internet. This system allows you to transfer files between computers on the Internet. Although to a great extent it's been superseded by the World Wide Web (which also allows you to transfer files), there are still many FTP sites around the world. More importantly, when you set up a Web site you'll also get an FTP account, so you can transfer files from your computer to your Web site.

newsgroup—A discussion group. There are tens of thousands of newsgroups around the world, of which almost 30,000 are distributed internationally. Think of a subject, and there's probably a newsgroup dedicated to it, which means that whatever you are trying to sell or promote, there's a newsgroup with people who are interested. To read newsgroup messages, you need a program known as a newsreader. These discussion groups are distributed via a system called Usenet, so you'll often see them referred to as Usenet groups.

mailing list—Another form of discussion group. To read this type of group, though, you'll need nothing more than your e-mail program. There are tens of thousands of mailing lists, some private, many public.

There are a few other things you should know about, though you may not actually use these systems:

Archie—This is a system used to search for files at FTP sites.

Gopher—This system was supposed to revolutionize the Internet, taking a complicated command-line system and turning it into a simple menu system. Then came the Web, and Gopher dropped out of the race. But there are still many Gopher sites around, and Web browsers can display Gopher menus and pages.

Telnet—This system allows you to log onto a computer across the Internet and work on that computer, running programs, searching databases, and so on. Very few Internet users know how to use Telnet or even what it is.

chat—You type a message and someone else across the Internet—perhaps a whole lot of people—can read it. They can respond immediately, generally with dross. You can respond to the response, perhaps with dross of your own. Peter can't stand chat; many people love it.

talk—This is similar to chat, though it's intended as a private system. Programs such as ICQ and AOL Instant Messenger are *talk* systems.

IRC—This stands for Internet Relay Chat, which was the first popular Internet chat system. Dross personified.

VON—Voice On the Net, a way of holding "phone" conversations on the Internet. You'll need a microphone, sound card, VON software, and someone to talk to who has the same setup.

Learn as much as you can about the Internet … we won't be explaining too much of the basics in this book.

ADVANCED RESEARCH AND MARKETING SOFTWARE

So far we've discussed a basic Internet system, but if you're going to set up and promote a Web site, you'll need a variety of programs to help you along the way.

You'll need software to help you create your Web pages, for instance. You may want a program that will help you register your site with the Web search engines, programs that you can use to do research, and so on. We'll discuss these programs as we go along. We'll give URLs to lead you to some of these programs. In some cases you may wish to buy commercial software. There are thousands of different Internet programs, and it's impossible to keep up with all of them. We'll mention programs that we use, like, or know about, but you may find equivalents that you prefer.

Where Will You Get the Software?

As we mentioned earlier, when you sign up for Internet service the ISP will provide you with basic software to get you started. Later you'll want more. You'll see ads for Internet software all over the place, of course—in the computer press, in the software catalogs you get in the mail by the dozen, and so on.

You can also find really great software at shareware libraries on the Internet. These sites contain several types of software:

Public domain—Free software that belongs to nobody. The program author has given away all rights.

Freeware—This type of software belongs to someone, but the owner is giving away the rights to use it, sometimes in particular circumstances—it's free to individuals, but companies have to pay, for instance.

Shareware—Take it, use it, if you like it, send money.

Demoware—Take it, use it, if you like it, send money and they'll send a program that actually works.

Crippleware—A demo that's substantially disabled—the save function doesn't work, for example, or it won't print. Take it, use it, if you like it, send money and they'll send a program that has all the features enabled.

There are other kinds of 'ware—postcardware, where if you like it you send a postcard, and linkware, where if you like it you link to the developer's site— but the ones listed above are the main types of 'ware. We'll be talking about all sorts of software in this book. Here are a few addresses of shareware libraries to get you started. We'll point you to particular sites for particular programs as we progress, but if there's ever something you think you need but which we haven't helped you find, check these sites:

Info-Mac HyperArchive
    http://hyperarchive.lcs.mit.edu/HyperArchive.html

Jumbo! (Programs of all sorts for Windows, UNIX, and Macs)
    http://www.jumbo.com/

Macdownload.com
    http://macdownload.com/

Shareware.com (All types of programs for Windows, UNIX, and Macs)
http://www.shareware.com/

Tucows—The Ultimate Collection of Winsock Software (Originally just Windows software, it now carries Mac and OS/2 programs)
http://www.tucows.com/

The Ultimate Macintosh Site
http://www.flashpaper.com/umac/

The University of Texas Mac Archive
http://wwwhost.ots.utexas.edu/mac/main.html

Winfiles (A large archive of 32-bit Windows software)
http://www.winfiles.com/

Winsite (A huge archive of Windows software)
http://www.winsite.com/

You can also search for software at Yahoo! and other Web search sites. As you've seen in this chapter, Yahoo! has several useful software categories. We've mentioned the e-mail page, but you can also find pages with information about **FTP programs** (http://www.yahoo.com/Computers_and_Internet/Software/Internet/FTP/), Usenet newsreaders (http://www.yahoo.com/Computers_and_Internet/Software/Internet/Usenet/), programs for converting word processing documents to Web (HTML) documents (http://www.yahoo.com/Computers_and_Internet/Software/Internet/World_Wide_Web/HTML_Converters/), links to Macintosh programs (http://dir.yahoo.com/Computers_and_Internet/Hardware/Personal_Computers/Macintosh/Software/Shareware/), and so on.

TEXT AUTOMATION TOOLS

Promoting on the Internet can be very hard on your fingers—you'll find you do an awful lot of typing. The frustrating thing is that you seem to be typing the same thing over and over again—your e-mail address, your Web site's URL, a description of what you are promoting, a suggestion for a particular type of cooperative promotion, and so on.

Finding Software at Yahoo!

To search for Internet software at Yahoo! go straight to the **Internet Software** *page (http://www.yahoo.com/Computers_and_Internet/Software/Internet/), select Just This Category from the drop-down list box next to the Search button, and then type the search term. That way you'll limit the search to useful categories.*

Don't do this! It simply doesn't make sense to type this stuff over and over again! You need to spend a little time figuring out how you can work more efficiently. The very simplest method is to set up a "boilerplate" text file—a file containing all the things you have to type frequently. You can then copy these pieces and paste them in when necessary.

But even that's pretty inefficient. You should seriously think about investing in a few tools to help you. Let's see what's available:

- Clipboard Utilities
- Text-Replacement Tools
- Programmable Keyboards

Clipboard Utilities

One of the annoying things about Windows is its clipboard. Its clipboard can only hold one "clip" at a time. That means if you need to move several clipped items you have to cut it out of one application, move to the other application, paste it, and repeat several dozen times or until you get sick of it.

Fortunately this problem bothers lots of people. We say fortunately because a lot of people have come up with programs that address this Windows limitation. Tara's absolute favorite clipboard utility is **ClipMate**, which you can get from http://www.thornsoft.com/. This little program is everything the Windows clipping utility should have been.

ClipMate allows you to clip several different file formats—both text and graphics. You can save text that you use often in a "long-term" collection so you don't have to type it over and over again. You can use a "glue" feature and clip several things together at once. You can edit the text clips right in ClipMate without having to use a text editor. You can even open a "picker window" and rearrange the clips you've made into different collections, add them together, etc.

When you're doing research leading up to your promotional effort, you'll be moving around your data a lot. You'll make that clipping a lot easier if you invest $20 and download a copy of ClipMate. (If you want a disk and a manual, that'll cost you $25 plus shipping.)

There are a number of other clipboard programs for the PC:

Click And Paste
   http://www.btsunlimited.com/
Click&Paste
   http://bigmeg.net/

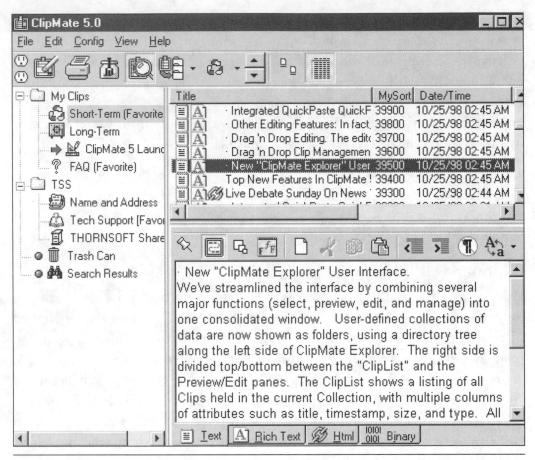

FIGURE 2.1: ClipMate makes it easy for you to work with large amounts of clipboard material.

ClipAid

http://www.stpt.net/shareware/clipaid/

Clipper

http://runsoftware.hypermart.net/

CoodClip

http://www.aha.ru/~deep125/

CopyPaste

http://www.scriptsoftware.com/

Mini Clipboard

http://www.olemiss.edu/~cvpsmith/

SmartBoard

http://www.wintools.com/smtbrd/

You can also find these programs at the shareware libraries we mentioned earlier in this chapter.

There are also Macintosh clipboard programs, such as **CopyPaste** (http://www.scriptsoftware.com/) and **MultiClip PRO** (http://www.olduvai.com/products.html).

Text-Replacement Tools

Another way to quickly automate typing is to use a text-replacement tool such as **ShortKeys** (http://www.shortkeys.com/). This Windows program lets you replace a small piece of typing with something longer or more complicated. For instance, if you want to type your mailing address, phone number, and e-mail address, all you need to do is type, say, *adr*, and ShortKeys types it all for you.

It works like this. You create entries, and assign some kind of keystroke sequence to them. You might, for example, assign your e-mail address to *e-*; whenever ShortKeys sees that you have typed *e-*, it will back up and delete the typed characters, then type the full e-mail address for you (see Figure 2.2). You can create different files, too. Each file can hold a set of replacement instructions, so you can use files for different purposes. For instance, you might use a

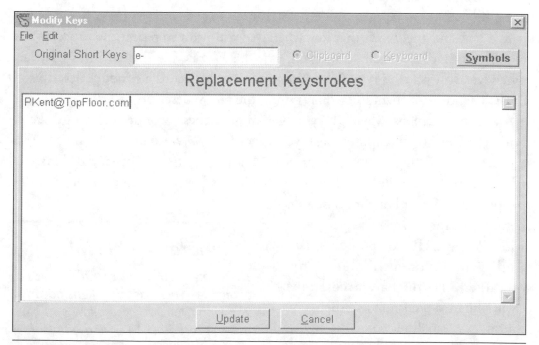

FIGURE 2.2: Tell ShortKeys what you'll type—in this case *e-* —then tell it what you want it to type for you.

file full of replacement texts for when you are replying to journalists after doing a mass mailing (see Chapter 16), another file for when you are wandering around the Web asking people to link to you (see Chapter 8), and so on.

ShortKeys is a $19.95 shareware program; there's also a free version, ShortKeys 98 Lite. The publisher has several other automation tools, too, such as **Keyboard Express** (http://www.wintools.com/smtbrd/) and the SmartBoard clipboard utility we mentioned earlier.

We haven't found many other text-replacement tools, though there probably are others. We have run across a Mac program that's supposed to be pretty good: **TypeIt4Me** ($27 registration—http://www.users.dircon.co.uk/~r-ettore/ or http://www.hebel.net/~rettore/).

Programmable Keyboards

Programmable keyboards are a godsend to the serious computer user. Yet network administrators hate them, because the inexperienced computer user often accidentally programs something into the keyboard and ends up getting completely confused. If you know how to use one, though, they can save you scores of hours of work each year.

A programmable keyboard allows you to "record" keystrokes on particular keys. If you have to repeat a process, you can quickly record the process and assign it to a key, and then press that key whenever you want to repeat the process. You could record your e-mail address on, say, the F12 key, and then press that key whenever you want to type the address. You could record a product description on F11, and press that rather than typing the entire description.

The problem is, where do you get one of these wonderful things? Peter bought a **Gateway** computer a few years ago (http://www.gateway2000.com/), at a time when all their computers came with a programmable keyboard. He's still using it. But new Gateways don't come with this keyboard—they'll sell them to people who have bought Gateways before, but the keyboards won't work with Pentium II computers (they'll work with Pentiums, Pentium Pros, or earlier). If you have a computer earlier than a Pentium II, then you might try to find someone who's bought a Gateway in the past and get them to buy the keyboard for you.

Programmable Mice

There are also programmable mice available, such as the Kensington Thinking Mouse. These allow you to assign procedures to a mouse button or a mouse/keyboard combination.

There are several other programmable keyboards, though it's hard to find them in the stores:

Maxim keyboard, Kinesis Corporation
http://www.kinesis-ergo.com/

MCK-142 Pro, Kbtek America (Their Web sites are awful—at the first you can view product information but not order ... at the second you can order but not view product information.)
http://www.ortek.com/
http://www.eagle-touch.com
626-855-0325

Avant Stellar keyboard, Creative Vision Technologies, Inc.
(Recommended by Jerry Pournelle in BYTE magazine.)
http://www.cvtinc.com/

Datadesk (various keyboards, for Macs and PCs)
http://www.datadesk1.com/

Floating Arms Keyboard, Workplace Designs
http://www.wpdesigns.com/

InterFatron-BBc, Ltd. (This company designs keyboards, but doesn't sell them ... they link to sites where you can buy them, though.)
http://www.ifbbc.com/

Grabbing E-Mail Addresses

One procedure we *haven't* found a tool for is the automated saving of e-mail addresses. While you are wandering around the Internet you'll come across a lot of useful e-mail addresses: newsletter editors, owners of Web pages containing link directories that you want to be listed in, owners of Web pages who are probably interested in your products, and so on. You'll want to collect these e-mail addresses for use later.

We'd really like to be able to point at a mailto: link in a Web page, press a keyboard combination—Ctrl+G, for instance—and have the program grab the e-mail address from the link and save it in a file. So far we haven't found anything like this. The best we've figured out so far is this: if you're out researching something, wandering around the Web grabbing e-mail addresses, you can start a text editor such as Windows Notepad, and copy mailto: addresses into there quite quickly if you have a programmable keyboard.

So, for instance, here's what you could do: right-click with your mouse on a mailto: link, and up pops the menu. Quickly press the key that's associated with the recording, and the recording plays; it selects the Copy Shortcut command on that pop-up menu, then presses Alt+Tab to switch from the browser to the text editor. It presses Ctrl+End to move the cursor to the end of all the text in the text editor, then presses Enter to move down a line, then presses Ctrl+V to paste the mailto: line into the text editor. Then it presses Alt+Tab to go back to the browser.

That's it; the address is quickly copied with a single mouse click and a single keystroke. All the e-mail addresses captured this way now have the mailto: prefix, but they can be quickly removed in a word-processing program.

We suggest that you build address books while you're doing your research; one could be a list of addresses of people maintaining link directories, another a list of Web-site owners who might be interested in a cooperative promotion of some kind, and so on. Later you'll be able to mail to everyone in an address book very quickly.

OFFLINE BROWSERS

Another tool that can be very handy is the offline browser. This is a program that grabs Web pages that you specify. For instance, you tell it to go to a particular Web page, look at all the links on that page and grab the referenced pages. You can even tell it to grab pages referenced by links on those pages, and even grab the pages referenced by links on that set of pages … I'm sure you get the picture. Most of these products allow you to state how many levels down you want to go. One's usually enough—if you do too many, it can take forever and end up filling your hard disk.

This is the sort of thing you set up to work over lunch or overnight. Once it's finished, it stores the Web pages that it's downloaded in a special directory on your hard disk, so your browser can view them very quickly. You can then decide which are useful and which are not.

The following are some ways to use these programs:

- If you find a Web page with a lot of links to pages associated with your business—a link directory, which we'll discuss later in this chapter—you can use the program to download the pages linked to this site and view them to see if they can be useful to you.

- If you use a search engine to find sites of interest to you, you can save the results page on your hard disk. Then you can remove links that are clearly of no use—links pointing back to other areas of the search site, for instance, and links that clearly point to sites that are of no use to you. Then use the offline browser to grab the pages referenced by the links you're interested in learning more about. Some offline browsers make it difficult if not impossible to work on pages stored on your hard disk, so you may have to store the page at your Web site and then continue the operation.

- Do a number of searches, save the results pages on your hard disk, and then merge them, keeping just the links that look as though they might be useful. Then use the program to get the referenced pages.

- Use the program to check links on your own site. There are programs that will check links to make sure they work, but they're "dumb." They can tell you if there's a page at the URL in the link, but not if that page has the information you think it has. So you can use one of these programs to make sure the links on your site really do reference the information you say they do: run the offline browser on your links page, and then you can quickly view each page one by one.

These programs vary in price from free to around $70. Unfortunately, most are not worth anything. Peter's used a number of these programs, and had all sorts of problems with them. In general this software category is of a pretty low quality, so it's hard to find a good one; even the ones highly rated by the computer press are often pretty awful.

For instance, FlashSite seems to work pretty well, with the exception that it will pull pages from only a single domain—it won't follow links across to other Web sites, which makes it almost useless for our purposes. Of all that Peter's tried, he's found NetAttaché to be the best of the lot, but perhaps the others will improve over time. Tara likes WebSnake, which can do a certain amount of searching in addition to downloading pages. Try a few and see which you prefer. It's worth spending a little time finding one that works for you, because these systems can really save you a lot of thumb-twiddling time. Don't sit in front of your computer waiting for things to transfer—let the computer do it for you while you're doing something else. Here's where you'll find a few offline browsers.

FlashSite (Windows 95/NT)
   http://www.incontext.com/

HotCargo Express (Windows 3.1/95/NT)
   http://www.documagix.com/products/hotcargo_express/

NetAttaché (Windows 95/NT, Windows 3.1)
   http://www.tympani.com/

SurfBot (Windows 95)
http://www.surflogic.com/

Teleport Pro (Windows 95/NT)
http://www.tenmax.com/

Web Buddy (Windows 95,
Macintosh)
http://www.dataviz.com/

WebFetcher (Windows 95/NT,
Macintosh, UNIX)
http://ontv.com/webfetcher/

Websnake
http://www.anawave.com/
websnake/

WebWhacker (Windows
95/NT)
http://www.bluesquirrel.com/

Overnight Problems

Leaving a process to run overnight is often a problem, thanks to the unreliability of Internet connections. There's a good chance your connection will drop five minutes after you walk out of the door. A better solution may be to let the program run while you're doing something else—filing, talking on the phone, or working on a different computer, for instance. Some of these programs can restart the process if the connection drops—an essential feature.

WEB PAGE ARCHIVES

Here's a class of software you may not have heard about … in fact, there aren't many of these programs around. But they can be very handy. A Web-page archive program is one that saves Web pages for you. For instance, you find a page containing useful information, something you want to save for later. Perhaps it's a review of your product, or a competitor's site you want to take a closer look at when you have time. You could set a bookmark on the page. But as you probably know by now, Web pages don't always hang around for long; the next time you try to return to the page it may not be there.

You could use the browser's Save As command, but that's a nuisance; it won't save all the images in the page, and it'll just drop the page into a directory—the browser will provide no tools for retrieving the page later.

A Web-page archive program (we just made up that term, by the way) will save the page for you, images and all. For instance, take a look at Figure 2.3. This is **SurfSaver**, a shareware program that you can find at http://www.askSam.com/. In the top of the browser you can see a review of *Poor Richard's Web Site.* In the bottom of the screen you can see a list of Web pages that Peter added to the archive. The page you're seeing here is being pulled from the archive, not from the Web itself. Long after this page has disappeared from the Web, it'll still be in the archive.

FIGURE 2.3: SurfSaver provides a great way to save and later retrieve Web pages.

SurfSaver allows you to create multiple folders; to categorize your pages; to add keywords and notes to help you find and recognize the pages later; to see a list of all the pages in a folder; or to search by keyword, title, URL, date, or even search the actual Web-page text. It's an easy program to use, too. To save a page into the archive all you have to do is click the button that the installation program placed on your browser's toolbar, then click QuickSave (to save it in a predetermined folder) or click Save and select the folder where you want to save the page. (One tip, though—SurfSave's documentation doesn't mention this, but if your browser has JavaScript turned off, SurfSaver won't work properly.)

Are there other archive programs? We don't know—SurfSaver is the only one we've run across, though there may be more.

CONTACT MANAGEMENT SOFTWARE

Relationships are what marketing and promotions are all about: making relationships with your customers, prospects, and vendors, and maintaining those relationships to (hopefully) everybody's benefit. To efficiently juggle all the details about the people you interact with regularly, you can use contact management software.

Contact management software helps you—that's right—manage contacts. This covers everything from keeping address information all in one place, to tracking when you've made particular calls, to when you need to make a follow-up call, when appointments are scheduled, and so on.

Contact managers have a couple of problems. First of all, one size doesn't fit all. Few people have needs that are likely to be met by many of the contact-management forms. If you have particularly complicated needs, you may find that a free-form database works better than a contact-management program for you. Let's take a look at both.

Standard Contact Managers

You've probably seen standard contact managers. They have forms that you fill out to indicate certain very standard information—name, phone number, fax number, e-mail address, etc. Many of them also have calendars, to-do lists, and other efficiency-boosting features.

Some contact managers are little more than basic address books. Some contact managers can do everything up to and including developing telemarketing scripts and helping you with contact management. Which one you try depends on your needs. Do you simply need to keep track of names and addresses? Do you have a lot of scheduled appointments? You can probably get by with a simple contact manager. Do you use the contact information you have to do a lot of different things—make follow-up sales calls, for example, or send letters? Do you analyze the information or try to break out different groups based on type of contact or where they live? You probably want a contact manager with more features. Do you share contacts across a network at your company? Do you use your contacts for one particular function—sales, for example—and use them very aggressively, constantly making and tracking contacts? You probably want an extensive or specialty contact manager.

There are dozens of contact managers you can choose from. Let's take a look at a few of the most popular.

Sidekick

http://www.sidekick.com/

Sidekick is a basic contact manager, helping you maintain an address book, do basic scheduling, and write letters and memos. And that's pretty much it. You can specify fields but you can't design your input screen. You can't dial a phone or track your expenses with the latest version of Sidekick. Its main function is to keep your address book.

Tara uses Sidekick extensively and finds it very useful. She appreciates the fact that you can export the address books in a variety of formats, and that it's easy to create address labels from within the program. Sidekick also uses little enough memory that you can keep it open while you're running several other different applications. If you have peripheral programs you're happy with—like e-mail and word processing—don't want to spend a lot of money, and need just an address book as your contact manager, Sidekick is a good one to look at. However, should you ever get into heavy contact management—making lots of contacts, tracking calls, keeping track of client expenses, and so on—Sidekick probably won't be the program for you.

ACT!

http://www.symantec.com/act/

ACT! is a powerhouse of a contact management software package, but you need to make sure you can use everything that it offers—and it'll take a little while to learn. ACT! offers all the features you would expect of a standard contact manager—address book, to-do list, calendars and alarms, and so on. But ACT! also offers more—configurable contact screens (you can design your own screens and figure out what you want to keep track of), callback reminders, integration with the Internet (you can use Internet search tools to find contact information and download

It Won't Work if You Don't Use It

You can have the greatest contact management software in the world and it won't do you any good if you don't use it. When you're shopping for a good PIM, make sure that you look for something you can actually use. Don't get something so simple that you're immediately frustrated by what it can't do. Conversely, don't get something that's so complicated that you're immediately frustrated by what you don't understand. Lots of contact managers offer demos—take advantage of that! Try before you buy.

them to ACT!, send e-mail directly from the program, and so on), caller ID, and more. There's even a little feature called SideACT! that allows you to enter information into the program without keeping the entire program open.

All of this would be great for you if you're willing to put most of your contact needs into one program, and you don't rely heavily on external programs to make contact. If you don't need all the bells and whistles, however, you might find this program to be a little more than you bargained for.

GoldMine

http://www.goldminesw.com/

Wow. GoldMine will do just about everything but butter your toast. It's a very highly rated program with features not available in other programs. But it is expensive, and it's very hard to learn. In fact, Peter rants about this one—he believes it's the epitome of a program created by a software-publishing company that thinks that as long as it creates software with lots of features it doesn't have to worry about making it easy to use or provide good documentation. The publisher is definitely losing business by making this program so complicated—they lost Peter, for one.

GoldMine is used by many sales people; it can be used to track contacts through sales cycles, schedule follow-ups, work with other people across a company network (GoldMine is perhaps the only full-featured contact-management program with complete network integration), and even go through telemarketing scripts. It also has Internet integration and a built-in e-mail center. If you have to work in a group, sharing contact-management data, you might want to look at GoldMine.

But whatever you do, don't buy before you try. Download their software first, and see if you can figure out how to use it. Or, as was the case with Peter, see if you really want to spend that much time figuring out how to use it. ACT! is a very good alternative—much easier to use—though it doesn't have the network integration.

These three software packages are just a sample of the contact managers available. You can also check out the following to get an idea of the different kinds of contact managers available:

ACE Contact Manager

http://www.sfsace.com/

Third-Party Helpers For Your Contact Manager

ACT!, GoldMine, and many of the bigger contact manager programs have third-party and add-on products available. If you have unique contact needs, or are working in a niche industry, check these add-ons to see if any of them are appropriate to your needs.

Not Just Software

Don't be afraid to mix high-tech and low-tech. Tara uses Sidekick, but she finds it very handy to periodically (every few months or so) print out the addresses in Sidekick and keep them in a Rolodex next to her computer. That way she doesn't have to open the contact manager every time she needs a phone number or e-mail address.

Pursuit for Windows

   http://www.pursuitsw.com/

SaleSmarz

   http://www.eurosmartz.co.uk/

Janna Contact Managers

   http://www.janna.com/

Maximizer

   http://www.maximizer.com/

Sharkware

   http://www.sharkware.com/

Time and Chaos

   http://www.isbister.com/

Free-Form Personal Information Managers

The above software packages offer very strict forms of information management. They're based around address books that have forms for input, with fields for each piece of information. In some cases you can modify the fields—rename or add fields—but in general there's a limit to the type of modifications you can make.

> ### The Web is All You Need?
>
> *There are free online services that duplicate some of the things that a contact manager will do.* **When.com,** *at* http://www.when.com/, *will set you up with a free Web-based scheduling calendar.* **Yahoo!** *has a free calendar and to-do list at* http://calendar.yahoo.com/. **Dataferret** (http://wwwdataferret.com/) *can store up to 10 contacts and provide you with a free web-based calendar service. People who do a lot of group scheduling might want to check out* **JointPlanning** *at* http://www.joint-planning.com/, *which offers free group scheduling, address book, calendar, and to-do list. Some of these products may be handy, but they in no way replace a contact-management program on your computer.*

Sometimes the information you have to manage doesn't fit into these neat little packages. Instead, you might want to save large things—clippings of news stories, lists of URLs, ideas, memos, what-have-you—things that don't fit into neat little packages and that can't be expressed in a form.

In cases like this, you might want to look at free-form information managers. These hold information that can't be categorized well and which may not fit into a standard form. There are two very well-known information managers: AskSam and InfoSelect.

AskSam

   http://www.asksam.com/

Sometimes you want to maintain large blocks of text-based information, like e-mail records or memos. At the same time, you want them to be searchable quickly. For something like that you could use AskSam, which allows you to dump large chunks of text in one database for quick searching and organization. You can specify form fields to enter data, like you use with standard contact managers, but you don't have to.

Let's take an example of how you'd use AskSam. Say you do media monitoring for your company and a couple of competitors. You want to stash the full text of any magazine or newspaper articles you find in a database. With AskSam, you could simply take the electronic versions of the documents and drop them into a database without specifying any form fields. The articles would be completely searchable and all together in one place. On the other hand, you could specify form fields for the name of the publication in which the article appeared and the publication date. With the form fields added, you would be able to both search the full

What Should You Track?

As you evaluate different types of contact-management software, a question might occur to you: what kind of information is essential to track? That's a difficult question to answer; everyone has his own idea of what is essential. Name of Web site, URL, and name and e-mail of contact person, surely. Name and postal address of the organization behind the Web site—good to have but not always essential (and not always available.) After that you get into details—how often the online publication updates, how the online journalist prefers receiving news releases, fax numbers, a site's policy for reciprocal links. All these details aren't things you'll need immediately, or even often. But the more details like that you can keep track of, the more effective you can be in promoting your Web site.

text of the articles and list the articles by publication name or date. AskSam also has several filters allowing you to import information from various sources—Eudora and Microsoft Word, for instance.

If you handle a lot of free-form information like articles, you'll appreciate the quick searchability of AskSam and its capacity for a lot of information. However, this system won't work well for normal contact management. And AskSam is a little expensive, ranging from $200 to $400.

InfoSelect

http://www.miclog.com/

InfoSelect provides contact management, a calendar, free-form information organization, and an easy way to maintain lots of information snippets and organize them over time. It's unusual and will take a little getting used to, but if you do a lot of information gathering you'll get a lot out of it.

InfoSelect offers an outline format from which you can organize various different types of information—text, calendars, images, outlines, databases, forms, and so on. Tara uses InfoSelect to organize snippets of information she comes across in the course of a day. Since she administers two newsletters and several different Web sites, she's constantly finding information in different categories that is relevant to her work. Instead of organizing these in a contact manager (since she'll need them within a few days of finding them) she uses InfoSelect's outline format to file different snippets under different topics. Each week she can gather these snippets into newsletters—InfoSelect allows her to make templates for her newsletters. She opens a new template, drops the information into it, polishes it up a little bit, and sends the newsletters away!

InfoSelect has a few drawbacks. It's an unusual program, so it takes a while to understand. If you need more standard contact management, you'll find this a little awkward to use for that purpose. And if you've already got an external e-mail program you like, you won't have any use for InfoSelect's e-mail features.

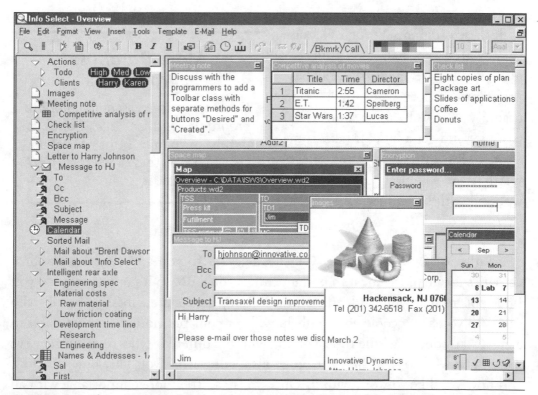

FIGURE 2.4: This snap of InfoSelect may look complicated, but it's really not so bad. The outline format—the "tree" on the left side, evolves over time as you add information.

But Tara loves it, finding it invaluable for managing collections of very different information.

Full-Blown Databases

You may find a need for a full-blown database, a program designed to work with large numbers of records. For instance, in Chapter 16 we'll discuss how you can take a database of media contacts—perhaps 12,000 individuals —and select appropriate ones to receive press releases. Working with large numbers of contacts like this is best done using a full-blown database program, such as **Microsoft Access** (http://www.microsoft.com/), **FileMaker Pro** (http://www. filemaker.com/), or **Alphasoftware's Alpha Five** (http://www.alphasoftware.com/). It'll take you a long time to sift through very large databases using a contact-management program—you really need the features of a database program.

There are a couple of problems with these programs, though. Because they are specialized things— few people use powerful database programs—prices are high, and usability is low. In other words, you pay a lot and get a little. It takes some effort to learn these programs, but it's worth it in the long run if you're working with big contact lists.

MS Outlook

Many Windows users have Microsoft Outlook available, which can be used as a contact-management program. It can store contact information, tasks, appointments, and so on, but it lacks some of the advanced contact-management features that these other programs have.

More Database Programs

If you want to investigate database programs further, see **Yahoo!'s database page:** http://dir.yahoo. com/Computers_and_Internet/ Software/Databases/.

Gathering information on Web sites relevant to you and your promotional activities is one of the most important things you'll do, so it's important that you find tools to help you work efficiently. Building a strong database of people who can help you and people you can help will get your promotional activities off to a great start. Spend a little time working with the different types of software we've recommended—trying different programs, seeing what you like, how it works, and how you like to work with it. Once you're a little more comfortable with all this software and with the Internet in general, it's time to think about putting up a Web site. The next chapter will introduce you to all the Web site basics.

CHAPTER THREE

Web Site Basics

Y ou don't have to have a Web site to do business on the Internet—but if you don't, you're missing out on a huge opportunity. Most businesses working online have Web sites, or are perhaps in the planning stages. Your Web site can be your operational headquarters, the center around which your other promotions are based. It seems, in fact, that many of the businesses that are choosing to work online *without* a Web site are spammers—companies using e-mail spam as their only promotional tool, companies that are to some degree "in hiding" in cyberspace, trying to generate fax and mail orders.

Most people reading this book probably want, or already have, a Web site. That's easy enough, isn't it? Everyone and their dogs seem to have Web sites these days. You get an Internet account with an ISP, the ISP gives you some Web space, and away you go … you set up your site.

The reality is very different. Sure, it's easy to set up a Web site with a few pictures of your spouse, kids, and assorted pets, as half of AOL's members have proven. But if you're in business, your needs are more complicated.

A few months ago Peter received a call from a jeweler in Texas who wanted to buy his book. The jeweler was having problems, he said, because he couldn't seem to get secure forms set up (that is, Web forms that would transfer credit-card information in an encrypted manner). It turned out he couldn't set up secure forms because his hosting company didn't have a secure server. Of course he should have asked the hosting company if they had one before he ever signed up with them, but, well, he didn't know enough to ask!

We're going to talk about some issues like that in this chapter, including domain names and hosting companies. But this chapter provides only a very cursory introduction to the subject. We strongly recommend that you read *Poor Richard's Web Site: Geek-Free, Commonsense Advice on Building a Low-Cost Web*

Site, by Peter (Top Floor Publishing, ISBN: 0-9661032-8-9). This book contains, for instance, an entire chapter explaining the different types of locations for your Web site, an entire chapter on the things to ask a hosting company, an appendix with a checklist to help you compare hosting companies, two chapters discussing domain names, and so on.

WHERE TO PUT YOUR WEB SITE

Too many people begin their Internet presence with the idea that there's only one place to put their Web site—on the Web space provided by the company they use for Internet access. In fact there are a number of choices. You can put your Web site at one of these types of locations:

> ### Poor Richard's Web Site
>
> **Poor Richard's Web Site** *may be the most widely reviewed and praised title in computer-book history. It's been mentioned in well over 100 media reviews … it's been recommended by* **BYTE** *magazine,* **The Philadelphia Inquirer, Windows Magazine, Keyboard** *magazine,* **Fortune.com, Web Server Online Magazine,** *and many others. You can see the reviews for yourself at* http://PoorRichard.com/review.htm. *If you need (in the words of David Methvin, writing in* **Windows Magazine***) "a practical, no-nonsense guide" to setting up a Web site, then (in the words of David Garvey, writing in* **The New England Nonprofit Quarterly***), "Buy This Book!"*

- **At an ISP's personal-page site**—When you sign up for Internet access, you'll probably be given a bit of Web space. This is not appropriate for most businesses; you need your own domain name (which you can't use on personal space), and the personal space probably doesn't have all the services you need.

- **At a free-page Web site**—There are a number of places, such as GeoCities (http://www.geocities.com/), XOOM (http://www.xoom.com/), and Tripod (http://www.tripod.com/) that will allow you to set up a Web site for free. Again, you won't be able to use your own domain name, and you won't get all the services you need. Many of the free Web site services also have restrictions on how you can use their space. Many, for example, frown on commercial sites.

- **At a cybermall**—Forget the malls. A mall is a stupid idea—geography is meaningless in cyberspace—and the online malls seem to be stacked with really badly designed Web sites.

At a Web store—There are some places that sell a particular type of product—books, for instance. They'll sell you a generic page or two (a specific size and format). Again, you can't use your own domain name and you'll have limited services.

At a Web host's site in a subdirectory or subdomain—A web-hosting company is one that sells you space on their server, and you can do whatever you want with it. A subdirectory or subdomain means that you are dependent on their domain; you don't have your own domain name, so if you move, your site will have a new address.

At a Web host's site as a virtual domain—This is the best choice for most small businesses and organizations. You can use your own domain name, and, if you choose the right company, get all the services you need.

On your own Web server—This is very expensive and complicated; not something the average small business should do!

You should understand that there's a lot of overlap. You may find that your local Internet Service Provider, the company you pay to provide you Internet access, is also a good Web-hosting company. You may run across a cybermall that is also a hosting company. And the free-page sites may also sell more advanced Web services, like sites with shopping carts. What we're saying here is that it's important for you to pick the right type of service at the right company. We're not implying that if a company provides free space it can't also be a good commercial host.

GETTING YOUR OWN DOMAIN NAME

We've just mentioned that some of these services are not suitable because you can't have your own domain name. So what? What's it matter? It really matters a lot. If you're serious about doing business or maintaining a long-term Web site, you should register your own domain name.

When we say *domain name,* we're really talking about a second-level domain name. For instance, look at this domain:

```
cnn.com
```

The .com bit is what's known as a top-level domain (TLD). The cnn bit is the second-level domain name. So CNN, the cable news channel, registered its own domain name as cnn.com.

If you set up your Web site at your online service or service provider, you'll have to use that company's domain name in your Web address—your URL. So the Web site's URL may be something like http://www.members.aol.com/acmekites/, or http://ourworld.compuserve.com/homepages/acmekites/. If you set up with a free service, such as GeoCities or Xoom, you'll end up with a URL such as http://www.geocities.com/Paris/LeftBank/54312/acmekites.html or http://members.xoom.com/acmekites/.

Why, then, is it so important to get your own? For a variety of reasons:

- It looks more professional. It's hard to take http://www.geocities.com/Paris/LeftBank/54312/acmekites.html seriously; this company should use http://acmekites.com/ so that it looks like it plans to stay in business.

- It's shorter. It's easier for your visitors to remember acmekites.com than http://www.geocities.com/Paris/LeftBank/54312/acmekites.html/.

- It won't change when you move your Web site, and one day you *will* move your Web site. If you don't own your own domain name, you'll have to change it ... and change your business cards, letterhead, catalogs, etc. And your old visitors won't know where you've gone, unless you pay to keep a redirection page at the old account.

- Once you have your own domain name and an account set up with a hosting company, you'll also have an e-mail account at that domain name, so you can create multiple e-mail addresses (sales@acmekites.com, fred@acmekites.com, etc.)

- Yahoo!—the single most important search engine on the Web—has a bias against subdomains; they're much less likely to add http://www.geocities.com/Paris/LeftBank/54312/acmekites.html to their index than http://acmekites.com/.

Don't try to save a little money at the expense of doing things right; it costs as little as $70 to register a domain name for the first two years, $35 a year after that.

How do you register a domain? If you want to register a .com (the most popular domain), .org, or .net domain, you have to do so through an organization called **InterNIC**; go to http://www.internic.net/, where you can find information about registering a domain. (Be very careful; that's .net, not .com! If you go to http://www.internic.com/ you'll find a private company selling domain names—which they have to register with InterNIC for you—and charging $220.)

One problem. Before you can register a domain name, you have to have somewhere to "point it." You need to provide InterNIC with IP (Internet Protocol) numbers for two *name servers*. If you sign up with a hosting company, the company will provide these numbers to you.

What if you have a domain name you want to register—and want to do

---

Do It Yourself

It's a good idea to register domain names yourself, rather than allowing a hosting company to do it for you. We've heard a number of stories of people arguing with hosting companies and then finding their domain names hijacked!

---

it right away before someone else grabs it—yet you don't yet have a hosting company you're working with? You can *park* the domain. There are a number of parking services. In fact InterNIC even has a commercial parking service you can use, **WorldNIC**; go to http://www.worldnic.com/. This will cost $119, so in effect you're paying an extra $49 to park your domain. (On the other hand, the WorldNIC service is easier to use than the regular InterNIC service, so you could say that part of that $49 pays for ease of use—in fact WorldNIC charges $80 for domains rather than the $70 InterNIC price.)

It's possible to park your domain for free, though. A number of companies allow you to register your domain to their name servers—they're hoping that eventually you'll sign up with their hosting service. A good place to start looking for a free parking service is at **Yahoo!'s Domain Registration page**: http://dir. yahoo.com/Computers_and_Internet/Internet/Domain_Registration/.

What if you want to register another domain, other than .com, .net, or .org? There are scores of different top-level domains—one for every country connected to the Internet, for instance. A good place to begin your search is the above Yahoo! page, or **Yahoo!'s Network Information Centers** page: http://dir. yahoo.com/Computers_and_Internet/Internet/Domain_Registration/Network_Info rmation_Centers/.

Picking a Domain Name

How do you choose a domain name or domain names? You may want several names for different purposes: one for your company (Peter has http://TopFloor. com/, for instance), one for a particular product (he also has http://PoorRichard. com/), one that identifies your general area of business, and so on. Here are a few guidelines:

- Try to get a domain name that matches your business name, or even create a business name that matches a domain name. CDnow.com, for instance, is the domain name of CDnow; Amazon.com is the domain name of Amazon.com; BizBlast.com is the domain name of BizBlast.com.

- Try to get a short domain name, though sometimes that's difficult. Barnes and Noble had two major problems, for instance. It's been in business with a long name for a very long time. Yet they got into the Internet business way too late to pick a domain name such as books.com, so they ended up with barnesandnoble.com.

- Look for a *keyword*.com domain name if possible, such as word.com, football.com, skydiving.com, or scuba.com. (Sorry, those are all taken, but it's still possible to find them in more obscure subjects.) Many users type a plain keyword in their browsers' Location boxes to see where it takes them; in many browsers if you type a single word the browser will add www. and .com for you, so these keywords can be very valuable. On the other hand, Netscape recently changed the way its browser works, so in many cases the keyword won't work in that manner—rather, the browser searches a database at Netscape's site.

- If you can't get quite what you want at first, use some imagination to pick an imaginative name. If you have a lawn service (or sell hemp products, perhaps), try GrassGrassGrass.com. If you paint houses in Denver, try DenverPainters.com. If you sell footwear, try BootsAndShoes.com. Sometimes it seems that all the good domain names have gone, but at the time of writing all these domain names are still available.

Clarifying Your Domain Name

You'll notice, no doubt, that we've done something unusual with the domain names above; we've used both uppercase and lowercase in these domain names. Rather than typing grassgrassgrass.com, we wrote GrassGrassGrass.com. For some reason you don't see this very often. People just assume that a domain name has to be lowercase; it doesn't. Browsers ignore capitalization in the domain name, so you can capitalize any way you choose when advertising your URL.

Using mixed case is a good way to make a domain name much more readable. For instance, Peter's Poor Richard's site is http://poorrichard.com/. However, some people don't notice that there are two r's in the middle of poorrichard, so he writes it http://PoorRichard.com/ to make it clearer. This is a simple way to make a URL easier to understand and remember, especially if you have a very long URL (http://SunriseSunsetBreakfast.com/, for instance), or repeating letters. (It's easy for the eye to miss two r's or two n's.) For instance, there's the http://spannet.org/ site. The owners realized that the name was easier to read, recognize, and remember if they spelled it this way: http://SPANnet.org/.

There are two basic rules for using this little trick.

- You can write the domain name whatever way you want, it makes no difference to a browser or Web site: http://PoorRichard.com/, http://POORRICHARD.COM/, http://poorrichard.com/, http://PoOrRiChArD.cOm/. Capitalization of the domain name doesn't matter as far as the browser is concerned. (Try these URLs and you'll see that they all work.)

- It does matter, though, how you write the rest of the URL—the directories and filename. For instance, http://PoorRichard.com/newsltr/archive.htm will work, but http://PoorRichard.com/Newsltr/Archive.htm will not. You should not change case of the text that follows the domain-name portion of the URL.

By the way, you can generally do the same with e-mail addresses; they are rarely case sensitive, so if it looks better to use uppercase letters in some positions (PeterKent@TopFloor.com, for instance), go ahead and try it. Try to send a message written in that manner. Most e-mail systems will handle it fine; if the message gets through, then you can start writing your addresses in that manner.

Here's another clever way to clarify URLs. **Computer Literacy's** URL is http://www.computerliteracy.com/. That's a little long, but in printed materials they make the individual parts of the URL stand out using different colors. They print the www. and .com pieces as white or gray; that makes sense, because it pushes those pieces to the background. After all, you don't really need to remember these bits; they "go without saying." Then they print the computer piece in bright red, and the literacy piece in black (that's how they display the name of the company on their main Web page, too). It really is quite effective when printing a URL in a color publication.

Finally, why bother with www. at all? You'll notice that many of the URLs we've shown in this chapter—http://PoorRichard.com/, for instance—completely omit the www. piece. In fact, Computer Literacy seems to have dropped it, too, at least in the logo at the top of their Web page. Amazon.com doesn't use it in their logo at the top of their page either. (They use Amazon in bold, with .com in a lighter type.) There's one catch here, though. Some Web-server administrators simply haven't caught on, and they set up the servers so that you *must* use the www. piece. For instance, at the time of writing you can get to http://www. schwab.com/, but you can't get to http://schwab.com/. So before you write your URLs like this, make sure they'll work (and if they don't, ask the administrator why!).

CHOOSING A HOSTING COMPANY

We said that in most cases the best place for a Web site is at a hosting company. There are now thousands of hosting companies. It's easy to track them down; just try one of these sites:

budgetweb.com
http://www.budgetweb.com/budgetweb/

The Budget Web Hosts List
http://www.callihan.com/budget/

Host Find
http://www.hostfind.com/

Leasing a Server
http://union.ncsa.uiuc.edu/HyperNews/get/www/leasing.html

Leasing a Server List at budgetweb.com
http://budgetweb.com/hndocs/list.shtml

Microsoft FrontPage Web-Presence Providers
http://www.microsoft.com/frontpage/

NerdWorld-WWW Servers
http://www.nerdworld.com/nw1642.html

The WDVL (Web Developers Virtual Library) Providers page
http://www.stars.com/Vlib/Mall/Providers.html

Web-Quote Central
http://www.centeroftheweb.com/webquote/

Checking Domain Names

If you want to find out if a .com, .net, or .org domain has been registered, use the **Whois system at InterNIC:** http://rs.internic.net/cgi-bin/whois/.

Type the name you want into the text box (remember to include the .com, .net, or .org bit at the end) and press Enter, and Whois will search to see if the name has been registered.

If you want more options for checking domain names, visit **AskReggie** *at* http://www.askreggie.com/. *This system makes it easy to search for domain names in different ways, and to search for specific companies to see what domain names they own. (You can do all this at the InterNIC site, but AskReggie simplifies it just a little.)*

Yahoo!-Web Presence Providers page
http://www.yahoo.com/Business_and_Economy/Companies/Internet_
Services/Web_Services/Hosting/

What to Ask a Hosting Company

These places will help you find low-cost hosting services—you may end up paying only $15–$30. But how on earth do you figure out which one to pick? That's a problem. There are a lot of different services available, so before you can possibly choose a host you have to understand what those services are. Here's a quick summary. (Remember, *Poor Richard's Web Site* has an entire chapter on this subject.)

Does the Company Have Microsoft FrontPage Server Extensions?

This is important only if you plan to use Microsoft FrontPage (a very popular Web-authoring program). If the hosting company doesn't have the server extensions installed, some of the FrontPage features won't work.

How Much Does It Cost?

Most services charge a setup fee, and then a monthly charge. Some don't have a setup fee, and some will waive the setup fee if you are transferring an existing Web site and domain from another location. Even if they don't advertise that they do so, if you are transferring a site it might be worth asking whether they will waive the fee.

Minimum Contract and Guarantee?

Some Web-hosting companies want you to pay a year's fee at once, but you should ask if you can pay for, say, three months. Some simply go month by month, others charge by the month and give the first month free—the ideal situation. Also ask what sort of guarantees they offer; some companies offer a 30-day money-back guarantee. And get the guarantee in writing if you can.

How Much Disk Space?

Your Web site will be limited to a certain amount of disk space, though you can buy more. Small, low-cost accounts may have just a couple of megabytes of disk space; larger sites will get tens, even hundreds of megs. You can actually get quite a lot into a megabyte or two, and a really huge site will need only a few hundred megs.

How Much Are Hit and Data-Transfer Charges?

Some companies charge you for the number of hits—the number of times someone transfers one of your pages to his browser. Others charge according to the amount of data transferred out of your Web site. Either way, the busier your site, the more you'll be charged under these pricing schedules. Others have no limit.

Unlimited use may not be so good if it means that all the sites handled by the server are very busy, of course. And in any case, most companies provide a certain minimum data transfer for free, which is usually plenty for most sites.

How Much Are Upgrades?

If your Web site grows, so will your hosting needs. Check to see how much it'll cost you to add more disk space, transfer more data, create more e-mail accounts, and so on.

How Much to Host Multiple Domain Names?

If you have more than one domain name, you can have them all point to the same Web site. For instance, you might have one domain name for your company and other domain names that you are using to promote specific products. There are different ways to handle this. All the domains can point to the same directory, or you can have separate directories for each domain. Of course, there are different ways to charge, too. You may be allowed two domains for free, perhaps, with an additional fee for extra domains. Or maybe you'll pay an additional fee for all extra domains.

Is There a Charge for E-Mail Accounts?

You'll generally get an e-mail account with your Web site. Sometimes you'll get several accounts even though you may need no more than one. Some companies, however, may charge extra for the accounts.

With a single e-mail account, you can retrieve e-mail that has been sent to various addresses: info@acmesewercover.com, sales@acmesewercover.com, joe@acmesewercover.com, susie@acmesewercover.com, and so on.

How Many Mail Forwarding Accounts?

You may also want to make sure the Web-hosting company allows you to set up mail forwarding—automatically defining certain types of incoming e-mail messages to be forwarded somewhere else. For instance, messages to susie@acmesewercover.com could be forwarded to susiesewer@aol.com. Ask how many accounts can be forwarded.

Do You Have Mail Responders?

A mail responder, or autoresponder, is a program that automatically responds to incoming mail. For instance, if someone sends e-mail to info@acmesewercover. com, an informational message can be sent back. These can be very useful, so I recommend that you use a host that provides these. There are several things a good autoresponder should be able to do:

- Quote the incoming message in the autoresponse
- Save the incoming message
- Redirect the incoming message somewhere else (to a mailing-list server, for instance)
- Grab the e-mail address from the incoming message and put it in a text file

The last of these is particularly important, as it allows you to collect e-mail addresses from messages sent to your autoresponders. Here's the problem: you almost certainly won't find an auto-responder system that does all these things. (This is really Peter's "this is the way auto-responders *should* work list.)

Do You Have Mailing Lists?

A mailing list is a discussion group based on the e-mail system. You may want to set one up; they're very useful promotional tools, as we'll discuss in Chapter 11. Even if you don't want to host a discussion group, you can use a mailing-list program to distribute a newsletter. Many companies have mailing-list software available for their clients to use. If your host does, ask whether there's an additional cost, how many mailing lists you are allowed to have, and how many members per list.

Do I Get a Shell Account? (Telnet Access)

A shell account allows you to log onto the Web site using Telnet, and modify files and directories. This can be useful, and you'll find that most companies provide a shell account. Some don't, though, and this can present problems. For instance, if you want to install your own CGI scripts (see below), you may need Telnet access so you can get to the scripts and modify their permissions, rename files, and so on.

Do I Get FTP Access?

You'll need FTP (File Transfer Protocol) access. This allows you to transfer files to and from your Web site, so virtually all companies provide this service. Some may provide a different way to transfer files, such as using FrontPage. But even if you use FrontPage, it's nice to have FTP access too.

Can I Set Up an Anonymous FTP Site?

This is not the same as FTP access to your Web site. Rather, it allows you to set up an FTP site that people can access to download files. You might want to do this if you are distributing software, for instance. While it's possible to transfer files directly from your Web site, it's sometimes handy to have an FTP site, too. People without good Web access can still use the FTP site. Further, some FTP sites can resume interrupted downloads. If someone tries to transfer a file, gets halfway through, and his ISP or phone company drops the line, he can come back and continue the transfer where he left off—a very handy feature for large downloads.

Do You Have a Secure Server?

If you plan to take orders online or transfer sensitive information, you'll need a secure server. (You'll often see it referred to as an SSL server, meaning a Secure Sockets Layer server.) For instance, credit-card information typed into a form will be encrypted before being sent from the user's Web browser to the server. There may be an additional fee to use the secure server. You don't have to have a secure server to take orders online, but many people won't place orders unless you do.

Do You Have Shopping-Cart Software?

If you plan to sell products and want to offer users some kind of catalog combined with an order form, you might want to find out if the Web-hosting company has any shopping-cart software already available and, if so, what are its capabilities and its cost. If not, ask if you can add your own shopping-cart software. We'll discuss this further in a moment.

Can I Use CGI Scripts?

CGI means Common Gateway Interface. It's a way to provide interactivity to Web pages, in particular to handle the input from forms. For instance, you can use CGI to take information from a form and send it to your e-mail account, and many shopping-cart programs use CGIs. Many Web-hosting companies have libraries of CGI scripts you can use. Some allow you to install your own CGI scripts, but don't provide a library. Others don't allow you to add any CGIs. I recommend that you find a company that at least allows you to add your own.

Do I Get Access Reports?

Access reports show you information about visitors to your site. You need this information, as it can show you where visitors are coming from, when they arrive, which pages they view, and so on. Some companies send reports to you automatically via e-mail each day or week. Some create charts to show access information.

Can I Have Password-Protected Pages?

If you need to set up a private area at your Web site, some companies will help you create password-protected areas. This is quite easy to do for yourself using Microsoft FrontPage, by the way.

Do You Have Telephone Technical Support?

Ask about the type of technical support available. Can you call and talk with someone? And if so, is it a toll-free or local call? This is a significant issue, as you'll almost certainly have to get help at some point. Some Web-hosting services try to handle all their support through e-mail, but the problem with this is that it's too easy to ignore e-mail or delay responses. You must have some way to talk to someone. Toll-free numbers are relatively rare for low-cost Web-hosting companies; you may end up having to use a long-distance number. But a long-distance number is better than no phone support at all. Some companies charge extra for phone support; some don't.

These are some of the most important issues involved in choosing a hosting company. Other things to consider are …

- Is Commercial Use Allowed?
- Do They Have a Discount for Non-Profit Organizations?
- Do They Provide Online Credit-Card and Check Processing?
- Do They Allow Imagemaps?
- Do They Allow Server-Side Includes?
- Do They Provide Database Access?
- Do They Allow Java Applets?
- Do They Have a RealAudio Server?
- Can You Resell Web Space?

- Do They Have Promotional and Design Services?
- Who Owns the Server?
- How Many Computers Do They Have?
- What's the Size of the Company?
- What's the Connection Speed and Distance to the Backbone?

In addition …

- Ask for References.
- Consider the "Look and Feel" of the Hosting Company's Own Web Site.
- Do a Real-World Check on Their Other Clients.

CREATING YOUR WEB PAGES

How are you going to create your Web pages? Well, the simple answer to that is "pay someone else to do it for you." Unfortunately we don't all have that option. And in fact it doesn't have to be terribly complicated to create Web pages.

There are two ways to create Web pages. One is to work with the "raw" HTML (HyperText Markup Language). Want to see what HTML looks like? Load a Web page in your browser, then use the View|Page Source command (or similar). You'll see something like Figure 3.1.

These little codes tell the browser what to display, and how to display it. It tells whether the text is a heading or just body text; whether a picture should be placed in a table; where the picture comes from; whether to create frames; whether a word is red or blue; and a multitude of other details.

If you don't already know HTML, this is all a very big hassle. There's a lot to learn. Luckily you don't have to learn it. There are many *authoring tools* you can use, word processors that create Web pages. If you can use a word processor, then you can create Web pages. Sure, there are a few differences, but it shouldn't take you long to learn how to use one of these programs.

Peter often recommends Microsoft FrontPage. He often gets e-mail from people thanking him for recommending FrontPage—people saying how easy it made creating Web sites. Then again, he often gets e-mail from people telling him that he shouldn't recommend FrontPage (though often these comments are based on the fact that it's a Microsoft product more than anything else). There is one important thing to be aware of, though: while Microsoft FrontPage for

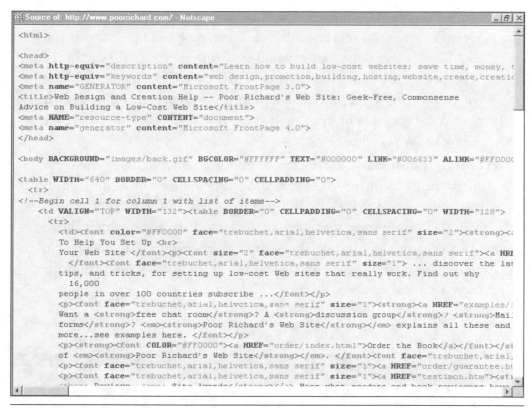

FIGURE 3.1: This is what a Web page looks like "behind the scenes." The stuff between < and > are the HTML codes.

Windows is a very good product, Microsoft FrontPage for the Macintosh is lagging way behind, and nowhere near as good.

In any case, FrontPage isn't your only choice. There are many, many authoring programs available to you. These are the different types of programs:

Simple HTML Editors—Simple HTML editors display all the codes but help you enter them. Instead of typing a code for something, you can click a button, and the editor drops the code in for you. These are like beefed-up text editors.

Sophisticated HTML Editors—A step up from the simple HTML editor is the sophisticated HTML editor, for people who like to see their tags but want to speed up the process of creating pages. These editors have a plethora of tools to enter the codes more quickly. Many expert HTML authors use this sort of tool.

WYSIWYG HTML Editors—WYSIWYG means What You See Is What You Get. In other words, while creating your pages, you can see, more or less, what a user would see while viewing the page in the Web browser. You don't see the HTML tags. This is like working with a modern word processor, and for non-experts it is much easier than using a simple or even sophisticated HTML editor. (FrontPage is a WYSIWYG editor.)

HTML Converters—There are a number of programs used for converting files into Web pages: converting them from various word-processing and desktop-publishing formats, for instance. This is very handy for companies that have a lot of paper documents that they'd like to convert and put on the Web. You generally use a converter in conjunction with a good HTML editor, because converters do little more than convert.

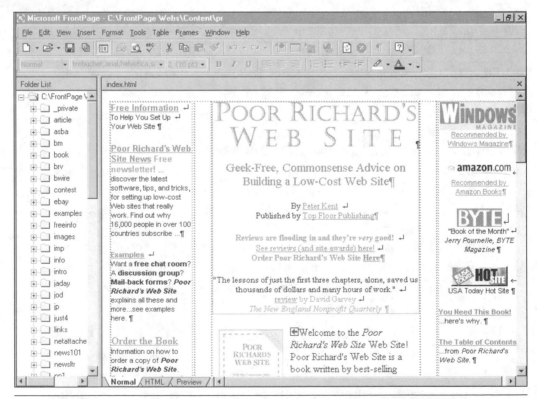

FIGURE 3.2: This is MS FrontPage, a WYSIWYG HTML Editor. On the left you can see the structure of the Web site—the individual directories. On the right is one of the pages being edited.

Built-in Converters—There are now many programs that contain built-in HTML converters; a number of word processors, for instance, allow you to save documents in HTML format.

Here's a sampling of WYSIWYG programs to get you started:

Claris HomePage (Macintosh, Windows 95/98/NT)
http://www.claris.com/products/homepage3.html

CorelWEB.DESIGNER (Windows 3.1/95/98/NT)
http://www.corel.com/corelweb/webdesigner/

Dreamweaver (Windows 95/98/NT, Macintosh)
http://www.macromedia.com/software/dreamweaver/

Internet Creator (Windows 95/98/NT)
http://www.formaninteractive.com/

Microsoft FrontPage (Macintosh, Windows 95/98/NT)
http://www.microsoft.com/frontpage/

NetObjects Fusion (Windows 95/98/NT, Macintosh)
http://www.netobjects.com/

PageMill (Macintosh, Windows 95/98/NT)
http://www.adobe.com/prodindex/pagemill/main.html

Symantec Visual Page (Windows 95/98/NT)
http://www.symantec.com/vpage/

Symantec Visual Page (Macintosh)
http://www.symantec.com/vpagemac/

WebExpress (Windows 3.1/95/98/NT)
http://www.mvd.com/

Yahoo!-HTML Editors
http://www.yahoo.com/Computers_and_Internet/Software/Internet/
World_Wide_Web/HTML_Editors/

Here are a few sophisticated HTML Editors:

BBEdit (Macintosh)
http://www.barebones.com/

HotMetal Pro (Macintosh, Windows 95/NT, UNIX)
http://www.softquad.com/

HTMLed (Windows 3.1, 95, NT)
http://www.ist.ca/

Sausage Software's HotDog Pro (Windows 3.1, 95, NT)
http://www.sausage.com/

WebEdit (Windows 3.1, 95, NT)
http://www.luckman.com/
http://www.greymatter.co.uk/gmWEB/Items/BND01156.HTM
http://www.nesbitt.com/

Yahoo!-HTML Converters
http://www.yahoo.com/Computers_and_Internet/Software/Internet/
World_Wide_Web/HTML_Converters/

Remember that you can also find many, many shareware programs at the software libraries we mentioned in Chapter 2.

SETTING UP A SHOPPING-CART

If you're planning to sell products online, you will need to set up a shopping-cart system. (*Shopping-cart* is the term commonly used to mean the system of forms employed to take orders at a Web site.) It should be simple to do this, but at the time of writing it's really not quite so simple, especially if you want a full-featured system.

Well, you may have seen a few products advertised, perhaps in software catalogs. You may have heard claims like these:

Just install the program on your computer, create your Web site, and then transfer the site to the Internet quickly and easily with the automatic upload feature.

Or how about these "system requirements" stated on a product box:

• MS Windows 95, or Windows NT 4 or higher
• Internet connection

Sounds simple. Buy the packaged software, install it on your computer, create your site, and publish it to the Web. Unfortunately, it's not that easy, as Peter discovered during his research into shopping-cart software. Unfortunately many software publishers are exaggerating how easy it is, and Web-site owners are buying products that they discover they can't use, or can use only if they move their Web sites to a hosting company that supports the software they've just bought.

First, some background. If you know a little about HTML—the "coding" required to build Web pages—you probably know that HTML can be used to create forms. But HTML cannot make a form actually *do* anything. In order to get the form to do something, you need a special program running on the server. That program might be a CGI (Common Gateway Interface) script, or it may be a special set of "server extensions" installed on the Web server.

When a site has a shopping-cart system, the buyer sees a series of forms. When the user enters information in those forms, and submits the forms, the data is taken by the program on the server and manipulated—sales tax, shipping costs, totals, and so on are calculated. Then the information is sent back to the user's browser. So when you buy a product that will create a shopping-cart system, there are two important questions to be answered:

a. How does this product create the program required to handle the forms data?

and, more importantly,

b. Will the program run on the Web server I'm using?

Here's an example. Foreman Interactive sells a product called Internet Creator, and that product can set up an online store. At Foreman Interactive's Web site you'll learn that:

E-mail ordering, shopping basket management, and searching capabilities are just some of the features included in Internet Creator's E-Commerce Edition.

You'll also learn that the system requirements are a Windows PC, 10MB hard-disk space, and 8MB RAM. After reading the blurb you might be ready to buy. And in fact you can navigate from the main page, through the promotional text, and into an order form, without discovering that the only way to set up a store with this product is to sign up for service with SiteAmerica (Foreman Interactive's partner Web-hosting company). If you already have a Web site, and don't want to move it, this program won't work for you (or rather, it will allow you to build Web pages, but the shopping-cart won't work unless you host with SiteAmerica).

This program is not alone; there are other products that claim you can quickly set up a shopping-cart system … until you look closely at the small print (if you can find it).

Picking a shopping-cart system is not easy. There are basically four ways to set up a system:

1. Buy the software and install it on your own server.

2. Buy the software and install it on your hosting company's server.

3. Sign up with a Web-hosting company that has shopping-cart software available.

4. Sign up with a shopping-cart service; the shopping-cart software runs on their server, linked to from your Web site.

As we noted before, option 1 is out of the question for most small businesses—it's way too complicated and expensive. So you're left with the other three options. Before you buy a product, you have to be sure what you are getting into. Internet Creator, for instance, really falls into category 3; although you can create Web pages with this program for use on any server, if you want to use it to create an online store, you'll have to sign up with a certain hosting company.

When you go looking for shopping-cart software, make sure you ask the following questions; don't rely on the company's product blurbs or declared system requirements:

- How does the system create the program that runs the forms? Does it require special extensions at the server, does it install CGIs, or does it require a particular server?

- Can I use this at any hosting company, or do I have to work with a particular company or choose from a list of companies? (Some products are set up to work at a few dozen companies.)

- If I can use it with any hosting company, which types of Web servers will it run on? (Make sure it's compatible with the one you or your hosting company uses.)

- Who will install the program on the server? (It's not a simple task to install these programs, so at the very least you need good technical support available.)

Let's look a little closer at the three options applicable to most small businesses.

Install Software on Your Hosting Company's Server

There are many products that you can install on your host's server. These are generally products that use CGI (Common Gateway Interface) scripts running on the server, so you must make sure that you're allowed to use CGIs on your server, that the ones you are buying are compatible with the server, and that you're sure that either you are capable of installing them or that you can find someone to install them for you. These things can be *very* tricky, but some software companies will install the products for you.

Such programs vary widely in cost. There are actually freeware programs available, but they're generally difficult to set up; perhaps you can hire a consultant to install them for you. Prices go up into the many thousands of dollars.

Use a Hosting Company With Shopping-Cart Software Available

Perhaps the simplest thing is to sign up with a Web-hosting company that already has shopping-cart software available for use. At least you know it's already installed on the server, so it should be relatively easy to get running … well, perhaps. Just because your hosting company chose it doesn't mean it's either easy to use or has all the features you need. Check it out carefully. (We'll discuss this in a moment.)

Use a Shopping-Cart Service

There are a number of companies that will host your shopping cart. They are not necessarily Web-hosting companies—they may not be interested in hosting your entire site—but they will run the shopping-cart system, with your products, on their server.

In other words, you can have your Web site at one location, the shopping-cart at another, and link from one to the other. Most customers won't even realize that they've jumped from one site to another during the order process.

The advantages? You may find a Web-hosting company you really like, with the exception of its shopping-cart system; you can keep your Web site where it is, and pick and choose between shopping-cart services. They're usually relatively easy to set up (*relatively* easy we said, not easy!). It's someone else's responsibility to keep the thing going. (If you install your own system, in contrast, you'll have to worry about maintenance.) And they can be quite affordable. But they're often rather weak systems, lacking important features.

Picking a Shopping-Cart

Right now, choosing a shopping-cart system is an exercise in compromise. There's no perfect solution. You'll be juggling features, price, and ease of installation. Here, to help just a little, are a few things to watch for when picking a shopping-cart system:

- Will the program be able to handle as many categories and products as you need?

- Does the program allow the buyer to add products to a basket, then continue shopping and add more products?

- Can you import items? If you have a lot of products, you really need to be able to import a list. If you only have a small number of products, you can enter them by typing in the information.

- Can a buyer leave, come back later, and continue shopping where he left off? (This is a nice feature, though not essential.)

- Can buyers search for products? (This is not important if you have a small number of products.)

- Will the program allow you to add fields? For instance, you may want to add a check box that allows buyers to sign up for a free newsletter, or a "where did you hear about this product" drop-down list box. (Of course, this information must then be included in the order information provided to you by the program.)

- How does the program calculate state sales tax? You should be able to specify sales tax for particular states—ideally for particular ZIP codes. But some programs don't calculate sales tax well. (For instance, if the user types Colorado instead of CO, the sales tax may not be calculated.)

- Does it allow you to specify all the shipping methods and rates you want to use? Some programs provide little flexibility, or even don't allow the customer to choose a shipping method at all but only tack on a set shipping price. (A ridiculous situation when you consider that the Internet is an international forum.)

- Will the program verify that credit-card numbers and e-mail addresses were entered in the correct format?

- How does the program provide confirmation to the user? It should display a confirmation page, but it should also send an e-mail message.

- Will the program e-mail a message to you letting you know that an order's been taken?

- Does the system require that buyers register before making a purchase? (It probably shouldn't, but some do.)

- How is the order information delivered to you? It should be easy to import into a database, so you need a text-file format (comma- or tab-delimited text) or a database format. Some systems deliver in an e-mail message, which is usually inconvenient. (How do you get it into a mailing-label or credit-card processing program?)

- Try entering information in many different ways—foreign phone numbers and provinces, different country names, and so on. Does the program handle different situations well, or does it give error messages?

- Do you like the overall "look and feel" of the product? Is it confusing, or simple to use? Does it make your customers "jump through hoops," or is it quick and easy?

A Quick Word about Transaction Processing

There are two basic processes involved in selling products online. First, you must take the order. Then, you have to process the financial transaction, which generally means processing a credit-card order, though there are other types of money: checks, debit cards, and even 900 numbers. (That's right, you can charge a transaction to a telephone bill by having the buyer call a 900 number.)

Most small companies take orders online, then do the transaction processing offline. In other words, they download the orders, then use a credit-card terminal to process the orders.

It is possible to do online transaction processing: to set up a system that takes the order, processes the credit-card, then saves the completed order information. Transaction processing is often expensive to set up, though: $200 to $500, depending on the shopping-cart system you're working with. And then there may be a monthly fee, plus a per-transaction fee—perhaps $1 per transaction, perhaps more (on top of your normal credit-card transaction fees).

Most small businesses will probably want to wait awhile before they use online transaction processing. However, prices are definitely on their way down, and we'll soon see online transaction processing available for little or no setup fee, and small monthly and per-transaction charges.

Finding Shopping-Cart Systems

Where do you begin your search for a shopping-cart system? With your choice of hosting companies. As we mentioned before, you might want to find a hosting company with a good shopping-cart system.

If you already have a Web site and want to find a system—or perhaps are not willing to compromise and use the poor products most hosting companies offer—then you'll have some research to do. Probably the best place to start is at

Peter's ***Shopping-Cart Software & Services Directory***, which you can find at
http://www.poorrichard.com/freeinfo/special_reports.htm. This currently lists
around 75 different programs and services. You might also try these Yahoo!
categories:

> **Yahoo!-Electronic Commerce Software**
>> http://dir.yahoo.com/Business_and_Economy/Companies/Retail_
>> Management_Supplies_and_Services/Electronic_Commerce/Software/
>
> **Yahoo!-Electronic Commerce**
>> http://www.yahoo.com/Business_and_Economy/Electronic_Commerce/
>
> **Yahoo!-Web Software Companies**
>> http://www.yahoo.com/Business_and_Economy/Companies/
>> Computers/Software/Internet/World_Wide_Web/

SIMPLE ONLINE TRANSACTIONS

Here's a quick description of a very
simple order-processing system for
Web sites, the one that Peter currently uses.

Step 1: The Shopping-Cart

Peter uses a shopping-cart system
called ***Hazel*** (http://hazel.netsville.
com/), a very flexible system that he
installed on the hosting-company's

Sell It On the Web

The **Sell It On the Web** *(http://www.
SellItOnTheweb.com/) site is a good
place to go if you want to learn more
about setting up shopping carts.
They review products, they examine
Web sites that sell products and tell
you what they like and don't like
about them, they announce new services, and so on.*

server himself. This system saves the transaction information—the person's
name and shipping address, the credit-card number and expiration date, and so
on—in a text file at his Web server, and then sends him an e-mail message telling
him an order has been taken.

Step 2: Download the Data From the Web Server

Peter transfers the order information from the Web server to his office computer.
Some shopping-cart programs and services provide a secure Web page from
which sales data is downloaded.

The data file created by Hazel is a comma-delimited text file, so he can
quickly and easily import the file into a database program. This is a very

important feature of a shopping-cart program: the format in which the data is saved should allow for database imports. Peter believes that this is a critical feature ... evidently some shopping-cart designers disagree with him!

Step 3: Import Into Access

Peter uses Microsoft Access to save all his transaction data. It's not the easiest program to learn to use ... but then he hasn't been able to find any other programs that will do everything he needs yet which are easy to use.

Peter has created an Access macro to process incoming orders. When he double-clicks the macro, it imports the order file that was downloaded from the shopping-cart system. Peter can then view the data in the database to make sure it looks okay—that the buyer provided all the information he needs to process the order.

Creating macros really isn't terribly hard, but if you don't know anything about Access it may take you a while to figure it all out. Perhaps you can find someone to help you set up a database and create a macro or two. Someone who knows how to use a database program should probably be able to do everything you need in an hour, two hours maximum.

Step 4: Export to PC Authorize

Peter created another macro to export the information into another text file, this time in the format used by PC Authorize. PC Authorize is the program he uses to process credit cards. Setting up an import template took ten minutes or so, and it allows him to import the data very quickly each day.

Step 5: Process the Credit Cards

Next Peter opens PC Authorize, and imports the text file that he's just created. Then he clicks on a button, and PC Authorize dials into the credit-card network and processes the cards. For every card that is approved, PC Authorize prints a receipt (which is sent with the book).

This is a great little program and, according to Peter, it's really fun to use. Peter's been working computer programs for almost 20 years, yet this is the first program he's ever worked with that actually takes money from someone else's bank account and moves it into his! By the way, for those of you who don't process credit cards and are wondering what proportion are approved ... Peter's found that the vast majority go through okay. He's experienced only around a 1 percent failure rate. Sometimes the problem is an incorrectly entered expiration date, or perhaps the buyer didn't realize the card was over limit. If he e-mails the buyers when there's a problem, a number of them will provide new information—a different expiration date or another card number. There's around a 50 percent chance that a bad order will eventually go through.

Step 6: Print Labels

For every order that goes through, Peter needs a mailing label. This is where it gets just a little clunky. The version of Access Peter's using has a bug that prevents it from printing mailing labels. So instead, he creates a report. (Actually, the macro that exports the data to the PC Authorize text file creates this report at the same time.) Then he clicks on a button at the top of the report, and the report is opened in Word for Windows. He then runs a macro in Word that cleans up the formatting in the report, removing tabs from it.

Next, he opens his LabelWriter program. LabelWriter is a little label printer connected to the computer's serial port. He selects the first mailing address in Word for Windows and copies it to the Clipboard, then clicks a button in LabelWriter and the content of the Clipboard is pasted into a mailing label and printed.

And that's it. The sold items can now be shipped.

How Much?

How much does a system like this cost? Here's a quick rundown.

Shopping-Cart Software—This can cost from a few bucks a month to thousands. Your mileage will vary.

Credit-Card Merchant Account—Prices vary tremendously, but if you look around you can find a good deal. Peter signed up with **Costco** (http://www.costco.com/), a warehouse club that has a special Business membership with a variety of special features—including low-cost merchant accounts. The annual membership is $100. It costs $25 to sign up for the credit-card account, which is a relatively low fee. Then there are per-transaction fees, which are also relatively low: 1.89 percent plus 25 cents for transactions in which you cannot swipe the credit card. (However, note that there are sometimes additional fees, in Costco's program and with all other merchant-account programs; for instance, there are fees for voice-authorization, for transactions not using "address verification," and so on.)

Database Program—Most people have a free database program available; many computers these days come with a copy of Microsoft

Access. The real cost is figuring out how to set up the databases and macros; it took Peter several hours, as he hadn't worked with a sophisticated database program in a number of years.

PC Authorize—Peter picked PC Authorize (http://www.Tellan.com/) because it was a Windows 95/98/NT program that would allow him to import a text file. Some of the other programs either won't run in Windows, or won't import text files. Whenever you sign up for a credit-card merchant account, you'll be offered various hardware terminals (which he didn't consider because he wanted an all-software order-processing system) and software. But you generally don't need to use the products you're offered; you can buy elsewhere. Costco's merchant-account program had a deficient software program, so he bought PC Authorize directly from the publisher, Tellan, and paid $358, including shipping.

Label Printer—There are several label printers available. Peter's using a CoStar LabelWriter, for which he paid about $140. It prints wide labels, which include a return mailing address at the top.

It can take a little while to set up a simple, low-cost system like this, but once it's up and running it's very quick and easy to work with.

FULFILLMENT SERVICES

So how do you ship? If you don't ship products already, it can be quite a hassle setting up to do so, and processing a few orders each day. If you automate it as much as possible, as we described earlier in this chapter, you may find that it's really not so hard. But perhaps you'd rather pay someone to do it for you.

That's where fulfillment companies come into the picture. These are companies that will ship products for you. They may even take the orders for you. Peter uses a fulfillment company called **Bookmasters** (http://www.bookmasters.com/). As the name implies, they ship mainly books, but they'll ship pretty much any small product. Peter allows Bookmasters to take all his phone orders—they have their own toll-free lines—but he ships his own Web orders. Occasionally—such as when he's traveling—he'll process Web orders on his computer or laptop, and then send the shipping addresses to Bookmasters so they can ship the products for him.

You can find fulfillment companies in a variety of ways. Check your local Yellow Pages, for instance, or use an online system such as **Yahoo!'s Yellow Pages** (http://yp.yahoo.com/) or **US West Dex** (http://www.uswestdex.com/). But perhaps you don't need a fulfillment service in a particular area. Perhaps, for example, you're with a company outside North America looking for a fulfillment company to ship your products for you within North America. In that case you should check **Yahoo!'s Fulfillment Services** page at http://dir.yahoo.com/Business_and_Economy/Companies/Marketing/Fulfillment_Services/. Also, if you search for the word *fulfillment* at Yahoo!, you'll find that there are other categories, such as lists of fulfillment services in Canada and Great Britain.

These are the things to consider when looking for a fulfillment service:

- Do they have staff who can take orders by phone 24 hours a day, or do they just ship products to lists of people that you send to them? (Many fulfillment companies ship, but do not process orders.)
- Will they ship orders you send to them if you process the payment first?
- Do they have their own toll-free lines, or do you have to provide your own line?
- Do you have to provide your own credit-card merchant account, or are they willing to process credit cards for you?
- Can they accept orders by fax and mail?
- Can you e-mail orders to them?
- What are their charges? Make sure you understand every little charge, as you'll probably be charged for every "touch" (that is, every little process involved in taking the order and shipping the product).

WEB DESIGN—IT'S SOFTWARE, NOT GRAPHIC DESIGN

How do you go about designing a Web site? We believe you should remember that a Web site is a piece of software. Few site owners seem to understand this, and even fewer Web designers do. Web design has become the domain of the graphic designer, which is a big mistake. Consequently there are many thousands of great looking Web sites ... that load slowly and are difficult to move around in.

A Web site is a piece of software. It has to *do something*. Unlike a piece of graphic design—a billboard or magazine ad, for instance—a Web site is interactive. People click on links and buttons to make the site actually do something. So the primary concern should be user-interface design. Does the Web site actually work properly? Does it achieve its aims? (By the way, a good place to visit to learn more about user-interface design, and in particular learn about its application to Web design, is the **User Interface Engineering** Web site: http://www. uie.com/.)

Once you have a Web site that *works*, you can make it look good. You shouldn't work the other way around.

Web design is a big subject, one that we have no space for here. But before we move on, we'd like to point out another important consideration. Your Web site must serve your visitors, but it must also serve *you*. There's a balance to be found here. If your Web site doesn't serve your

Long Pages or Short?

*Here's an example of the sort of thing you'll find at the **User Interface Engineering** site. You may have heard that it's better to create lots of short Web pages, rather than making users scroll through long pages. This is one of those graphic-design myths. User Interface Engineering studied this issue and discovered that in fact users don't mind scrolling, and that, more importantly, long pages often work better. People find it easier to navigate around the site and find what they need.*

visitors ... well, you won't have any visitors (or, at least, few repeat visitors). But what's the point in having a Web site if it doesn't serve you, too?

You must find a way to make the site easy to move around in for your visitors, and provide the information and services that they need. At the same time, you have to make sure that you get something out of it—for instance, that they see the sales blurbs that you want them to see, that they provide you with the information you need, and so on. Again, a Web site is not simply graphic design; it's more complicated than that. In some cases you may have to make compromises. Sometimes the site won't be as attractive as it could be because you want to make it easier to use in some way. Or perhaps a process is not quite as simple as it could be because you want to make sure the visitor "passes through" an area of the site. For instance, Peter often mentions his special reports in mailing-list discussion groups or his newsletter. He could provide a link directly to the report he's talking about. But instead he points people to the **Poor Richard's Special Reports** page at his Web site (http://www.poorrichard. com/freeinfo/special_reports.htm). It's still very easy for the visitor to find the report he's looking for. But Peter has made sure that the visitor sees a list of other reports, and sees links back into the main Poor Richard's site, where the visitor can find more information about the book ... and, Peter hopes, buy the book.

There is quite a lot involved in setting up a Web site, and it can take some time. The first step, though, is knowledge. (By the way, did we mention Peter wrote a book called *Poor Richard's Web Site: Geek-Free, Commonsense Advice on Building a Low-Cost Web Site*, with an ISBN number of 0-9661032-8-9?). So we'll leave this subject for now, and move on to the first step in your promotions: figuring out who you're going to target.

CHAPTER FOUR

Finding Your Targets

In Chapter 1, we took a look at some essential questions to consider before starting your promotion or marketing campaign, and then left you to think over those ideas while we explained what you needed before you got started.

We hope you did take some time to think over those ideas, because in this chapter we're going to show you how to find your targets by describing research resources that will help your promotion campaign. These promotional resources will give you an idea of the newspapers, periodicals, and other media outlets available that might have an interest in your product or service.

When you see how many are available—and there are thousands upon thousands—you might be a little intimidated. Don't be. Consider one of the focuses you decided on in Chapter 1, and start from there. Don't try to drink the river in one gulp.

If you have plenty of time, you might want to bypass the focuses and instead go methodically through a checklist of where you can find information specific and helpful to your Web site. You'll need a checklist, a few tips for using search sites, and possibly some search-site software. We'll be looking at ways to find information related to your promotional campaign in this chapter.

PLANNING YOUR SEARCH

When searching for sites that might be interested in you and your product or service, you can break down the sites for which you search by category. You want to keep your eye out for certain kinds of sites that can help you during your quest for online promotion. (We'll be more specific about how you can contact and use these sites as we continue through the book.)

    Specialty Indexes—These are sites that index sites like yours. You want to both pursue links in these indexes and investigate the sites that they index as possible promotional partners. (We'll discuss "partnerships" in detail in the second part of this book.)

Competitors' Sites—What are your competitors doing online? Who are they linking to? Who's linking to them? If you know what your competitors are up to you may get a few good ideas, or be able to "head them off at the pass" in some way … and people linking to your competitors may want to link to you, too.

Industry Update Sites—These may be formal publications, online newsletters, or simply Web pages that are updated a couple of times a week, but you want to keep an eye out for sites that keep their visitors informed about your industry. For one thing, you'll pick up valuable hints about new Web sites that pertain to your industry. For another thing, you'll have a nice list of media to alert when you offer new services on your site or launch a site overhaul.

Potential partner sites—These sites cover a broad range of possibilities: sites with whom you could swap banner ads, sites whose interests dovetail with yours, sites that could share promotional ideas with you—in other words, sites that don't directly compete with yours but in some way could partner with you for mutual benefit.

In this chapter we're going to cover how you can find media and promotional resources. But since we can't give you exhaustive lists of every type of site you want to find, we're going to kick off this chapter with some tricks for finding Web sites using search sites.

FINDING THE SITES YOU NEED: SOME HINTS

This book can't give you an exhaustive tutorial in Internet research. For that, you might want to check out Tara's *Official Netscape Guide to Internet Research*, co-authored with Jill Nystrom (Netscape Press). But we can give you a few hints that'll make your search easier.

You may know about Boolean searching: using the AND, OR, NOT, and other operators to make very specific queries. For instance, you could search for `rabbits OR hares` to find pages related to either rabbits or hares; or `rabbits AND NOT hares` to find pages related to rabbits but only if those pages are not related to hares; or `rabbits AND hares` to find only pages that are related to both rabbits and hares. Most search systems allow you to use some kind of Boolean logic, but you have to check each one to see how it works. For example, AltaVista doesn't understand `rabbits NOT hares`, while other systems might; in the case of AltaVista this would have to be entered as `rabbits AND NOT hares`.

Perhaps you've used these Boolean operators while searching. But you might not have heard of specialty syntaxes, which allow you to do even more specialized searching.

Special Search Syntax

Many search sites have their own special, advanced search syntaxes—special ways to put together search terms and keywords to create a very highly targeted search. You can find information about advanced syntax in a search site's documentation, but as an example we'll look at the special keywords offered by **AltaVista** (http://www.altavista.com/). AltaVista has a variety of keywords that help you do some really "fancy" searches, as

Bugs in AltaVista

Note that there are, at the time of writing at least, software bugs in AltaVista; a search that finds 4,557,231 pages one moment may find 9,099 the next. (These are real examples.) With luck this will be fixed soon! You can make sure AltaVista does a clean search, though, by going back to the first page each time; click on the AltaVista logo at the top of the page.

AltaVista calls them. There's the `anchor:` keyword, `applet:`, `image:`, `title:`, and so on. Let's see how some of these work.

domain:

The `domain:` keyword is one of Tara's favorites. Adding `+domain:com` to a query ensures that your results will come from a domain that ends with .com, like http://www.poorrichard.com/ or http://www.amazon.com/. That is, AltaVista will only show you pages from .com domains. If you use `-domain:com` instead, AltaVista will only show you pages from domains other than .com domains. This works for any domain, from the ones that are very common (.com, .org, .net, and .edu) to the less common or even downright obscure (.gov, .mil, and country codes like .jp, .us, and .fi). Try it for yourself. If you search for `rabbit hunting australia`, AltaVista will find literally millions of pages—almost four million when we checked. But if you search for `rabbit hunting australia +domain:nu` (which means "only find pages from the .nu domain"), you'll get only a relative handful (3,679 when we tried).

When you're looking for sites, you can narrow down your search results a lot by the kind of domain you're searching for. If you need academic resources, you can use `+domain:edu` to assure your results are at least mostly academically oriented. If you want just commercial results, like online stores, you can use `-domain.edu -domain.org` to make sure you have more commercially oriented results. But remember that such a search strategy won't work perfectly, because there are so many different domain suffixes—net, com, org, gov, all the country codes—and Web-site owners don't always pick the type of domain one might expect.

host:

The `host:` keyword allows you to narrow your search to a specific host, or computer, on the Internet, or to avoid finding pages on a particular host. For example, poorrichard.com refers to a particular host computer, so if you added `-host:poorrichard.com` to your search query you would eliminate all the Web pages which are hosted on poorrichard.com. If you added `+host: poorrichard.com` you would be specifying that only pages hosted on poorrichard.com should be included in your search results. This works well when you're searching for information in a particular area—for example, if you were looking for information at a particular college, you could search it by specifying its host. It's also useful when searching for links to a particular Web site. You can tell AltaVista to show you links to the site, but to omit internal links—links from other Web pages within that site.

title:

The `title:` keyword allows you to search *only* the titles of pages for particular keywords. This comes in really handy when you're looking for a particular type of resource but the resource has a common keyword. For example, say you were looking for sites pertaining to starfish. If you did a search for starfish in AltaVista, you'd find more than 50,000 results (at the time of writing, at least … these numbers will change, of course). However, if you searched for Starfish in the title of a Web page (`title:starfish`) you'd find just over 1,300 results. If you narrowed those results down to more academic sites by using the following query …

```
+title:starfish +domain:edu
```

… you'd find only 44 Web pages.

That brings us to another point. You can mix and match these keywords. They don't exist in a vacuum. You can use different ones, add Boolean query modifiers, and even mix in natural language searching (more about that shortly.) The Internet has millions and millions of Web pages; use every resource at your disposal to narrow down the number of Web pages you have to search.

AltaVista has these other important keywords:

anchor:*text*—Finds pages with the specified text in a link (links are known to the more geeky of us as "anchors"). This searches for the link text that appears on the page, not the URL specified by the link.

applet:*name*—Finds pages containing a particular Java applet.

image:*filename*—Finds pages containing a particular image name.

link:*URLtext*—Finds pages with links that contain specified text; unlike the anchor: keyword, this one actually looks at the URL specified by the link.

text:*text*—Limits the search to the actual text, ignoring the image tags and links.

url:*text*—Finds pages with a particular word or phrase in the pages' URLs.

You can find more information about these keywords at AltaVista—http://www.altavista.com/av/content/help.htm.

Don't Stop at AltaVista

Just because we're using AltaVista in these examples doesn't mean you shouldn't explore other search sites and the special syntaxes they have to offer. **HotBot** (http://www.hotbot.com/) *in particular offers many different types of specialty searching.*

Natural-Language Searching

Maybe you just can't be bothered to learn all these keywords. Maybe Boolean searching just confuses you. In that case, you should try a new search technology that's slowly getting better—natural-language searching.

Natural-language searching is just that—stating what you want in English (or, in some cases, a number of other languages—AltaVista claims to be able to work with a couple of dozen) and having the search site get it for you. You can visit **AskJeeves** at http://www.askjeeves.com/ or the **Electric Monk** at http://www.electricmonk.com/ if you want to see search sites that use only natural-language searching, but you can also visit AltaVista and use natural-language searching on that system, too.

Formulating questions when using natural-language searching is an evolving art. You have to make the question simple enough to understand, but thorough enough to get what you want. For example ...

```
Where can I find puppets?
```

... is probably not as good a query as it could be. You haven't specified what kind of puppets you want. The query ...

```
Where can I find hand puppets?
```

... may be a better query. Notice that you don't have to specify that you want sites about hand puppets; asking `Where can I find sites about hand puppets` might confuse the search sites. Keep it simple, simple, simple.

If you don't get the information you need with the first search, try rephrasing the query. The query ...

```
A giraffe is how tall?
```

... won't work well. Rephrased ...

```
How tall is a giraffe?
```

... works much better.

Mixing the Two Search Types

Here's a great secret that we're going to let you in on—in AltaVista you can mix natural language and keyword searching, and even include Boolean modifiers! For example, say you want to find sites that deal with cancer research in order to find possible partners for your non-profit cancer prevention site. Start with the natural language query *Where can I learn about cancer research?*

You'll get tens of thousands of results, which is a little too much to handle. But you can probably eliminate all or most of the sites selling cancer treatments by using -domain:com. You can make sure the site deals with cancer by adding the title:cancer. You could also add another search term, like chemotherapy. Your query will now look like this:

```
+where can I learn about cancer research?
-domain:com
+title:cancer
+chemotherapy
```

This will still find thousands of results, but perhaps one quarter of the original number. Still a lot, but you can narrow it down even further by using more keywords and search terms.

The Right Tool for the Right Occasion

If you're searching for really general topics, like cancer, use a topic index like Yahoo first. You'll save a lot of time.

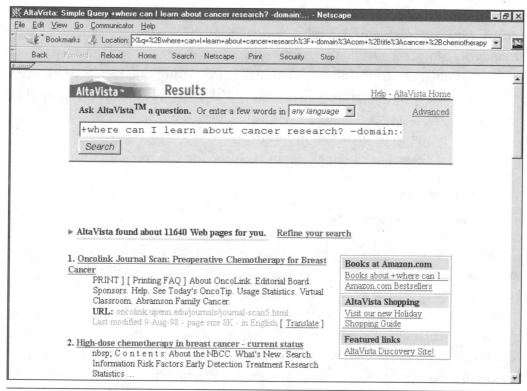

FIGURE 4.1: Use AltaVista's special keywords in conjunction with natural language searching to really pinpoint your searches.

If you're used to going to a search site and just typing in one or two search terms, it's time for an attitude adjustment. It's possible, using Boolean operators, special keywords, natural language searching, and so on, to do very carefully targeted searches, and to find just what you're looking for. Check a search engine's documentation before you begin, to see what's available.

META-SEARCH ENGINES ONLINE

In this chapter and other parts of the book, we talk about specific search sites—AltaVista, HotBot, Yahoo!, and so on. Wouldn't it be great if instead of visiting each of these sites individually, you could search them all at once?

Well, you can. Sites that can help you search several sites at once are called *meta-search engines.* You can use meta-search engines online, or you can get software packages that offer meta-search features.

Meta-search engines gather the results of several search sites into one big group of results. The more advanced meta-search engines even remove the duplicate results. Meta-search engines can come in really handy, since there's less overlap between search sites than you might think. Different search sites will return very different search results, so you probably need to search several of them; you can get a huge list of results all in one place.

The problem with meta-search engines is that using one results in an even larger pool of Web sites from which you can draw results. It's imperative that when you use meta-search engines, you use as specific a query as possible. Otherwise you're going to be drowned in results.

There are several meta-search engines online for you to choose from.

SavvySearch

http://www.savvysearch.com/

SavvySearch is actually a collection of meta-search engines. In addition to a meta-search engine for general search sites (Lycos, Excite, HotBot, WebCrawler, Google, Galaxy, AltaVista, Thunderstone, NationalDirectory, Infoseek, and Direct Hit), it also offers meta-searching in several different categories, including magazine articles, news, newspapers, and colleges. At the time of writing SavvySearch was in the process of implementing Boolean meta-searching, in which the Boolean modifiers to your query are applied to all the search sites. (Usually with a meta-search engine, applying Boolean modifiers to a query is iffy. Some search sites will get the modifiers; some won't.) This really is a must-try site.

MetaCrawler

http://www.metacrawler.com/

MetaCrawler is one of the granddaddies of meta-searching. Like SavvySearch, it offers specialized meta-searches in several categories, including news, finance, and health. Its general meta-search searches through a variety of sites, including Lycos, Infoseek, WebCrawler, Excite, AltaVista, Thunderstone, and Yahoo!. It can also search through USENET newsgroups (which can be handy if you're researching a topic that's the subject of much discussion).

Inference Find

http://www.infind.com/

Inference Find is a fast meta-search engine that doesn't offer the specialty searches of MetaCrawler or SavvySearch. It searches WebCrawler, Yahoo!, Lycos, AltaVista, InfoSeek, and Excite. While Inference Find admits that sometimes Boolean searches don't work properly with its meta-search engine, it's still worth a look. Tara finds that it's one of the fastest meta-search engines she's used, and she usually gets a result from all the search sites that Inference Find queries. (On some meta-search engines, some of the individual search sites "time out" before results can returned.) Inference Find also doesn't overwhelm you with results, so you can use it for more general queries without a risk of getting drowned in results. (If you do want to use really general searches, though, stick with a topic index like Yahoo!.)

These are just three of the meta-search engines available online. There are plenty of others, such as these:

Dogpile
   http://www.dogpile.com/
MetaFind
   http://www.metafind.com/
SuperSeek
   http://www.super-seek.com/
Mamma
   http://www.mamma.com/
byteSearch
   http://www.bytesearch.com/

While the meta-search engines are good, sometimes you might find yourself needing something with a little more flexibility. Something that resides on your own hard drive, perhaps.

SEARCH SOFTWARE

Search software—programs running on your own computer—can both conduct meta-searches and allow you to build your own databases of searches and results. They can give you a head start on your research, especially when you're doing very complicated or esoteric searches. You enter a search term, click a button, and off goes the program, searching the Web for whatever you've specified. It checks a set of search sites—you'll probably be able to add new ones to the list—and retrieves a list of hits. Then the magic begins.

Up to this point, you see, you've simply searched the sites and got a list of links back in return. You can do that for yourself—not as quickly as the search program, but reasonably quickly nonetheless. What really takes a long time, though, is checking all of those links. If you find 10,000 links that might refer to something interesting, how do you check them all? There's no way you can; it's just too big of a job. But you can let the search program run overnight and do it for you.

Come back in the morning and what do you find? Something like the window shown in Figure 4.2. This is a screenshot from Quarterdeck's WebCompass, one of the best of these programs. In this illustration the search is actually in progress, but you can still see the sort of

Mini-Search Engines

Many of the major search sites offer mini versions of their search technology for download. These are generally not meta-search utilities, however.

information that's presented. If you click on a link in the top-left pane, you see information about the Web page in the lower pane. In many cases this provides enough information for you to decide whether or not the search will prove useful to you. If it is, or if you're not sure but want to see more to check it out, you can double-click on the entry. Up pops your browser, and the page loads.

Another nice feature of these programs is that you can use them to repeat searches periodically to find new things that have appeared. Search once or twice a month, and you'll be able to keep up with what's going on on the Web.

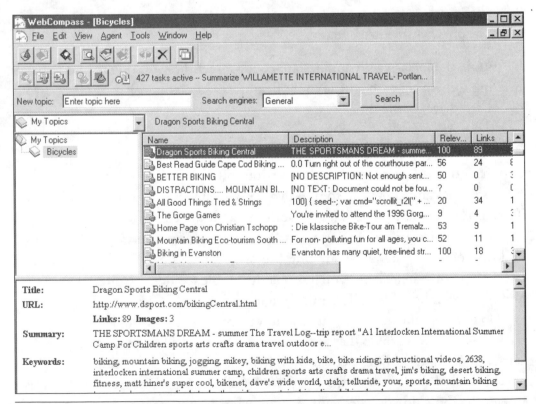

FIGURE 4.2: Quarterdeck's WebCompass is like a search engine on steroids.

There are a number of different meta-search-software packages to choose from. Here are a couple that Tara likes:

BullsEye Pro

http://www.intelliseek.com/

BullsEye Pro can search over 300 search sites and can refine searches, remove redundant results, and generally whittle down the huge ocean of search results to a small list. One of the benefits of BullsEye, indeed with most software packages, is that you can store a particular type of search and do it over and over again. BullsEye also allows you to monitor search sites for changes—a handy feature if you tend to do the same type of research often.

WebFerret

http://www.ferretsoft.com/

WebFerret allows Boolean support for search queries, and offers several extras, including the ability to eliminate duplicate results and save a list of search results. WebFerret comes in two flavors—freeware and professional—so you can try before you buy. FerretSoft has a number of other Internet research tools, too: InfoFerret, EmailFerret, FileFerret, IRCFerret, NewsFerret, and PhoneFerret.

There are many other search programs out there:

Arf (Windows 3.1/95/98/NT)
   http://www.dwave.net/~bitsafe/arf/
Copernic 98 (Windows 95/98/NT)
   http://www.copernic.com/
EchoSearch (Windows 95/98/NT)
   http://www.iconovex.com/
Hurricane WebSearch (Windows)
   http://www.gatecomm.com/websearch/
Inforian Quest 98 (Windows 95/98/NT)
   http://www.inforian.com/
Mata Hari (Windows 95/98/NT)
   http://thewebtools.com/
QuickSeek (Macintosh and Windows—provides a fast way to search at InfoSeek)
   http://www.infoseek.com/iseek?pg=quickseek/Download.html

Trawler (Windows 3.1/95/98/NT)
   http://www.dwave.net/~bitsafe/trawler/

WebBandit (Windows 95/98/NT)
   http://www.jwsg.com/

WebCompass (Windows 95/98/NT)
   http://www.qdeck.com/qdeck/products/wc20/

WebSeek (Windows 3.1/95/98/NT)
   http://www-personal.umich.edu/~jeffhu/webseek

WebSeeker (Windows 95/98/NT)
   http://www.bluesquirrel.com/

Websnake (Windows 95/98/NT)
   http://www.intermk.com/products.html

By the way, a few products will grab e-mail addresses from pages you find. You could use these to get the addresses of people to whom you want to offer cooperative marketing promotions, for instance—the people running Web sites that your prospects are visiting. Websnake and WebBandit, listed above, can both grab e-mail addresses.

Do you have to use a meta-search engine or search software when researching Web sites relevant to your promotional effort? Not really; the better you know how to use the search sites, the less you'll need to use the meta-search engines and software. Tara, who spends a great deal of her time doing online research, actually uses meta-searching very little. She works instead on creating as focused a query as possible and then makes the most of the results she gets. Most of the time, that focus is sufficient to do a good job on her research work. Of course, when you get into very esoteric research, you might find that using a meta-search tool is the only way you can get more than a dozen results. For example, this might be the case if you are working for a nonprofit organization that's trying to educate the public on a very rare childhood illness that has little exposure on the Web. These specialized tools can also be very handy in cases where you have a lot of time available to get into a very extensive and comprehensive promotional campaign, or when you simply have to know *everything* about a particular subject. But in most situations one search site at a time will probably be enough.

PROMOTION RESOURCES

Don't be daunted at the idea of doing all this searching. We know you want to get a jump start on your online promotional activities, and we want to help by getting you started with your research activities. There are some general site types that almost all of you will want to take a look at.

Let's start with promotional resources, Web sites that will help you track down places to promote your products and services. It used to be that if you wanted lists of media, you had to go to the library. That was, however, B.I. (Before Internet.) Nowadays all you have to do is get online and check into these resources. Let's take a look at various resources available to you.

All Types of Media

News365

http://www.news365.com/

News365 offers listings of newspapers, magazines, and TV stations—over 10,000 media listings. The listings are broken down by industry, so if you're looking for a vertical market publication this is a good place to start. You can also get media listed by American state or by country, from Albania to Iceland to Zimbabwe.

AJR NewsLink

http://ajr.newslink.org/

AJR NewsLink is a service of the American Journalism Review and has been one of the great online reference sites for years now. They feature listings of newspapers, magazines, broadcasters (television and radio), and news services worldwide. Their newspapers are broken down both by geographic location and by type (dailies, non-dailies, alternative, etc.). They also have an excellent collection of college newspapers.

NewsDirectory.com

http://www.newsd.com/

NewsDirectory.com (formerly Ecola) lists both newspapers and magazines. They list over 6,900 English-language media that offer unrestricted access. They're another one of the old-timers of Internet reference, having been around since 1995. They list their magazines by type and have a strong variety of industry/vertical-market publications. American magazines are listed first, followed by regional magazines listed by region and international magazines and their country of origin. Newspapers are listed by continent and country of origin, with business newspapers having their own geographically broken down section.

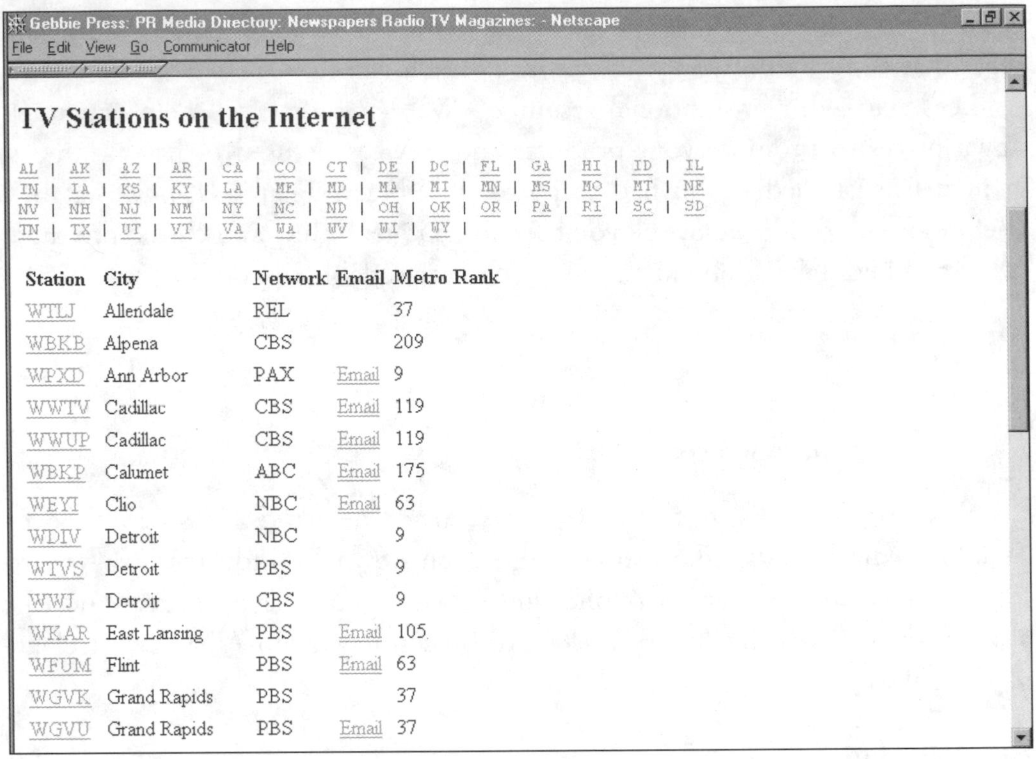

Gebbie Press: PR Media Directory: Newspapers Radio TV Magazines: - Netscape

File Edit View Go Communicator Help

TV Stations on the Internet

AL | AK | AZ | AR | CA | CO | CT | DE | DC | FL | GA | HI | ID | IL
IN | IA | KS | KY | LA | ME | MD | MA | MI | MN | MS | MO | MT | NE
NV | NH | NJ | NM | NY | NC | ND | OH | OK | OR | PA | RI | SC | SD
TN | TX | UT | VT | VA | WA | WV | WI | WY |

Station	City	Network	Email	Metro Rank
WTLJ	Allendale	REL		37
WBKB	Alpena	CBS		209
WPXD	Ann Arbor	PAX	Email	9
WWTV	Cadillac	CBS	Email	119
WWUP	Cadillac	CBS	Email	119
WBKP	Calumet	ABC	Email	175
WEYI	Clio	NBC	Email	63
WDIV	Detroit	NBC		9
WTVS	Detroit	PBS		9
WWJ	Detroit	CBS		9
WKAR	East Lansing	PBS	Email	105
WFUM	Flint	PBS	Email	63
WGVK	Grand Rapids	PBS		37
WGVU	Grand Rapids	PBS	Email	37

FIGURE 4.3: Gebbie Press breaks out media by state. Click on the state abbreviation for a media list.

Gebbie Press

http://www.gebbieinc.com/

Gebbie is specifically designed for promotions people, and combines a bevy of free resources with publishable resources to make your work easier. This site lists radio and TV stations, daily newspapers, weekly newspapers, and magazines online. Their more than 20,000 listings are broken up by state (they seem to be mostly U.S. listings) and provide both links to the appropriate Web sites and e-mail addresses when available. In the case of radio listings, programming format is provided. In the case of TV, the network is provided. Magazines are listed by category. This site has a very simple design, so if you've got a slow Internet connection or a simple browser, start with this site.

NeWo News

http://newo.com/news/

NeWo provides not only listings of newspapers and other media outlets, but also information aggregates like InfoJunkie and NewsIndex.com. Sites are listed by geographical area, and broken down from country to state or region as appropriate. NeWo's strength lies in its simple interface and the fact that it's easy to tell when listings were last updated. (You don't want to get stuck with a stale listing.) NeWo is decidedly not American-centric; it's a good choice if you're looking for media all over the world.

MediaINFO Links

http://www.mediainfo.com/emedia/

MediaINFO is a service of Editor & Publisher and includes links to journalism-related associations, city guides, magazines, newspapers, radio, syndicates and news services, and television. The City Guides are a good browse if you run a retail establishment that needs to focus its promotional efforts in a certain area. The magazine section especially has a lot of listings not found on most sites. It's broken down geographically, so it's another good site to consult if you're focusing on promotion within a certain area.

If you want to get an idea of the range of targets you can have for your promotion campaign, take some time to explore the sites above. If you want to concentrate on newspapers, magazines, or another specific media, check one of the following listings.

Newspapers

NewspaperLinks.com

http://www.newspaperlinks.com/

Hosted by the Newspaper Association of America, NewspaperLinks.com lists only American newspapers. It has an easy-to-use interface that enables you to search for a newspaper by city name or paper name or list newspapers by state. NewspaperLinks.com also provides links to special sections, like election coverage.

College Newspapers Online

http://www.cpnet.com/

CPNet is a lot more than just a list of links to college newspapers. It has two lists: a list of American college newspapers broken down by state, and a list of collegiate international newspapers broken down by country. It also has several resource listings and an excellent set of links if your product or service is aimed at college students. You can get a somewhat smaller list of college newspapers at http://beacon-www.asa.utk.edu/resources/papers.html.

Magazines

PubList

http://www.publist.com/

If you're looking for periodicals appropriate to your promotion campaigns, start here. You can find over 150,000 periodicals in this database, encompassing both online and offline publications. You can search by title, keyword, publisher, or ISSN. It lists both American and international publications. The listings provide a wealth of information, including frequency, publisher's mailing address, phone number, advertising rates, and circulation. (Different publications supply different amounts of information.)

LinxNet Magazine Index

http://www.linxnet.com/mag.html

LinxNet lists several different categories of magazines, and also lists them by first letter. All the links are checked weekly so you're not going to find a lot of stale stuff here. This site doesn't have tons and tons of listings, but the links it does have are well-maintained and easily navigable. LinxNet also has a couple of directories for TV and newspapers which, although not quite as good as the other directories we've listed here, may be worth looking at:

http://www.linxnet.com/tv.html

http://www.linxnet.com/news.html

Computer & Software WWW Magazines & Journals

http://www.internetvalley.com/top100mag.html

This is a great Web site with links to 100 computer magazines and journals on the Web; a fantastic resource if you're promoting a computer hardware or software product.

ZineVine

http://www.zinevine.com/

"Your one stop for magazines located on the Internet that have topics associated with computers and the Internet." This site has been recently updated, so we're not sure of the figures now, but at one time they claimed to link to over 330 magazines.

Radio Stations

RadioDirectory

http://www.radiodirectory.com/Stations/

RadioDirectory lists radio stations by geographic location (and even includes a listing of radio stations that exist solely on the Internet—148 at the time of writing.) They're grouped by continent (Africa, North America, etc.), then grouped by country and state. There's also a newsletter available so you can keep up with changes to the listings.

'Zines and Newsletters

A 'zine used to be a kind of fringe publication that was published by smaller organizations than publishers of large, slick magazines. (The term 'zine is commonly used on the Internet to mean any kind of e-mail publication. The term *e-mail newsletter* is also widely used.) With the advent of the Internet, however, 'zines and e-mail newsletters have begun to come in all shapes and sizes, from one person's essays and observations of life (with a readership of about 20) to a biweekly newsletter that's administered by ten people and has a circulation of hundreds of thousands.

Many people shrug off the possibility of promoting to 'zines, but it's wrong to paint them all with so broad a brush. Some of them aren't particularly good, and some of them are absolutely fantastic, and most of them fall somewhere in between. There are a number of very influential 'zines, and they can be a great place to get mentioned. When Peter's *Poor Richard* Web site (http://PoorRichard. com/) was mentioned in Lockergnome (http://www.lockergnome.com/), for instance, he received thousands of visits to his Web site, a couple of thousand new subscribers to his own e-mail newsletter, a couple of dozen book orders on the Web site, and more orders through bookstores. Lockergnome has around 130,000 subscribers, and despite the fact that Internet users often feel overwhelmed by the quantity of e-mail they receive, many of Lockergnome's readers really do pay attention to what the newsletter recommends.

Unlike large-circulation magazines, there isn't a certain level of quality you can assume with a 'zine. On the other hand, 'zine editors can often devote more time to listening to your pitch, tend to have loyal readers, and can give you valuable feedback on the way you're approaching people. And they're not nearly as intimidating as calling up *Business Week*.

Tara's favorite resource for e-mail publications is John Labovitz's e-zine list at http://www.meer.net/~johnl/e-zine-list/. At the time of writing, this list had

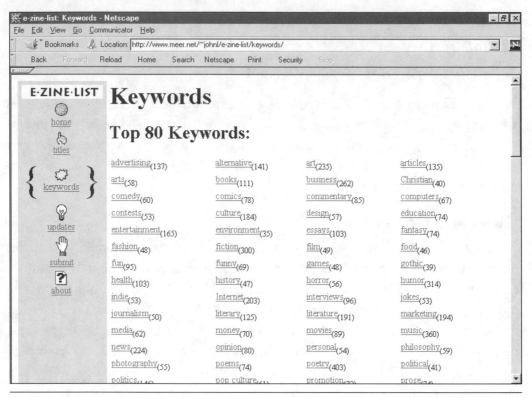

FIGURE 4.4: John Labovitz's e-zine list contains dozens of keywords, allowing you to zero in on the resources you need.

almost 2,500 'zines and newsletters listed. They run the gamut from the original fringe publications to daily newsletters put out by large computing companies.

There are scores of other places to find 'zines and newsletters, including a number of detailed directories that are for sale. Note that some of the directories listing mailing-list discussion groups also include newsletters. Here are a few sites worth checking:

Liszt
   http://www.liszt.com/

Publicly Accessible Mailing Lists
   http://www.neosoft.com/internet/paml/

Vivian Neou's List of Lists
   http://catalog.com/vivian/

Reference.com
   http://www.reference.com/

A1 Ezine Directory
   http://www.a1co.com/freeindex.html

ARL (Association of Research Libraries) Directory of Electronic
   Journals, Newsletters and Academic Discussion Lists
   http://arl.cni.org/scomm/edir/

Electronic Journal Access
   http://www.coalliance.org/ejournal/

Low Bandwidth—This site incorporates the data from Todd Kuiper's
   E-mail-zines List, a popular list that was closed recently.
   http://www.disobey.com/low/

Dominis Interactive Ezines—Around 3,000 publications.
   http://www.dominis.com/Zines/

The E-ZineZ
   http://www.e-zinez.com/

NewJour—A large directory of newsletters (almost 7,000)
   http://gort.ucsd.edu/newjour/

This should keep you busy for a while. But if you need more, see Peter's free *Places to Register Your E-mail Newsletter* report, which lists literally scores of places to find more information. You can find this report, along with various others, at http://www.poorrichard.com/freeinfo/special_reports.htm.

Most directories provide some kind of background information so you can figure out what a 'zine or newsletter is about. Before you approach one about advertising or promotion, read a few back issues to get an idea of what it's about and what it offers. And if you do want to advertise, make sure there's some way you can get a circulation statement.

When you first begin to look at all these resources, the sheer number of periodicals available online might possibly overwhelm you. That's why it's important to divide into subgroups the people who might be interested in your product or service. That way you can focus on one group at a time. Take the educational toy example we used in Chapter 1. You could focus on promoting to parents and teachers for three months, and then move on to work with grandparents and child-development. If you rotate through different subgroups, you'll:

• Keep your approach fresh
• Generate new ideas for promoting your product or service
• Keep yourself from saturating a particular subgroup

Instead of trying to gather all the contact information together at once, do a little at a time. Surf Web pages for 20 or 30 minutes at a time, as much as you can stand. (You'll be able to do more over time.) If you try to sit down and do too much at one time, you'll find yourself getting distracted, drifting over to the sports pages, checking out RealAudio, etc. Not getting any work done.

Once you've got your targets together, you're ready to think about promotion. But before you can really promote effectively, you need to examine your Web site. Is it ready for prime time? Is everything together? Check out the next chapter for information on how to get your Web site in good shape for the search sites.

PART II

WEB SITE REGISTRATIONS

CHAPTER FIVE

Web Site Checkup: Preparing for Indexing

How long have you had your Web site? Do you have tons of content, millions of guests, and the presidents of huge Internet companies calling you for advice? Well, it doesn't matter; however happy you are with your site, it probably needs "tuning up" for the search engines. Before you get started doing a big promotional push, you need to examine your site carefully, to make sure it's ready to be indexed.

GET YOUR OWN DOMAIN NAME

A quick word of warning. If you don't have your own domain name, you'll find it harder to get registered at some search sites, in particular at Yahoo! For instance, if you have the http://members.aol.com/~rocketry/ URL, you'll find it much harder to get registered in Yahoo! (which is, after all, one of the most important search sites out there—perhaps *the most* important) than if you were using, say, the following URL: http://Rocketry.com/.

I've heard many people complain about this, as if somehow it isn't fair. But look at it from Yahoo!'s point of view. They need a useful directory of Web sites, yet a major problem is that Web sites come and go quickly, so they have to reduce the link "attrition" rate. They can do that by avoiding sites that are likely to disappear. If you have a URL that clearly states "this is hosted at my ISP … who knows where it'll be next month!," they're not interested in you. If you have your own domain name, though, you've gone to some trouble to set up the site, so you're less likely to close it down—and even if you move it, you'll be able to take the domain name with you. So think seriously about getting your own domain name! (This sort of thing is discussed in detail in *Poor Richard's Web Site: Geek-Free, Commonsense Advice on Building a Low-Cost Web Site* by Peter Kent.)

109

IS WHAT YOU'VE GOT WORTH PROMOTING?

Before we get started, we're making some assumptions about your site. We have to assume that what you've got really is worth promoting. As we've discussed already, your site has to be worth visiting. This is for two reasons. Perhaps you can get listed in the search engines—but if your site isn't worth visiting, then you'll never get someone to visit you more than once, and you won't get people to recommend your site to others. But there's another reason—in some cases you won't even get listed at some important search sites (in particular Yahoo!), because some search sites evaluate sites before they add them to their directories. Let's consider, then, what makes a good site.

It's More Than One Page

There are a lot of rather sparse Web sites out in cyberspace. It may be possible to create a site that is useful to someone and yet not take up more than one page or so … but it's unlikely. Make sure you've got enough information at your site to make it worth visiting. Here's a good rule of thumb: the less unusual topic you've got, the more content you need. If you've devoted your site to the southeastern aerosol industry, ten information-packed pages could be quite a draw for your prospects. On the other hand, if you're putting up yet another site devoted to small businesses, you're going to need a lot of content—a lot of very good content, considering the competition—in order to stand out from the pack.

It's More Than Just a Brochure and an Order Form

Let us reemphasize something we pointed out in Chapter 1—no one cares about your product or service as much as you do. Therefore it's silly to think you can attract visitors to your Web site with nothing but the electronic equivalent of a brochure and an order form. That might work if you've discovered a foolproof, exercise-free diet or a cure for the common cold—maybe. But for most other products you're going to have to establish your expertise, build credibility, and define to your prospects why they need to "buy" whatever you're "selling"—and a brochure and an order form isn't gonna do it.

It's Been Updated Sometime in the Recent Past

Internet time isn't like real-time. Time moves a lot faster on the Internet. A week moves like a month. Three months move almost like a year. And a year—wow, you wouldn't believe how a year moves. That means that you probably can't update your site once every three months and think you're keeping up with Internet time.

So how often *should* you update your site? Well, we (the authors) don't completely agree on this point. Tara believes that you should be continually updating your Web site—daily if possible. (Was that the sound of a few of you hitting the floor?) If you can't manage daily, she believes, you should update your site weekly. And if you just can't manage weekly, you should definitely update your site no less than once a month.

Why do you want to update frequently? Because it'll affect how often visitors come back. If your visitors come to your site four or five times over a three-month period and nothing's going on, they will stop coming back. You can bring them back later by keeping them updated about you and your business via newsletters (more about that in Chapter 11), but a better way to keep their attention is to update your pages regularly and condition visitors to expect additions if they visit regularly.

Tara learned this through administering three very different sites. One site she updates almost every business day. Another has been growing for over a year and she has backed off to the point that she's updating it only once a month. The third site is updated only once every few months. Guess which site gets the most consistent traffic? That's right, the most frequently updated site.

Peter has a different view. He believes that if the information is still up-to-date—still valid today—then it's still of value, regardless of whether the information has been changed in a couple of weeks or not. What's important is *timeliness*, not age. Daily changes are, for most people, impractical, and they're probably not necessary. What counts is whether the information is useful to people. If it is, then you don't have to keep changing it! It all depends on what you are trying to achieve. If you are selling advertising at your site, then you want as many people as possible to come to your site, and to come as often as possible. Constant change may be useful in that case. If you are selling a book, however, you don't care how often people come back ... as long as they buy your book on their initial visit. So it's not necessarily true that you must be constantly changing your site.

The most important thing, though, is something we mentioned in Chapter 1. Your Web site must be useful today. If you've got something that's useful today, you can attract viewers.

It's Useful!

More than anything, what really counts is that there's a reason for people to visit your Web site. If you haven't given people a *reason* to visit, then there's not much point in trying to get them to visit. Here's an example. CDnow wants to sell you

CDs. But that's not a reason for you to visit them. After all, do you really care if they make money? CDnow understands this principle well, so they set out to give people a reason to visit their Web site—lots of reasons, really. They've created a site that's full of information (hundreds of thousands of pages), and full of sound clips (over 250,000 of them). They've created special personalized areas—the *My CDnow* pages—that are Web pages in which people can store information. Visitors can keep a list of music they'd like to buy sometime, and even allow their friends and family to view the list (hey, maybe Gran will buy you that *Beastie Boys* album you want). They provide links to your favorite bands' pages; they recommend music based on your previous purchases and responses to questions; and so on. They have given people a reason to visit by building what the founders of CDnow call *the better music store.*

Why would anyone want to visit *your* Web page? If you can't come up with a good answer to that, you've got problems.

———————

Have you got your stuff together? Do you have a site worth marketing and a page worth promoting? Great. Make sure you've got all the details down. And remember this one important idea:

> *Think about what your visitors care about, not what* you *care about.*

Your visitors don't care what you want. They care only about what *they* want. So give it to them, and they will come.

SEVEN STEPS TO WEB-SITE READINESS

While the big picture of "why" and "what" is very important, you must also focus on the details that make a site look professional. Don't overlook proofreading and other site housekeeping. You should take these seven steps to make sure your Web page is ready before cranking up your promotions.

1. **Spell check it!**—You may have the most beautifully written copy in the world, but if it is not free from spelling errors, it will leave a bad impression on the reader. Nothing cuts into your credibility more than a bunch of typos littering your pages. (Visitors may forgive one or two typos, but don't push your luck.) Many HTML editing programs, like FrontPage, have spell-checkers built in. If you don't have such a program, you can get a spell check online. (See the section on online resources at the end of this list.)

2. **Proofread it!**—Spell checking works when words are actually misspelled, but it doesn't point out faulty word choices and grammar errors. Go over your page with a magnifying glass, if you have to, and get rid of those mistakes. That doesn't mean you have to use the Queen's English, of course. (Substitute "proper French" or whatever language you're writing in for "Queen's English.") If your Web site is oriented towards teenagers or a particular aspect of pop culture, the use of vernacular and not-quite-proper English might be appropriate, but make sure your use of that vernacular is deliberate, and not a result of sloppy proofreading.

3. **Get someone else to proofread it!**—When you write something, your eyes are so close to it you will miss mistakes. Go out and find some fresh eyes—preferably someone who's never seen your site before—and get that person to proofread it. Not only will he help you find mistakes you might have missed, but he might be able to point out where your copy is confusing or difficult to understand. Ideally this person should be an editor, someone who understands the rules of the language.

4. **Check your links!**—Have you ever heard of link rot? Link rot occurs when someone puts up a list of links and never checks the links. With the natural, high-speed rate of change of the Internet, more and more of the links become inaccurate over time, and the list becomes less and less valuable. Clicking on bad links leads to *404—Link Not Found* errors in your visitors' browsers. It's irritating, and gives the impression that your site is old and out of date. Check your links regularly—once a week is ideal, though once a month is okay. FrontPage allows you to do this within the program, and there are also standalone products that'll check your links for you.

Link Checker Problems

Link checkers show you whether a link is broken, but not whether the page that the link points to still contains the information you think it contains. The page might now be nothing but a "This page has been removed" message, and a link checker would not see a problem with that. Periodically you should probably use an offline browser to transfer all the pages referenced by links at your Web site, then take a quick look at each page. (You can find more information about offline browsers in Chapter 2.)

5. **Make sure your site can be navigated without graphics, Java, or JavaScript!**—One of the problems with Internet time being so fast is that people are always adding "doodads" to their sites. Doodads make the site more interesting—they flash or buzz or click—but they don't add real, usable content. Doodads are mostly harmless, but it becomes a problem when doodads become essential to the navigation of the site. For example, Java is very interesting and can be used to create fabulous programs that do neat things, but you should not use Java as the only navigation tool. Some sites have nice little Java buttons that change color when the user places the mouse pointer over them, but in some cases those buttons won't work in browsers that don't use Java or don't have it activated. The result is that people who don't have Java capability can't navigate around the site!

   Sites that provide navigation links only via graphics are almost as bad. Such sites make things difficult for the visually impaired and those who surf without graphics (as many people do). At the very least, you should make sure that every important graphic has an ALT tag to tell what it is. The best solution is to provide a text menu as an alternative to your graphic navigation links.

6. **Add an "about this site"! page**—If you've put up a site that's a fan club for old 60's shows, you need one. If you're building an e-commerce solution for selling widgets, you need one. If you're setting up a city for the city transportation system, you need one. Somewhere on your site you need a mention—at least a brief paragraph—of what your site is all about. If you're a corporate site, you also want to have a section for press releases as well.

7. **Make sure your site is compatible with most browsers!**—Don't rely on a single browser running in a single video mode on your computer to be sure that your Web site looks reasonable in all browsers. There are lots of different browsers out there, and lots of different screen sizes. Your visitor might be checking out your site on a 21-inch monitor, or the small screen of a Palm Pilot. Checking your site from as many different viewpoints and browsers as possible will make sure it looks good to the majority of visitors. (You might find you can't look great to *all* visitors and screen sizes. That's okay; just go for *most*.) Checking your Web site from many different browser types and screen sizes will also teach you how long your Web site takes to load in different browsers.

ONLINE DIAGNOSTICS

There are lots of online resources to make sure your Web site is running as well as it can. One of the most popular is **Web Site Garage** at http://www. websitegarage.com/. Web Site Garage offers several free services for a one-page check: browser compatibility, load time, dead links, popularity, spelling, and HTML compatibility. Remember that the free service checks only one Web page at a time, so if you've got a 50-page site and want to check each page, you'll be here awhile. The Web Site Garage also offers several pay services, like browser-compatibility snapshots and site promotion.

NetMechanic, at http://www.netmechanic.com/, offers similar free services. NetMechanic can do a load-time check of your Web pages, a link check, and an HTML check. It even has a free image compressor to reduce your image sizes so your pages load more quickly. NetMechanic can check an entire site instead of just one page at a time like Web Site Garage, but they send you your results by e-mail so you'll have to give them your e-mail address.

LinkAlarm (http://www.linkalarm.com/) is a pay service that provides extensive link reports; they summarize the type and number of broken links and provide a detailed list of problems. The services costs only about $20 a year, and you can get the first two months free.

Bobby, at http://www.cast.org/bobby/, helps you determine whether your site is accessible by the disabled and whether your site conforms to different HTML standards (that browser-compatibility thing again). This site presents its results in rather technical terms, so try a different service first if you're not very HTML-savvy.

Doctor HTML, at http://www.imagiware.com/tools.html, will perform a variety of tests on a single Web page: spelling, image analysis, document structure (making sure all HTML code is properly executed), image syntax (making sure each image has a height, width, and ALT tag), table structure (making sure HTML tables are set up properly), hyperlink verification, form structure, and command display (showing the HTML commands in a document). You can specify which tests should be run. Doctor HTML is a good analysis to run if you've put together a page with very complex HTML, such as a page with lots of tables.

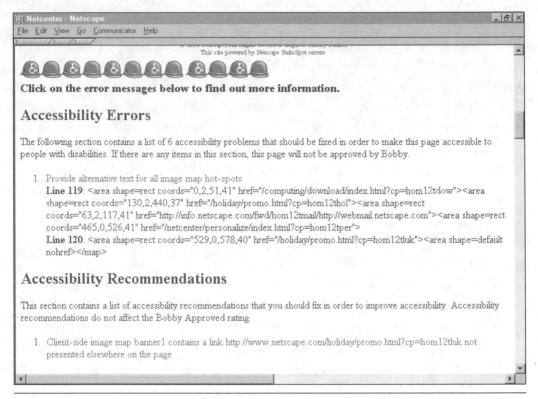

FIGURE 5.1: Oops, the Netscape site has some problems! Bobby found accessibility errors—links that can be used only through imagemaps.

> **Lynx** is a text-based browser that many UNIX machines run—no graphics, no doodads. You can see what your Web page looks like in a Lynx browser thanks to the **Salt Lake Community College Lynx page** at http://www.slcc.edu/webguide/lynxit.html.

With the help of all these resources and the seven steps, your Web site should now be ready. You've ensured that it's visitor-friendly and ready for real, live visitors. But there's another step. Now you have to make it ready for another type of visitor—it has to be search-engine friendly.

GETTING FRIENDLY WITH THE SEARCH ENGINES

Most search engines use programs called *spiders*, *'bots*, or *crawlers* to visit your site, index your content, and put it on the search engines. Of course they can't reason like humans do, so they make some assumptions about your content when indexing it. They don't always choose the most important words as the words that they index on.

You can, however, point out to the spiders what words are most important on your page by using two elements: META tags and Title tags.

META Tags

META tags aren't viewed by your site's visitors, but instead are reviewed by the spiders and 'bots that index your site. They're strictly to tell the spiders which words on your site are most important, exactly what your site is all about, and so on.

Without META tags, the spider can't make sense of the contents of your site; it views every word as a keyword. With META tags, you can supply a description and keywords that are given more weight when your site is indexed. That is not to say all search engines support META tags; they don't. But many do. Out of the several different types of META tags, the three that should concern you are the `description`, `keywords`, and `robots` tags.

Different META Tags

We don't have the space to go into all the different kinds of META tags, and you don't need to know about all of them anyway. We strongly recommend that you use the description and keywords META tags; the robots one is optional.

The META tags go within the HEAD part of your Web pages' HTML code, like this. (Notice the inclusion of the title tag; we'll talk more about that one in a minute):

```
<Head>
<Title>A Code Example</Title>
<META name="description" content="An example of how
to include descriptions in your Web pages and make
them as accessible as possible to spiders and other
Web crawlers.">
</Head>
```

Description

The `description` META tag is for describing your Web pages—see above for an example of how it's used. You want a 20- to 40-word description of your Web site to put in there. Try to avoid using dates, unless you feel that you really have to use them:

```
The model train Web is devoted to the collector of
1920-1950 model trains, with an emphasis on news,
pricing, and model train shows.
```

Spend some time coming up with a good description, because you can use the same description later in submitting your site to search engines (see the next chapter).

Keywords

The keywords META tag gives you the opportunity to enter a list of appropriate keywords for your Web site. This is especially appropriate when your Web site contains words that might be somewhat misleading.

For example, say you've got a site devoted to a new heartburn treatment. The treatment is designed for use by professional healthcare providers, and therefore you don't want consumers coming to your site looking to purchase this treatment.

```
<Head>
<Title>The Burn B Gone Anti-Heartburn Treatment
Solution</Title>
<META name="description" content="A revolutionary
no-pain, low-side effect heartburn treatment
designed for professional health care providers">
<META name="keywords" content="heartburn,
healthcare, doctor, nurse, heart, acid reflux,
gastroesophageal reflux disease, GERD">
</head>
```

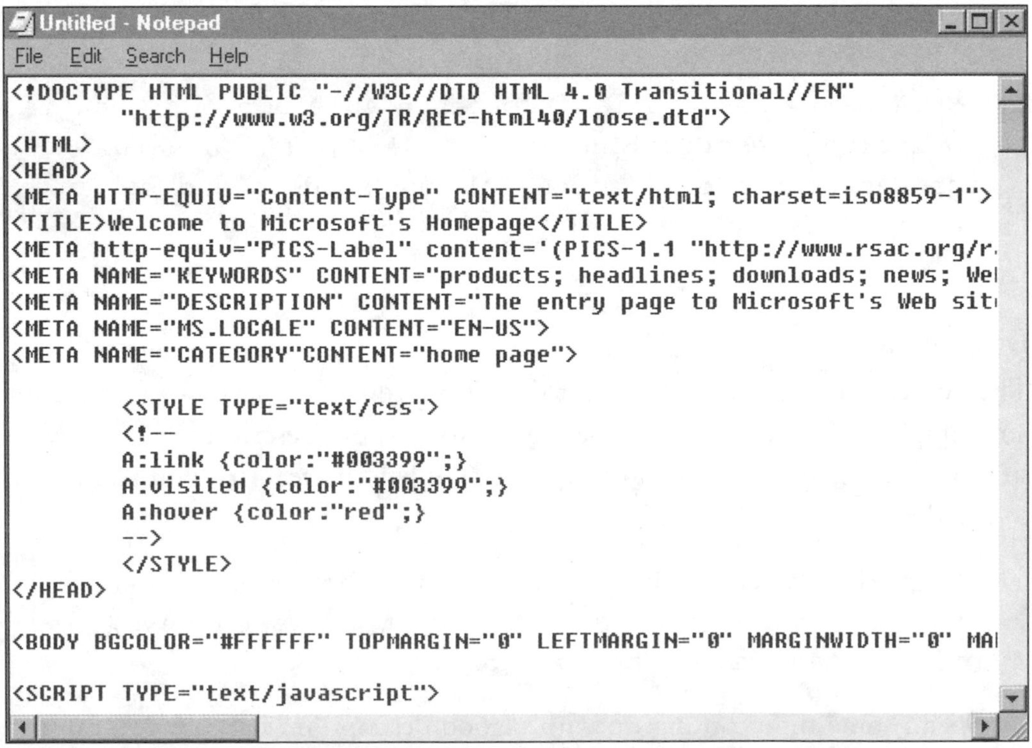

```
Untitled - Notepad
File  Edit  Search  Help
<!DOCTYPE HTML PUBLIC "-//W3C//DTD HTML 4.0 Transitional//EN"
        "http://www.w3.org/TR/REC-html40/loose.dtd">
<HTML>
<HEAD>
<META HTTP-EQUIV="Content-Type" CONTENT="text/html; charset=iso8859-1">
<TITLE>Welcome to Microsoft's Homepage</TITLE>
<META http-equiv="PICS-Label" content='(PICS-1.1 "http://www.rsac.org/r.
<META NAME="KEYWORDS" CONTENT="products; headlines; downloads; news; Wel
<META NAME="DESCRIPTION" CONTENT="The entry page to Microsoft's Web sit
<META NAME="MS.LOCALE" CONTENT="EN-US">
<META NAME="CATEGORY"CONTENT="home page">

        <STYLE TYPE="text/css">
        <!--
        A:link {color:"#003399";}
        A:visited {color:"#003399";}
        A:hover {color:"red";}
        -->
        </STYLE>
</HEAD>

<BODY BGCOLOR="#FFFFFF" TOPMARGIN="0" LEFTMARGIN="0" MARGINWIDTH="0" MAI

<SCRIPT TYPE="text/javascript">
```

FIGURE 5.2: Here are some of the META tags used by Microsoft's Web site.

We could go on, but you get the idea that professionally oriented keywords like "gastroesophageal reflux disease" and "acid reflux" are more likely to attract professional healthcare providers than consumer-oriented keywords like "chest pain" and "stomach acid." (In retrospect, perhaps this is kind of a gross example. Sorry... .)

Do you need to add META tags to every Web page you have? Probably not. However, you do want to add tags to every major page, such as index pages, introductions to sets of articles, and, of course, your home page.

The Content of the Page

Engineering the content of a Web page to look good to a search engine is almost an art form, and a very new one at that. The rules are changing constantly, so you may want to do some experiments to see what works for you. (This is not your high school algebra class; there isn't just one answer.)

Some search engines look at the first few lines of the page and collect them as a short abstract of the page. So make sure the headings at the top of the page and the first few lines of text are really descriptive of what you want the search engines to index. Try to use lots of words that your prospective clients are likely to be searching for in that first important paragraph.

Even after the first paragraph, some search engines continue looking. AltaVista indexes everything, so the rest of the text on the page is important, too. Some people try to fool such search engines by including large lists of keywords at the bottom. This is sometimes known as *spamdexing*. You may run into pages in which the authors have tried to camouflage a list of hundreds of keywords by changing the color of the words to match the page background, for instance. Other authors put hundreds of keywords in the Comment tags within the page, so they're not visible. Does this work? Almost always no. Most of the search engines in action these days are clever enough to figure out what's going on, and they ignore repetition. And many no longer index any text within HTML comment tags. Some will actually punish obvious spamdexing. They won't simply ignore the spamdexing; they'll actually dump the site from the directory and perhaps even blacklist the owners from the site so they can't get back in.

Some page designers feel that you should have pages that are focused on one topic and one topic only, and therefore have many small pages whose fewer words will count for more in the search engines. Tara disagrees with this, feeling that administering many small pages makes your site more likely to have update problems and linkage errors. On the other hand, if you do have distinct areas in your Web site, it's a good idea to register each area. For instance, if you have a site related to model rocketry, you might have a newsletter archive; a directory of model-rocket resources on the Web; and an article about the history of rocketry. It's a good idea to register all these areas individually.

ALT Text in Images

Some search engines are now indexing the IMG tags so that people can search for graphics. Infoseek does this, for example. And even sites that are not creating image indexes may still read and index the text to get an idea of what the page is about. So it's a good idea to include a description of the images on your pages in the ALT attribute (not to mention the fact that it makes your Web site much more usable to people using text-only browsers and to the disabled.)

If You're Using Frames

If you are using frames at your site, search engines may have trouble figuring out how to index pages. When the spiders or crawlers arrive at the site, all they get is the frame-definition document, a document that tells a browser how to set up the frames—how many frames, their sizes, their positions, and which document is displayed within each frame. But most search engines don't bother examining the documents referenced by the frame-definition document, the documents that will actually appear in the browser window.

If your site has frames, you can provide information for the search engines in two ways. You can add META tags to the top of the frame-definition document, and you can use the NOFRAMES tags (`<NOFRAMES>` and `</NOFRAMES>`), which enclose information that is not displayed inside the browser window unless the document is loaded by a browser that can't work with frames. It's a good idea to copy the information from the main frame into the NOFRAMES area of the frame-definition document. Then not only will non-frames browsers be able to see something, but so will the search engines.

Robots

As was said earlier, many search engines create a searchable database by sending out programs, called spiders and crawlers, to index your Web site. But what if you don't want your page indexed? You might have a page that you'd like to keep out of the search engines because it changes constantly, because it doesn't provide meaningful information, because you want someone to visit the site to get to the information, or for whatever reason. The robots META tag tells the spider and crawler how to treat your Web page.

The robots META tag has six variables, as you'll see below. You can use these variables in combinations to specify certain actions by the robot. We'll give you an example in a moment.

```
<META name="robots" content="variable">
```

All: Tells the robot to "crawl" through your site, following all the links, and to index all the files in your Web site. (This value is the default for your average crawler, so it is probably not necessary to insert this command.)

None: Instructs the crawler not to crawl through any of the site. It will not index the site and will not follow any links away from the site. (Using this command is a great idea when you're still putting the site together and don't want the draft version accidentally inserted in a search engine.)

Index: Indicates that the page itself may be crawled through but that every other page should be checked for its own META tag.

Noindex: Indicates that the page itself may not be crawled through.

Follow: Allows the crawler to follow the links on the page to other Web sites; this works well in combination with the Noindex command, as you'll see in a minute.

Nofollow: Instructs the crawler to *not* follow links to other sites.

Let's see how you could use this in certain situations. Say you've got a Web site whose content changes every day—it's a "tip of the day" page or something. Therefore, you don't want the page to be indexed by the search engines because it's changing all the time. However, the links from the site are good, and you want them to be followed. You could use the following META tag:

```
<META name="robots" Content="Noindex, Follow">
```

On the other hand, perhaps you've got a page that's stable and you want it to be indexed. However, you don't want the links away from the page to be indexed—perhaps they have content that's meaningless without the context of other pages. You could use a tag that's the opposite of the above tag:

```
<META name="robots" Content="Index, Nofollow">
```

And of course, if you just want to tell the crawler to go away, you could use:

```
<META name="robots" Content="Noindex, nofollow">.
```

If you'd like more information about working with robots, see the *Standard for Robot Exclusion* document at http://info.webcrawler.com/mak/projects/robots/norobots.html.

META-TAG TOOLS

If you're intimidated by the idea of generating your own META tags, look online.

There's the **META-Tag Generator** at http://www.websitepromote.com/resources/meta/. Enter the title of the page, a few keywords, and a description, and the META tag code will be e-mailed to you. From there you can cut and paste it into a Web page.

If you want to create many kinds of different META tags, try **META Tag Builder** at http://vancouver-webpages.com/META/mk-metas.html. You'll find a form to insert a whole lot of META information above and beyond the keywords and description. For example, you'll see forms for adding contributor names, owner names, and expiration dates, and even a couple of robot instructions.

WebPromote's META Tag Builder at http://metatag.webpromote.com/ also offers a META tag building service much like the one at Web Site Promote. They also offer several tips for META tag generation and site promotion.

There's also **Meta Medic** (http://www.northernwebs.com/set/setsimjr.html), a Web site that will check your META tags and tell you if they're too large or if you are repeating words too many times. (A more advanced version called SET SIM PRO is available for purchase.)

> ### *Meta Medic*
>
> *Meta Medic is a handy tool, but make sure each META tag on your page is on one line, not split into two or more lines, or Meta Medic will be unable to do its job.*

If you don't like the idea of doing all your META tag generation online, you can download a freeware META tag generator, **SiteUp Networks Meta Tag Generator**, at http://www.siteup.com/meta.html. Registration is required. There's also **Tag Master**, a $20 Windows shareware program (http://www.designmaker.com/). This program comes with a spell checker, a 100,000-word keyword library, and a template tool that allows you to add META tags to scores or hundreds of pages at the same time.

For more META Tag resources, visit the **Yahoo! META Tag page** at http://dir.yahoo.com/Computers_and_Internet/Information_and_Documentation/Data_Formats/HTML/META_Tag/.

TITLE TAGS

The `title` tag is not a META tag; it's a regular old HTML tag. But you'd be amazed at how many folks don't use it, even though it's so helpful.

The `title` tag looks like this:

```
<Title>This is the title
tag</Title>
```

Whatever appears within the `title` tag markers shows up as the page's title in the browser's title bar. For example, if you were using Netscape and you visited Yahoo!, the title of the page would be shown as *Yahoo!* in the title bar.

META Tag Training

There are lots of different META tags, used for various purposes, such as Expires, Pragma, Refresh, and so on. If you're interested in learning more, and in finding more META-tag tools, see the **WebDeveloper.com META Tag Resources** *page* (http://webdeveloper.com/categories/html/html_metatag_res.html) *and* **A Dictionary of HTML META Tags** *at* http://vancouver-webpages.com/META/.

Why use the `title` tag? Because search engines weigh the words in the title tag more carefully than the other content of your Web page. As a matter of fact, some search engines can search just Web page titles. At **AltaVista,** for instance, you can tell the system to just search page titles (http://www.altavista.com/).

The text in your title tag may have a significant effect on where your page is placed in a search engine. In addition, the title loads almost immediately, so viewers on slower Web connections can get some idea of what your Web page is all about without having to load the entire thing.

Leaving the `title` tag off your Web page is like leaving the headline off a newspaper article, or a company name off business cards. Make sure all your Web pages have `title` tags—even the ones that you think aren't major enough to have META tags!

With all this discussion of META tags and `title` tags, you might be getting the idea that they're great inventions. You're right. You may also be getting the idea that they're open to a lot of abuse. You're right again. If you're not friendly to the search engines, as explained in the following section, you might get labeled as a Search Engine Jerk (SEJ)—by Tara, anyway.

HOW TO BE A SEARCH ENGINE JERK (SEJ)

You can get your Web site set up to be friendlier to search engines—or you can set it up to manipulate search engines and try to get your Web page the highest listings and most hits possible. The second course isn't a good idea, because these techniques can get you kicked out of search engines. We advise you to avoid the following courses of action unless you want to be known as a Search Engine Jerk, and, more importantly, risk losing your place in the search engines.

1. **Add keywords that have nothing to do with your site**

   Some people add keywords to their META tags that have nothing to do with the content of their site. The theory is the more keywords they have, the more hits they'll get in the search engine and the more people will visit their site. But this is a silly idea. The extra people who visit their sites will be visiting because of keywords that have nothing to do with the content, so they're not likely to be interested in the content. Furthermore, they're unlikely to look kindly upon the Web-site owner for playing such a trick.

2. **Add multiple instances of keywords to your META tags**

   Instead of adding a keyword one time in your META tags, you might add the same keyword ten or fifteen times. That's one way to try "keyword stuffing" and most of the time, it won't work—spiders are too smart for that. (Note that putting "dogs, dogs, dogs, dogs" in your description META tag is not okay. However, putting "German Shepherds, Welsh Terriers, Boxers" is okay—as long as your page has something to do with each of these breeds.)

3. **Use copyrighted or trademarked terms in your META tags**

   SEJ's might use copyrighted or trademarked terms to which they are not entitled as META tag descriptions. For example, if they've set up a site to promote one particular brown fizzy drink, they might use the names of other brown fizzy drinks to attract visitors to their site. At best they'll be deceiving visitors. At worst— and this is pretty bad—they'll be sued for misuse of a trademark.

Want a Lawsuit?

Some people actually steal the entire META tag structure of a competing site that's at the top of the search engines. This is called metajacking *and it's very naughty. In fact, it's a good way to get sued. Don't do it.*

And yes, there have been META tag lawsuits already, at least five of them (three of which involved Playboy magazine trying to stop Web sites using the words Playboy and Playmate in their tags), one of which ended in a $3 million settlement. See the **Meta Tag Lawsuits** *page at* http://searchenginewatch.internet. com/resources/metasuits.html *for more information.*

4. **Add invisible words to the bottom of your pages**

   Sometimes to increase the incidence of keywords on a page, Webmasters resort to a sneaky form of keyword stuffing. They set up text the same color as the page background—so viewers can't ordinarily view it—and add lines and lines and lines of keywords. (In the search-engine business this is sometimes called *fontmatching*.) This could get your page—and sometimes your entire Web site—kicked out of search engines. Some spiders also consider a preponderance of very small text as possible evidence of keyword stuffing, so be careful how much tiny text you're using on a page.

5. **Set up multiple entrances to the same site**

   Other Web sites set up several copies of the same page so they'll show up in several places on a search-engine's results list. These pages are often known as *doorway pages*. There's a chance that using these will get you into trouble with the search engines, but we'll look at this subject in detail in a moment.

6. **Title Stacking**

   Title Stacking (also called *Title Packing*) is when you use a perfectly legitimate way to enhance your search engine ranking—that is, using a title tag—in a nefarious manner. Specifically, you use several title tags at a time, like this:

   ```
   <Title>The Best Example Title Tags Online</Title>
   <Title>Thousands of Free Example Title Tags</Title>
   <Title>Learn All About Example Title Tags</Title>
   ```

   The theory is that search engines will add the information from all the title tags. It probably won't work anymore—if it ever did—and it might get you into trouble with the search engines, so don't do it.

All of these techniques may work in the short run. But they'll cost you a lot more in the long run by wrecking your credibility, attracting to your site visitors you don't want, and getting your site kicked out of a lot of search engines.

CREATING "DOORWAY" PAGES

Some people in the "search-engine optimization business" recommend the use of *doorway* pages, also known as *bridge* pages, *portal* pages, *jump* pages, *entry* pages, and so on.

The idea is that you create a number of pages—perhaps half a dozen or a dozen—and set them up with META tags and keywords. Then you register all these pages individually in the search engines. In theory you'll get more search engine hits, so you'll get more visits.

Does this work? Probably. Is it dangerous? In other words, can it lead to problems with the search engines? Possibly—though at the time of writing, probably not. Things change quickly, though. Kris Carpenter, of the search engine *Excite*, was recently quoted as saying, "I'm sure they're looking at [doorway pages] and saying, 'But I'm having such good success.' In three to six months, it may have the opposite effect."

Take that as a warning. The search engines don't like you playing these sorts of games. They're interested in providing a good service to the people searching at their sites, and these sorts of tricks make it harder for them to do so. All of the search-engine companies are looking for ways to make searching easier and more productive, and that means finding ways to filter out the effect of tricks. Infoseek has reportedly already banned redirection pages from their directories—pages that automatically redirect someone from one page to another (see Chapter 14).

So, it's up to you. You could try it … or not. We're not advising either way. If you'd like to learn more, though, see these articles:

What Is A Bridge Page Or Entry Page?
http://searchenginewatch.com/webmasters/bridge.html

A Bridge Too Far
http://searchenginewatch.com/sereport/9802-bridge.html

Promoters Call For Certification
http://www.searchenginewatch.com/sereport/9808-certification.html

MUCH MORE INFORMATION

You can spend a great deal of time fooling around with your Web pages, trying to get them just right. We're not convinced that all this time is necessarily time well spent, but if you'd like to investigate further, check these Web sites and newsgroups and their associated reports and newsletters:

comp.infosystems.search (a newsgroup related to search-engine issues)

META Tagging for Search Engines
http://www.stars.com/Search/Meta/Tag.html

PlanetOcean—Search Engine Secrets ($97 for a book)
http://www.hitmasters.com/

Search Engine Secrets ($15 for a book)
http://ww.lr-publishing.com/SES2/

Search Engine Tips—Submit It!
http://www.submit-it.com/subopt.htm

Search Engine Watch (free newsletter)
http://searchenginewatch.com/

Search Engines—Submission Tips, Help and Use
http://www.sofer.com/research/

Secrets to Achieving a Top 10 Ranking and the Marketposition Monthly Newsletter (free with purchase of the WebPosition software)
http://www.webposition.com/

The Brick (tips on optimizing your site for search engines)
http://207.217.39.6/thebrick/

The Secrets of Search Engine Positioning
http://yellowpage.com/ses.htm

VirtualPromote (a discussion forum related to search engines, along with articles and services)
http://www.virtualpromote.com/

Web Ranking Tools
http://www.bruceclay.com/web_rank.htm

WebPromote (free newsletter)
http://www.WebPromote.com/

Yahoo!—Site Announcement and Promotion Placement Improvement
http://www.yahoo.com/Computers_and_Internet/Internet/World_Wide_Web/Information_and_Documentation/Site_Announcement_and_Promotion/Search_Engine_Placement_Improvement/

GET PROFESSIONAL HELP

If all this seems a bit much, there are many companies waiting to help you. These companies will play the search-engine tricks for you … for a price, of course. They may charge a set fee, or perhaps a per-click fee. We've seen rates between 12 cents and 25 cents per click. That is, for every new customer they bring in, they'll charge you that much. They set up pages on their Web sites, register those in the search engines, then charge you each time someone reaches one of those pages and is redirected to your site.

For instance, one major search-engine optimization company, Did-It.Com, charges $399 to set up the system, and then 25 cents for each "clickthrough." In other words, you pay them 25 cents for each person who visits your site as a result of the Did-It.Com listing. Now and then they'll run promotions; We've seen the setup as low as $150, with a clickthrough rate of 12 cents.

The good news? That's not a bad price, compared to advertising (see Chapter 12). The bad news? It could still be a significant cost. At those rates, 100 visitors would cost you from $12 to $25. That may be too much for some businesses, laughably cheap for others. Another problem, though, is that if you decide to drop their services, they have pages pointing to your site, carefully designed to catch searchers, but now they're directing searchers *away* from your site.

A number of the Web sites mentioned above (under *Much More Information*) provide these services. You might also try these sites:

Beyond Interactive
http://www.gobeyond.com/

AAA Internet Promotions
http://www.websitepromote.com/

Did-It.com
http://www.did-it.com/

SearchPositioning
http://www.searchpositioning.com/

Site-Promotion.com
http://www.site-promotion.com/

Yahoo: Search Engine Placement Improvement
http://dir.yahoo.com/Business_and_Economy/Companies/Internet_
Services/Web_Services/Promotion/Search_Engine_Placement_
Improvement/

IS IT WORTH IT?

Is it worth it? We're not sure. But here's the way Peter looks at this sort of service: in effect, it's just another form of advertising. They send you people interested in your product or services, and you pay them for it. And 12 cents per click-through is actually a very good price when compared to other Web advertising systems.

The search-engine optimization services say they can put your Web site in the major search engines near the top of the relevant category, boosting traffic to your site. Unfortunately a lot of the claims are hype. Here are a few of Peter's thoughts on the subject.

The first thing to consider is that these services cannot boost your rating in the most important search site of all, Yahoo!. More searches are done at this site than at any other—according to at least one survey more than all the other search sites combined. The submission services can't fool Yahoo!, because search-engine optimization relies on tricking a computer program—some kind of search-engine "bot" that looks at your Web site—into giving you a high rating. But Yahoo! uses real live people to rate your site. If they like it, they'll add it; if they don't, they won't. And in any case, you'll just be added to a list in alphabetical order (although you can try using an "A" word in your page title to get near the top, Yahoo!'s people may not use your page title to enter you into the list).

Also, the search-engine optimization services may not really be as successful as they claim. An employee of Did-It.Com, one of the better-known services, told Peter that on average they were sending around 800 people a month to their customers, hardly a deluge. (On some days Peter's Web site gets that many or more.)

The whole concept of promising large numbers of people that you'll push them to the top of their categories is a little strange; we can't all be at the top, can we? And even if you can find a way to trick a search engine into doing what you want it to do today, the search engine may change how it works tomorrow. The search-engine guys are constantly trying to keep ahead of the optimization people; it's a sort of battle of wits, with each side looking for the other's weaknesses.

You can spend an awful lot of time and energy—and money—trying to optimize for search engines, but you'll never be finished, because you'll constantly have to keep up with what the search engines are doing. In fact search-engine optimization can sometimes have the opposite effect. If you're too aggressive it can get you banned from a search engine.

There are some simple things you can and should do to make your Web site attractive to search engine spiders and crawlers. Make sure you have a descriptive title tag in your Web pages, including the sort of key words people are likely to use when searching for sites of your type. Use the META keywords and description tags. Make sure the main page at your site includes text that contains the keywords that search engines are likely to look for.

But here's the most important secret for search-engine optimization, or at least for drawing people to your site, a secret you don't often hear when people discuss this subject. Make sure your site is worth visiting. Consider why somebody would want to visit your site, and ask yourself a simple question: if it wasn't my site, would I want to visit it? If you create a really useful site, and register with the major search engines, it will probably get listed. And eventually the word will get around, and people *will* visit.

A final thought. If you think getting your Web site listed in the search engines is all you need to do to bring people to your site, you've got a problem. That may have been the case a couple of years ago, but today there's too much stuff out there. Unless you're really active in getting the word out about your site, people are not going to visit, regardless of how well "search-optimized" your site is.

This chapter has given you a good idea of what to do (and what not to do) when it comes to making your site friendly for search engines. We believe that it's worthwhile doing the basic things we've outlined in this chapter. However, we're not convinced that it's worth spending a great deal of time playing tricks on search engines; that time could probably be better spent concentrating on providing something really worthwhile at your Web site, and working on the other promotional techniques we'll discuss in this book. You can think of the search engines as being similar to the telephone Yellow Pages. Yes, you need to be listed, and yes, they can bring your Web site visitors. But most companies get only a small portion of their business from the Yellow Pages; they get most of their business from other promotional and advertising techniques. And so too, with search engines—you'll probably get most of your visitors elsewhere (and if not, you're probably not trying!).

Now that you've got the site ready, you must submit it to the search engines. That's what we'll look at in the next chapter.

CHAPTER SIX

Registering with the Search Sites

Got your page set up? Great. Filled to the brim with META tags? Fine. Got all your links checked, grammar confirmed, t's crossed, and i's dotted? Terrific. *Bring on the search sites!* In this chapter we'll explain how to go about registering with various types of search sites, places that people go to find the information they need. If someone's searching for the sort of information you have at your site, they should be able to find your site when they search. But unless you do a good job of registering with the search sites … they won't.

A GREAT DESCRIPTION

No, wait a minute. You have to do one more thing. You have to write a description. Your description is what brings in your viewers. It's what attracts them to your site before they even get to your site. As you might imagine from this fact, a description is critically important. You might have the best site devoted to bass fishing in the world, but if the description reads "Really neat site on bass fishing. You have to come visit. Look at my bass fishing page.", you're going to have trouble getting visitors.

Write down a description of your Web site. Put down everything you can think about your site. Now see if you can boil it down to 75 good words. Now see if you can reduce that number to 50. Now cut down to 25. Now take that all the way down to 10 good words.

Use a Text Editor

Don't write your description in a word processor, or you may end up with various typesetting characters (such as curly quotes and emdashes) that won't work properly when you fill in forms at the search sites. Use a text editor such as Notepad (in Windows) or SimpleText (on the Mac); or, if you use Windows, get **TextPad** (http://www.textpad. com/), which is a great text editor with word-processing features.

Here's an example. Say you've got a site dealing with origami. Start out with about a 75-word description:

```
Example Origami, the site devoted to paper folding.
Covers traditional paper folding as well as dollar
bill folding, toy-making, and other types of
origami. Information available for beginners to
experts. Several patterns on the site, with links
to other origami resources online and a gallery of
classic origami. A directory of worldwide origami
organizations is also here. Free monthly newsletter
available on origami folding. Origami paper, books,
publications, and tutorial videos for sale.
```

That about says it all, and in a way that makes an origami enthusiast want to come visit. (Note how we didn't make every sentence in the description grammatically perfect—sometimes you have enough space to get your information across but not enough space to impress your English teacher. On your Web page you have more room to pay attention to your grammar.)

Now, let's take that example and boil it down to 50 words:

```
Example Origami, the site devoted to paper folding.
Covers traditional paper folding as well as dollar
bill folding, toy-making, and other types of
origami. Information available for beginners up to
experts. Several patterns available, with links to
other origami resources online. Paper, books, and
tutorial videos for sale.
```

You've pulled out some information and left in what you consider the critical stuff. Now, pare it down further to 25 words:

```
Example Origami, the site about paper folding. Also
dollar bill folding and paper toy-making. For
beginners to experts. Free patterns. Origami
materials for sale.
```

Now you really start getting squeezed, and your ability to describe what your site offers suffers. But as you can see here, this description lets the viewer know that:

- A wide variety of things are available on your site (covering many types of origami folding)

- It's appropriate for a wide audience (beginners to experts)
- There's something there they might be interested in (free patterns)

Finally, if they need some paper, they know that this site has origami materials for sale. Get as specific as you can! Every specific note (beginners to expert, materials for sale, dollar bill folding) is a great keyword, helping your site stand out to visitors who want to find you.

Getting down to ten words can be a pain, especially if your site has a lot to offer. But it can be done:

```
Example Origami. All types of origami. Beginners-
experts. Free patterns.
```

Of course you don't have any room to be descriptive, but you can maintain the fact that the site covers all kinds of origami, that it's appropriate for beginners to experts, and that it offers free patterns. You have to both tell what your site is about and give them a reason to come (thus our leaving in phrases like "free patterns" and "materials for sale"—not critical to the description of the site but a good incentive to visit for the casual browser).

You may be wondering: if you have only ten words to work with, why not make them all keywords? There are a few reasons you don't want to do that:

- Keywords all strung together are hard to read.
- You might choose a keyword combination that's confusing to your readers. Better to state what you're all about in plain English, even if it's grammatically fractured English.
- If you use straight keywords it's harder to make statement/phrases like "free patterns;" the viewer will see every individual word as an independent keyword.

You'll have opportunities to use descriptions of all these lengths, so once you've put your descriptions together, save each of them. If you're using a clipboard utility (see Chapter 2), stash them there so you can cut and paste a description every time you have to use one.

You've seen an example of a good description set above, but there are some other rules of thumb to follow when putting together a description.

Good Descriptions Are Not Dated

Putting dates in your description automatically makes them look really, really old. For example, say we put in the description "Tara's example descriptions. The best descriptions of 1998." That looks fine in 1998. Two years after 1998 it's going to look horrible. Far better to put "Tara's example descriptions. Fine selections of example descriptions including satirical, metaphorical, and traditionally boring."

The same rule applies to mentioning time. For example, don't put in a description that you've been in business for two years. If you absolutely must, you can put that you've been "in business since 1996" but we wouldn't recommend even that. The Internet and its culture are unfriendly to time. Time on the Internet means non-updated pages, outmoded technology, and ancient resources. (Thankfully, it means something much different in the offline world.)

Good Descriptions Are Catchy

Tara's got a thing for words like *pep* and *verve*; they're so 1920's. Your description needs to have pep, and lots of it. It needs to be *catchy*. Consider ...

```
The Example Cartoon Page has a very extensive
collection of example cartoons, like several
cartoons devoted to certain industries.
```

Yawn. There's little that's specific in this description, and the addition of *very*—one of the most dreadful words in our language—makes it drag. Let's take another thwack at it:

```
The Example Cartoon Page contains a plethora of
example cartoons, including cartoons devoted to fire
fighting, pumpkin tossing, and creosote production.
```

Isn't that a much more interesting description? Not only is it more interesting, but you've also put more specific keywords in there to attract searchers who are looking for information about fire fighting, pumpkin tossing, and creosote production.

Good Descriptions Are Not Mere Puffery

Puffery is an advertising term that means a description that's so subjective, or so hyperbolic, that it can't be taken as an objective measure of the quality of a product or service. The problem is that people can see through puffery. (Perhaps that should be part of the description of this term; if it's quite clearly hyperbolic nonsense, it's puffery.)

We believe that puffery won't get you far. (Very occasionally it'll get you into a lawsuit, though, as in the case in which bookseller Barnes & Noble sued Amazon.com for claiming to be the world's largest bookstore.)

Once you've got your descriptions together, and have assured that they're non-dated, specific, and puffery-free, you're finally ready to approach the search sites and subject indexes.

SEARCH SITES: THE BIG 'UNS

In this section we'll list the URLs for submitting to certain search sites and hit the highlights as to what these search sites do and don't want. However, don't take our word for it—check the pages yourself! Unfortunately things change so quickly online that it's hard for a mere book to keep up. Oh, and don't run out and register quite yet—not until you've read about the submission services and programs later in this chapter.

Yahoo!

Main Site:
   http://www.yahoo.com/

Site Submission Page:
   http://www.yahoo.com/info/suggest/

Yahoo! is the most popular search site around, which means you really, really want to get listed there. However, they don't automatically list everything, and we're not aware of anything that clearly explains what they list and what they don't, and why. The process is very subjective, because Yahoo! uses real people to

Sites, Engines, and Indexes

You'll hear a variety of terms related to sites where people can find information about other Web sites. They're often called search engines. *We prefer to call them* search sites, *though, because the term* search engine *often really means a highly automated system with little human interaction in the indexing process. For instance, AltaVista is a true search engine. It uses programs to go out and index Web sites, and it provides a search system for users to find things.*

But then some of these places have much more human interaction— Yahoo! actually has a staff of people who try to assess each site and decide whether it should be in the directory. Yahoo! has a directory of categories and subcategories—yet it also works in a similar way to many search engines, in that you can simply enter keywords and search for them.

There are other differences, too. Some search engines (such as AltaVista) index just about every word in every page. A site such as Yahoo!, though, indexes just the URL, page title, and description. You may hear sites such as Yahoo! and Excite called subject indexes, *in fact.*

Then there are various other types of sites—directories and listings. They are often much smaller and more specialized. But all these sites have one thing in common, regardless of the terminology; they are used for finding information on the Web.

check all the submissions; most systems use programs to check submissions. If the person looking at your site doesn't like it, then you're out! (Try again.)

Their submission procedure—find your category first, and then submit it— is a lot like LookSmart. First, you've got to find the most appropriate place in *their* index for *your* page. (As you probably know Yahoo is broken down into a series of categories and sub-categories.)

Once you do that, you'll be asked if that's really the category you want to submit to. You'll also be asked for the site name, URL, and a description, (they have some guidelines for what they do and don't want in a description), then you'll have the chance to suggest a second category. Then you'll be asked for your name and e-mail, and the geographical location of the site (if applicable.) Finally, you'll be asked if your listing is time-sensitive and if you have any comments.

Use the time-sensitive feature if it's applicable. The time-sensitive feature will set your site to be removed from the Yahoo! database after a certain date. This is a great feature if you want to promote a convention, seminar, or some other

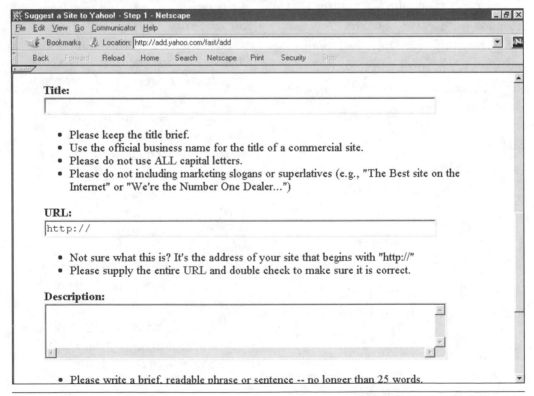

FIGURE 6.1: Yahoo! has very specific guidelines for suggesting Web sites. Be sure to follow them!

date-related event. You'll be able to promote something and get some exposure, and you won't have to worry about it sitting in Yahoo!'s database, getting moldy.

If Yahoo! accepts you, they'll drop you an e-mail and let you know that your site will appear and when it will appear. Don't hold your breath, though. It can take literally months to get listed on Yahoo! In fact, you probably *won't* get listed in Yahoo! the first time you try. On the other hand, the last time Tara submitted a site to Yahoo! she received notification that she'd been accepted within about three days.

Yahoo! is the single most important search engine. At one point not so long ago, more searches were carried out at Yahoo! than at all the other search engines combined. Although that may not be the case today, it's certainly one of the busiest—if not the busiest—search site around, so it's essential that your Web site is listed there. But that's easier said than done. There's a good article on this subject (from August of 1998) at the Search Engine Watch Web site: http://searchenginewatch.internet.com/webmasters/yahoo/results.html. This article, based on a small, informal survey, indicates that most people who try to get listed at Yahoo! don't succeed (72 percent), and that in order to get listed the successful site owners had to try, on average, almost four times—about the same number of times as those who didn't get listed!

One important criterion noted by this report was that sites are far more likely to get listed if the submission is for a "root URL" (the domain name without subdirectories) than for a URL at a "members page" Web site (a site at America Online, CompuServe, and so on). We've said it before, and we'll say it again … you need your own domain name!

AltaVista

Main Page:

http://www.altavista.com/

Site Submission Page:

http://www.altavista.com/av/content/addurl.htm

AltaVista asks that you submit only one URL per site; its site crawler (named Scooter) will index the whole site eventually. AltaVista supports META tags, but will kick out sites that abuse search sites with keyword stuffing and META-tag abuse. They also note that they occasionally rebuild their site from scratch, and some sites might get lost. If your URL vanishes from the site and you know you're not a Search Engine Jerk, just resubmit the page.

Excite

Main Page:

http://www.excite.com/

Site Submission Page:

http://www.excite.com/info/add_url/

At this writing, Excite is in the process of changing its submission procedures, and it is currently taking two weeks to add new URLs to the site index. Definitely read the "Getting Listed on Excite" page at http://www.excite. com/Info/listing.html. This page will inform you that Excite doesn't support META tags in an attempt to protect searchers from misleading information. Excite reviewers will review sites on occasion, but will not accept nominations for sites to be reviewed. They also recommend that you improve your site's rankings by creating Web pages for very limited subjects, thus decreasing the number of keywords (and the importance of each keyword) per page.

HotBot

Main Page:

http://www.hotbot.com/

Site Submission Page:

http://www.hotbot.com/addurl.asp

HotBot's site submission information page is at http://www.hotbot. com/help/. HotBot does index META tags, but warns that META-tag abuse will lead to site rankings being "severely penalized" (whatever that means; they don't specifically mention kicking a page out of their index, but perhaps that's what they mean). You can check to see whether your site has been indexed at http://www.hotbot.com/help/checkurl.asp.

InfoSeek

Main Page:

http://www.infoseek.com/

Site Submission Page:

http://www.infoseek.com/AddUrl?pg=DCaddurl.html

With InfoSeek you can either submit pages by e-mail or by the Web site. Adult-oriented sites must submit to InfoSeek via e-mail, which will take up to seven days or longer. (InfoSeek wants to make sure that such sites aren't inappropriately categorized.) InfoSeek, at its submission guidelines page (http://www.infoseek.com/Help?pg=new_guidelines.html), also notes that it isn't "responsible for sites submitted by third parties on behalf of Web-site owners," whatever that's supposed to mean. We'll talk about the URL-submission services later in this chapter.

InfoSeek also blocks the URL submissions of certain domains because of previous problems, and if your Web site is from one of those domains (they're not specific in listing them) and you submit a URL through the Web page, you won't get listed in their index. If your URL is banned, it may not be your fault. If you don't have your own Web site domain, then the actions of another user of that domain could be what's causing the ban. The other user may have spammed InfoSeek, or submitted really inappropriate content, or done something else against InfoSeek's terms of use.

However, you can submit a banned-domain URL via their e-mail address to be considered for inclusion. If it's clear your site has nothing to do with the site that was banned, and that you're playing by the rules, we suspect you'll get listed (but this is yet another argument for having your own domain name).

If you're getting the idea that InfoSeek is pretty strict, you're right. InfoSeek devotes an entire page to what it considers spamming, at http://www. infoseek.com/Help?pg=spam.html. They pretty much describe what we talked of as the actions of a Search Engine Jerk in the last chapter; InfoSeek may be one of the strictest search engines we've seen.

Lycos

Main Site:

http://www.lycos.com/

Site Submission Page:

http://www.lycos.com/ addasite.html

Lycos does not permit sites with certain characters in their URLs— ampersand (&), percent sign (%), equals sign (=), dollar sign ($), and question mark (?)—to be added to their index, as their spider (the program that runs around the Internet

Adult Sites Beware!

You may notice that the proprietors of "adult" sites need to adhere to different standards from owners of sites viewable by a more general audience. That's because there's still a lot of controversy of what is and isn't appropriate content. We're not going to get into that in this book; however, we do suggest that if you have any content that's appropriate only to the over-18 set—pornography-related, drugs- and alcohol-related, gambling-related, whatever—pay extra careful attention to the search-site submission rules, because there may be exceptions that apply to you.

looking at the submitted Web pages) doesn't recognize them. Lycos will also delete from their "rolling catalog" any sites that cannot be indexed after four weeks. (If your site goes down, or you move a page, or something else makes your Web page unavailable, you might be deleted from the rolling catalog. You can add the site back to Lycos again once it goes back up.)

Northern Light

Main Site:

http://www.nlsearch.com/

Site Submission Page:

http://www.northernlight.com/docs/register.htm

Northern Light is different from most of the other major search sites. It includes a "special collection" of material—news articles and the contents of press wires—in addition to indexed Web sites. Northern Light asks that you submit only one URL per day, and points out that they will only accept 120 submissions per user per day. (Any submissions over that will be discarded; Northern Light asks for your name and e-mail address when you submit an URL so they probably track your submissions that way.)

WebCrawler

Main Site:

http://www.webcrawler.com/

Site Submission Page:

http://www.webcrawler.com/Help/GetListed/AddURLS.html

WebCrawler has a very small index compared with the other search sites we've mentioned here, and it isn't used as often as the other ones. However, it is still an important search site—it's one of the earliest, and still fairly popular. (WebCrawler is owned by Excite; it's intended to be more family-oriented and friendly, while Excite is supposed to be more "hip" and cutting edge.) WebCrawler has a help page for their URL submissions at http://www. webcrawler.com/Help/GetListed/AddURLS.html. They will index "every word on your page up to 1MB of text"—that'd be some huge page. WebCrawler will kick your page out of its index if you're a Search Engine Jerk. They also note that their spiders won't necessarily index your entire site from the URL you submit, so be sure to submit your main URL or the URL that contains the most important information about your site. (They ask that you not submit more than 25 URLs for any server.) WebCrawler also applies a lot of importance to Title tags, so make sure all the pages you're submitting have titles—good ones!

A FEW INTERESTING SMALL ONES

The sites we've looked at so far are a fantastic resource for finding information, with many millions of words and hundreds of thousands of Web pages indexed. But there are many, many more, hundreds of them. The following is a tiny sample of a few of the not-so-big ones.

Dig

Main Site:

http://www.dig.com/

Site Submission Page:

http://www.disney.com/dig/youdig/today/

This is the Disney Internet Guide (DIG, get it?). DIG asks for your e-mail address, the name of the site, site URL, and a description of why you "dig" it. (A little advice here. Admit straight up that you're plugging your site; don't pretend that you're recommending it as an impartial observer. Editors are apt to view your site more critically if they suspect that kind of misrepresentation. Anyway, if they really like your site, they're not going to hold the fact that you recommended it against you.) DIG notes that they review every site that goes into their index, and they do their best to avoid listing "inappropriate" material. (We wouldn't even consider submitting a site to this index unless it was G or PG rated.)

eBLAST

Main Site:

http://www.eblast.com/

Site Submission Page:

http://www.ebig.com/feedback/submit.html

eBLAST is the directory service of the Encyclopedia Britannica. eBLAST doesn't contain articles from the EB—just reviewed Web sites. They don't ask that your site be about anything in particular; they just ask for your name, your e-mail address, the site URL, and a description of the site. eBLAST editors say they "sift out sites of questionable value," but do not state explicitly that they review all sites. (They have a 1- to 5-star rating system.) eBLAST does allow surfers to restrict their search to "kid-friendly" sites, but they accept submissions of all kinds of sites. (They note in their site reviews whether or not something is appropriate for kids.)

LookSmart

Main Site:

http://www.looksmart.com/

Site Submission Page:

http://www.looksmart.com/h/info/subsite.html

You may not have heard of LookSmart; it's a searchable subject index a lot like Yahoo!. We're including it here for a couple of reasons: a) they've got excellent partnerships and push, so you'll probably be seeing more of them as time goes by, and b) they have an interesting way of displaying their category listings that's easy to use. We think it'll attract a lot of repeat users. (If you're reading this three years after we wrote it, and LookSmart has long since vanished into obscurity, feel free to have a laugh at our expense.)

LookSmart admits that "many sites will be rejected because they do not meet our current content needs." We're not sure what that means. They also say a paragraph later that they're in the process of developing a new "self-publication" site that will be launched in the "near future," as of November 1998. You can get a better idea of what LookSmart wants by checking their submission FAQ at http://www.looksmart.com/h/info/submitfaq.html. (Don't bother to submit pornographic or adult-only sites; LookSmart doesn't want 'em.)

Surf the LookSmart categories and find a category that fits your site. (Don't submit to the "Best of the Web" categories because your submission will be discarded.) Click on the "Submit" button. You'll be asked for a variety of information, including the title of the site, the URL, description, keywords (these are optional), date the site was launched (optional again), and contact information. LookSmart has some rather exact guidelines for how long a description and keywords can be, so pay attention to those. It can take up to six weeks for your site to get listed, so don't expect your site to appear here overnight.

FINDING SPECIALTY SEARCH SITES

As we noted, there are lots of other search sites out there—literally hundreds. They don't get as much traffic as the big ones we've mentioned here, but their visitors are often interested in specific subjects. If your subject and the search site's match, you've got a unique opportunity to attract qualified traffic to your site. The following list includes sites that list both search sites and specialty subject indexes. These are a great way to find places to register your Web site, places that focus on the same subjects that you do.

Beaucoup

http://www.beaucoup.com/

Beaucoup is a great place to start—it has links to over 1,200 search sites, indexes, and meta-listings to help you submit your site to targeted sites. Sites are divided by category and subcategory; if you cover a lot of categories, check out the Beaucoup BIG page, which lists almost all the categories on one page.

Argus Clearinghouse

http://www.clearinghouse.net/

If you want more information about sites and directories before you start submitting to them, check out the Argus Clearinghouse. Argus has policies for accepting new listings into their directory (they say they accept only about 5-10 percent of the guides submitted), and they review each resource and give it a rating so you can check that before visiting a search site or specialty index.

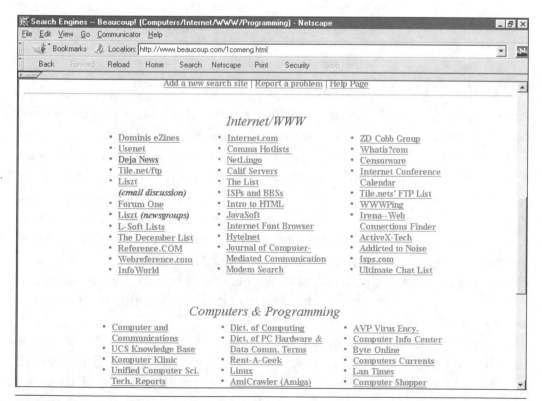

FIGURE 6.2: There are many different search engines in lots of different categories.

iSleuth

http://www.isleuth.com/

iSleuth links to over 3,000 searchable databases. You'll see that the name of the resource is a clickable link—that's how you get to the site itself. If you just want to search it to see if your Web site is already there, use the search form. This is a fantastic resource, well worth visiting.

FinderSeeker

http://www.hamrad.com/
search.html

Meta Lists

A meta-listing is an exhaustive listing of sites in one category. For example, if Peter had a site devoted to lighthouses, and he created a huge list of links devoted to lighthouses and nothing but, then he has a meta-listing devoted to lighthouses. Meta-listings are sometimes better than general subject directories like Yahoo!, since site owners often invest a lot of energy in indexing sites of only one type.

If you want to use a search site to find the search sites, check out Finder-Seeker. This is especially good for those of you who might be looking for rather obscure categories, because you can search by keyword. You can also narrow your search by category or geographical location. (Sometimes when searching you'll find things besides search sites; FinderSeeker also lists software archives, site-rating services, and so on.)

AUTOMATED SUBMISSIONS

After reading all these listings, you may have tossed this book across the room a couple of times and decided this was all too much trouble. You don't have to do each site manually—though we recommend it if you want to be absolutely sure of how your site was submitted and when. If you want to save time, you can try third-party software and submission services. It's probably a good idea to submit Yahoo! by hand, and perhaps a few major search sites such as Excite, HotBot, InfoSeek, and so on. Some search sites require that you provide quite a bit of information—descriptions, keywords, and so on. There's really not much point submitting to some of them by hand, though; there's no real need to submit to AltaVista or WebCrawler by hand, because all that these require is a URL. You can use a service or program to submit to these.

There's a wide variety of software and third-party services that will help you get your sites submitted to the search sites. These software packages and services ask you for a lot of information initially—your site name, URL, description, keywords, and other information that search sites and specialty indexes want. Then they take that information and send it to the search sites in the form in which they need it. This saves you from typing the same information over and over again, and saves you time by submitting to search sites automatically. The downside is that some search sites, such as InfoSeek, don't seem too keen on submissions from automated packages. We recommend that you only use software and third-party services for search sites and subject indexes that aren't top priority for you.

Some services advocate things like keyword stuffing and multiple doorways in order to get better search-site ratings. Check out what's being offered before you get too much into it.

> ## Goodbye Automated Submissions?
>
> *The major search sites don't much like the idea of automated submissions, because they're the cause of so much abuse. If the search sites really wanted to, they could easily stop almost all automated submissions, by continually changing the way in which the submission programs work, making it virtually impossible for the submission services to keep up with the changes.*
>
> *The submission services are worried about this, and have been lobbying the search sites for some kind of "certification" for submission services.*

SUBMISSION SERVICES

Submission services are Web-based systems that you can use to submit to hundreds of search sites at a time. You enter your information into a Web form, include your credit-card number, and that's it—the service does the rest.

Submit It!

http://www.submitit.com/

Submit It! is one of the oldest submission sites on the Web. Currently they offer automated submission to over 400 search sites and directories. They also offer free verification of pages and the ability to re-announce changed pages. At the time of writing the price of a 12-month license was $59 for two URLs. (Since many of the search sites automatically index your entire site if you submit one URL, that's not as skimpy as it sounds.) You also get the use of Site Analyzer, which analyzes browser compatibility, link rot, load times, popularity, and spelling, among other things.

!Register-It!

http://www.register-it.com/

Another one of the older submission services on the Web, !Register-It! offers you the ability to submit to up to 400 sites on the Web, and lets you get an idea of how it works by offering a free version that allows you to submit to up to 11 search sites. !Register-It! offers a 30-day money-back guarantee and the ability to use a visitor-tracking service, and a service (*Hitometer*) that allows you to track how many visitors have been to your Web site and what pages they were looking at (we'll discuss this subject in Chapter 14). At the time of writing the price of a 12-month license for one URL is $39.99. Two URLs are $59.99, and discounts for multiple URLs beyond that are available.

Shotgun

http://www.peachmedia.com/shotgun/

If the prices for the above services are getting you down, check out Shotgun. They're linkware—meaning that if you like their service they'd like you to link to their site—but beyond that there's no cost. There is an extensive signup process, though. (If you've got a pornographic or adult-only site, do not submit it using this service. Peach Media will bill you for removing your sites from the lists that Shotgun adds it to.) You have to enter a lot of information to Shotgun—whether your site uses VRML or Java, your complete contact information, your address, a description of the site, keywords of the site, target audiences for the site, and so on. Set aside a block of time to work on this one.

There are many other services on the Web; check out the following to get an idea of what's available:

@Submit! (Register with 30+ sites free)
  http://www.uswebsites.com/submit/

1 2 3 Register Me (100 sites for $45)
  http://www.123registerme.com/

A1 WebSite Promotions (50 sites for $89.95, 100 for $159.95, or 200 for $299.95)
  http://www.a1co.com/

AAA Internet Promotions (50 sites for $99, 100 for $199. Also options to submit once a month for a year)
  http://www.websitepromote.com/dls/

did-it.com (10 sites for $99)

    http://www.did-it.com/

JimTool Free Site Submitter (12 sites for free)

    http://www.virtualpromote.com/submitter/

PostMaster (350 sites for $249)

    http://www.netcreations.com/postmaster/

QwikLaunch (7 sites for free, 400 sites for $9.95)

    http://www.qwiklaunch.com/

SiteLaunch

    http://www.sitelaunch.net/

SmartAge Submit

    http://www.smartage.com/submit/

TrafficBoost.Com (530 sites for $49, or 530 sites submitted four times for $99)

    http://www.contactdata.net/

WebStep

    http://www.mmgco.com/top100.html

Yahoo!'s List of Services

    http://dir.yahoo.com/Business_and_Economy/Companies/Internet_Services/Web_Services/Promotion/

SOFTWARE

The other submission option is to use software programs that run on your own computer. There are literally dozens of software programs that can help you promote your Web site. The following few are noted as being at the top of their class at **Tucows**. (Tucows is one of the best repositories of Internet software. When you need some Internet software and don't know where to turn, start there first—http://www.tucows.com/.)

Why would you use a software package instead of the third-party services we mentioned above? A few reasons. With a software package you can submit to search sites as many times as you want. You can submit multiple URLs, without having to pay individually for each. And, if you're the suspicious type, you'll know the submission work is being done if you do it yourself.

AddSoft

Publisher's URL:

http://www.cyberspacehq.com/

Product URL:

http://www.cyberspacehq.com/addsoft/

If you're trying to promote a piece of software, this is the program for you. AddSoft enables you to automate submitting your software to several shareware sites and software directories. The software is presented in a series of tabbed windows; you submit information about your company and software, and then click on the Sites tab. The tab will give you a list of directories to which you can submit. (In the demonstration version, you can submit your software to only a limited number of sites.) Since software tends to go through many permutations, this is an excellent tool for you to use when your site undergoes an update, and you know that not every shareware directory will pick up on it. AddSoft is currently $89.

AddWeb

Publisher's URL:

http://www.cyberspacehq.com/

Product URL:

http://www.cyberspacehq.com/addweb/

By the same publishers that put together AddSoft, AddWeb is for promoting Web sites. Once again, it's a series of tabbed screens. You enter all your vital information about your Web site (and your company) in one, choose the search sites to which you want to submit in another (AddWeb currently works with 565 search engines and sites), then begin the submission process that AddWeb will update for you in a kind of digital "control panel."

AddWeb also offers a "page-builder" that will build a page for you that's set with the description and the keywords you specify, so you can submit that page to the search sites. (See *Creating "Doorway" Pages* in Chapter 5.) This page will also automatically redirect visitors to your main Web page. While this sounds great, bear in mind that some search sites don't approve of automatic redirects like this.

AddWeb has a search-site-analysis feature that checks several search sites to see where your Web site shows up. (On the trial version, this feature works 14 times.)

AddWeb has three versions. The standard version costs $49. The "Gold" version costs $89, and adds the ability to customize and edit e-mail reports, and the ability to automate report and e-mail generation. (This is a good option if

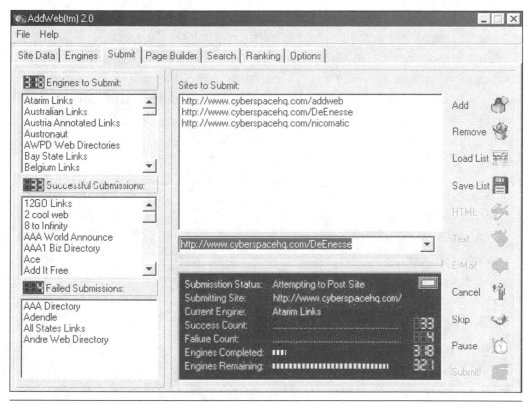

FIGURE 6.3. This is AddWeb, a submission program that gives you plenty of control over the process.

you're doing a lot of URL submissions, or you're doing URL submissions on behalf of a lot of different people and you want to send them reports.) The "Pro" version costs $129 and has everything the AddWeb Gold version has plus the ability to add new search sites to the database.

SubmitWolf

Publisher's Site:

http://www.msw.com.au/wolfhq.htm

Product Site:

http://www.msw.com.au/swolf/

SubmitWolf currently has information for over 1,200 search sites. These sites are divided into several different categories: Engines (search engines and sites), Links (Lists of links available), Manual (sites that have complicated submission arrangements or are fairly minor listings), Custom (a subset of engines and lists that are of particular interest to you and your Web site), and

RIP (sites that aren't at this moment responding to SubmitWolf; you can try to submit to them but there's no guarantee that you'll get through).

Clicking on one of the buttons next to a listing will give you a wealth of information, including the name of the search site, the URL, the submission URL, and the various rules for submission. (It's a violation of SubmitWolf's terms of usage to break these rules.) This program requires a little more work than AddWeb, but in return it gives you a lot more search-site information. SubmitWolf costs $95.

For more submission software, check out the following Web sites:

007 Submitter
   http://www.007software.com/

GlobalSpider
   http://www.globalspider.net/

Hired Hits
   http://www.hiredhits.com/

Hurricane WebPromo
   http://www.theoffice.net/webpromo/

HyperHits
   http://webmastertools.com/

Net Submitter Pro
   http://softwaresolutions.net/

Register Pro
   http://www.registerpro.com/

SoftSpider
   http://www.designmaker.com/

Submission Wizard (Windows 95; 500 search sites—the program
   will run for one month for $25, six months for $80)
   http://www.exploit.com/
   http://www.exploit.net/
   http://www.submissions.com/

Submit Blaster (Windows 95; 120 sites for $100)
   http://www.rtlsoft.com/

Web Promotion Spider ($50 to $100, 250 to 300+ search sites; also
   configures META tags for you and checks search sites to see how
   your site is listed)
   http://beherenow.com/

WebPosition

http://www.webposition.com/

www.SitePromoter (Windows and the Mac—the only Mac program we've found)

http://www.sitepromoter.com/

Check Your Search Site Position

Want to know how you're showing up in those search sites once you've been added? Some of the services we've mentioned above will give you an idea of your position with search sites—they have built-in utilities for providing feedback. But there are also independent services that focus solely on showing you how you're doing with the search sites. Check the following Web sites for more information.

MetaMedic (online META-tag checker for free, with a pro version available for pay)

http://www.northernwebs.com/set/setsimjr.html

MyRank (free search-site rankings delivered by e-mail)

http://www.myrank.com/

Position Agent (free trial for a commercial rank-checking service)

http://www.positionagent.com/

Rank This! (free rank check with 10 different search sites)

http://www.rankthis.com/

ScoreCheck (a free trial of a commercial rank-checking service)

http://www.scorecheck.com/

SmartAge SiteRank (a free trial of a commercial rank-checking service)

http://www.smartage.com/rank/

WebPosition (rank-checking software; download version available)

http://www.webposition.com/

Yahoo!'s Listings

http://dir.yahoo.com/Computers_and_Internet/Internet/World_Wide_Web/Information_and_Documentation/Site_Announcement_and_Promotion/Search_Engine_Placement_Improvement/

Search-site submission isn't something you can do in five minutes, so plan to spend a lot of time with it. A good rule of thumb is to start with the major search-site listings first, go to the searchable subject indexes second (concentrating on the groups you think are most important to your product or service), and then work on the specialty directories.

Even after you've registered your site, you're not finished. The next step is to try to get certified, recognized, notified, and awardified. Some of these will just make you feel good, while others will help build your visitors' confidence in your site. Check out the next chapter for more information on awards and certifications. Then visit Chapter 8, where we'll tell you about yet more places to register your Web site.

CHAPTER SEVEN

Getting Certified:
Assurances, Awards, and Alliances

If you're fairly new to the Internet, you may remember how you felt when you first logged on. You had questions about the safety of your information. You didn't know how Web sites could accept your credit card without anyone else getting the number, you didn't know how to confirm the trustworthiness of the businesses with whom you shopped, and so on. Over time you got the answers to those questions and your Internet experience became more comfortable.

Your Web site visitors are all in various states of Internet enlightenment. Some of them know exactly how the Internet works—possibly better than you do. Some of them have a pretty good idea of what's going on, and are comfortable visiting your site and buying online. Still others are very nervous about giving out personal information online and need lots of assurance.

It's easy for you to post huge assurances about how great you are, how trustworthy you are, how wonderful your Web site is, and so on, but you are not going to be immediately credible. While reading all those accolades about your company, viewers will keep constantly in mind that the accolades are coming from … your company. (When you're reading a newspaper, which do you attach more credence to: an advertisement or a positive product review?)

There are companies out there that will "vouch" for your Web site in several areas—how you handle privacy, how suitable your content is for children, whether your Web site is accessible by any browser, etc. By getting in touch with these sites and participating in their programs, you can assure your visitors you're complying with certain Internet standards.

Some companies award sites with special recognition for having great content, being especially appropriate for kids, and so on. By nominating your

153

site for these kids of awards, you can build your credibility to target audiences and increase overall traffic to your Web site.

Finally, you can make a statement about your beliefs and the causes you support by joining many of the alliance programs online. (Your jaw will drop when you see how many "ribbon" campaigns are being perpetrated online.) With these programs you can establish a bond with your visitors by letting them know you believe in something that they also believe in. Of course, this has the potential to backfire if you show that you believe in something that they disagree with, but we'll get to that later in the chapter.

ASSURANCES

We've had friends who asked if the Internet could "steal" their credit card numbers from their computer. Upon questioning, it turned out that they had never made a transaction online, didn't intend to, and in fact had never entered their credit card numbers into their computer. But they were still worried.

Their fear might sound a little irrational, but perhaps they have the right to be irrational. It seems like every week brings a new privacy problem or "security bug" in the major browsers, or some talk of an HTML-based virus. Further, parents have concerns about the content their children can see, and may question whether your site is suitable for youngsters. Other visitors, who might have special needs, have other questions. It's hard to know everything—the Internet changes so quickly—and easy to feel overwhelmed.

You should not dismiss concerns like these out of hand. At the least you need to take some time to educate your visitors and help them understand why these kinds of things aren't a problem with your site.

This is where the third-party "assurances" come in. The third parties provide complete explanations of the issues and standards they support. By joining a program you're connecting your visitors to its explanations, and getting a little of the credibility of those third parties. The assurances can be simple (that your Web site conforms to an open HTML standard) or more controversial (that your Web site has a clear and easily-accessible privacy policy, or that your Web content is suitable for children.)

There are a variety of programs with which you can get involved. A few are listed here in alphabetical order. Don't feel you *have* to work with any of these programs, but in some circumstances you may find them useful or beneficial.

AnyBrowser

http://www.anybrowser.org/campaign/

When the Internet first got started, there was Mosaic. Then there was Netscape and Mosaic. Then there was Internet Explorer and Netscape. (These are the popular graphical browsers, programs that can display pictures. Lynx, a text-based browser, has also been around the whole time.)

These days, things are more complicated in the browser market. There's AOL, Internet Explorer, Netscape, WebTV, Opera, browsers on WindowsCE and Palm computing devices, and Lynx, of course. You can hardly guess who's going to be looking at your site or what Web browser they're going to be using to look at it. And of course some things work on one browser that don't work on another browser.

The AnyBrowser program advocates that Web designers use HTML code that's accessible by any browser. If your Web site is standard text-and-graphics, you'll have no trouble adhering to this. If you're getting fancy with ActiveX, Java, or other bells-and-whistles, you'll have to check your code carefully.

This site has several "buttons" you can use showing that you adhere to an AnyBrowser standard, design guides to make sure you're using compatible HTML, and links to like-minded assurance programs and resources.

Bobby

http://www.cast.org/bobby/

That's Bobby as in British policeman. Bobby checks out your Web pages to make sure they're HTML-compliant and easily-accessible to the handicapped. It checks for accessibility errors—like making sure all your images have ALT tags attached to them—and accessibility recommendations; that is, what you can do to make your Web site more accessible to people with disabilities. Bobby will also ask you accessibility questions related to your page to help identify problems that Bobby can't diagnose on its own, and give you its own accessibility hints. (These hints will open your eyes to possible accessibility problems we bet you haven't even considered.) It'll also give you a summary of how long it took your Web page to load and which images took how long.

If you don't have any accessibility errors, Bobby will give you a banner to put on your site. (Incidentally, Bobby doesn't like the way LinkExchange banners work, so if you are a LinkExchange member Bobby will not give you a banner—

see Chapter 12 for information about LinkExchange.) The banner assures your visitors that your site is accessible to viewers with disabilities and that you've taken steps to be compatible with the HTML standard.

BBBOnLine Privacy Program

http://www.bbbonline.org/privacy/

BBB stands for Better Business Bureau, an organization dedicated to protecting consumers against fraud. An offline mainstay for decades, the Council of Better Business Bureaus has in the last few years moved online and created Web sites to educate consumers about online frauds, hoaxes, and other things that online buyers need to be wary about.

Recently they've started accepting applications for a new BBBOnLine Privacy Seal Program. This program is designed to assure site visitors that any information they submit will not be misused. It's a lot like the TRUSTe program discussed later in this chapter, except that there's an offline component to it.

Applicants to the program must have a U.S.-based Web site and have a satisfactory rating with the BBB. Other requirements include:

- The adoption of a clear privacy statement (what sites are doing with information they collect from visitors)
- An agreement to participate in the BBBOnLine Privacy Policy Dispute Resolution Program, a program through which the BBB helps consumers who have a disagreement with a participating company resolve the issue
- Adherence to a compliance program set by the BBB

The site must also agree to participate in "consumer education activity," helping visitors understand what online privacy means.

This program is not cheap (depending on what you regard as cheap, of course). Annual registration prices range from $150 (for sites with annual sales of less than $1 million) to $3,000 (for sites with over $2 billion in sales). If you're selling products online, consider it an investment in consumer trust.

You might also wish to investigate the **BBBOnline Reliability Program** at http://www.bbbonline.org/reliability/. This is more similar to the traditional work of the Better Business Bureaus. The Reliability Program is a pretty neat idea; the participating site agrees to adhere to the BBBOnline's standards of honest advertising and customer service. (This includes, of course, having a satisfactory record with the offline counterpart of the BBB.) The participating site puts up a BBB seal, and the BBB hosts the company's profile on the BBB server. When a visitor clicks on the BBB seal, they're taken to the profile page, which lists essential information with the company (how long it's been registered with the BBB, and so on.) It's an easy way to create a credible repository for important company information.

TRUSTe

http://www.etrust.com/

Privacy is a huge buzzword online. Everyone wonders whether his information is kept private, what Web sites are doing with registration information, and whether his e-mail address is going to end up on spam mailing lists.

In response to this, a lot of Web sites are developing "privacy policies." These policies make clear what information a Web site is gathering about visitors, how that information is being protected, what the site will and won't do with it, and so on.

That's where TRUSTe comes in. TRUSTe is "an independent, non-profit privacy initiative dedicated to building users' trust and confidence on the Internet and accelerating growth of the Internet industry." They've spent a lot of time putting together an organization that educates users about online privacy and teaches Web publishers how to develop fair and sensible privacy policies.

With that in mind, TRUSTe has developed a "trustmark" that participating sites can put on their sites. The trustmark certifies that the site has an easily available privacy statement that makes it clear what's being done with visitors' personal information, and gives users a choice for how their information is used and shared. (There are other requirements as well. You can read the entire list of requirements at http://www.etrust.com/webpublishers/pub_join.html).

The TRUSTe program is one of the best-known on the entire Web, and many major businesses subscribe to it. That's the good news. (We would guess they are better-known online than the Better Business Bureau's assurance services, though of course not nearly as well-known offline.) The bad news is that it's going to cost you. The annual license fee depends on your company revenue, ranging from $299 to $4,999. However, the fee may be a good investment since it carries so much credibility and it does help you build a comprehensive privacy statement for your site.

We recommend you seriously investigate the TRUSTe programs if one or more of the following conditions apply to you:

- You require a lot of personal information from your visitors. A privacy statement backed by TRUSTe can help alleviate their fears that the information will be used inappropriately.

- You are participating in e-commerce, which also requires the online use of sensitive personal information.

- You are running a site that's child-oriented and requires registration or submission of personal information by children. Parents are rightly concerned about any Web site that asks children to register; you should be very precise about why you want the information and what you're going to do with it. TRUSTe has a special program and trustmark specifically dedicated to children's Web sites.

If you view this as a good idea but prohibitively expensive, take a look at the credibility TRUSTe has built up, and take a look at how much trust you're asking from your users in the way of personal information. It may turn out that for building customer relationships and making them comfortable in dealing with you, it isn't that expensive at all.

Incidentally, certifications such as this may become increasingly important over the next few years, partly due to government pressure from the European Economic Community (EEC). The EEC is creating very strict privacy laws, and mandating that data gathered in Europe not be transferred to countries with less stringent privacy laws. This is putting pressure on U.S. companies that want to do online business in both Europe and North America—and even on the U.S. government—to follow suit.

RSACi

http://www.rsac.org/

Parents thought keeping track of what their kids are watching on cable TV was hard! The World Wide Web has many more than 50 channels, and there are all kinds of, um, interesting things on display! If you're trying to attract kids or families to your Web site, you need to make sure they know your content is safe to view by all ages, or if it's not, that the pages about which they should be cautious are clearly delineated.

RSACi stands for *Recreational Software Advisory Council on the Internet.* They've taken it upon themselves to help parents control their children's access to objectionable material. RSACi's ratings are integrated into Internet Explorer (IE); an IE user can use this "content advisor" feature to avoid sites that have certain RSACi ratings, or to actually avoid every site that isn't rated with RSACi!

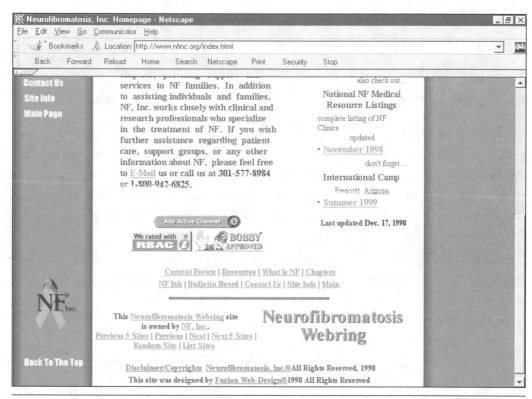

FIGURE 7.1: This page has registered with RSACi, so browsers can determine if it's for children, and with Bobby, to show that the site can be browsed by the disabled.

Web-site owners are invited to register their site with RSACi and get both an RSACi banner and a special PICS-Label META tag to include in their HTML code. The registration process is fairly simple. First, you'll be asked to specify for what amount of a site you're generating a tag; you can rate an entire site, a section of a site, or a single page. Next, you'll be asked to complete a one-page questionnaire and to give contact information—address, phone number, etc.

After that, you'll get into content rating. You'll be asked to give your site's level of nudity, sexual activity, language (from slang all the way up to making horses blush), and violence. Definitions are clearly provided for everything so there shouldn't be any ambiguity as you create your ratings. You'll then be asked to agree with RSACi's terms and conditions. Finally, you'll be given your rating. Along with the rating you'll be given a META tag and an RSACi logo to use with your site. Registration is free.

If your site attracts any younger viewers at all, we urge you to consider this tag. If your site contains content that could be considered unsuitable for kids, you really should get this certification. Because it's supported by Internet Explorer, it will become more widely used as time goes by, and shows that you've made a good-faith effort to warn people about potentially offensive/harmful content on your site. This is a good message to get across.

SafeSurf Rating System

http://www.safesurf.com/

Internet Explorer has RSACi; Netscape has SafeSurf. The SafeSurf rating system, like RSACi, is intended to protect children from inappropriate material online. We don't know of any law that says you can't rate your site with both RSACi and SafeSurf, so we recommend you take the time to do both if your site is designed for families and young viewers, or if it contains material inappropriate for children.

Like RSACi, SafeSurf has a self-rating form. Initially you'll be asked whether you want to rate a single page or an entire directory. After that, you will be asked to provide the site's URL, the title, and your full name and e-mail, along with the recommended age range for site visitors (from "all ages" to "explicitly for adults.")

In the content arena, you will be asked to identify the presence of any one of nine themes, including profanity, glorifying drug use, and different sexual themes. SafeSurf's definitions are not as extensive as RSACi's; you may find yourself confused at certain points. (Be sure to check the ratings FAQ for more information.)

When you've completed your self-assessment of all the themes, a Web page will be returned to you with your rating along with an explanation of how to use it. The same information will also be e-mailed to you. This service is free.

Banner Placement

At this point you might be thinking, "These are an awful lot of little banners to put on the front page!" You don't have to put them all on the front page. Put the ones that offer reassurance or guarantees on the front page, like the BBB banners or the TRUSTe seal. But the other ones, the ones that are concerned more with operability questions than consumer concerns, you might want to put on your "about this site" page or your awards page.

Web Interoperability Pledge

http://www.zdnet.com/anchordesk/wip/pledge.html

One browser company develops one standard, another company develops another standard, and second-tier Web access devices like palmtop computers are forced to try to navigate some happy medium. There are lots of different ways for browsers to look at Web sites. It's frustrating for Web masters to try to second-guess which standard will end up being prevalent, and it's frustrating for viewers to figure out which standard they want to use.

ZDNet, a division of publisher Ziff-Davis, is trying to end all that with the Web Interoperability Pledge. The pledge for Webmasters is pretty simple: "I pledge to use only recommended HTML tags as defined by W3C." **W3C (The World Wide Web Consortium**—http://www.w3.org/) is the body that sets and creates new HTML standards. Taking this pledge will show a good-faith effort towards creating a usable Web site.

You can get assurances from the BBB and other online agencies that you're a square company and okay to do business with. You can get assurances from other sites that you're doing your bit to create one Web standard and make your site as accessible to as many people as possible. But to get assurance that you're cool, admired, and beloved in all corners of the Web? You need awards, of course!

AWARDS

Awards started off slowly. There was a *Cool Site of the Day*, *The Top 5% of All the Sites on the Web*, and so forth. But Web site awards have exploded. There's a *Cool Site of the Second*, for crying out loud, a site devoted to cataloguing the best 404 errors online, awards for Best Dog Sites, sites approved by cats—there are all kinds of awards available. (Peter's favorites: *The Absolutely Meaningless Site Award* and *The Bottom 95% of all Web Sites Award*.)

As you might guess from the fact that there are so many awards, they're not quite as meaningful as they used to be. Reams of meaningless awards can be bought for the price of a few e-mails. Some sites will give you awards simply if you link to them. You probably want to avoid these; they don't do you or your site a lot of good. (However, award collecting can be fun! ... if not particularly profitable.)

On the other hand, there are some great awards that can have a big effect on traffic. We'll point you to some good ones, and, if you really want to learn about every last one of what's available, we'll give you some links to those too.

Submitting Your Site

The most popular awards get lots and lots of nominations. You want your nomination to stand out even before an editor takes a look at your site. Keep these rules in mind when nominating your site for an award:

- Abide by the guidelines for submitting your nomination. If they want a 50-word essay in purple text, give 'em a 50-word essay in purple text. And don't nominate your site for an inappropriate award—your consumer-protection cat-litter site will not be served by winning a "Cool Dog Site" award, and you'll waste everyone's time by nominating it.

- Create a precise description of the site that you can send with your nomination. Make sure it's free of spelling and grammar errors.

- Double-check, triple-check, quadruple-check the URL you submit! You don't want it to be incorrect.

- If your site requires anything for optimum usage (like RealPlayer, Shockwave, etc.) make sure the editors know about it. (You don't want them to visit and then leave because they don't have the right software to make the most of it.)

Really Good Awards

Might as well start at the beginning. Let's look at some particularly useful awards.

Project Cool

http://www.projectcool.com/sightings/

The first big award, where it all started, was *The Cool Site of the Day*. The guy who created this award in mid-1994 has developed Project Cool Sightings, which dishes up a new Web site every day. This is a great award, but it's not for sissies. Make sure you're good, and darn good, before you submit here. (And if you've got a pornographic site, a site glorifying crime, or a site that's just a link list—don't bother.) Project Cool judges sites on the basis of content, use of the Web as a medium, and well-thought-out navigation.

To Win or Not to Win …

It's Tara's opinion that having no award is better than having an almost worthless award. Peter's not quite so sure, having had a lot of fun collecting awards through multiple-submission engines (which we'll discuss in a moment). But he'd certainly agree that you should be very choosy when looking through available awards. Ask yourself, "Do I want to display this banner on my Web site?" Don't go for quantity; go for quality. Fifty awards that no one has ever heard of will be beaten hollow by one USA Today Hot Site Award.

Once you've submitted your Web site, explore the rest of the Project Cool site. You'll find some great resources for site developers and a community for people who build Web sites.

USA Today Hot Sites

http://www.usatoday.com/life/cyber/ch.htm

Every weekday except Friday, USA Today dishes up five hot sites that you should take a look at. (On Friday there's a "Weekend Edition" with an extended list.) Tara's won two of the awards and noticed a serious pop in her site visits after she won them. Peter won one for his Poor Richard site, and had 2,500 extra visitors in two days.

USA Today's hot site awards are won by a wide variety of sites—new search engines, educational resources, media, whatever. But they've all got a lot of great content, and more than occasionally a good sense of humor. The USA Today technology editor chooses the sites on the basis of content and appearance, sites that "push the envelope," etc. If you do win a USA Today Hot Site award, your site has a chance to be listed in the offline, print version of USA Today—another great perk, probably more valuable than the Hot Site award itself. In fact one of Tara's sites (her **Louisa May Alcott Web** site, http://www.coppersky.com/louisa/) *did* make it into the printed paper.

Regularly reading the USA Today Hot Site Awards gives you a good feel for what's out there and can also point you to some sites that are making great use of online technologies.

Yahoo! What's New

http://www.yahoo.com/picks/

When Yahoo really likes a site, they put a pair of sunglasses next to it in the directory. They also list their favorite sites in the "pick of the day." There is an e-mail address at the bottom of that page, so you can suggest your site as a Yahoo! pick. Get mentioned in Yahoo! What's New, and the number of visitors to your site could skyrocket.

Media Hot Lists

There are many, many media sites—papers, magazines, TV shows, and so on—that provide hot lists. They're generally great sites to get mention on because they provide the credibility of print publications in addition to an online presence. And they have an infrastructure of editors who are already used to reviewing and evaluating. Keep an eye out for awards that are provided by media, and in the meantime, if you have a computer-related site, check out an example ... the **Computer Currents Link of the Week** *at:* http://www.currents.net/resources/link/linkweek.html.

NetGuide's Internet Sites of the Day

http://www.netguide.com/

Each of NetGuide's various subject guides has a Site of the Day. Go into each guide and look for an e-mail link to submit your site. These are the various guide subjects: Computing, Entertainment, Health, Internet, Living, Money, News, Shopping, Sports, Travel, Women, and so on. And if you're really lucky, eventually you may end up in the overall Net Guide. At the time of writing they're doing *Net Guide 99*, which lists 99 of 1998's top Web sites.

Lesser-Known Awards

There are literally hundreds of Web-site awards—over 2,000, actually—and it would take another couple of books to list them all. Unfortunately, a lot of them aren't worth the electrons on which they're printed. Anybody can make a little banner for an award, but that doesn't make them useful! Furthermore, an award that's impressive to your target audience—that Yak Stalking Site of the Day award, perhaps—is meaningless to a different group of users.

You're going to have to judge a lot of awards for yourself. Some are not going to do you any good, yet some specialized awards may turn out to be well worth having. There are a couple of enormous directories you can use to check out what's available:

Awards Cave

http://members.tripod.com/
~AwardsCave/

This site lists over 2,000 awards, both in alphabetical order and by specialty. The site is in English and French and has a special section for "sites francophones." This is an exhaustive list and should be one of your first stops.

Nomination Fees

The vast majority of awards are free. Sometimes, however, a site award may ask you to pay a nomination fee. There are enough site awards going around that we wouldn't recommend doing this. If it's an award you really want, or which you personally consider very prestigious, then explore the award thoroughly before handing over any money.

AWARDS SITES!

http://www.focusa.com/awardsites/introduction.htm

This site not only lists over 900 awards, but the awards are also rated—from 1 star to 5 stars. Awards that are rated from 3 to 5 stars are given a description and a graphical link (usually their award badge). Awards that get 1 to 2 stars get a text description and link to the home page. This site also breaks down the site listings by higher ratings versus lower ratings. Check out their specialty ratings to see if there are any awards especially suited for your type of site.

The Awards Connection

http://www.citeweb.net/theAC/

A huge listing—over 1,700 awards—with almost 1,000 of the award images so you can go after attractive ones.

Awards Jungle

http://207.49.108.198/flamingo/chowch/aj/

This site lists around 130 different awards. Furthermore, it has a submission form that allows you to nominate your site for a whole bunch of awards at the same time. Peter tried submitting to many on this list (don't bother submitting for inappropriate awards, of course), and within a few days had won several awards:

- The Element Design, from Jerry Tong or someone or other ...
- Quatec's Web Site Design Award
- The Critical Mass Award
- Computer Magic's Magical Business Web Award
- The Website Innovation Award
- Approved Web Design
- DDC Bronze Leaf Award

He almost didn't accept the DDC Bronze Leaf Award, being slightly miffed that he didn't get the Gold Leaf, but eventually accepted it, based on the theory of "what the heck, might as well have it." (If you'd like to see the awards, and various others, visit Peter's **Poor Richard's Web Site awards** page: http://www. poorrichard.com/awards.htm.)

As you've seen, there are many, many awards. For a list of around 20 award-related sites—including directories that will point you to hundreds of awards—read the special report **Getting Awards for Your Web Site** at http://www. poorrichard.com/freeinfo/special_reports.htm.

GIVING AWARDS

Before we move on from awards, consider another way to promote your site, something that many award sites are doing. You might want to give awards to other sites. Each time an award is placed, the recipient has to put a link from the image back to your site. This may be a good way to bring people to you.

Giving awards can turn into a major operation if you're not careful, and can take up a great deal of time. But you may be able to get something out of it without too much effort if you play your cards just right. For instance, perhaps you can tightly target the awards. If you're in the model-rocket business, give awards for model-rocket sites; if you're selling homeopathic medicines, give awards for alternative-medicine sites; and so on. If I owned Estes Rockets, for instance, I'd be handing out awards to every really good rocket site on the Web ... but then, if I owned Estes Rockets I'd have a Web site, too, and they don't seem to have one. (At least, if they do, it's well hidden.)

Begin by seeking out sites, and picking the ones you like, the ones that are really useful. Later, if your award becomes well known in your business, sites will seek you out pleading for awards.

Things to consider:

- Make sure your award image contains your domain name, so even if people don't click on the link back to you (and they probably won't very often), they may remember your site. Few awards contain the URL, but it's a good way to make the most of what is really a promotion for you.

- Don't give in to the temptation to award undeserving sites! Yes, every award is a link back to you. But if you present awards to sites that are of no use to anyone, you'll dilute the value

Fake Awards

If you've got kind of a wild and crazy Web site, and you don't find awards to your liking, you might want to check out some fake certifications, awards, and banners—awards such as This Site is Made in the USA by Illegal Immigrants certification and the Titanic Navigation Award. These are only for those who have a sense of humor and want to show it off. They're not appropriate for most corporate Web sites (unless you manufacture whoopee cushions or something). Since they tend to mock things in which people believe strongly, you may find something in these sites offensive. Visit:

The Boodle Box: http://www.jwp. bc.ca/saulm/html/award.htm

The Corporation's Icon Gallery: http://www.thecorporation.com/ icon/icon.html

of the award, and people won't pay any attention to it. Maintain your award's credibility by having it really mean something.

- Make sure you have an attractive award logo. There's something about a well-designed image that lends credibility to the award. Besides, nobody wants to display an ugly award. If it looks good, more people will display it.

- Consider linking awards to other promotions. For instance, if you present a site with an award, ask if the site would like to hold a drawing for one of your products.

- Make the name of the award descriptive—the Estes Web Rocketry Award rather than The Estes Award, for example. It'll be more memorable, and you'll get fewer inappropriate submissions! For instance, it's tempting, when using systems such as Awards Jungle and Award It!, for people to submit their site to all the awards. If it's clear what your award is all about people are more likely to exclude it if the award isn't appropriate for their site.

ALLIANCES

Once you've set up your assurances to your visitors, and shown off the awards you've won for your site, you might want to tell a little more about yourself. What you believe in, what you support—in short, your alliances.

There's a lot of politics on the 'Net. It's not political party type of politics, but rather controversies over what's good for the 'Net and what isn't. People have different and strong beliefs about free speech, filtering, spam, and other 'Net activities. Remember that the Internet is still being formed. There are still policies being created. Speaking up about what you believe in can change the shape of the Internet.

People speak up about what they believe in through ribbons. We can't say for sure, but we think the whole ribbon thing was started through the EFF (Electronic Frontier Foundation) Blue Ribbon free-speech campaign that started several years ago. (More about that in a minute.) Since then there have been dozens of ribbon campaigns—from black ribbons to invisible ribbons to tie-dyed ribbons to plaid ribbons.

Why should you join an alliance when joining has the potential to alienate people as well as cause them to feel they have something in common with you? Sometimes it's appropriate to your Web site. If you're an online publisher, you might feel that supporting free speech is important to your Web site. If you've

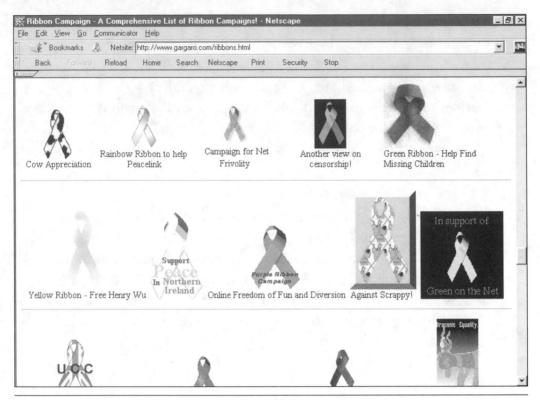

FIGURE 7.2: We told you there are a lot of ribbon campaigns!

put up a site that provides computer support services, you might want to join the lime-ribbon campaign, which supports the notion that all computer users aren't geeks. Since that notion is appropriate to a Web page offering support services, and says a little bit about the people who run the site ("Hey, we don't want to be considered nerds. We just happen to be good with computers."), it's a good fit. You could also find yourself attracting links from other like-minded—and lime-ribbon-wearing—Web sites.

Maybe you don't want to wear your opinions as ribbons on your Web page. That's okay. But at least check out these campaigns:

EFF Blue Ribbon Campaign

http://www.eff.org/blueribbon.html

The Electronic Frontier Foundation's Blue Ribbon campaign was started as a reaction to the United States government's attempts to legislate what kind of information could and could not be transmitted on the 'Net. The campaign also opposes mandatory filtering of Internet content. This was the first big ribbon campaign on the Internet, and a casual check with AltaVista shows over 40,000 pages linking to the EFF Blue Ribbon campaign page.

Golden Key Campaign

http://www.privacy.org/ipc/index.html#Key

This isn't a ribbon but the idea is the same. The Golden Key Campaign supports privacy for Internet users. They support the right for users to send information privately and the right for users to have access to technology, like encryption, that protects their privacy. They specifically want users to have the right to these technologies without government restraint. (In several countries around the world, there is a limit to encryption access, for instance.)

These are a couple of pretty serious campaigns, but don't get the idea that every campaign is this heavy. (These are just examples chosen because they're fairly well-known; we're not endorsing them or advocating that you join these or any other ribbon campaigns.) For a list of almost 200 ribbons, check out **The Ribbon Campaigns** Web site at http://www.gargaro.com/ribbons.html.

Among other things, you'll find the "I can't type and I'm proud of it" campaign, the "Be nice to newbies" campaign, the "Save the hamsters" campaign, and of course the "No more ribbons" campaign.

Why all these campaigns? Because the Internet is full of varied and eclectic people. They've all got different agendas, different ideas, and, as you'll see, a lot of different senses of humor. Signing up for such campaigns can help you convey your beliefs to your audience. You don't have years to get to know someone through their Web site. You can't meet up with them and have lunch and learn what they're all about. So one of the ways you can get to know about them and learn about them are ribbon campaigns like these. You can make a stand, let people know what your concerns are, give some insight as to your beliefs, or show the world you've got a sense of humor, by your choice of campaigns. Don't go crazy with these ribbons, though. A few will make a lot more impact than a dozen, and still serve to give your visitors some idea of what you're all about.

Every page addition we've talked about in this chapter has its own purpose. An assurance lets visitors know you're serious about your business and want to establish yourself as a credible merchant, organization, or information resource. An award (at least a good award) shows that you've established an excellent Web site in your field—and will also push a lot of visitors to your site. An alliance is a shorthand way to let visitors to your site know what you're all about and what's important to you, and perhaps attract links from other sites that feel the same way.

In summary, you want to make a good impression on your visitors and make them feel comfortable. (We're not advocating that you lie and put up a banner you don't believe in. You can make someone feel comfortable without compromising your own beliefs.)

Over the last few chapters we've covered a lot of information about preparing your Web site for indexing, registering with the search engines, and attracting visitors and confidence with assurances, awards, and alliances.

But there's still a little ground left to cover, some things that haven't yet been mentioned. In the next chapter we'll cover "and the rest"—miscellaneous and unique places where you can promote your site.

CHAPTER EIGHT

Other Places to Register Your Site

If you've followed our advice this far, you've spent a lot of time getting your Web site ready and registered. At this point your site should be optimized for search engines, and you should have submitted your site to all the major ones. By now you've set up whatever alliances or affiliations you find necessary, and you might have even picked up a couple of awards.

But you're not finished. Before you start looking beyond the Web for your promotional efforts, you can go a little further and make the most of the Web. In this chapter, we'll be looking at more places to "register" your Web site.

There are three major ways to promote your Web site besides the traditional Web services:

Announcement Services. These are part mailing list, part newsletter, and part town crier. The Web grows so quickly that the announcement services are essential to anyone who wants to keep up.

Free-For-All Link Pages (FFAs). The FFAs allow anyone to add a link to a list without editing or reviewing the link. In limited situations these might be useful, but they do have serious drawbacks.

Web Rings. Web rings are sites that are gathered together by subject. Web-ringed pages have HTML code at the bottom of their pages, allowing interested visitors to move from one site to another. In effect the sites are joined together in a "ring."

Like-Minded Links. This is Tara's term for sites that link to your site for some reason. They're not necessarily set up as search sites or directories, but their proprietors may like your site enough to link to it.

You can use any or all of these methods to help promote your site—we'll show you how in a minute. But we're saving the most powerful method for the last part of this chapter. Announcement services can be *very* effective, but probably the most powerful of all these techniques is finding sites that have interests similar to yours and asking them to link to you. Doesn't seem like a big deal, does it? But each of those links is a doorway, as we'll explain later. But first, let's talk announcement services, Free-For-All link lists, and Web rings.

ANNOUNCEMENT SERVICES

In the spring of 1998, a study announced that there were over 320 million pages on the World Wide Web. Most mere mortals despair of ever keeping up with the changes, since thousands of Web pages are added every day.

Paper and online publications, like NetGuide and USA Today, review Web sites, but there's usually a lag time between the announcement of the site and their coverage. They also have limited editorial resources, so they can't take a look at and review every site. Traditional news outlets like television and radio shows can review and announce new sites, but they usually stick to announcing major sites, and don't provide much of an outlet for "small players."

With all that being the case, it's not a surprise that editorial services have evolved that are limited to solely announcing Web sites. They don't review 'em, and they don't package 'em into well-rounded stories—they just announce 'em.

The most famous of these services is probably **Net-Happenings** at http://scout.cs.wisc.edu/scout/net-hap/. Net-Happenings is moderated by Gleason Sackman, who's going to get a medal for it one day. Every day he skims several mailing lists and reviews lots of submissions. He picks the best 40-60 entries and sends them on to his mailing list. Since his list is distributed both via mailing list and on USENET, he reaches a lot of people.

Gleason does a lot of work for one guy. Because Net-Happenings is a one-man operation, you have to be very careful about how you submit. For example, you can't submit on the weekends because weekend submissions are automatically deleted (so he doesn't have a backlog when he comes back Monday morning). When he goes out of town he announces it in advance, and you can't submit during that time because, again, submissions are deleted. When you do have an item to submit, you must go to the submission page (there's a link from the URL we gave you above.) You'll be asked to give your name, resource title, category, URL, and description.

Tara's been on Gleason's announcement list for about 3,000 years now, and based on the many announcements she's read, she has a few suggestions to make when you use Net-Happenings.

- Remember that you're announcing to a global audience. Tara's seen dozens of announcements talking about "Scenic Hedgefield" and "Beautiful Spring County" when the announcements don't bother to mention the city, state, or even country the resource is referring to. Similarly, local business announcements and conference announcements that apply to a limited geographical area should be considered twice before being submitted to this list.

- Make sure your description is clear. You don't have to write War and Peace, but make sure that the description of your Web site is quite clear. In Chapter 6 we asked you to write several different descriptions, of varying lengths, of your Web site. Take the longest one, add a few more words if you like, and use this as your description. Some people use press releases as their descriptions, but Tara isn't too keen on that. She thinks that's too much for a busy surfer to read. If they want the whole release, they can get it at your Web site.

- Announcements that are riddled with spelling and grammar errors reflect poorly on the Web site, as do announcements IN ALL CAPS, overloaded with punctuation!!!!, and so on.

- Limit the number of times you use this service. Unless you're doing major content updates every week, we wouldn't announce to Net-Happenings more than once a quarter. We wouldn't want to wear out our welcome.

Not as widespread as Net-Happenings, but still an excellent service, is **Net-Announce** at http://www.erspros.com/net-announce/. Net-Announce doesn't accept pornographic sites, sites promoting multi-level marketing, sites that sell things, hate sites, or sites that don't have an English version.

Net-Announce asks that you submit your site to their service only once a quarter. Net-Announce also asks that you avoid HTML code in your announcement. Net-Announce further requests that you return your tray table to an upright, locked position before landing. (No, wait—that's American Airlines. Sorry.) Anyway, Net-Announce does have several rules for how you can announce to their list and how often, but by employing these rules they can create a stream of high-quality submissions that their readers are eager to read. Abide by the rules and benefit! Also, with Net-Announce you can use a more extensive description. You could even go so far as to write an article discussing the high points of your site and of what benefit it is to viewers. Make it engaging, lively, and grammatically correct.

The announcement services covered above are the "biggies," but there are several other announcement services you can use. Here's a sample:

BUBL Link Updates (updates to the Catalogue of Internet Resources)
http://www.bubl.ac.uk/link/updates/current.html

Hersh Web Site Observer
http://www.cyberjournalist.com/

LinkMaster
http://linkmaster.com/

Nerd World: What's New
http://www.nerdworld.com/users/dstein/whatsnew.html

Netscape What's New
http://home.netscape.com/netcenter/new.html

Netsurfer Digest
http://www.netsurf.com/nsd/

The NewPageList
http://web-star.com/newpage/newpage.html

The Scout Report (mostly academically-oriented resources)
http://wwwscout.cs.wisc.edu/scout/report/

UK Yell
http://www.yell.co.uk/ukyw/whats_new/index.html

Whatsnew.com
http://www.whatsnew.com/whatsnew/

What's New (a search engine and weekly bulletin of what's new on the Web)
http://www.whatsnu.com/

What's New in Canada
http://whatsnew.canadasearch.com/

What's New in the UK Index
http://www.ukindex.co.uk/whatsnew.html

What's New Too!
http://nu2.com/

Yahoo!'s What's New list
http://dir.yahoo.com/Computers_and_Internet/Internet/World_Wide_Web/Searching_the_Web/Indices_to_Web_Documents/What_s_New/

FREE-FOR-ALL LINK PAGES

Free-For-All (FFA) link pages are just that: link lists that anyone can add to without paying a fee. Sometimes they're so quick that your link appears immediately. That's good for quick exposure on the Web that slower-adding search engines can't provide.

Free-For-All link pages really *can* drive traffic to your Web site. That doesn't mean you should necessarily use them, however; the disadvantages may outweigh the advantages. So what's the problem with them? Well, one reason is that anyone can add to a link list. Unfortunately, a lot of Web pages that aren't accepted by standard search engines resort to link lists to get exposure on the Web. This includes questionable business sites, poorly written sites, adults-only sites, and so on.

Does that mean every site on an FFA link list is going to fit into one of the above categories? Of course not. However, it does mean you don't know into what kind of company your listing is going. There are a number of other reasons not to work with these systems, which we'll discuss in a moment. First, though, let's have a look at where to find these things.

Finding Free-For-All Link Lists

There are thousands of FFA pages. How do you find them all? There are a variety of directories of FFA link pages. Here are a few of them.

AccuSubmit Free Links Submit Station

http://accusubmit.com/ffa/

The AccuSubmit Free Links Submit Station is a free service listing hundreds of FFAs in a frame on the left side of the browser; click on one of the links, and you'll see the referenced FFA site itself in a frame on the right, so you don't have to flip back and forward between sites. This is a good place to start looking for FFAs if you're determined to work with FFAs but have absolutely no money.

Stealth Promotions Free-For-All Links (FFA) Page

http://www.stealthpromotions.com/ffa.htm

This list offers links to over 700 FFA links. Stealth Promotions also offers a service where they submit to these sites on your behalf for $19.50. This listing also offers you a link where you can get your own FFA link page. If you really have to work with FFA pages, pay the money for this or some other service; it simply isn't cost-effective to register with all these pages by hand.

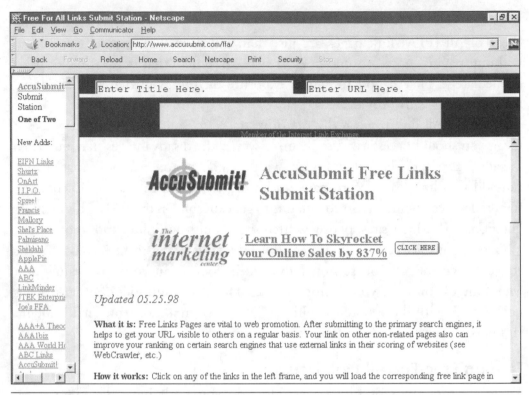

FIGURE 8.1: AccuSubmit lets you put your Web-site title and URL at the top of the screen so you can cut and paste it into each FFA Link Submission Form.

Jill Studholme's Free-For-All Links Pages Directory

http://www.users.zetnet.co.uk/
studholme/freelink.html

This site lists only about 40 FFA lists, but they seem to be of high quality—lists that are long-lasting and concentrate on having good content. This site seems to be updated often as well.

Lots and Lots of Errors

You'll learn something else about FFA links when you start using these link indexes—many FFA link lists have about the same life span as a fruit fly. Expect lots of 404 errors when you're checking out these sites.

Link-O-Matic

http://www.linkomatic.com/

This is one of the better FFA sites. You can submit to over 470 FFA pages in one fell swoop. For $100 you can buy 16,000 credits—16,000 individual submissions. That's currently 34 submissions to the entire list.

If you want to find more of these sites, check **Yahoo!'s Free-For-All Pages** page: http://dir.yahoo.com/ Computers_and_Internet/Internet/ World_Wide_Web/Searching_the_ Web/Indices_to_Web_Documents/ Free_for_All_Pages/.

To give you an idea of what FFA pages are all about, let's look at a couple of individual ones, starting with **The Vortex** at http://vortex. bytetech.com/vortex/. The Vortex is one of the oldest FFA lists on the Web, having started in February 1995. The Vortex takes the time to validate the links placed on the site (not to check them for appropriate content, but rather to make sure they

Are FFAs really Free for All?

They're called Free-For-All link pages, but sometimes they're not really for all. Some link sites restrict the type of links that can be posted, refusing adults-only sites or multi-level-marketing sites. Still other sites are restricted to links pertaining to a certain topic—check out a **Reiki FFA list** *at* http://www.reikilinks.com/ *and the* **All-Comers Christian Link Page** *at* http://www.jesus.org.uk/links/. *There are caving sites, and sites devoted to all sorts of other things. Be sure that you know of any restrictions before posting to FFA lists.*

actually lead to a page and not to a 404 error) and therefore maintains a more useful page of links.

The Vortex is an example of a great FFA page. Visitors can view the list of links in a variety of ways—commercial links, links excluding adult links, non-commercial links, and so on. The list is searchable, and every day statistics are released showing how many pages are added to and removed from the list. (At the time of writing there are over 19,000 links.) Finally, The Vortex "ideally" adds submissions to its list immediately (although sometimes it may take a little longer than that.)

Leave-A-Link at http://www.toocool.com/guest/cool.htm is a little different from The Vortex. Leave-A-Link requires that its links be listed by category (Vortex does not), and Leave-A-Link's search box is at the top of the page, more like a traditional subject directory. Only 20 of the most recent submissions are included on the front page. Leave-A-Link also doesn't add the links instantaneously; it takes 1 to 3 days to add a link, according to the site's FAQ. (Spammers submitting the same site multiple times will be banned.) This site's strengths lie in its ease of design and searchability.

There are hundreds—perhaps thousands—of FFA sites. You could easily spend many hours finding them, evaluating them, and then submitting to them (or not). Tara recommends that you work on FFA listings with the scraps of your time—when there's not much else going on promotion-wise. Peter recommends that you don't bother with FFA sites at all unless you're really desperate for visitors; your time is probably better spent some other way. In any case, don't make them a high-priority activity, and definitely don't choose them as a promotion vehicle over the other methods described in this book. FFAs can give you a good quick burst of promotion, but you pay for that in the time it takes to find them and the company you might find your site in.

Here's a real-life account of an FFA campaign. This comes from Peter's newsletter, Poor Richard's Web Site News. (This is a free newsletter—visit http://PoorRichard.com/newsltr/ to subscribe. It's sent out every two weeks; this article will give you an idea of the sort of information you'll get.)

Beginner's Column: Announce Your Site Here

[This article contained information about the What's Nu service, mentioned earlier in this chapter. Then Peter talked about FFA sites …]

You can also get a few free links at this site:

http://www.linkomatic.com/

It only takes a few seconds, and you'll get links placed at 10 "Free-For-All" Web pages. (These are long lists of links.) Of course, the question is: *Is it worth the time it takes to place the links?*

If you sign up for the Link-O-Matic service (it costs $100, but don't do it yet … I'll explain why in a moment), you'll be able to automatically submit your link to a list of 445 Free-For-All pages. You'll get 16,000 credits—that is, 16,000 individual submissions—so you can submit to this list around 40 times. In theory that's 6.25 cents per link. In practice, however, some of the submissions fail for various reasons. (You'll get a report telling you which ones succeeded and which didn't.) The actual cost per link is probably more like 7 or 8 cents.

However, I suggest that you don't use this service, at least not for the moment. I've wondered about these Free-For-All Link pages for a long time. I've always thought they probably don't work particularly well, but after reading Link-O-Matic's sales blurbs and testimonials from users talking about how much traffic they'd got by using the program, I just couldn't help plunking down 100 tax-deductible dollars.

So wait a little and I'll let you know whether this service does anything for me. So far, I've got to say, it hasn't sent enough traffic to my site to even turn up on my hit logs. (I set up a page to link to, so I could measure hits.) Right now I'm feeling a bit of a sucker; I knew it wouldn't work, and so far it hasn't. I'm rationalizing the whole thing by telling myself that I'm doing research for this newsletter, but did I really need to test something I knew couldn't work? I'm just hoping I'll prove myself wrong ... but I doubt it. I'm just glad that the Internal Revenue Service is paying part of the cost. But in any case, I'll give it a while, use up all my credits, and then let you know the results.

Well, Peter did try Link-O-Matic, and he did report back to his readers ...

A few weeks ago I wrote about Link-O-Matic, a service that automatically submits your URL to hundreds of free link pages (sometimes known as Links-For-All or Free-For-All pages). At the time I was a little skeptical, but said that having paid my $100 I'd run the course, submit all 16,000 times, and report back.

I haven't yet submitted 16,000 times, but I think I've got enough information to update you. It really can push some traffic to a site. But it may not be worth the hassle. I just looked at my logs and found that about 200 people have visited my site over the past few weeks. I still have 13,088 submissions left, so once I've finished with them all I may have brought 1,000 to 1,100 people to my site. At a cost of $100, that's around 10 cents per visitor, which is reasonably cheap as far as advertising costs go.

At this point you've probably got two questions. First, why aren't I more enthusiastic?, and second, why haven't I used all 16,000 submissions?

Well, there are a few problems. Right now there are 500 link pages in the Link-O-Matic system. (There were around 450 when I started, a month ago.) Most of the sites don't accept duplicate URLs, so you can't use all 16,000 submissions at once; either you have to submit around 32 times, with about a week between submissions—if you submit too soon, the link pages will simply reject your submissions—or you have to set up a number of different URLs, and then submit links for those different URLs. I could create 32 different URLs, then create 32 different submission sets, to 500 pages each, on the same day, I guess, but I decided that spreading them out, doing one set of 500 every week, would be less hassle and probably more effective—the links would be seen by far more people if spread out. So although this free-link scheme may be effective to some degree, it's a bit of a nuisance to use; there have to be easier ways to bring people to a site than this!

There's another problem. You'll get an awful lot of e-mail back; when you register, many of the sites, perhaps most, send a message back to you thanking you for your submission … and trying to promote their own products, from Internet marketing services to tongue cleaners (no, really). So if you're going to do this, you'd better set up an e-mail address for just this purpose (I used links@topfloor.com, for instance), and then use your e-mail program's filtering system to filter all mail to that address into a folder, or perhaps have the filter delete it automatically. The problem is, though, now and then you'll get real messages. People who own the link sites want to contact you about something—perhaps a broken link at your site—and they use the special e-mail address you set up.

Here's another tip, in case you decide to use free-link pages. Make sure you write your link text like a mini advertisement. Don't simply give your Web site's title or even a plain description of your site. Give people a *reason* to visit. I used links such as "Save Time, Save Money, Save Hassle Building a Web Site" and "It's been called the 'best investment in Web design.'"

Well, I'm going to use all 16,000 registrations if it kills me. I've set my Schedule program to remind me every Monday morning to go to Link-O-Matic, so I'll get into the habit. It should only take until next March or so to use them all up.

Well, Peter never did use up his credits—it was just too much of a nuisance to keep going back. In fact, writing this chapter reminded him, so he checked back and found he still had 12,656 credits left.

WEB RINGS

Web rings are a completely different animal from FFA lists. FFAs can have all kinds of different content, while Web Rings are generally devoted to one topic at a time. Web rings can bring a lot of interested visitors to your site, but they might leave just as quickly.

Web rings are pretty simple. Sites participating in a ring use special HTML code that creates several Web-ring navigation links. These links allow visitors to

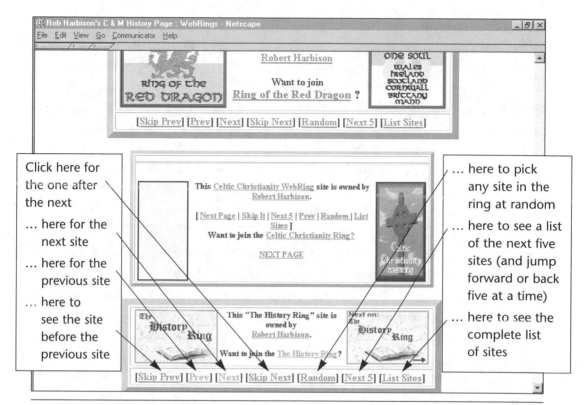

FIGURE 8.2: What's better than joining one Web ring? Joining several, perhaps, as the owner of this site did.

move to the previous or next site in the ring, to go to another page in the ring that is selected randomly, and perhaps to visit the ring's main page, where they can see a list of all the sites within the ring. In theory all the sites are strung together in a big "circle," so by clicking on the Next link over and over, it should be possible to travel all the way around and come back to your starting point.

The largest coordinator of Web rings on the 'Net is **WebRing** at http://www.webring.org/. At this writing, WebRing sponsors over 40,000 rings, with over 500,000 sites participating.

When you visit WebRing, you can start a new ring, join an existing ring, or just check out what rings are available. Do the latter right now—take a look at what rings are available. (There's a search box at the bottom of the page.)

You'll see that there are all kinds of rings—rings dealing with religion, romance, science, news, and lots more. There are rings for people who are clumsy and rings for people who consider themselves unenthusiastic. You get the idea. Rings range from five participating sites to over 400 sites!

The advantage to being a part of a ring is obvious. You'll have visitors coming to your site who are interested in your topic. The disadvantage is more subtle; if your site isn't immediately useful and compelling, the visitor can keep going on the ring and pass your site right by. Furthermore, very general rings might serve less of a purpose. If you've got a ring dealing with unusual museums or the visual arts in Russia, you've developed a ring of content that won't be available many other placcs on the Web. On the other hand, if you have a Web

Another Potential Problem

If you have a commercial site, you might want to avoid a ring. Besides sending viewers away from your site, you might end up in a ring with your competitors or with sites you wouldn't want people to think that you "endorse."

ring devoted to Texas, or football, or nothing in particular, your ring won't be that unusual in terms of content. The more specific the better.

You have to consider the company you're keeping, too. Do you want to live in the same "neighborhood" as the other sites in your ring? Some rings are very exclusive about what they accept, while others aren't exclusive at all. Guess which rings we prefer.

Go over the available rings carefully and see if there are any that fit your site. If there aren't, you can start your own.

Create Your Own Web Ring

To start your own ring, go to http://www.webring.org/cgibin/ wrnewring/. The site warns you that

A Rose By Any Other Name

*You'll hear Web rings referred to in other ways, such as loops or railways, but a ring is a ring; for instance, see **LoopLink** at http:// www.looplink.com/.*

starting a ring is not for HTML beginners and can be time-consuming, and that as a free service they can't make guarantees as to reliability.

If you're not scared away, creating a ring takes a series of steps. First you choose an identifier for your ring (just a brief series of letters and numbers— "new-ring," "ring-123," etc.). Next, you need to name the ring, provide the home URL of the ring, provide contact information (your real name and e-mail address), and choose a password for administering your ring. After that, you need to categorize your ring, describe what audience rating your ring has (from G to XXX), and describe your ring in 100 words or less. Finally, you must provide 20 keywords that visitors can use to find your ring when searching the WebRing directory. Once you've done that, WebRing will set you up with your own ring.

A few things to keep in mind if you decide to go the ring route:

- Please, one ring at a time. Some Web sites join four or five rings. Besides giving up a lot of real estate to the rings' HTML code, it's awfully confusing for the viewer.

- Make your entrance page—the one on which you put your site's entry point to the ring—as engaging and interesting as possible. You don't want the visitor to look at your site for two seconds, get bored, and move on.

- Check out your neighbors. Learn who the other sites in the ring are. You want to know whom you're sharing the ring with.

Tempted by the Web ring thing? Here are a few places to look for more info:

People Chase
http://www.rainfrog.com/pc/

Sadiq's Webring Directory
http://www.users.dircon.co.uk/~majaffer/webrings/

Yahoo!—Web Rings Page
http://dir.yahoo.com/Computers_and_Internet/Internet/World_Wide_
Web/Searching_the_Web/Indices_to_Web_Documents/Rings/

FINDING "LIKE-MINDED" LINKS

Between announcement services, Free-For-Alls, and Web rings, you might think you've got all the bases covered. But the most important item is the last. You need to find yourself some "like-minded links."

You should think of every link to your site as a doorway. If you want traffic, it naturally follows that the more doorways you have the better.

But some doorways are better than others. Doorways that lead from similar sites to yours are the best of all, since the visitors to those sites are already interested in what your site talks about. The process of getting those kinds of doorways is what Tara calls hunting like-minded links. In the process of building and researching your site, you may have already developed a list of sites that cover ground similar to yours. That's great. Put those aside for a moment and we'll show you several more ways to find like-minded sites—awards and *backlink* checking.

Awards

In the last chapter we told you how awards might be good for your site. If you focus on specialty awards, they're awfully useful for finding similar sites.

If you've spent some time submitting your site for awards that were appropriate to your site type, go back and look at the awards list now. Look at the specialty stuff. Then go check those awards' archives. (Most awards sites have an archive list.) If you do this with specialty awards, you'll be able to assemble a list of sites whose interests at least overlap with yours—and which must be marginally good or they wouldn't have won an award (assuming you've chosen decent awards).

Backlink Checking

Sometimes if you want to find something, you've got to go backwards. Sites like **HotBot** (http://www.hotbot.com/) and **AltaVista** (http://www.altavista.com/) allow you to search for Web pages that link to another Web page for which you specify the URL. By backlink checking someone else's URL, you can see who is linking to them. If you have a site related to sheep herding, you might want to find other sheep herding sites, do backlink checks on them, and see who is linking to them. (Why? We'll get to that ... you're going to ask for links, or, as we'll explain in Chapter 10, perhaps propose some kind of promotion at those sites.)

Here's how you do it:

- Find one Web site that covers the same topic you do. This can be a Web site you found with the awards trick above, or a site that you found when you created your site, or maybe a competitor's site. Choose a site that's reasonably popular, so it's likely to have a good number of links to it.

- Find a search site that supports backlink checking, such as AltaVista or HotBot.

- Search for that site's URL—you'll be given a list of the sites that are linking to it.

Here are a couple of examples of how to backlink search—at AltaVista and HotBot:

- **Hotbot**—Type the URL for which you are looking for links to (complete with the `http://` part) in the search box and then choose *Links to this URL* in the search drop-down list box.

- **AltaVista**—Use the `link:` keyword (we talked about AltaVista's keywords in Chapter 2), like this: `link:poorrichard.com`. (Don't include the `http://` bit. Don't even include the `www.` bit; you may reduce the number of hits if you do.) Of course you'll want to omit links to the page from the same Web site. You can do that by using `-host:`, like this: `-host:poorrichard.com`. So the complete search string would be `link:poorrichard.com -host:poorrichard.com`.

You'll find that you get some good results, a few *great* results, and a few results that aren't any good at all. But you will get enough that you'll find some places that would look good with your site linked to them.

Here's a really neat little service you can use to automate this backlink process: **LinkPopularity.com** (at, you guessed it, http://www.linkpopularity. com/). This site has a form into which you enter your URL—or the URL of some other site you'd like to check up on. The system does a backlink search at

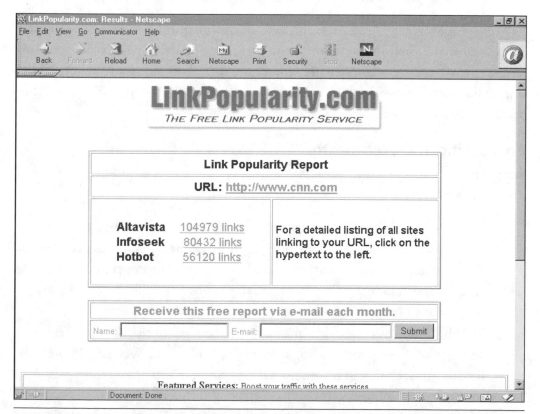

FIGURE 8.3: LinkPopularity.com will let you search for links to a URL at three search sites at once. (One day, if you're really lucky, maybe you'll get a result like this for your Web site!)

AltaVista, HotBot, and InfoSeek at the same time.

Gather a list of appropriate sites together using the tools we talked about in Chapter 2. Once you've got a list together, start cruising these sites. Don't spend more than a few minutes at each site, but keep the following questions in mind:

> ### Try Different Ways
>
> *You may need to search a few different ways. For instance,* **HotBot** *treats the URLs* http://www.poorrichard.com/, http://poorrichard.com/, *and* http://www.poorrichard.com/index.html *differently when searching for backlinks.*

1. How's the overall composition of the site? Is it a professional presentation?
2. What are the other links like? Are they links you'd want to be associated with?
3. Is there a site counter available? If so, does the site seem to get a lot of traffic? Does it seem to be updated often?
4. Does the Webmaster seem receptive to adding links?

The reason we ask you to keep these things in mind is because you visit a Web site for the first time only once. And in that one time, you get impressions that a lot of other visitors to the same site get. You need to analyze those impressions and ask yourself, "Is this the kind of company with which I want to be associated?"

Contacting the Webmaster

Suppose that you've found a great site, and you want to get a link from it to your site. Here's how to do it:

1. Find the Webmaster's address, and e-mail him or her. Address the Webmaster by name if possible. If not, address the message to Webmaster, or Site Owner, or whatever seems appropriate. Don't address the message "To Whom It May Concern"; that looks like a form letter or, worse, spam.
2. Tell the Webmaster you like the Web site and *name the Web site!* Tara gets e-mails from people saying things like, "I like your Web site. Please link to my Web site." The problem is that Webmasters often administer multiple Web sites which cover completely different subjects, so they may have no idea which site you're talking about. If you're asking for a link from a popular Web site, be aware that the site administrator probably gets tons of e-mail. Make things as easy as possible.

3. Don't say "I love your site" unless you mean it. And if you *do* mean it, give an example ("I thought your bibliography page was great; I can't believe you've found over 200 references.") so you don't sound like you're just trying to get a link. ·

4. Ask if the Webmaster would consider linking to your site; give the Webmaster a reason! Why would your site be of interest to the Webmaster's visitors?

5. It's a good idea to provide a brief description of your site in addition to asking for the link. It gives the Webmaster something to use so he can put the link up quickly. The description no-no's we talked about in Chapter 6 apply doubly here—no puffery, etc.

6. Thank the site administrators for their time, no matter what they decide.

To Reciprocate or Not to Reciprocate?

Sometimes when you contact people and ask them to link to your site, they ask that you link to their site in return. Trading a link for a link is known as a *reciprocal link.*

Do you have to offer reciprocal links every time you ask for a link? No, you're not obligated to give a reciprocal link to anybody. And sometimes it's not appropriate. Let's take a look at an example. Say you administer a Web site that sells Toyota truck parts. You've also got lots of information on Toyota repair, parts lists, and so on. In short, your site is useful to a group whether they buy from you or not.

Perhaps you're already linking to lots of Toyota sites—racing trucks, repair information, and so on—so if you ask for a link to a new site about Toyota racing you've just found and the Webmaster has asked for a reciprocal link, you might as well give it. It fits in with your existing list, anyway.

But say you ask for a link from a broader site—like a specialty index that covers Japanese vehicles. That's probably too broad for you to link to, but your site is appropriate for *them* to link to. In that case a reciprocal link isn't necessary.

Also remember that when you link to a site, for whatever reason,

Let's Be Honest ...

... it's in your interest to get as many links as possible, and, perhaps, to give as few as possible. Don't take inappropriate links in return for links to your site.

you may want to contact that site and ask for a reciprocal link. Actually, when Tara is in this situation, she links to the site and simply informs the site of what she's done. She doesn't ask for a reciprocal link because she considers it a little pushy. Nonetheless, she has discovered that around half of those sites give her a reciprocal link anyway.

Finding like-minded sites and asking the Webmasters for links should be an ongoing part of your promotional efforts. Keep an eye out for appropriate sites. Try to contact five or ten of them each week. You'll find as you do this that your efforts will snowball. Other sites will link to yours without your asking them to. You'll get pointers to other resources. This should be a high priority in your promotional efforts, but it doesn't need to take a lot of your time.

Part II of this book has been the meat-and-potatoes part if you have a Web site. If you don't have a Web site, these chapters have probably given you a few new reasons to have one, and some design tips you can use before you even crack any HTML. If you follow all the directions in this part, covering all your bases, you will get traffic.

But as anyone who used the Internet before 1994 knows, the Internet is not simply the Web, and the Web doesn't come near to encompassing all of the Internet. You can go beyond the Web when it comes to your promotion and marketing; you can go to newsgroups, newsletters, and even other Web sites. Part III will help you learn more about how to get the word out.

Part III

Getting The
Word Out

CHAPTER NINE

Promoting in the Newsgroups and Mailing Lists

This is a sensitive subject. We're going to talk about promoting your products and services in the Internet's discussion groups—newsgroups, mailing lists, Web forums, and the online services private discussion areas (MSN BBSs, CompuServe forums, and so on).

It's a sensitive subject for a couple of reasons. First, many people feel that these discussion groups should not be used as promotional tools. And second, so many people have used these groups as promotional tools in such a grotesque and clumsy manner that it's easy to see *why* people think that discussion groups should not be promotional tools!

In fact, commercialism seems to be killing many newsgroups. It's so easy to push promotional messages into the newsgroups, thousands at a time, that many newsgroups are little more than junk repositories.

But that doesn't mean it's not possible to promote yourself or your products in discussion groups without upsetting people. It most certainly is possible. Many of the most active participants in discussion groups have an ulterior motive for participating. But the people who are most successful at discussion-group promotions realize something important. In order to get something, you have to *give* something.

The History of Spam

The term spam, *although today applied mainly to e-mail, actually originated with newsgroups. Spam messages were newsgroup messages sent to hundreds, perhaps thousands, of newsgroups at once.*

This shouldn't be such a strange concept to you by now. We've discussed earlier how Internet marketing and promotion often seems to rely on giving something away; some of the most successful Web sites are those that provide something for free, something valuable for free. The "freebies" are used, in effect, to draw people in.

Well, it's the same with discussion groups. There are many people who are successfully using discussion groups to promote themselves, by giving away information and advice. They turn themselves into discussion-group experts on a particular subject, they get known and respected within the group, and in turn people come to trust them and, perhaps, buy from them.

Before we go on, we have to make one very important point. Discussion groups can be a huge drain on your time, especially if you're not quite disciplined enough to stop yourself from being drawn in too deeply. It's easy to get off track, by jumping into every conversation and answering every question ... and the next thing you know you've spent far more time than you really have available. But the next time you look at your discussion-group messages you'll see that someone has responded to you, or asked another question, so you jump back in ...

Some discussion groups, including most of the really good ones, are based on the e-mail system. These are called *mailing-list discussion groups*, or just *mailing lists*. That means lack of discipline is even more of a problem, because the messages arrive in your mail program's Inbox every time you get your mail. You just can't escape. If you have a hard time keeping out of every discussion, keep this in mind. Your credibility in a discussion group is directly proportional to the amount of useful information you dispense. So if you pick your responses carefully, and try to provide useful information to a large group instead of fielding every last little request, you'll build up a lot of credibility on that newsgroup.

Despite the dangers, discussion groups can be an important part of a marketing and promotion campaign—for some people even the primary part of the campaign. So let's see how to use them.

FINDING THE DISCUSSION GROUPS

The first step is to find the discussion groups that are useful to you. There are probably a couple of hundred thousand mailing-list discussion groups (one major directory lists over 90,000) and more than 30,000 newsgroups (and tens of thousands more when you include newsgroups with relatively limited distribution). Then there are thousands more discussion groups in the online services, private groups that you can get into only if you are a member of that service. There are probably more than 30,000 other discussion groups on CompuServe, AOL, MSN, and the other major online services (okay, so that's a pure guess, but a slightly educated one).

In all, there must be about 300,000 discussion groups to which you could have access … if only you know where they were. That's the hard part, of course, tracking them all down. On the other hand, you don't need to find every single group that's related to your market. You want the most important ones, and that's a much easier thing to find.

Finding Newsgroups

The first thing to do to find newsgroups is simply use your newsgroup program. Your newsgroup program has a command that makes it go to your service provider's news server and grab a list of all the groups—not all the groups in the world, but all the groups your service provider has available. Some service providers may just subscribe to five or ten thousand newsgroups. Others may subscribe to thirty or forty thousand.

Newsgroup Programs

We don't want to get into an explanation of basic Internet knowledge, but if you're wondering where to find a newsgroup program … you probably already have one. Netscape Messenger not only works with e-mail, it also works with newsgroup messages. MS Outlook Express can work with newsgroup messages, too, and some online services have built-in newsreaders.

Your newsreader will have a command that allows you to search the list, so you can search for particular keywords. But what if the subject you're interested in turns up missing? Or you're sure that there are more newsgroups on your subject, but your service provider doesn't subscribe to them? Well, you could ask your service provider to subscribe, if you know the name of the group you're interested in. Or you can use a public news server, a service that allows you to read newsgroups that your service provider does not subscribe to:

DejaNews (Free service, with access to 80,000 discussion groups, including many newsgroups)
http://www.dejanews.com/

Randori (31,000 newsgroups for under $10 a month)
http://www.randori.com/

Newsguy (22,000 newsgroups for $10 a month)
http://co-op.newsguy.com/

RemarQ (Free access to 30,000 newsgroups through their Web site, or $12 a month to use your newsreader)
http://www.remarq.com/

Yahoo!—Public Access Usenet Sites
http://dir.yahoo.com/Computers_and_Internet/Internet/Usenet/
Public_Access_Usenet_Sites/

Of course if you're not sure what's out there, you can't know if your service provider doesn't have one of the newsgroups you need. You can find lists of newsgroups at these places:

Liszt
http://www.liszt.com/news/

Tile.Net
http://www.tile.net/

Usenet Info Center
http://metalab.unc.edu/usenet-i/

Yahoo!—Newsgroup Listings
http://dir.yahoo.com/Computers_and_Internet/Internet/Usenet/
Newsgroup_Listings/

Finding Mailing-List Discussion Groups

Finding mailing-list discussion groups is a little more difficult. Because of the nature in which newsgroups are distributed—a sort of centralized distribution system—it's relatively easy to build directories of newsgroups. But anyone can set up a mailing-list discussion group, as we saw in Chapter 11. These groups can be running on expensive software such as Lyris or Listserv, or on shareware or freeware programs such as AKmail or Pegasus. So you'll never find a complete list of mailing-list discussion groups. Nonetheless, you can probably find the groups that are most important to you. Here are a few places to look:

Liszt (Over 90,000 discussion groups indexed)
http://www.liszt.com/

Publicly Accessible Mailing Lists
http://www.neosoft.com/internet/paml/

NEW-LIST@LISTSERV.NODAK.EDU
(Archives of new-mailing-list announcements)
http://scout.cs.wisc.edu/scout/new-list/

TILE.NET (Lyris, majordomo, and listproc lists)
http://tile.net/lists/

Vivian Neou's List of Lists
   http://catalog.com/vivian/

Also, try searching at Yahoo!—or whatever your favorite search engine happens to be—for the term *mailing list*. At Yahoo! you'll find entries such as *Entertainment: Music: Mailing Lists, Arts: Humanities: History: Genealogy: Mailing Lists,* and *Recreation: Sports: Football (American): Leagues: National Football League (NFL): Teams: San Diego Chargers: Mailing Lists.*

The Online Services

The online services have a combined membership of tens of millions of people. AOL alone was over 15 million last time we checked. So somewhere on those services are thousands of people discussing subjects related to your business … in private discussion groups that you cannot get into unless you join the service.

The discussion groups in these online services are similar in many ways to Internet discussion groups, though they're generally not as convenient. In the online services, you have to visit each group individually, changing to a completely different area of the service each time, whereas with Internet newsgroups you can set up your newsreader so that just the groups you want to work with are displayed in the program, and then click on one to read its messages. With mailing lists, you can read all the messages in your e-mail program. Still, the online services are well worth checking into and can bring you into contact with many people you won't find on the Internet proper.

In some cases, for historical reasons, the online services have discussion groups that are very important within a particular industry or business. For instance, there used to be a very popular Mystery Writer's discussion group on GEnie, and many people in the Windows-help authoring business used to hang out in a CompuServe forum. If you discover that *the* place for you to be is in one of these online-service discussion groups, then maybe you'd better join. On the other hand, if you find that out on the Internet proper you have more work than you can manage, perhaps you should save your money and forget about joining an online service.

WORKING IN THE DISCUSSION GROUPS

Here's how to make a lot of enemies when you join a discussion group. Just jump straight in and pitch your product. Tell everyone how wonderful your product is, how you've got a special offer going on, why they should all come to your Web site *right now* or they miss out—there's only five days left—how your product has won the top awards in your industry, and so on.

That's just blatant commercialism. You just posted an ad to the discussion group, and people don't like that too much. It's as if someone called you at home on the phone during supper trying to sell you something—how would that make you feel?

There are more subtle ways to go about things. We're not talking trickery, we're talking about what we mentioned earlier; you've got to give something in order to get something in return. Here, then, are a few ideas on working in the discussion groups.

Get a Feel for What's Going On

Before you begin posting messages to newsgroups and mailings lists, you should just visit for a while. Just *lurk*, to use a little discussion-group jargon. That is, read the messages but don't take part in the discussion. Unless you take a look, you don't know for sure the slant of the discussion group. You won't know what types of messages you can post without upsetting people. And for the moderated groups this is especially important, because if you send an inappropriate message, the moderator won't post it to the group. Many newsgroups and mailing lists have FAQs (Frequently Asked Question documents) and charters that explain the purpose of the group and what sorts of messages are acceptable. In the case of newsgroups, you'll sometimes find a FAQ posted to the newsgroup once or twice a week so it's always available. In moderated groups, you may find that the moderator puts his signature at the bottom of every message, with information about where to find the FAQ or charter. In the case of mailing lists, when you subscribe you'll generally be sent a document describing the group and explaining what is acceptable.

Another reason to visit without posting is to make sure you're in the right place. Is the discussion group really suitable for your purposes? Are there many people taking part? Is there anything you can contribute to help the other members?

Creating a Signature

Before you start posting to newsgroups and mailing lists, design a good signature. A signature is a little block of text at the end of your e-mail or discussion-group message that says something about the person who sent the message—something the person wants other people to know. These are great forms of advertising, especially if your message is intelligent and useful to other people in the discussion group. If people read a message and find something useful or interesting, they may want to know about the person writing the message, and they may spend a few moments visiting the person's Web site to learn more. Signatures are often used to carry little promotional ads, too, and this seems to be more or less accepted these days, as long as the signature isn't too large.

So think about what you want to tell people and how you can fit it into a few lines at the bottom of every message you send. You'll want to design several signatures and use the most appropriate for each discussion group. How many lines? It used to be said that four or five were about the maximum, but these days people often use nine or ten without too many complaints. Don't be too pushy in the signature, though. Try to give the person a reason to visit your site. For instance, which is likely to be the more appealing of the following two signatures? This one ...

```
Buy from us! The best prices and the best rocket
products on the Web! http://www.podunkrocket.com/
```

Or this ...

```
Meet Buzz Aldrin in our discussion group next week!
(March 3-7, 1998) Also, free classified ads, great
link pages, fantastic selection of model rockets and
accessories. http://www.podunkrocket.com/
```

Think about what you can offer people to come to your site. Certainly the first signature may bring some people in, but the second is likely to be stronger because it's not selling, at least not until the last few words. Rather, it's talking about how your site gives something to its visitors.

What sort of things should you remember to include in your signature? The following:

- The URL to the particular page at your Web site that you want people from this group to arrive at—which may not be the same page for each group. You may want to present different information first depending on who's arriving at your site. (And, as we'll discuss in Chapter 14, you can use this method to track how many people from the discussion group visit your site.)
- The e-mail address of an autoresponder—many people still have slow Internet connections or minimal Web access, so they may prefer to obtain more information from an autoresponder.
- The e-mail address of a real person to which questions can be directed.

- Reasons for people to visit your site. Don't list reasons why you want them to visit, but give them reasons why *they should want* to visit—these are two very different things.

How to Write Messages

Now you're ready to post messages to the discussion groups. Let's say you want to promote your model-rocket site to various newsgroups. You could, if you were really reckless, write a message like this:

```
CHECK THIS OUT!
THE BEST MODEL ROCKET SITE ON THE WEB!!!!!!
COOL STUFF, REAL CHEAP, SAVE $$$$$!!!
COME VISIT US AT HTTP://WWW.ROCKETFOOL.COM/!!!
```

This sort of message is obnoxious, and people generally hate them. You'll probably make more enemies than friends posting messages like this. It's clearly an ad, and it sounds like a poorly written ad, too. But it's similar to thousands of messages being posted to newsgroups every day, and people are getting sick of them.

Think of newsgroup messages in a different way. Don't think of them as advertisements but as informational messages. Don't *scream* your message at people—talk to them. Try a message like this:

```
Hi, I've just started checking out the model rocket
discussion groups on the Internet. This one seems
like quite an active group. I run a mail-order
model-rocket business in Podunk, Texas, so I wanted
to find out a little about how other model-
rocketeers are using the Internet. We just set up a
Web site (come visit us sometime: http://www.
podunkrocket.com/ ). We figured we'd try to provide
some services to other people who love rockets, so
we've got links to all the rocket sites we can find
(not just model rockets, but the real things, too—
lots of cool NASA links). We've got a discussion
group running, too—we're starting celebrity
discussions, soon, as well, so you'll be able to
post messages to the rocket designers at Estes, some
top prizewinners and so on. Let us know if you've
```

```
got any suggestions for people you'd like to talk
with. And my partner says I'm crazy to do this—why
risk losing business? he says—but we set up a free
classified area. If you have any rockets or
accessories you want to sell, you can post a
classified ad (that's right, no charge!).

If anyone else has any ideas for services we could
provide at our Web site, please let us know. Oh,
and if we're missing a link you know about that we
really should have, you can fill in a form at our
site to add it to the list.
```

Which message is more annoying? Which is more of an ad? They're really both ads, but the first is nothing but an ad, while the second has some character. You can *hear* a person's voice in that message—there's a real person there, not just a bulk-mail program. Notice also that this message isn't directly selling something; it's actually giving something away—three things, really: free classifieds, a rocket discussion group, and a useful link page. It's also asking questions: Have you any ideas for people we could invite to answer questions in our discussion group? Are there any services you'd like to see us provide? Any links we've missed? Nowhere in the message do we ask people to spend money; we just suggest that they might like to visit our site, and give good reasons why.

Now, it's quite possible that a message like this one could get complaints. But because it's clearly from a real person and because it's chatty, any complaints are more likely to be similar to this: "Fred, we try to avoid ads in this group; could you be more careful in the future?" Not so much a flame as a gentle rebuke.

So remember these basic principles about advertising in discussion groups:

Pure ads (Buy, Buy, Buy!) irritate people.

"Ads" in which you give people something are usually acceptable.

Look at your message carefully. Are you providing something useful to the members of that list? Is your message something that a significant proportion of the list is likely to find useful or interesting? Or is it purely an ad?

Not Sure about a Group?

What about groups that probably attract people who are interested in your products, but which are not directly related? Groups about rockets, though not specifically about model rockets, perhaps? I'd be very careful about what I posted in these groups, and I'd keep it short. And I'd try to think about the services that my Web site provides that are more directly related to this newsgroup. For instance, you might try something like this:

```
Anyone out there want to swap or sell rocket-
related products—books, videos, magazines, NASA
souvenirs? I run a Web site with loads of links
to rocket sites, and we've got a free classified ad
section too. You can post messages to sell your
stuff, for no charge. And we're going to be
having question-and-answer sessions in our rocket
discussion group soon; we're trying to track down
an astronaut or two to take part. If anyone knows
someone knowledgeable who might be interested,
please let us know.
```

In this message I've mentioned the things that might be useful to people on this list. It's a rocket discussion group, though not a model-rocket group, so I've mentioned the rocket-links page and the discussion group. I've mentioned the free classified ads, as well; after all, it's likely that there's a lot of overlap, that many people who are interested in rockets are also interested in model rockets, and so may be interested in the classifieds. I also kept it low key and chatty again—it's not a Buy, Buy, Buy! posting.

But That's Not an Effective Ad

Now, I know that some people, particularly people who are used to the world of direct mail, feel that this sort of discreet advertising in discussion groups is not real advertising—it's not direct enough. And indeed, you'll see many ads in discussion groups, in particular in newsgroups (because it's so easy to post messages in newsgroups), that look something like this:

```
**********************************
MAKE MONEY WITHOUT PRINTING MONEY
**********************************
SIXTY THOUSAND DOLLARS IN ONE YEAR
**********************************
```

and this:

```
Register for a free Internet downline and receive,
absolutely free, your own Internet Web site. Sign
```

```
up now and get a massive Internet downline and a
Web page absolutely free. It's FREE! It's easy and
it can be your answer to financial security. Visit
my web site at ...
```

(What's downline? It's a bit of multilevel marketing—MLM—jargon, referring to income from people who you recruit; unfortunately, MLM discovered the Internet some time ago.)

Am I saying that ads like this can't work? No, they probably can. There's no doubt that spam can work—you need only a tiny response to make it pay. There are programs that will send your message to 20,000 newsgroups at once very quickly and cheaply. Of course you may not like the reaction you get—everything from insulting e-mail to eventually, perhaps, prosecution. And there are systems out there designed to look for this sort of cross-posting and destroy cross-posted messages.

But even if this type of advertising can pay, you should be more interested in the long term, in building a good reputation for your products and services, rather than in a get-in-get-the-money-and-get-out type of scheme. This book is about building a presence in the Internet, not hiding in cyberspace, which you'll have to do if you do too much of this sort of thing. (You may have noticed that a lot of ads are anonymous, in the sense that they don't provide a Reply To e-mail address or a URL; rather, they use phone numbers and mailing addresses, so the perpetrator cannot be "attacked" in cyberspace.) You're trying to build a very visible presence, and that will be difficult to do if you make a habit of this kind of advertising.

How Often Can You Post?

Don't post the same message over and over to the same places. If you do so, your chatty announcement turns into a blatant ad, the very thing you're trying to avoid. That doesn't mean you can't remind people about your Web site, of course. You can announce new services now and again. In fact you may not want to mention everything in your first post; keep something back for later.

If you have an active chat or discussion group, you can announce activities such as celebrity chats or extended question-and-answer sessions in your discussion group. And, as we'll discuss next, you can provide information and become an advisor as another way to keep a regular presence in the discussion groups. Your signature will still act as a reminder and an ad, and if you've set up a truly useful Web site, you'll find that other people will start to talk about your site; you'll often see group members recommending another member's site.

Provide Information At Your Web Site

Another technique many people use is to provide information and post it at their Web sites. Then they can post messages in newsgroups and mailing lists that are directly related to the subject of that information. For instance, a lawyer who works in employment law might write an article about a particular issue related to that area of law, then post messages to the discussion groups related to employment law mentioning that the article is available.

Also, if you see someone asking for information—something that requires more than just a few lines in reply—and if you have the answer, why not post it at your Web site and then send a message saying where the information is available? This is very commonly done, and isn't regarded as a "teaser." It's not a matter of: "I've got the information, you can have it, but only if you come to my site." It's more a case of: "I have an entire article on this subject, but it's way too big to post to the mailing list because most members probably aren't interested, so if you *are* interested why not view it at my Web site?" You're not only providing a service, but doing it in such a way that you don't annoy people by posting a huge message to the discussion group.

Note, by the way, that you need to remember to set up your Web site so that people coming to your site for the information will see other things at your site. Some people doing this provide the main URL of their Web site, so the visitor must look for the information—don't make it too difficult to find, though—and at the same time is bound to notice other things at your site. Alternatively, you can give a URL to take people directly to the information while ensuring that there are obvious links to other information at your site.

Become an Advisor

Most discussion groups have a small core of regulars and a large number of lurkers—people who read the messages but never post responses or new messages. A group may have 600 or 1,000 members, for instance, but if you watch the group for a while you'll notice that it only has around 30 or 40 regulars who seem to post messages frequently.

Among the regulars there's often a smaller group—maybe only five or ten—who are what might be termed *advisors*. When people send messages posing questions, members of this group are the first to answer, and they provide the best and most useful answers.

Get involved in a few of the active groups. Get known to the members as someone who understands the subject being discussed and can answer questions and provide leads to useful information.

The problem with this level of involvement, though, is the time it can take. You'll need a lot of discipline, and you'd better learn to use the Delete key. Immediately delete messages that are of little importance—the very chatty messages or messages about subjects that don't particularly interest you. And pick and choose what you get involved with carefully. You can't be expected to answer every question; just answer a few now and again with helpful information. Occasionally point people to your Web site, and make sure you have a good signature on all your messages.

Get to Know the Advisors

The advisors and moderators in newsgroups and mailing lists can be very useful to you. Get to know these people; send them free goods, in the same way you would with people who run Web sites associated with your area of business. (We'll discuss this a little in Chapter 10.) Send them e-mail and chat with them a little. They'll remember you and may well check out your Web site. If you've got something of value, they'll remember that and mention it to other people. And their status as advisors gives their comments and opinions great weight with many group members.

These people are often useful product reviewers, too. Sometimes they write in real-world magazines, and sometimes they have Web sites that review products. So keep a watch for people who can leverage your marketing campaign by talking about your products for you. Remember, the very best advertising you can get is product endorsements from people who are not directly affiliated with or paid by you or your company.

Here's an example. Peter wrote a book called *The Technical Writer's Freelancing Guide* in the early 1990s; this book was reviewed in four periodicals. In 1997 he revised the book, and it was republished as ***Making Money in Technical Writing*** (http://www.mcp.com/mgr/arco/techwr/). This time Peter actively recruited reviewers. Many came to him after he announced the book in mailing lists and newsgroups and asked for reviewers. Others read other messages he'd written, visited his Web site, saw the invitation to reviewers, and contacted him. By the time *Making Money in Technical Writing* was published he had 90 reviewers lined up, some claiming to be planning multiple reviews.

Bear in mind, however, that the easier you make it to get a review copy, the more likely you are to be ripped off. Some of these 90 people perhaps asked for a free book without any intention of ever publishing a review. But even if only half of them publish reviews, it's still well worth the cost. And the rip-off rate is almost certainly much lower than 50 percent—probably less than 5 percent. If you ask for some kind of "proof of purpose"—for instance, ask reviewers to provide you with the names of the publications for which they're writing the reviews, for the dates when the reviews will be published, and the editors' contact information—then the rip-off rate is likely to be pretty low. The Internet provides a really easy and convenient way to contact reviewers—a way to leverage your promotional efforts tremendously.

By being willing to make this and other books readily available to everyone who wants to review them, Peter gets a lot more coverage than if he vigorously screened every potential reviewer. For every hoop you make a prospective reviewer jump through—whether it's asking for their credentials or for clips of other reviews—you'll lose some reviews. Concentrate on getting your products to reviewers, rather than on keeping them away from scammers. As small-publishing guru Dan Poynter puts it, "if in doubt, send it out."

Announcement Newsgroups

There are a number of newsgroups designed specifically for announcements, where you can post blatant ads and nobody cares. Some of these are general; comp.infosystems.www.announce, for instance, accepts announcements about new noncommercial Web sites. Others are more specific; comp.security.pgp.announce, for instance, contains announcements related to the PGP encryption program.

In your newsreader, search for these words: `announce`, `forsale`, `market`. Or better still, search one of the newsgroup directories we talked about earlier. If you search in your newsreader, the program will find only those groups in which the word you are searching for is within the group name; at some of the directories a group description is also searched.

You'll find groups like the following:

- alt.fandom.cons—Announcements of conventions (SciFi and others)
- chi.places—Announcements of Chicago-area events
- alt.aquaria.marketplace—Fish and aquariums
- alt.art.marketplace—Art for sale
- biz.marketplace.computers—Computers and computer equipment
- ithaca.marketplace—Stuff for sale in Ithaca, New York
- alt.autographs.transactions—Ads related to autographs for sale
- edm.forsale—Stuff for sale in Edmonton, Canada

There's a flip side, too. There are also groups that take "Wanted to Buy" ads, and though you're not supposed to post messages selling things, you can look in these groups for people who may be searching for the products or services you provide. And if you search for the word *wanted* in the directories, you'll often find groups that accept both for-sale and wanted ads, such as the following:

- alt.auto.parts.wanted—Described by its members as alt.american.automobile.breakdown.breakdown.breakdown
- aus.ads.wanted—Goods for sale or wanted in Australia
- comp.binaries.ibm.pc.wanted—People seeking software
- nj.market.autos—Vehicles wanted and for sale in New Jersey

Note, by the way, that some groups are really intended for classified-ad-type ads rather than for businesses. Also, many of the *announce* and *announcement* groups are for announcements that are not necessarily goods for sale—announcements about upcoming events, for instance. Another category of newsgroup that takes announcements of various kinds is the net-happenings groups, such as comp.internet.net-happenings. There are also a few newprod groups for announcements of new products, such as the following:

- biz.next.newprod—New product announcements for the NeXT computer
- can.newprod—New products/services of interest to Canadian readers
- comp.newprod—Announcements of new products of interest
- eunet.newprod—New products of interest to Europeans

Also take a look at the biz newsgroups, many of which contain announcements about commercial products. And there are also the Clarinet releases newsgroups, though you can't post messages directly to these groups. Rather, you must send a press release through one of several press-release services, which we'll discuss in Chapter 17.

Finally, there are scores of mailing lists and newsgroups that review products—books, software, music, theater, restaurants, bicycles, cigars, and so on. Search for the word `review`, and you'll find these groups. Then visit the appropriate ones and see if you can find someone to review your product. With luck, you may be able to contact a review writer who also sells reviews to magazines and newspapers. Some of these review groups—such as alt.books.reviews—allow redistribution of reviews, so a review of your product may end up going further than just the newsgroups—into newsletters and on Web sites for instance.

The Internet's discussion groups provide a tremendous resource for the promoter. Many people have used them successfully, in particular to promote themselves as experts and consultants. This is real grass-roots promotions, a low-cost technique for reaching people, though it does require a large investment of time and patience. In the next chapter we'll look at other grass-roots promotional techniques, such as giving away products at other people's sites.

Grass Roots Marketing

You've probably heard the term *guerrilla marketing*. It was coined long ago, many years pre-Internet, by Jay Conrad Levinson, who has written a series of books about the subject. Guerilla marketing is all about how small businesses can market their products using low-cost techniques. Like a guerrilla army fighting with whatever weapons it can scrape together, taking on a much more powerful military force, small businesses can use guerrilla-marketing techniques to win their battles in the marketplace.

The Internet provides a multitude of guerrilla-marketing opportunities. Of course many of the techniques we speak about elsewhere in this book could be regarded as guerrilla marketing—using large databases of journalist contact information, listing your Web site in appropriate places, and so on. All these things are low-cost yet effective techniques for getting the word out about your products and services.

TOTAL PERSONAL MARKETING

In a sense, the Internet is all about grass-roots promotions. It's about you-scratch-my-back-I'll-scratch-yours, it's about friends helping friends to get the word out. We've entered what **Christopher Locke** (http://www.rageboy.com/), Internet commentator extraordinaire, calls the era of *Total Personal Marketing*.

This is the era in which a kid with a cheap computer and an Internet connection can sign up a hundred thousand subscribers, and have his words read by those hundred thousand people—and by thousands more people to whom they forward his words—every week or so. This is the sort of power that just a few years ago was unimaginable. To reach that sort or audience you had to own a magazine, or have a low-paid job at a magazine, or be willing to spend $50,000 each time you wanted to reach 100,000 people.

"The net is not a passive medium," Christopher Locke e-mailed us recently. "Which means (to me) you gotta *work* the thing! Everyone now has a say, even 11-year-olds (and by the way, I know some sharp 11-year-olds). Being an anarchist at heart, I think this state of affairs is just terrific. You just need to call in a few favors and get your pals to the barricades."

Now look at what we've just done ... well, what Peter just did. Some time ago Peter mentioned Christopher's publication, *Entropy Gradient Reversal*, in his newsletter, *Poor Richard's Web Site News*. It's not huge, but 15,000 subscribers is still something worthwhile (it has many more subscribers than that now). Later, when a few bad reviews turned up at Amazon.com related to Peter's **Making Money in Technical Writing** book (http://www.amazon.com/exec/obidos/ASIN/0028618831/ref=sim_books/002-2052570-0953861), Christopher jumped in and boosted the ratings a little, then encouraged another reader of this book to do the same. Now Peter's mentioning Christopher's site in a book ...

In fact, the Amazon.com *Making Money in Technical Writing* page is an interesting illustration of this principle in action. It's not a very widely read book, which is not surprising considering the subject matter. But it does get a lot of good reviews and testimonials from people in the technical-writing business. It also gets a number of complaints, from people who simply don't believe it's possible to make much money as a freelance technical writer. When the book first appeared at Amazon.com, it wasn't long before someone posted a review—a glowing, five-star review. Then no more reviews appeared for a long time, until almost exactly ten months later in fact, when two reviews appeared, both negative. All of a sudden the book's five-star rating dropped to a one and one half-star rating.

Christopher jumped in with a few comments of his own—not saying that he'd read the book (he hadn't), but praising Peter's writing and pointing out fallacies in the other reviewers' comments. Then another friend reviewed the book, giving it a five-star review. And Peter posted a number of comments, both replying to the criticisms in the earlier reviews and posting readers' testimonials. Then another five-star review turned up, pushing the total up to four stars.

Around this time, the book's Amazon.com ranking started to rise. (Amazon.com assigns every book a sales rank—the higher the number, the more copies are being sold.) The book's rank rose from somewhere around 40,000 to about 17,000. Was this caused by these little comments and reviews? Hard to say ... in fact probably not, at least not directly. Something else may have happened—a press review, for instance—but at least when people visited the Amazon.com page to take a look at the book, perhaps after reading about it in a magazine, they saw a four-star book rather than a one-star book, and they read plenty of glowing praise. Does this help sell books? Yes, absolutely.

Christopher mentioned two other authors "who have benefited hugely from hot debate about their work on Amazon.com: David Siegel (*Killer Web Sites*) and Michael Wolff (*Burn Rate*)." Take a look at the Killer Web Site reviews (currently over 147 of them), and you'll find comments ranging from "pathetic" and "hype" to "excellent" and "a must read." (Which just goes to show, *different strokes for different folks*, and *you can't please all of the people all of the time*.)

So this is what Christopher Locke refers to as "getting your pals to the barricades." It's a new way of looking at the manner in which your products and services are represented to the world. You can react to criticism—or praise, for that manner—immediately, if you're paying attention to what's going on. And you can recruit friends and well-wishers to help you, to man the barricades for you.

GIVEAWAYS

Now let's look at a specific grass-roots technique: giving products away in high-traffic regions of the Internet. Let's say, for instance, that you are Mr. Estes Rocket. (The Estes Rocket company still doesn't know that the Internet exists, apparently, so if anyone from Estes Rocket reads this and puts these ideas into action, please contact us so we can send you the bill.) By the time you had read this far into the book you would have had a good idea of what Web sites are of interest to you: the model-rocket-related Web sites. You may also have found a number of discussion groups related to model rocketry, and perhaps some e-mail newsletters.

Now, the next step is to pick which of these are getting a lot of traffic. That's not always easy—you have to take an educated guess. Is this a site (newsgroup, newsletter) that people talk about a lot, and refer other people to? Is it a Web site that is obviously very well designed, with really useful resources for model-rocket hobbyists? The sort of site that requires a lot of time and energy, and perhaps even money? It's generally not hard to figure out the busiest sites.

Next, contact the site owners, the discussion-group moderators, the newsletter editors, and suggest a giveaway. The principle is simple. You offer to give away a number of your products—a few of your mid-level rocket kits, and perhaps one of your top-of-the-line products as a grand prize. You might hold a contest for one particular Web site, discussion group, or newsletter, if it's big enough to warrant that, or perhaps combine a few together into one contest.

You'll set up a form at your Web site, in which entrants can provide their information: at a minimum their e-mail addresses, perhaps also their names and some sort of survey information that you may find useful. (But don't overdo things; if you make it too difficult to enter, you won't get many entrants.)

The Web sites, discussion groups, and newsletters can now publicize the giveaway. Why would they care? It adds value to them, of course. You'll find that many people are quite happy to be involved in such an arrangement; they like to be able to tell their visitors or subscribers about such offers (especially if it's an exclusive).

What's in it for you? First, you get mentioned in these places; it's low-cost advertising. Not only will you get mentioned in the places publicizing the giveaway, but you may even find that Web-site owners go to *other* places and say "come to my site—we're giving away stuff."

Secondly, you get people to visit your site. You need to set up the entry form so that visitors can also see links enticing them further into your Web site. That shouldn't be hard. If they're interested enough to be at the other site, in the discussion group, or reading the newsletter, and if they're interested enough to enter your contest, then they're "well qualified," to use a sales term. That is, these are people you can be fairly sure are interested in your products.

Finally, here's another benefit. On your entry form you'll have a couple of option buttons, with the label "Would you like to receive the Internet's best Estes Rocket newsletter free every couple of weeks?" or something similar. You should set the option buttons so that the Yes button is already selected. The entrants can change the button to No if they wish, and some will, but probably not many. Peter's found that only around five percent of entrants will decline to receive his newsletter.

Essay Contests Don't Work

We'd recommend that if you carry out this kind of promotion, you do a simple drawing. Use a form to save all the entries in a text file, and then, at the end of the contest, pick the winners. You might do so using a random-number generator (you can find these at the shareware sites listed in Chapter 2), or even print them out and throw darts at the pages.

There's one form of contest that we don't recommend: the essay contest. This is the sort of contest that many magazines used to hold: "tell us, in 20 words or less, exactly why you feel you should be running the country," and that sort of thing. Do they still hold these contests? They used to be popular, didn't they? Perhaps the reason we don't see many anymore is that people probably don't enter them anymore. Nobody has time.

That's certainly been Peter's experience with such contests on the Web. The first one he did was for *Entrepreneur Magazine*, which has a very busy Web site. It wasn't his idea—he simply suggested a drawing, but the staff of the magazine wanted to try an essay.

There were fewer entries than drawings Peter had held at Web sites with a tiny fraction of *Entrepreneur's* traffic. He tried another such drawing recently at a different site, another busy one. Again, almost no response. It seems that few people are willing to spend the time for this sort of thing anymore. So Peter's conclusion is that drawings really do work. Essay contests don't.

Is It Legal?

Are these contests legal? That's difficult to answer, because it depends on where you happen to be. It seems that within the United States at least, they are. Now, we're not lawyers, so you can take whatever we say here with a pinch of salt if you wish. (In other words, don't come complaining to us if your state government doesn't like what you're doing; it's up to you to make sure it's okay.) However, it seems that if you are running a simple drawing, with no money changing hands—the entrants are not paying an entrance fee—then you're okay. There's a little confusion about this. Some people assume that a drawing is a *sweepstakes*, but it's not. In a sweepstakes, there's money being exchanged—the entrants pay to enter, and the winnings come from the combined entry fees, for instance. Contest laws are generally aimed at sweepstakes, not at drawings in which the entrant paid nothing.

The laws are really aimed at contests in which the organizer charges money. If you're just giving away products, without any entry fee, you should be okay. But don't take our word for it. Call your local city or state government and ask if there are any regulations in your area covering these sorts of things. Make sure they understand what you're doing, that you're not selling lottery tickets, for instance. (And yes, we know that the Internet raises all sorts of questions about legal jurisdiction, but that's getting way out of our legal league.) You might also look at the **Sweepstakes and Contests** page (http://www.arentfox.com/features/sweepstakes/articles/sweep.html) published by Arent Fox, a law firm in Washington.

WATCH FOR NEWSLETTER OPPORTUNITIES

While most of the media seem to be focusing on the World Wide Web, they're missing an incredibly important development in communications: the e-mail newsletter. The media spends so much time fussing about glitz—pretty Web sites with cute little graphic-design tricks—that they've really missed the point about the Internet. People are not going online looking for eye candy. They get enough of that on TV, videos, and movies—the Web can't compete with those media. (One important exception—a very big exception, admittedly—is online pornography.) People really are interested in *content*. And content means information. Preferably well-written, well-presented information.

It's possible to present information very effectively through the use of an old technique—typed words. Just plain text, in an e-mail message. As we discuss in Chapter 11, there are now many very influential newsletters, with subscriber lists in the hundreds of thousands. They're written by a wide range of people, with many different writing styles. They're often a love 'em or hate 'em sort of thing, with some people unsubscribing after the first issue and others hanging on every word.

These newsletters can be *very* influential. When Chris Pirillo featured *Poor Richard's Web Site* in his newsletter, Peter got thousands of visitors to his site and over a thousand new subscribers to his newsletter. (By the way, Chris is the author of *Poor Richard's Email Publishing*, to be published by Top Floor Publishing in June of 1998.) When Dan Butler's **Naked PC** (http://www.thenakedpc.com/) was mentioned in Fred Langa's **LangaList** (http://www.langa.com/), *The Naked PC* received 1,000 new subscribers in just one morning.

There's only one thing better than getting mentioned in one of these newsletters—it's getting mentioned in them more than once. Peter's now trying to convince Chris to hold a drawing for copies of Poor Richard's Web Site. Cultivating newsletter editors can be a very worthwhile endeavor. Try to get mentioned; try to give things away. Whatever you do, don't miss out on this very powerful way to reach people. To paraphrase a popular *Placebo* song, "A friend in need's a friend indeed, a friend with a 100,000-subscriber newsletter is better."

LOOK FOR OPENINGS

Keep your eyes open and your wits about you; this is a guerrilla operation. Make friends with people in the same business as you, get to know newsletter editors, spend time finding out who's running the discussion groups that are important to you, and so on. You'll see opportunities turn up out of the blue, and you can go searching for them. And read some of Conrad Jay Levinson's *Guerrilla Marketing* books. Most of these are about marketing in the real world (though he also has a book about marketing on the 'Net). But you'll find that many of the principles and ideas he discusses in his books can be applied in cyberspace. What it all comes down to is keeping a lookout for opportunities in which you can, at a very low cost, reach people with a message about your products and services.

CHAPTER ELEVEN

Creating Newsletters and Discussion Groups

The Web has a lot going for it. It's huge, it's accessible practically world-wide, over 340 million Web pages are available online, and millions of people surf them every day. (340 million pages? Maybe 400 million, or 250 million, who knows—just pick whatever very large number you like.) The Web also has a lot of disadvantages, though. For example, it's huge, it's accessible practically worldwide, over 350 million Web pages are available online, and millions of people surf them every day.

When you put your Web site online, you are competing with millions of other sites. That's quite a daunting thought. You have to get a visitor's attention, keep it long enough to make a pitch, and then make enough of an impression on the visitor for him to keep coming back.

Fortunately, you do not have to end your promotional efforts with the Web, as we've discussed in earlier chapters. Not only can you mention your site in subtle, appropriate postings to newsgroups and mailing lists (which we discussed in Chapter 9), but you can also push content beyond your Web site through your own newsletters and discussion groups. You can even put a discussion group on your site and leave it to your visitors to create site content! You can do both these things—creating discussion lists and newsletters—without paying a dime.

When you put together a mailing list and deliver it via e-mail, you're not asking people to remember to come to you; you can come to them. This is an easy way to stay in front of your visitors, keep them thinking of you, and give them something to pass on to other people. Similarly, creating an e-mailed discussion group gives you a forum through which you can help solve problems and share your expertise.

Creating this kind of content can have a big payoff, as it can increase your credibility and visibility. On the other hand, it takes a lot of work to create good content.

NEWSLETTERS

You've probably seen newsletters put together by offline businesses. They show up in your mailbox every month or every quarter, and hold your attention for at least a few minutes, causing you to think about that company and helping bring their name to mind when you need something from their industry. Offline newsletters are a big investment in time and money, because printing and postage have to be paid for. Online newsletters are just a big investment in time.

To get a newsletter together, you need three things: content, a good format, and an audience.

Newsletter Content

You might think that doing a weekly newsletter is no big deal. Believe us, do it for a few issues and you'll realize that it is indeed a big deal. Putting together all that information can turn into much more work than you might at first realize.

How do you think of what to write? It's best if you start from the perspective that you're writing for an audience that needs a problem solved, or wants to learn more about your industry, or uses products similar to yours and wants to know how to use them better. You're not writing for an audience that loves hearing product pitches, or wants to hear your slogan four billion times, or just can't wait for your next clever marketing idea. Your audience doesn't give a fig for your company or product; they just want you to help them fix their problems. Keep that in mind.

If you look at things from that perspective, you'll find you've got plenty of content. How did you solve that last customer request for a software feature? How did you handle that last rush job for your client? (Don't present it as bragging; instead, make it a point to go over what you did with enough detail that the reader could use it too.) What are some things you've learned in working with your industry? All of these things can make a great series of articles.

Tara calls developing content this way *Industrial Editorship*. Nobody knows as much as you do about your product or service. Therefore, it stands to reason that you're always learning

---

Be Subtle

Don't make every third word in your newsletter the name of your company. You're trying to increase visibility and mindshare, not ram your product down somebody's throat. Make it a soft sell.

lots of little things about your industry—how this thing works, where to go to find that thing, how to make the most of this service or invest most effectively in that product. You can use those bits and pieces of information to establish your expertise and share your knowledge with prospects and customers alike.

If you're from the old school of entrepreneurship, the idea of sharing the fruits of your work might strike you as a bad idea. Why should you give away all your secrets? Well, naturally, if you've built an economic empire on a secret crispy chicken formula, we don't want you to give it away. It's the heart of your organization. But we bet you know a lot about how to drain fried chicken so it doesn't get too greasy, and how to reheat it so it doesn't taste rubbery, and how to make a great chicken salad out of leftovers. You can share that information without mentioning one ingredient of your secret formula. You can use every scrap of information and knowledge this way to your benefit, by sharing with your customers and prospects and establishing yourself as a center of expertise.

The mantra on the Internet is "give it away, give it away, give it away." Only by giving away some of what you know can you establish credibility and expertise. Only by giving away can you make a name for yourself. So keep in mind that you want to protect the essential secrets of your organization, but consider also what you can give away.

If this is still a little fuzzy to you, let's use Tara's work as an example. A lot of her work involves Internet research. She's written a book about it and does a lot of research in her consulting business. For that reason, she has to keep up with the latest

What's the Frequency?

How often are you going to put your newsletter out? Weekly? Monthly? Daily's probably too often unless you're a real net-head or several people are sharing publishing duties. Tara finds once a week comfortable. More than that and she feels too pressured; less than that and she finds herself forgetting about it; it's hard to put it into a "routine." Less than once a month is a hard schedule to maintain; it's too easy to forget about it or make it a low priority that somehow never gets done. (Some newsletters, like the Dilbert Newsletter, seem to thrive on that occasional schedule, but the Dilbert Newsletter has a huge audience and constant promotion through other arenas.)

Peter's newsletter goes out every two weeks, though he's considering changing to a short bulletin five times a week, and a compilation once a week. To do this, though, he'd do all the writing at the same time, and split the information into smaller pieces ready for transmission each day.

research resources and changes to the major search engines. Instead of hoarding that information, she shares it via her Web site and a free newsletter. When she figures something out about how a search engine works or how searches can be performed better, she shares that too. She wants everyone to learn how to search better, while realizing that not everyone will have the patience to perform the kind of detailed, exhaustive research that she does in the course of her work.

You got content? Great. Let's talk about laying it out.

Laying out the Newsletter

A newsletter doesn't have to be 10 or 12 pages—a couple of medium-sized articles (400 or 500 words), a few newsbits of a couple dozen words each, and a little editorial comment on the state of the world, and you've got a newsletter. More is not always better—you don't want to intimidate your readers with something that's several pages long. Tara's of the opinion that you should create something just large enough that the viewer can go through it without investing a lot of time. If you create a really long newsletter, it may sit around in a reader's e-mail box until they "get around" to reading it. They never do get around to

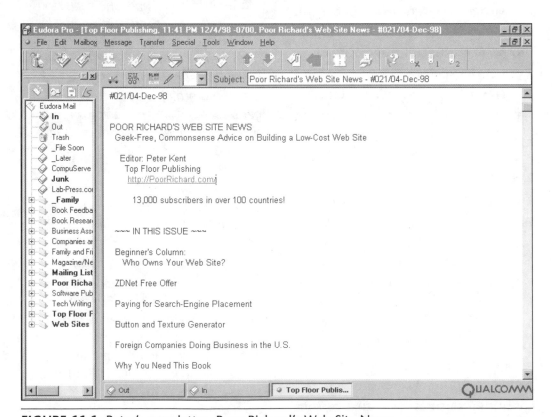

FIGURE 11.1: Peter's newsletter, Poor Richard's Web Site News

reading it and eventually it's deleted unread. On the other hand ... it depends. Peter's biweekly newsletter is quite long, but he also has a very loyal readership that doesn't seem to have a problem with it; a number have said that they print the newsletter out and put it in a binder.

You may want to develop departments and "regular features," though perhaps it's better to let these evolve over time and as a reaction to feedback from your readers.

Regardless of what you decide on your newsletter content, be sure to follow these rules for putting together a readable newsletter:

1. Unless you're absolutely sure your entire readership can handle it, no HTML. Make everything plain text. (If you put your archives up on the Web later, you can add HTML then.)

2. Be sure to write out URLs with the http:// included—some e-mail readers can interpret this kind of text as a clickable link. You should probably write URLs in such a manner that they stand alone—no other character touches the beginning or end of the URL. For instance, don't put the URL inbetween <> characters (for a discussion of this subject, see Peter's newsletter: http://www.poorrichard.com/newsltr/019.htm#begin).

Archiving Your Newsletters

Many of the mailing-services we'll discuss in this chapter offer a way to archive your posts into a Web archive. You can also archive your newsletters on your own Web site, or let someone else archive them if you don't want to manage them yourself. The point is this: have an archive available somewhere so your readers can check out back issues and take advantage of all your expertise. Peter prefers to archive his newsletters at his site—these archives act as a way to draw people to the site (see http://PoorRichard.com/newsltr/). *Since Tara compiles her newsletter from updates she posts daily on her Web site, she doesn't archive her newsletter at all (but she does archive the updates.)*

If your newsletter covers Web sites and other Internet news, it won't age well. We recommend that you include a disclaimer that says something like, "The links are checked periodically to avoid 404 errors, but the facts of the Web site—cost or content—can change at any time. These are archives, after all." That way someone who found your archives via a search engine avoids a shock if they find something different about a Web site than what you describe in the archives of your newsletter.

3. Put a line of space between paragraphs. Don't just run paragraphs together; it turns your text into a giant block that's hard to read. Also try to keep paragraphs short. Keep one line between paragraphs in the same story, and two lines between different stories and different sections.

4. Keep your columns 60-65 characters wide or less. That'll keep the lines from breaking up strangely on most e-mail readers.

5. Don't try to create justified text, in which each line is the same length. Let the text be ragged, where each line is a different length. (The text in this book is justified.) Long stretches of ragged text are easier to read.

6. You can use text characters to break up sections in your newsletter—like this: - - - - -, or ===== , but don't overdo it.

7. Don't try to center things and line up columns; many mail programs these days display messages with non-proportional text, so centering and lining up things doesn't work well. Try to make your newsletter look good using a font such as Times New Roman, rather than a "monospace" font such as Courier. (Monospace means a font in which every character—including spaces—takes up the same amount of space.) If you do use a monospace font—because you want to display information in tables or something like that—put a disclaimer at the top of the newsletter. If it says something like "this newsletter best read in 12 point Courier font," the

HTML Mail

The term HTML mail *refers to e-mail messages that are formatted using HTML coding—the tags used to create Web pages. HTML mail messages are much more attractive than plain text; you can use color, tables, images, and so on. But there are two problems with HTML mail. First, many users are working with e-mail programs that cannot display these messages; they'll probably display a jumble of codes making the text unreadable. Second, even if the recipient is working with an e-mail program that, in theory, can display HTML mail, it may not do so well. All the HTML-compatible programs work slightly differently, so what works well in one doesn't work well in another.*

For this reason most newsletters are still plain text. That's not to say HTML mail should never be used. There are a number of extremely successful HTML-mail newsletters.

reader will know how to adjust the fonts they're using to read the newsletter properly.

8. Before you send out your newsletter, send it to yourself—make sure that it looks okay when it comes back. Look in the header of the newsletter for this line:

```
Content-Type: text/plain; charset="iso-8859-1"
```

If you see something else, then you have a problem. You may have some kind of typesetting character—curly quotes, an emdash (—), or an ellipsis (...), for instance. That's a problem for many mail programs, which may display all sorts of strange characters within the newsletter. It's a good idea to write newsletters in a text editor, such as Windows Notepad or SimpleText. (A really good text editor for Windows, with many word-processing features, is **TextPad**— http://www.textpad.com/.)

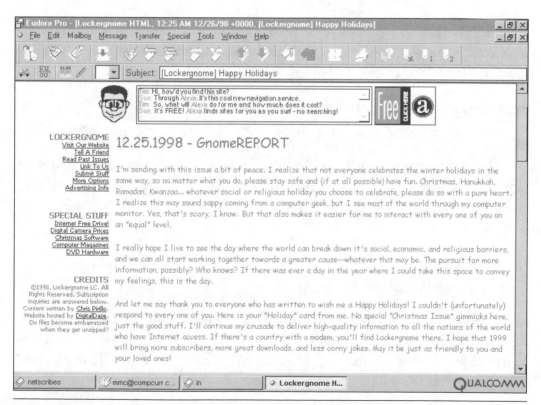

FIGURE 11.2: An HTML newsletter, Lockergnome (http://www.lockergnome.com/)

Resources for Creating a Great Newsletter

For more information on creating a great newsletter, check out these sites on the Web.

Inkspot

http://www.inkspot.com/

Inkspot is both a wildly successful newsletter and a great clearinghouse for writing resources on the Web. As a newsletter, it reaches over 44,000 subscribers with each issue, and contains regular market information and columns from a variety of writers and other professionals with writing-related information. As a Web site, you'll find links to all kinds of writing and writing-related resources. Especially check out the article ***How to Start an Online Newsletter*** at http://www.inkspot.com/bt/craft/newsletterinfo.html.

Church Street Publishing

http://www.churchstreet.com/

This site has an excellent resource list of articles and newsletter-publishing resources. Their articles cover topics such as "Developing an e-zine for marketing purposes" and "8 reasons new publishers don't make it."

The Newsletter Editors' Resource List

http://www.tedgoff.com/erlist.html

This is a lengthy, and we mean *lengthy*, list of Web sites found useful by newsletter editors. You'll find media links. You'll find links of use to editors. You'll find reference links. And you'll find a great section covering online publishing.

InfoBot.Net

http://www.infobot.net/

InfoBot.Net has a great list of articles on e-mail publishing (and promises to have a tutorial later). They also have an onsite publisher's forum, links to e-mailed publishing resources, and a database of free content for use in e-mailed newsletters. There's a lot of great stuff here.

E-ZineZ

http://www.e-zinez.com/

E-ZineZ claims to have "everything you need to know about starting an E-Zine." They do have plenty of stuff here—including a template sample for a plain-text e-zine, elements of essential e-zines, and a huge resource list. Put this site on your surfing list!

Distributing the Newsletter

Once you've got your content together, and used the sites above and your own resources to put the first issue together, you need to figure out how to distribute it. You have three choices: do it yourself, go for a freebie, or pay for it.

Newsletters don't distribute themselves, and once you've got more than a couple hundred readers, you're talking about a serious administrative task. If you decide to do it yourself you're in for a lot of work. If you decide to get a freebie, you'll get a lot of administrative chores taken off your hands but it comes at a price. Nothing's really for free, after all. If you pay for it, you'll get premium service but it'll hit you in the wallet. Which way you should distribute depends really on how large a subscriber base you expect to have and how often you're planning to distribute your newsletter.

Doing It Yourself

Tara doesn't recommend this. Tara administered her own weekly newsletter on Internet advertising issues for a little over a year. She had a couple hundred subscribers and administered the list by hand—adding and removing subscribers, dealing with bounced messages, etc. She did all this in Eudora Pro. While Eudora could handle the newsletter, Tara had a hard time keeping up with the bounced messages, manually handling the subscribes and unsubscribes, and basically doing things besides producing content, which is what she wanted to do most.

On the other hand, Peter thinks it's okay to do it yourself, if you set things up carefully. His list was up to almost 2,000 subscribers, handled through his own e-mail program, before he switched to a for-pay system. It may take a little fooling around to get everything set up correctly—you may have to install a particular e-mail program, too—but it can be done.

There are two things you need to be able to do in order to administer a newsletter mailing list yourself. You need a program that can filter e-mail addresses into and out of the address book, and you need a program that allows you to import lists of addresses from text files into the address book.

Unfortunately only a few programs can do both of these things. We only know of three: **AK-Mail** (http://www.akmail.com/), **Pegasus** (http://www.pegasus.usa. com/), and **Postmark**. Worse, the first, though available, is no longer in development, and the last doesn't seem to be available any more. The major e-mail programs—Eudora Pro 4.1 and Outlook 2000, for instance—cannot do these things.

Your options are therefore limited. If you want to run a list from your own system, we advise you to use AK-Mail or Pegasus. You can use the filters in these programs to grab an e-mail address from an incoming message, and then drop it into an address book (or *distribution list*, as it's called in Pegasus). For instance, take a look at Figure 11.3. This is the box in which filters are set up in Pegasus Mail for Windows, and it's fairly straightforward; we've selected **In These Headers** and the **To:** check box to tell Pegasus to take a look at the address in the To: line. In the **Trigger text** text box we've told it to look for the word **info**. And in the **Action to take** drop-down list box we've selected **add user to List**. When we did so, a box opened in which we could create or select a distribution list; we created one called **info**.

What these sorts of filters allow you to do is publish subscription information for your newsletter, then set up the e-mail program so that whenever you receive

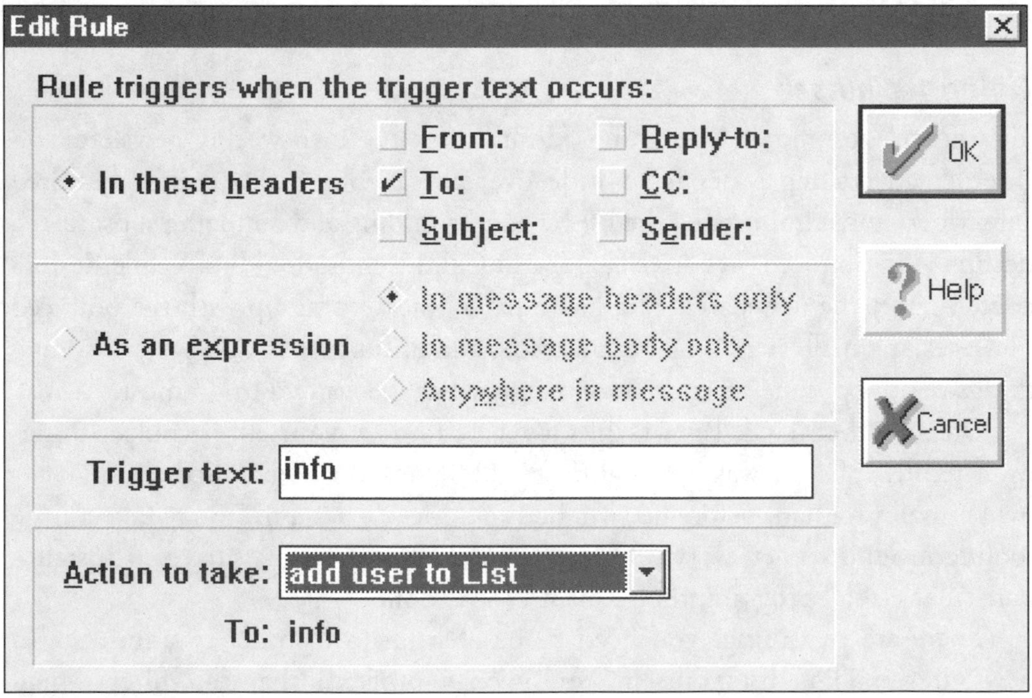

FIGURE 11.3: Setting up a filter in Pegasus Mail for Windows

a message using the particular address or code word in the Subject line, the address of the sender is placed into the address book. You can do the same for unsubscription information, too; whenever you receive a message to a particular address or using a particular word in the Subject line, the address is *removed* from the address book.

Another way to get addresses into the program is to import them from a text file that has been created by an autoresponder or by a Web form. Some programs can do this, but the most popular ones—such as Eudora, Netscape Messenger, and Microsoft Outlook—*cannot*.

Sending Out Your Messages

Once you have a subscriber list of e-mail addresses, what do you do with it? How do you mail to all these people? It's important to get this right, or you'll upset a lot of recipients.

Most mail programs allow you to mail to an address book, a distribution list, or an "alias" or "nickname" that contains multiple addresses. But if you simply enter the address-book or distribution-list name into the To: text box and send the message, you've just committed a faux pas; everyone who receives the message will see everyone else's e-mail address in the To: line. (And it's no longer a To: line so much as a To: page if you have a big list.) I've received e-mail messages containing literally hundreds of addresses in the To: line.

Instead, you must use the Bcc: line, which stands for Blind Carbon Copy. It means that everyone on the list gets a copy of the message, but nobody can see who else got a message. Although you place the address-book or distribution-list name on the Bcc: line, when a recipient views the message, he'll see his address on the To: line and won't see any others. We'll discuss using e-mail headers properly in Chapter 16.

Some e-mail programs won't let you mail just to the Bcc: line; you must have an address in the To: line as well. So you can put your own address on the To: line, then the address book or distribution list name on the Bcc: line.

Bcc Works Differently ...

Unfortunately different programs handle the Bcc: line differently. Some will place the address from the Bcc: line onto the recipient's To: line. Others display the Bcc: address on a Bcc: line, and display the original To: line as well. Experiment to see how your program works; mail to a few friends and to yourself.

Using a Freebie

If you're a non-commercial or non-profit enterprise, if you want to send out issues once a day or more often, or if you have a very small list, freebies are probably the way to go. Free services host your mailing list—they use their programs to handle your subscription list and send out the messages. That's the upside. The downside is that there are usually some restrictions with how you can handle your mailing list, and the services keep the sites free by selling advertising on the mailing lists they host. Several Web sites offer such free services.

Be Careful!

It's a good idea to set up your mail program so that the Cc: field does not normally appear on your message composition screen. Turn on the Bcc: line so it's always there. Not all programs will let you do this, but many will.

If you leave the Cc: line visible, one day you will send a couple of hundred messages on the Cc: line. If you're very lucky, people won't be too mad at you.

eGroups

http://www.egroups.com/

eGroups offers free discussion-type mailing lists (and moderated ones that can be set up as newsletters). eGroups' service can also poll newsletter readers and will archive your newsletter on its Web site if you like. eGroups protects Internet users from bogus subscriptions by sending confirmation messages to eGroups users before adding them to a mailing list. They do sell advertising within the mailing lists they host, but they will guarantee no third-party ads in your newsletter if you pay $4.95 a month. They have a limit on the size of messages (individual messages of over 500K are not allowed, which we don't think would ever be a problem for the average newsletter publisher) but do not have a limit on the number of subscribers a newsletter may have.

ListBot

http://www.listbot.com/

ListBot is affiliated with LinkExchange, one of the first and certainly the most famous banner-exchange program on the Internet (see Chapter 13). Like eGroups, ListBot does not have a limit to how many members you can have or how many messages you can send to your list, and like eGroups, ListBot doesn't sell or give away the e-mail addresses of subscribing members. ListBot is advertiser supported, but they do have an option called ListBot Gold.

ListBot Gold does not have a 50K-per-message restriction (we assume that the free version of ListBot does, but can't find a statement to that effect on the Web site), does not contain advertisements, and allows you to import existing mailing-list subscribers into the new list. In addition, you can set up a series of demographic questions by which you can track what type of person is reading your newsletter. ListBot Gold costs $79 a year, which provides you with 1,000 message credits a month. One message to one person equals one credit. Therefore, if you sent out a monthly newsletter to 1,000 people, you'd use 1,000 credits. If you sent four weekly newsletters to 250 people, you'd use 1,000 credits. If you

Newsletters Vs. E-mail Discussion Groups

In the section below we'll be talking about distribution options for your newsletter, and you'll notice that a lot of the services that can distribute a newsletter can also maintain an e-mail discussion list. What's the big difference between a newsletter and an e-mail discussion list? Technically speaking, not much. Newsletters go from one entity to many readers, while an e-mail discussion list goes from many writers to many readers. In the case of a newsletter, it's one person's editorial content being distributed to many readers, like a newspaper. In the case of a discussion list, it's many people inserting their own content—like a telephone "party line" or a discussion group.

sent ten issues of a newsletter to 100 people, you'd use 1,000 credits. You get the idea. If you think you'd use more than 1,000 message credits, you need to contact ListBot for a price quote.

OneList

http://www.onelist.com/

Tara used this service for a little while, and she was happy with it for the most part, though she eventually decided to use the pay service **Liszt** (more about that shortly). OneList has a registration process that gathers information about users, and they use this information to create demographic profiles to help them sell their advertising. It's not possible to subscribe to the newsletter without registering. Like eGroups, they have a 500K e-mail size limit. They also offer a no-ads option, which costs $59.40 a year and does not appear to use the "message credit" system like ListBot does.

Tara did have an experience with OneList that should serve to illustrate the problems with free services. OneList has a feature that allows one to send an invitation to a prospective subscriber describing the newsletter and inviting them to subscribe. Tara sent this invitation to someone as a test, and was distressed at the kind of message that was sent—it had a definite feeling of "mail merge" and "fill in the blank" about it. It was completely counter to the impression she wanted to give as a friendly, accessible newsletter filled with easy-to-use information. The fact that the "list invitation" feature is there at all

---

Registration Before Subscription

Some free services require that participants register at the Web site before they can sign up for a newsletter or discussion group. They do this so they can get enough demographic information to sell advertising on the mailing lists they're sponsoring. The problem is, it's one more hoop that a potential subscriber has to jump through. For every hoop you make potential subscribers jump through, you lose a certain number of the subscribers. Keep the hoops to a minimum.

---

is good, and in many circumstances would be quite useful. But overall such an impersonal invitation would be more appropriate to something like a discussion list, where the participants set the tone, than a newsletter.

Web Site Post Office (WSPO)

http://www.websitepostoffice.com/

WSPO is an affiliate of Web Site Garage, which we mentioned in Chapter 5. It offers a free mailing-list service for announcement lists only—like newsletters. They currently don't support discussion lists. They have no limit on the number of members or the number of messages you can send out, but they do not support mailing-list attachments or HTML mail. Just like the other services discussed in this chapter, they do not rent or sell the e-mail addresses of the mailing lists they host.

WSPO offers a premium service that removes the advertising from WSPO messages. In addition to removing the advertising, it also allows you to import up to 2,000 current members of your mailing list. (The

---

What Happens When You Leave

Make sure there's some easy way to get your subscription list out of the system before you sign up! Consider what will happen when you want to move to another service.

ability to import members is a "premium" service for many of these free newsletter distribution services—one more reason to choose the one you want carefully and stick with it. You don't want to have to haul lists of e-mail addresses around from place to place!)

One of the neat things about WSPO's commercial version is you can send out e-mail based on demographic data. For example, you could send an e-mail to all readers who have identified themselves as coming from California, who use Linux, etc. This would be a great feature for a newsletter "supplement" if you were going to sponsor an activity in a given area, for instance, or give an online seminar for a particular project. The commercial version of WSPO costs $9.99 a month for 1,000 messages (which works like the 1,000 "message credits" in the ListBot service.) You can also buy a year's worth of credits—12,000—for $99.99. You can also purchase the ability to send additional messages in blocks of 10,000.

If you don't know if you want to pay for a mailing list, using a freebie is a good way to get your feet wet. You can run a mailing list for a while, see if you can keep up with the content responsibilities, and get reaction to your writing. The problem is, if you decide to move to a different mailing list provider, you have to do several things. You have to move what could be a substantial mailing list to a new provider, alert everyone who knew about your old service to your new service, and make sure that there are no places on the 'Net or your own Web site that mention your old newsletter. To get around that, you might use a free service for six issues or so without promoting your newsletter to make sure you can handle the schedule of doing a newsletter, and then move to

There's More

*There are other free and for-pay services that we haven't reviewed here. There's **CoolList**, for instance, at http://www.coollist.com/. And you can find more links at **Yahoo!'s Mailing List** page: http://dir.yahoo.com/Business_and_Economy/Companies/Computers/Communications_and_Networking/Software/Electronic_Mail/Mailing_Lists/.*

Upgrading Service

Another option in addition to going straight to a pay service is to go to the pay version of one of those services we listed above. But if you have a large newsletter—more than a few thousand subscribers—the "premium" offerings of services like ListBot and Web Site Post Office are going to get expensive very quickly. Services that are strictly pay services, described in the following section, are usually much less expensive for high-volume newsletters.

a pay service and seriously promote. If you decide you don't want to direct your energies into the newsletter, you can simply shut it down without having paid any money.

Pay Service Newsletters

If you want to control the advertising in your newsletter, or you want lots of administrative control—or if your newsletter is getting very big—you can't beat a pay service.

Lyris

> http://www.lyris.net/

We both use **Lyris** for our newsletters, and we're both happy with it. In fact Lyris may well be the best program available; many major newsletter publishers are working with this system.

Lyris gives you extensive control over the different messages your list sends out (the welcome message, goodbye message, etc.) and gives you very precise information about your list. You can view a list showing the number of subscribers who joined per day, for example. You can also merge each reader's name into each message (if you feel like using that much personalization). Lyris uses a simple subscribe/unsubscribe function that makes it very easy for people to unsubscribe even if they didn't bother to save the directions for doing so. Their tech support is quick and they're very good at unraveling problems. Lyris is stacked full of features, such as these:

Schedule messages to be sent at particular times.

Customize headers and footers that are automatically added to the message; place ads, announcements, subscription information, etc.

Customize welcome and good-bye messages so you can include information about your newsletter and your Web site, for instance.

Archive all the messages at the Lyris Web site, so visitors can search and view old messages or newsletters.

Produce detailed delivery reports, showing how many messages were sent out and when, and how many bounced back.

Carry out sophisticated "bounce" management. Tell the program how long it should accept bounce messages before putting a bad e-mail address into a "held" list; what message to send to held addresses and how often; when to purge held addresses if the address remains bad; and so on.

Carry out mail merge operations. You can incorporate the recipient's name into the message body. I could, if I wished (but I don't), start each of these newsletters with Dear John (or whatever a reader's name happens to be).

Provide sophisticated management tools. You can send messages to the server to carry out various commands, or use a Web form.

Display different types of subscriber lists, such as a list of all the "held" e-mail addresses, lists sorted by country code, lists sorted by name, and so on.

The people at Lyris have some other important features in the works:

Split runs: This feature will enable you to send half the subscribers one newsletter, and half another (so you can sell ads to people who can't afford a full run), or perhaps send one newsletter to all AOL addresses and one to all the rest (so you can send a newsletter formatted for AOL's e-mail program).

Circulation verification: Newsletter publishers need the ability to prove to advertisers how many subscribers they have. Pretty soon they will be able to, with verification reports coming directly from the Lyris server.

If you'd like to see exactly what Lyris can do, you can see the **Lyris User's Guide** at http://www.lyris.com/help/. It looks a bit daunting, but remember that most features are optional so you don't have to learn it all! If you want to buy software and run it on your own server, see http://www.lyris.com/. (You'll need somewhere between $500 and $8,000.)

On the other hand, you can pay monthly for the service (you can find information about using the **Lyris service** at http://www.lyris.net/). Lyris ain't cheap, though. They charge $1 per thousand messages, with a minimum of $50 in charges a month. (1,000 messages is 1 message to 1,000 people, or 10 messages to 100 people, or 500 messages to 2 people, etc.) Furthermore, those prices are based on an average message size of 4K—messages over 8K are charged an extra $1/thousand per 4K of message. If you have a small mailing list of a couple hundred people, the cost minimum will be very unattractive to you. However, if you have a large list, or even a small list that's daily instead of weekly or monthly, Lyris is more cost effective than the "premium" versions of the free lists.

There is another way to get the service, though; find a company that has bought the Lyris server and is selling the service. For instance, **Dundee Internet Services** (http://www.dundee.net/) sells Lyris at a much lower rate.

SparkLIST

http://www.sparklist.com/

SparkLIST also offers mailing list hosting services—both for discussion lists and newsletters—and a Web-based interface for managing the newsletter. They don't seem to offer as much micro-management as Lyris from the looks of their demo page, but they structure their prices differently—by member count rather than message count. The first level of service, for an announcement list with 1,000 members, costs $49 a month for three months. (You'll get a discount if you sign up for a longer stretch of service.) They list prices up to 100,000 users for $999 a month, and will give quotes for larger lists. There does not seem to be a limit on the number of messages that may be sent to a member list. SparkLIST also offers several different promotional packages to help get the word out about your newsletter.

L-Soft EASE

http://www.lsoft.com/

L-Soft EASE is produced by the same folks that brought the Internet Listserv, at one time the most popular mailing-list management software on the Internet. L-Soft offers several different kinds of services, but EASE is probably the one you want to look at. EASE offers several different kinds of services—EASE Business, EASE Bulk, or EASE Home.

Your Hosting Company

Before you take advantage of one of these services, you may want to check with your own Web-hosting company first. Some companies offer free mailing lists if you use their Web hosting service. However, these services are generally not as easy to use or as powerful as the services we're looking at here.

EASE Business—This is for smaller lists, those that have between 150 and 500 subscribers. Costs vary depending on how much technical support and L-Soft involvement you require—it ranges from $500 a year to over $3,000 a year. These lists can support 150 postings a day, so they're really more for discussion lists rather than newsletters.

EASE Bulk—EASE Bulk is for newsletters and other one-way services. EASE Bulk charges as if for a minimum of 1,000 users, so unless you plan to build up to that many readers quickly, you won't want to start with this service. EASE Bulk offers a wide variety of pricing options, depending on how many readers you have, how regularly you send out your newsletter, what time of day you want to send it out, and so forth.

EASE Home—If you're a non-commercial entity, you definitely want to check this service out. EASE Home supports very small lists—for 25 to 100 users—at really cheap prices. Twenty-five subscribers will run you $8 a month; 100 subscribers will run you $15 a month. (EASE Home lists will support up to 1,000 readers, but you'll need to contact L-Soft for a price quote.)

If you want to get information about L-Soft's software, **Listserv**, check out the software's Web site at http://www.lsoft.com/.

OakNet Publishing

http://www.oaknetpub.com/

OakNet offers list hosting with a little twist. They offer newsletter distribution accounts that can work with up to 10,000 subscribers. The newsletter may be sent no more than once a week. This costs $25 a month and OakNet Publishing will place advertising in your newsletter. They do offer another plan, though. Once your newsletter has over 3,000 subscribers, OakNet Publishing will act as a newsletter-advertising broker. They'll sell advertising for your mailing list (they'll work with you to set a price) and they'll keep one-third of the revenue or $20, whichever is greater. They will not place an ad in your newsletter that you don't want; you have the right of veto. If you don't anticipate your list ever getting over 10,000 subscribers and you want to phase into selling advertising, this service could be a good option for you. It doesn't provide options for daily or high-volume (over 10,000) subscribers, however, and it doesn't offer as much micro-management as Lyris.

If you're a non-commercial or non-profit organization, or you plan to run a really small newsletter, free services (or "premium" free services) are probably the best idea for you economically. There's no point in footing a minimum pay charge for a list that only has 50 subscribers. (In fact, a list with only 50 subscribers is probably small enough for you to manage yourself.) If you want to make money off advertising or send out very high volumes of e-mail, check out a paid service.

What do you want once you've got content and a distribution mechanism? You want readers, of course! And to get readers you need to promote your newsletter. We'll look at that next.

Publicizing Your Newsletter

There are lots of places you can go to publicize your newsletter:

ETEXT Archives (A huge repository of zine and newsletter information; if you need a place to archive your newsletter, check this out.)
http://www.etext.org/Zines/

E-Zine Ad Source (If you plan to sell advertising make sure you're listed here. It's free, but they ask that you run a small ad for their service twice a year.)
http://www.ezineadsource.com/

E-ZineZ (A search engine and searchable subject index just for e-zines)
http://www.e-zinez.com/

InfoBot.net (A zine subject index)
http://www.infobot.net/

John Labovitz's E-Zine List (This should be one of your first stops to register your newsletter. It's one of the best-known zine sites on the Web, with over 3,000 zines.)
http://www.meer.net/~johnl/e-zine-list/

Liszt (Lists over 90,000 discussion groups and newsletters)
http://www.liszt.com/

Low Bandwidth
http://www.disobey.com/low/

NewJour (An e-mail publication carrying announcements about online publications)
http://gort.ucsd.edu/newjour/

NEW-LIST (Another publication dedicated to announcing new newsletters. It's got some of the same restrictions as Net-Happenings—see Chapter 8—so pay attention.)
http://scout.cs.wisc.edu/scout/new-list/

Newsletter Access (Paper and electronic newsletters. You can add a little information for free or a full listing for $19.95 a year.) http://www.newsletteraccess.com/

Newsletter Library (Currently lists over 11,000 newsletters. Free samples of any are available. Cost to be listed in this resource is $50.) http://pub.savvy.com/

There are more, many more. Peter has a special report called *Places to Register Your E-mail Newsletter*, which you can find at http://www.poorrichard.com/freeinfo/special_reports.htm. The report currently lists over 48 useful sites.

Search Engines

If you have a Web site associated with your newsletter, don't forget to register it with the search engines; see Chapter 6.

Finding Readers

Though you can do a lot to simply promote your newsletter—make sure it's in all the newsletter search engines and subject indexes, run an announcement in Net-Announce, and so on—you can also do a lot to court readers themselves. Perhaps the single most important thing you can do is to put a form at your Web site in which people can subscribe to the newsletter. If you're working with one of the for-pay or freebie services we talked about, you'll be given a form that you can incorporate into your Web site. Otherwise you'll have to create a form using a CGI script or perhaps the form tools in MS FrontPage, if you're using that tool.

Send your newsletter to a few of your friends and ask for their reaction. (Send each sample copy to each person individually and let him or her know why you think they'd like the newsletter.)

Make it as easy as possible for someone to subscribe to the newsletter. Most of the services we've

Where Will You Put the Form?

Newsletter publishers often put introductory information about their newsletter at the "front" of the site, and lead people to a subscription page. You may find you get more subscriptions if you put that page right up front. Randy Cassingham, publisher of the **This Is True** *humor newsletter (http://www.ThisIsTrue.com/), told us that his subscription rate tripled after moving the subscription form up front. So make the form obvious and easy to get to. In fact, consider putting it on several pages at your Web site.*

described above will give you some HTML code to put on your Web page. The code usually creates a small form in which readers can enter their e-mail addresses and click a button, which will sign them up for the newsletter. Some mailing list services use an authentication process, which means that the new subscriber will get a validation letter that they'll have to return before they're signed up for the newsletter. (The authentication process is so people can't be signed up for newsletters or mailing lists without their consent.)

However, there's a problem with this. If you set up your mailing list so that the person has to confirm receipt, then you'll lose 15-20 percent of all your subscribers—that is, somewhere between one in seven and one in five will not confirm the subscription. Some publishers set up the system so that a confirmation letter is sent, but no reply is required in order to complete the process. This way you won't lose so many subscribers, yet the subscriber has received a notification, so if he's been subscribed by someone else (which is actually relatively rare) he can quickly remove himself from the list. (The ability to play games like this, configuring your system in different ways, is one of the big advantages of working with a system such as Lyris.)

Make it very clear what your policies are. When Tara moved her newsletter to Lyris and began promoting it, she didn't make it clear on her sign-up page that she would never rent or sell the list of subscribers to her newsletter. To her, it was a no-brainer—of course she wouldn't do anything like that. But enough people e-mailed her and asked if she was going to rent or sell her mailing list that she appended a privacy disclaimer to her Web page. Then she started getting e-mail asking if her newsletter was free. That was another no-brainer to her. So she added the word *free* to her Web page.

Are you making any assumptions about your newsletter policy? Have you made it crystal clear how much it costs, what its frequency is, what its copyright statement is, and how you will treat the aggregated list of e-mail addresses? Don't get blindsided by a no-brainer.

Make it easy to spread the word. Your newsletter should always have a copyright statement, though under current copyright law, copyright does not have to be explicitly stated. Copyright is secured automatically as soon as the work is created. (For more information on this, visit the **US Copyright Office** and check out their copyright primer: http://lcweb.loc.gov/copyright/circs/circ1. html.) However, stating an explicit copyright allows you to grant certain rights. For example, you might want people to feel free to pass your newsletter along via e-mail, but you don't want them to use it as part of a book or include it in a CD-ROM. You could issue a copyright disclaimer like this:

```
The example newsletter is copyright 1999 by so-and-
so. All rights reserved. Feel free to forward this
newsletter to others as long as you forward it in
its entirety and leave this notice. This newsletter
may not be included in any compilation, electronic
or printed, or as part of any commercial endeavor
without written permission.
```

That's all you have to say. If you want to attach very specific details—like granting reprint permission for single articles, or excerpt information—create a Web page for your details and include the page's URL in the copyright disclaimer.

This copyright disclaimer does a couple of things. First, the disclaimer makes it very clear to your readers what they can and cannot do with the newsletter (and perhaps helps them feel free to pass it on to other interested potential subscribers). Second, if someone does perhaps do something inappropriate with your material, they can't claim ignorance of your wishes; you made it very clear how your material was to be used.

Give Them Plenty of Opportunities

Give visitors to your Web site plenty of opportunities to subscribe to your newsletter. For instance, if you sell a product at your Web site, include option buttons on the order form that allow people to sign up for your newsletter. Peter does this on all his forms, and sets the option buttons to Yes. People filling out the forms can change the setting to No, of course, but only five percent do. If people are interested enough to place an order or fill in some kind of response form, chances are they're interested enough to get your newsletter, too.

Spread the word yourself. When you mention another mailing list, Web site, or other Internet resource in your newsletter, be sure to let them know what you're doing and send them a copy of your newsletter. The owners may find it interesting enough that they subscribe. Better, they might find it interesting enough that they mention your newsletter or link to it from their Web sites.

Keeping the Momentum Going

When you first start your newsletter, you probably won't lack for ideas. After all, you wouldn't have started the newsletter unless you had a good idea of what you wanted to write about. But as time goes by, you might find that the well's running a little dry and you're finding it hard to fill a newsletter. Don't wait until you're completely out of ideas; anticipate the problem and answer it before it threatens the existence of your newsletter.

Recruit your readers. From your very first issue, ask your readers for feedback. Ask them for ideas. Ask them what they want to learn from your newsletter. You can't keep up with the Internet all by yourself, but if you get a couple thousand readers who know what you're interested in, you're well on your way to making the most of the Internet.

Pay attention to your company communications. Pay attention to what's going on with your corporate structure. What are callers to technical support asking about? What features arc sales prospects after? You might also want to pay attention to what's being said about your products and services on the Web and USENET, and build articles around exploring strengths and answering criticisms of your product.

Trade writing for promotions. Sometimes you might find someone whose interests dovetail the topic of your newsletter, but who does not compete with you. Once the circulation of your newsletter is high enough, you could approach someone like this with the idea that they provide you with a certain amount of material—like a column a month or a certain statistic every week—in exchange for a certain amount of promotional consideration. The only potential problem with something like this is that you've got to coordinate with this person on a regular basis and make sure they make your deadlines. Try to get a lot of material in advance if possible.

Selling Advertising

One way to offset the cost of your newsletter is to sell advertising. In fact one way to make a living is to sell advertising; a number of newsletter publishers make a good living from their newsletters. Some e-mail newsletters may be bringing in hundreds of thousands of dollars a year. These levels are rare ... but partly because this is such a new game that few people know how to play it right.

How many subscribers you need in order to sell advertising depends a lot on how specific your newsletter is. If you have a rare-book restoration service and your newsletter is read by 500 rare-book sellers, then you've got a highly-targeted audience and something you can easily sell to potential advertisers. On the other hand, if your newsletter has 5,000 subscribers and it's about "cool stuff on the Net," you probably have a more vague demographic which would be less valuable for potential advertisers.

If you do have enough subscribers to take a mailing list, check out the competition. How much are they charging? (If you have a targeted demographic, you can charge more than if your newsletter is general interest.) We've seen advertising rates varying from a cpm of 45 cents to a cpm of $40.

When you've got an idea of how much you can charge, consider whether it's worth your time. You might be someone who can keep track of ads, work with prospects and sell advertising spots, keep track of who's paid what, and pester those folks who have problems with their payment. If so, then it might be worth your time. But if merely thinking about all those chores makes you itch, you might want to bypass advertising entirely or take on an agreement like OakNet Publishing's—or find an advertising broker of some kind.

---

cpm

cpm *means "cost per thousand" (the m coming from the Roman numeral for 1,000). Newsletter publishers who know what they're doing sell advertising according to a cpm of some kind (publishers who don't know what they're doing often publish flat rates without even explaining how many subscribers they have, so you don't know what you're getting for your money).*

For instance, a cpm of $30 means "for every one thousand e-mail messages in which your add appears, you'll pay us $30." Thus if the list has 10,000 subscribers, the ad costs $300 ($30 x 10).

Another option, if you don't want to formally sell advertising, is to swap ads with Web sites and other newsletter publishers. This helps publicize your Web site and your newsletter without you having to spend money on advertising and without you having to keep up with a lot of accounting. **List City**, at http://list-city.com/, maintains a list of e-zine publishers who are interested in exchanging advertising.

DISCUSSION GROUPS

Newsletters can be difficult to create because you have to come up with all that "content"—the *stuff* that goes into the newsletter. It takes one person, or a team of people, to produce a set amount of content on a regular schedule. It's hard enough to do that in itself, but when you're doing it as a sideline, or to promote the thing you're truly interested in, it becomes even more difficult.

As we said earlier in the chapter, newsletters are one-to-many. You create the content, and send it to everyone on your list. But there's a way to cheat. Why not let someone else create the content for you? You can do that by setting up a discussion group based on the e-mail system; all the services we looked at earlier can be used to do this. With a discussion group the people involved in the discussion are, in effect, providing the content. (Though you could also publish small, occasional articles as part of a discussion list.) But in some ways discussion lists can take as much time as creating a newsletter, and the content is sometimes not as good.

E-mail discussion groups—or discussion lists, as they're often known—are "free-for-all" conversations. Everybody can talk to everybody. Discussion lists come in a couple of flavors.

Discussion lists that are *unmoderated* have no restrictions on how posts can be made to the list. If a member posts something, it goes to all the members of the list immediately. There are also *moderated* mailing lists. Postings to a moderated mailing list go to the list moderator (there may be just one or more than one) who must approve the messages before they can go to the rest of the list. Messages that aren't approved are deleted so that most list members never see them.

Between these two extremes there are several different degrees of list control—for example, a mailing list may not be formally moderated but the list owner may exert a high degree of control over what kind of topics might be discussed on a list. (If you're concerned about your moderation skills, information moderation is the best way to go; everyone sees the posts and can see for themselves how off-topic they are.)

The smaller the discussion group, the less difficult it is to control. Smaller groups seem to be cozier, and peer pressure seems to make people behave. Once you get more than a hundred people, however, you have to watch out for fighting, harsh words, straying way off the topic, and so on. (On the other hand, it's also possible for a list to be *too* small; there's a point at which there are not enough people on the list to keep the list going, so if it's too small it may just die.)

Remember Copyright

Be sure if you add newsletter-type content to a discussion list—like articles and newsbriefs and such—that you attach copyright disclaimers to it. You want to protect individual articles as much as you'd want to protect an entire newsletter, but at the same time you want readers to know they can forward articles if you want them to.

Moderation

Some people view moderated lists as too controlling and restrictive of freedom of speech. Some others view moderated lists as a reasonable way to control excessive amounts of traffic and keep a list of traffic. If you choose to moderate a mailing list, you have to be careful of how you moderate and how objectively you evaluate contributions to your mailing list. You want your moderation to be considered fair and evenhanded.

Some of this you won't be able to avoid. Tara actually thinks it's healthy to stray a little off-topic; it helps keep the list fresh. (Without going off-topic a little, mailing lists can fall into a rut of covering the same topics over and over again.) But sometimes discussions can get quite ugly—fighting and wars of words are not healthy and not something you want to happen under the aegis of your discussion group.

Whether you choose to formally moderate a list or not (and if you're creating a list for support of your product or service, we do recommend that you impose some sort of moderation, formal or informal), you will have to keep up with reading your own list. It's like an ongoing editorial

Who's Responsible?

Remember, if you sponsor a discussion group or mailing list, everything that happens on that mailing list may appear to reflect on your company, for better or for worse. You'll want to make it clear that you are providing the forum, but are not responsible for everything that is said. Also, there's a danger to moderating a group. If you are clearly moderating the group, you may become legally liable for things that are being said in the group. By taking up the position of moderator you are, in effect, screening out "the bad stuff." So if someone doesn't like what's being said, he can claim that you are partly responsible.

process—there's all this content coming and you need to make sure it stays appropriate, focused, and on topic. The more you work to maintain the quality of that content, the better and more valuable the list will be. If you do not have that kind of time to invest, an out-of-control discussion group can reflect poorly on you and your company.

Discussion groups can, properly administered, be a very powerful promotional tool. David Rogelberg, founder of Studio B (a company providing services to the computer-book business), says that the single most important promotional technique he used to build his business was the **Studio B discussion group** (http://www.studiob.com/).

You can set up discussion groups via e-mail with many of the lists we covered earlier in this chapter—the ones that also handle newsletter lists. For that reason we won't rehash that list of resources.

WEB FORUMS

You can also set up discussion lists on the Web, using what are often known as *Bulletin Boards* or *Web forums*. A Web-based discussion list may be useful if you do a lot of updating, expect your board to be very busy, or have periodic events or product releases that would lead to a lot of activity at one time. (For example, suppose you have a mailing list that covers Christmas ornaments and is only really busy three months of the year. It's hard to promote it, and it's hard to justify paying a mailing list pay service a minimum usage fee that your mailing list won't even use two-thirds of the time.) However, there's a big problem with Web forums: you have to rely on people visiting your site in order to take part in the discussion. This will greatly reduce the number of people who are likely to be involved over the long term; it's just way too easy to slip out of the group. With mailing-list groups, however, the information goes to each subscriber—the subscriber doesn't have to take time out to go get the information.

Everything we said about maintaining a good flow of content on a mailing list goes double for a bulletin board. In addition to maintaining order on the board, you also have to maintain a steady list of postings. Nothing is more disheartening than going to a bulletin board and seeing there have been no postings on it for two or three months. You'll need to fight off spammers who plaster your list with XXX advertisements and get-rich-quick schemes, too.

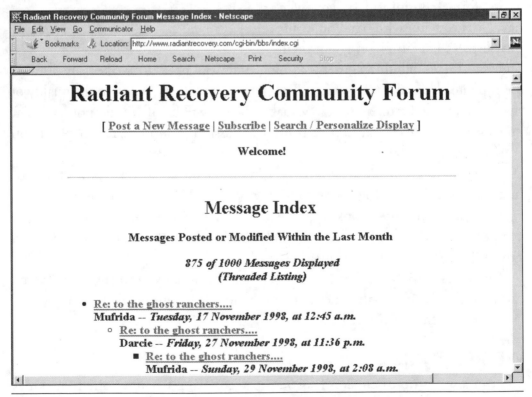

FIGURE 11.4: This Web forum is used to promote a book.

There are several places where you can get a free online bulletin board.

Inside the Web

http://www.insidetheweb.com/

Inside the Web hosts your discussion board on their Web site for free. They offer options for moderated and unmoderated message sites. Moderated sites have messages that stay on the board until you delete them, while unmoderated boards have message

Using CGI

*The resources listed below are places you can get a free discussion board for your Web site without having to mess with CGI (Common Gateway Interface) scripts or server-side programming. If you like messing with CGI, however, check out the **CGI Resource Index:** http://www.cgiresources. com/Programs_and_Scripts/Remote ly_Hosted/Bulletin_Board_Message_ Systems/.*

expiration times that you can set between 0 and 999 days. (We recommend you don't let messages stay on the board for more than a couple of months, unless you're very comfortable that the information on the bulletin board won't get stale.) They offer a hit counter to track how many people are coming to your bulletin board. Inside the Web notes that spammers are getting clever in invading online bulletin boards and state that they're trying to figure out how to stop it. If your board is inactive for 45 days it will automatically be deleted.

Netbabbler

http://forums.netbabbler.com/

Netbabbler is another free forum service. They make money from the forums by putting an advertising banner at the top of the site. For about $25 a year you can upgrade to the premium version of the service, which removes the banner. Netbabbler requires you to register in order to use their service. Once you've registered (they ask only for your e-mail address), you're asked to give a name and description to your new forum. Netbabbler will automatically create your forum and give you a URL to link to for access to your forum. Once you've created the forum, you've got a lot of control over it. You can block users based on IP (Internet Protocol) address, change the table forum (you have several different options for displaying messages), turn censors on and off, and change the "escape link" to get back to the Web site from the bulletin board. NetBabbler struck us as the best option for a beginner.

YourBBS.com

http://www.yourbbs.com/

YourBBS is another advertiser-supported free bulletin board service. It's got lots of options, including requiring users to enable cookies before they can post, removing HTML from posts, banning certain IP addresses, password-protecting your BBS (so that users have to enter a password before they can post), and setting up different templates. Be sure you have your Web browser's cookies enabled before you try to use this service.

By using mailing lists and discussion groups, you're taking content beyond the Web and into mailboxes (or onto dynamic Web pages, if you're hosting discussion groups on a Web page). While discussion groups allow users to generate lots of content, you've got to stay vigilant; making sure content stays on topic and is useful to the readership of a discussion group makes your discussion group or newsletter very valuable. Similarly, giving away plenty of information and helping your readers solve problems makes your newsletter a very valuable property. Trumpeting about your great sales and bragging about yourself does not.

You Need This Book!

Publishing using e-mail is quite a new thing; the vast majority of all e-mail publications, over 99 percent, are less than three years old. (Peter just made up that statistic, so it's fresh; feel free to use it if you wish. It's almost certainly correct, though he can't prove it.) There's a lot to learn, much more than we can cover in one chapter. So if this is an area you're interested in, look for Poor Richard's Email Publishing: Newsletters, Bulletins, Discussion Groups and Other Powerful Communications Tools *(ISBN: 0-9661032-5-4), which will be published by Top Floor Publishing in June of 1999.*

*This book will include a chapter by someone who owns a four-year old humor e-mail newsletter that goes to 175,000 people; a chapter by the owner of a literary agency who used a mailing-list discussion group to build his business; and a chapter by Peter, who built his e-mail newsletter (**Poor Richard's Web Site News:** http://PoorRichard.com/newsltr/) up to 15,000 subscribers in one year.*

CHAPTER TWELVE

Advertising Your Site

Here's another of those good-news-bad-news things that we seem to run into so often. We'll start with the bad news. The bad news is that much of what you may have heard about advertising on the Internet is completely wrong. Advertising, contrary to the claims of many pundits (and, of course, of the companies selling advertising), is *not* a sure-fire affordable way to bring people to your site. Yes, you'll bring people to your site, but can you afford what it's going to cost per visit? In many cases the answer is No. We'll come to that in a minute.

The good news, though, is that advertising *can* work, if you don't pay too much attention to people pushing banner ads. The real advertising bargains are often elsewhere. We're not saying that banner ads never work, nor that you should stay away from banner ads completely. We're just saying that if you decide to try banner advertising you should enter into the process with your eyes wide open—and with just a little skepticism to guide you along the way.

WHAT'S CPM?

Before we get started, let's just clarify a little terminology. Advertising prices are generally stated according to a *cpm*—cost per thousand. (Why *m* for thousand?; M is the Roman numeral for 1,000.) This isn't just an Internet thing; it's an advertising thing.

A *cost per thousand* what? Generally a cost per thousand "impressions." An impression may be one of several things. If we're talking about banner ads, then 1,000 impressions means that the banner ad is loaded into Web pages 1,000 times. That doesn't mean that the ad was seen 1,000 times, though. The visitor to that page may not look at that particular ad; and in fact the ad may even be at the bottom of the page, "below the fold," as it's known—invisible to the viewer unless he chooses to scroll down the page. (For this reason banner ad placement is important, and "above the fold" ads generally sell at a higher price.)

If we're talking about e-mail advertising, 1,000 impressions means that the ad is placed into 1,000 e-mail messages. Again, that doesn't mean that 1,000 people read the ad. Many recipients may simply delete the message without opening it. On the other hand, newsletters are often forwarded to the recipients' friends and colleagues. That's why a really good newsletter, one with a very loyal readership, is more valuable than some piece of badly written garbage thrown together to act as an advertising vehicle.

Here are a few more important terms you should understand:

Click through or clickthru: When someone clicks on a banner ad, or a link in an e-mail ad, in order to visit your Web site, that's a *click through,* also known as a *clickthru.* Note that a click through is not always the same as a visit to your Web site; while people clicking through may intend to visit, a proportion will change their minds and cancel before or soon after your first page loads.

Click-through rate: The *click-through rate* is the percentage of people viewing your ad who click through.

Targeted and untargeted: A *targeted* ad is one that is displayed to people who are probably interested in your product. An *untargeted* ad is one that is shown to a group of people whom you have no reason to believe want your product. These terms are relative, of course, and the targeting of ads is often very imprecise.

By the way, there's a myth that targeted ads are always more effective than untargeted ads. "All things being equal," this would be true. Show the same ad, at the same cpm, to a targeted list, and you'll do better than showing it to an untargeted list. (If you don't, it simply means that the list you thought was targeted actually *wasn't.*) But things are never equal; you'll pay more for a targeted list. In fact, you may pay so much more that even though you'll pull more sales, you won't cover your costs. So when you're talking with advertising salespeople, take what they say with a pinch of salt. Buying a targeted list may be a good idea ... *if* it's the right price. Also, remember that it's difficult to compare an untargeted ad in one medium with a targeted ad in another. In other words, an untargeted ad in one medium may actually be far more effective than a targeted ad in another.

BANNER SWAPS

The easiest way to get into the advertising business is by swapping ads. Don't worry—this won't take a lot of time. It's remarkably easy to do using a number of automated swap systems. Here's how it works. You go to one of the banner-swap sites and sign up for the service. You then take a little bit of HTML and insert it into one or more of your Web pages. This HTML uses the <IMG> tag to insert an image—the banner—into your Web page, and pulls the image from the banner-exchange site. The banner-exchange site sends a different banner each time, and has a program that keeps track of how many times your site pulls in a banner. This record is used to keep track of your credits and to assign your banner to other sites according to how many credits you accrue. Some services provide free credits when you sign up, so your ad starts displaying on other sites right away.

You have to have a banner, of course. This is generally a standard size; it's usually 468 pixels wide by 60 pixels high, though there are a few other formats used now and then. They have to be a particular file size, too, generally 10 Kbytes or less.

Some of these banner-swap systems sell advertising; that's how they make their money. In other words, you get your ad shown for free but you don't get equal time. Generally, your ad will be shown once for every two times that someone visiting your site sees an ad from the banner exchange. The banner displays that aren't given away are used by the exchange itself to advertise its services, or are sold.

Creating Banners

The banner's file size is determined by color depth—the number of colors in the art's palette. There are many services that will create low-cost, or even free, banners for you. Search for the words banner design at a search site.

Some of the services allow you to specify, to a limited degree, where your banner will be shown, so you can target your advertising. Others accept only certain types of banner ads to make sure you don't get inappropriate advertising at your site. Some even allow you to pick whom you will swap with; they provide a way for people wanting to swap to meet and arrange to swap.

Another service provided by these banner-swap sites—and a very important one—is statistic reports. You'll be able to find out how often you displayed an ad and how often your ad was displayed. This information is important because it can help you decide how effective the service is.

Check out these sites for more information about banner exchanges:

1-2-Free Banner Exchange
http://www.1-2-free.com/

Amiga Web Network
http://www.amicrawler.com/search2/amicrawler/banners/

BannerAd
http://businesspark.ipgnet.com/bannerad/

BannerSwap
http://www.bannerswap.com/

Cyber Link Exchange 2000
http://cyberlinkexchange.usww.com/

Do the Wave
http://DoTheWave.com/

Internet BannerExchange
http://www.bannerexchange.com/

Link Exchange
http://www.linkexchange.com/

NarrowCast Media
http://www.narrowcastmedia.com/

NetAdNet
http://www.netadnet.com/

NetOn's Banner Exchange
http://www.net-on.se:81/banner/

PostMaster Banner Network
http://www.PostMasterBannerNet.com/

Web Site Banner Advertising (A large list of banner-swap programs, including a number of European programs)
http://www.markwelch.com/bannerad/

WPRC Banner Exchanges (A list of banner-swap systems)
http://www.wprc.com/pldb/wprcpldb.shtml

Yahoo!—Banner Exchanges
http://dir.yahoo.com/Computers_and_Internet/Internet/World_Wide_
Web/Announcement_Services/Banner_Exchanges/

What's the advantage of using a banner-swap system? You get your banner posted on other sites, for free. The disadvantages? There are two main disadvantages. First, you'll probably have a limited choice in where and when your ad appears. And if your site is not very busy, your ad is not going to be placed on many sites. You're swapping placements, remember, so if you don't display many ads from the banner exchange, you won't get much in return.

PAYING FOR YOUR BANNER ADS

The other way to place banner ads is by paying for them. There are plenty of companies willing to take your money and place your ads for you. In fact once you have a banner ready to place, and you're signed up with a banner-advertising network, you can be running ads within a few minutes.

But is buying ads a good idea? There's a general principle in the PR business that money spent on PR is more effective than money spent on advertising, so you may want to forget about advertising, and think a little more about the public-relations methods that you can use to promote your site.

Obviously public-relations people are biased towards PR, but they're probably quite correct; remember, the most effective promotional claims are those that appear to come from people not directly affiliated with your company. Everyone knows advertising is biased toward the person paying for the advertising, whereas reviews and feature stories in the press are generally trusted. And using the techniques discussed elsewhere in this book you can get your products and services mentioned, for very little cost, in media spots that would cost hundreds of thousands of dollars if you had to buy the equivalent advertising.

Still, if your company budget can bear the burden, you might want to experiment with a little banner advertising. One of the best ways to experiment is using **Flycast** (http://www.flycast.com/). This company provides you with a program, which you run on your computer, to select where your ad will run. You pick the banner you want to use, select the actual Web sites on which the ads will run—or select a low-cost *run of the network* option, which means Flycast places your ad wherever it has space unsold—enter how much money you want to spend, click a button, and away it all goes. It's easy to get started, and also easy to see results. It's really quite fun, almost like a form of gambling. You can begin watching the results as soon as the first banner is placed; you'll see how much you've spent so far, how many click throughs the banner is getting, and even the cost per click through.

How Much Does It Cost?

Banner ads vary greatly in price, from a cpm of around $5 to $60 and up. You may occasionally hear of rates as high as $150 a thousand, though that's probably quite rare. Yahoo!, for instance, charges $1,000 for a one-week placement on its Web Launch page. This page contains just six ads in total, and each ad also appears in a banner that appears on the various Yahoo! category pages. Yahoo! guarantees that each ad will be seen by at least 120,000 people during the week, so that's a cpm of just $8.33, perhaps less. However, the Web Launch banners are not targeted—they appear in all areas of Yahoo!—and each ad gets one third of a banner, hence the low cpm.

If you want to put a banner ad of your own at Yahoo! and have it appear even in targeted categories, you'll be charged for each impression (that is, each time someone sees the page). Rates vary from 1.5 cents per impression ($15 cpm) to 6 cents per impression ($60 cpm) depending on the type of service. You can provide keywords for some of the service levels so that when someone searches for a particular word, your ad will appear. You can also target regions, through Yahoo!'s regional pages, and demographic groups—kids or women, for instance. Other major search engines have comparable prices.

By the way, these keyword banners may be a good deal, and can have fairly high click-through rates. If someone enters a keyword, and then almost immediately sees your banner, there's a good chance he'll click it. Jim Daniels, writing in an article that ran in Peter's newsletter recently (*Poor Richard's Web Site News*), says that he got an 8 percent click-through rate using the keywords "home business," "business opportunities," and "online marketing."

If you want to look into banner advertising, try some of these places:

24/7 Media
http://www.247media.com/

Ad.Up
http://www.ad-up.com/

AdCentral
http://www.adcentral.com/

ADSmart
http://www.adsmart.net/

BURST! Media
http://www.burstmedia.com/

DoubleClick
http://www.doubleclick.net/

Public-Service Announcement Banner Ads for Nonprofits
http://www.markwelch.com/bannerad/baf_psa_bann.htm

ValueClick

http://www.valueclick.com/

WAB Directory

http://www.wab.co.uk/

Yahoo!-Advertising on the Web

http://www.yahoo.com/Computers_and_Internet/Internet/Business_
and_Economics/Advertising_on_Web_and_Internet/

Banner Advertising May Not Work

Be careful about some of the advice you hear on the Internet; a number of
Internet publications have suggested, over the last year or so, that banner advertising is good, easy, and effective, and that every business should be involved. This
is simply untrue, and generally the conclusion of journalists who have investigated
banner advertising but never actually paid for a banner-advertising campaign.

What the truth is, there's a good chance that banner advertising won't work for
you. We've heard that banner ads are often quite effective for Web-hosting
companies. If you're charging, say, a $50 initial setup fee and $30 a month, and
you expect someone who signs up for an account to stay with you for perhaps 18
months, then each sale is worth $590. If you sell ancillary products and services,
too—design services, upgrade hosting services, and so on—then your income per
sale may be much more. In such a case banner advertising may be very effective.

What if you're selling a $20 or $30 product, though? Ah, well, it depends what
game you're playing. A number of large businesses, companies such as
Amazon.com and CDnow, are playing a "grab as much cyberspace real-estate as
quickly as possible" game. Advertising doesn't have to lead to profits right away for
them—as long as it leads to regular customers who, perhaps, will be profitable
over the long term. You can play this game only if you have a lot of money to play
it with, and are prepared to lose money for several years. (As Jim Bezos, the President of Amazon.com, has said, if Amazon.com turns a profit any time soon, it'll
be a miracle.) But what about the average small business? A business that has to
turn a profit, and can't afford to lose money this month, let alone for several years?
In that case, banner advertising is probably not a good way to sell a low-cost item.

Before you jump into an expensive banner-ad program, run all the
numbers—see what sort of click through you'll need in order to break even, and
if possible do a small test. And don't believe a salesperson who tells you that in
order to test properly you need to spend a minimum of $5,000, as one recently

told Peter. This ignores basic rules of statistics; you can get a damn good idea of your possibility of success with a *much* smaller sample than 100,000 impressions!

Here's a quick rule of thumb. Assume that one impression in five or ten thousand leads to a sale, and then figure out how much those impressions will cost you. One in five to ten thousand is a pretty common range for this sort of thing. Yahoo! claims an average click-through rate of 2 percent, while ZDNet claims click-through rates as high as 5 percent at its site. The **Web Site Promoter's Resource Center** (http://www.wprc.com/) claims an industry average of 3 percent. Not too long ago I/PRO Research and DoubleClick stated that an industry average click-through rate was 2.11 percent. But other research suggests that rates may be much lower, perhaps under 1 percent.

So let's say one or two people in 100 who see your ad will click on it to visit your site, and one in 100 visiting your site will buy something; that's one impression in five or ten thousand leading to a sale. (Your numbers may be better; but then, they may be worse.) Can't make money with one in five or ten thousand at the cpm you've just been quoted for a banner ad? Then there's a good chance the banner-ad campaign won't work for you, unless you've got good reason to believe you can get significantly more people clicking on the banner, and convert more of them to sales.

E-MAIL ADVERTISING

There's another important form of advertising, one that is too often ignored, one that presents the shoe-string marketer with a way to buy effective advertising at a low cost. And that's e-mail advertising.

We're not talking about spam. We're talking about advertising to people who have signed up to receive e-mail for some reason. There are essentially two types of e-mail advertising. The first is to advertise using "opt-in" lists. These are lists of people who have signed up to receive advertising. Some people sign up for "I'll scratch your back, you scratch mine" plans. In other words, they agree to receive e-mail in return for something else. For instance, a company may hold regular drawings, giving away computers to the winners. In order to be included in the drawing, you have to be on one of their mailing lists. Of course, the problem with this sort of list is that the people who sign up may have no interest at all in receiving the e-mail, and may delete it without reading it. All they want is the chance to win a prize.

The other reason people sign up for opt-in e-mail is because they have a genuine interest in getting information. For instance, hundreds of thousands of people who are trying to learn how to do business on the Internet have signed up to receive e-mail about doing business on the Internet, in the hope that some of the mail will lead them to information and services that will help them.

The other form of advertising is in e-mail newsletters (which we discussed in Chapter 11). In this case people have subscribed to a news-

---

Create a Doorway Page

When you advertise in e-mail, you should create a doorway page so you can measure the amount of traffic coming to your site in response to the ad. See Chapter 14 for more information.

---

letter and, if it's a good one, continue to receive it because they find it useful or entertaining. The newsletter has ads embedded into it. If it's a plain-text newsletter, then the ads are just text ads—generally six or seven lines, about 65 characters wide. If the newsletter is an HTML-mail newsletter, the ads will be banner ads.

There are a number of companies selling opt-in lists; you'll find lists targeted at about any group you can imagine, from antique collectors to writers. Here are a few places you'll find opt-in lists:

BulletMail
> http://www.bulletmail.com/

Business Link (600,000 business e-mail addresses at a very low cost; $59 for a small ad to the entire list, $1,095 for a large ad)
> http://www.businesslink.net/

DEMC (A 300,000 subscriber list—private mailings to the entire list for $477)
> http://www.demc.com/

Direct E-Mail List Source (A list of companies with opt-in e-mail lists, electronic newsletters carrying ads, "sponsorable" discussion groups and so on; a very useful site)
> http://www.copywriter.com/lists/

Direct Marketing Online
> http://www.directmarketing-online.com/services/opt-in.htm

Intellipost
> http://www.intellipost.com/

PostMaster Direct (One of the largest and best-known opt-in companies)
> http://www.postmasterdirect.com/

WebPromote
> http://www.webpromote.com/de/

Yahoo!—Direct E-mail
http://www.yahoo.com/Business_and_Economy/Companies/Marketing/
   Direct_Marketing/Direct_Email/

Some services charge by response rather than by recipient. In other words, instead of charging you, say, 15 cents for everyone who receives your message, they'll charge you perhaps 50 cents for everyone who visits your Web site as a result of your e-mail message. Negotiate with these people, and see if you can get a lower rate.

To find newsletters to advertise in, see these directories:

Direct E-mail List Source
   http://www.copywriter.com/lists/
E-Zine Ad Source Directory
   http://www.ezineadsource.com/
Internet Marketing Services—E-Zine Ad Directory
   http://foxcities.com/ims/ezine.htm
Lifestyles
   http://www.lifestylespub.com/
MeMail
   http://www.memail.com/
Places to Register Your Email Newsletter special report
   http://www.poorrichard.com/freeinfo/special_reports.htm

What Works, What Doesn't

Peter has tried a number of e-mail advertising systems, some of which worked and some of which didn't. Here's a comparison of two types, an opt-in list and a newsletter:

PostMaster Direct
   http://www.postmasterdirect.com/
Joke of the Day
   http://www.joker.org/

PostMaster Direct

PostMaster Direct is a company that sells many thousands of names, in hundreds of different lists, from lists for animal lovers to woodworkers and writers. Peter mailed to around 2,000 people for $300—15 cents per person. He sold a grand total of one book, and received not much more than 200 visitors to his site. Post-Master Direct later offered him a per-order campaign; that is, they'd provide him with orders, and he'd pay a fee per order. But it turned out that they thought he was going to sell the book on a billing basis; the book would be sent to customers free, then they'd receive a series of bills later, so they could make three payments or so. (PostMaster Direct works with Rodale Press, which sells books in this manner.)

They also told him that it's very difficult to get people to buy something outright using e mail, and when they discovered that was just what he wanted to do, they declined to carry out a per-order campaign.

Joke of the Day

The Joke of the Day mailing list is, not surprisingly, a list that transmits a joke to each—all 150,000 of them, reportedly—every day. Each joke is "sponsored" by a single advertiser; the ad comprises a few lines of text above the joke.

Now, the nice thing about Joke e-mail is that this is mail that people actually read. Jokes ... well, isn't that why the Internet was invented? To save fax paper? People really do read joke e-mail. They subscribe to joke mailing lists because they want that humor fix. And they open and read the e-mail because they want a laugh. And—this is really important from our point of view—if they think the joke is funny, they send it on to their friends. Often to many of their friends. With luck they simply click on the Forward button, and away it goes ... with the ad still in place. So although a joke list may be sent out to 170,000 people, who knows how much further it travels? To 175,000 people? 200,000? Many more?

Peter's ad in Joke of the Day cost $75. (At the time the list had only 110,000 subscribers, and rates have increased significantly since then.) It didn't bring in enough business to buy a new car or send him to Hawaii, but it did bring in around 930 visitors to his Web site, and sold about seven or eight books (around $220 to $260, not including shipping fees), more than enough to pay for the ad.

Notice, by the way, that he paid around eight cents per visitor. That's very cheap in the world of Internet advertising, far cheaper than most Web banners, which are measured in dollars per visitor.

Not All E-mail Advertising Works

E-mail advertising really can work. E-mail advertising is getting a good reputation these days, as people realize that it can be affordable and effective, but not all e-mail advertising is such a great idea. There are three main problems to watch out for.

Classified Ads

Some newsletters sell "classified ads." You buy a few lines, and your ad runs along with scores of others. These ads almost never work. Very few people will actually read these ads—in fact many of these newsletters probably don't get read at all, having been subscribed to in order to enter a drawing. Even if they do get read, people tend to quickly scroll past the classifieds.

If you can find a newsletter with very cheap classified ads, go ahead and try it. Create a doorway page to track incoming visits, and see how many people hit that page. Probably very few. Remember, the best way to place an ad in a newsletter is within the editorial content, separated from any other ads the newsletter may be carrying. The better the content, and the fewer ads in the newsletter, the better you ad is likely to work.

Classified Ads

Some people use the term classified ad to mean any text ad placed into an e-mail newsletter. By classified ad we mean a small ad that is placed together with a lot of other, similar ads. So some of the directories of "classified ads" that you may find can still be useful to you because they're listing newsletters that accept all types of newsletter ads, not just true classifieds.

Exorbitantly Expensive Ads

Some opt-in lists are way too expensive. We looked at a number of opt-in lists recently, and found that prices seem to be from eight cents up to as much as thirty cents a name. Eight cents per name is a cpm of $80, which is toward the high end for banner advertising. And thirty cents a name represents a cpm of $300!

Can you make money at those rates? In many cases the answer is clearly, No! It may be possible if you're selling a high-cost item. For instance, if you are selling Web-hosting services, and expect each customer to bring you $300 in the first year, you may find it effective. If you're selling a book that costs $19.95, however, the chance of you making money with this sort of advertising is slim to none. It's quite possible to find advertising in newsletters at *much* lower rates. The cpm for targeted newsletters is often around $35, but rates can be much lower, around a dollar or two.

Real Numbers?

This last problem is tricky, and right now there's no easy answer. If you buy advertising in a newsletter, how do you know you're getting what you paid for? If you pay for 50,000 subscribers, how do you really know that you're getting

50,000, and not 40,000—or 10,000? We can tell you that some newsletter editors are inflating their numbers … at least, that's the rumor among newsletter editors, and after all, it just makes sense that some would be doing so. It's too easy to get away with.

Right now most newsletter-advertising money is being spent on faith; people are simply taking the seller's word. In a lot of cases numbers are inflated. Many list owners probably don't clean their lists very often, for instance, and a large list can quickly build up thousands of bad addresses.

What we really need is some kind of independent verification service. By the time you read this at least one mailing-list program will probably have such a feature: **Lyris** (http://www.lyris.com/). A newsletter owner, for instance, would be able to direct a subscriber report to a potential advertiser. The report would come from Lyris, not from the newsletter owner, and would show how many people are subscribed to the list, and perhaps information about the number of successful deliveries of the last issue, the number of held (potentially bad) e-mail addresses, and so on.

A Few Things to Remember

Here are four points to remember when looking into e-mail advertising:

- Classified ad e-mails probably don't work. The message may be a newsletter with classified ads at the end, or may carry nothing but ads, but either way, why would people read these ads? Some will, but most won't.

- E-mail message ads sent by themselves to opt-in lists probably won't work well. If the message carries nothing but an ad, people will read the subject line, and unless it's a *really* good subject line, just delete the message. Remember, people are flooded with e-mail, so they're using the Delete key a lot!

- The most effective e-mail ads are probably those that are inserted into something that you know will be read, a newsletter or bulletin that people have asked to receive. If the information held in the message is entertaining or interesting, people will open the message and at least part of your ad will be read.

- Advertising rates are all over the place. Cpms vary from 42 cents to $300. Peter's had ads running at a cpm of 42 cents that far outpulled ads running at a cpm of $150. Look hard and you can find good deals.

OTHER FORMS OF ADVERTISING

Keep your eyes open for other forms of advertising that are not Web-based and that may be more direct and effective than Web advertising. For instance, a number of discussion groups sell sponsorships. Either they put a small text ad at the bottom of every message distributed to subscribers, or perhaps they have a special advertising bulletin that's sent out periodically.

For instance, once a day the **Studio B** discussion group (http://www.studiob.com/) sends out a message containing a few ads. Each ad costs $50 and is sent out five times. I've heard few complaints about this message—some people take offense to any advertising in e-mail whatsoever. But the fact that a single ad message is sent each day is made clear to new subscribers. Also, the messages are sent from a special e-mail address so if people really object to them they can easily delete the messages automatically using their e-mail program's filtering system. In any case, many of the people on the list want to see the ads because they are useful, containing job offers, for instance.

Another form of advertising is available through companies that build products designed to distribute information automatically. The user of one of these products doesn't go to a Web site to retrieve information; instead, the information comes to his desktop automatically through *push technology*. (The products that receive and display the "pushed" information are variously described as Web scrubbers, personalized broadcast products, micro-browsers, and push programs. Not so long ago they were hyped as the Next Big Thing, something that would be as big or bigger than the Web, but somehow that never happened.) Some of these companies sell advertising space, and will push your ad to thousands of desktops each day.

Then there are services such as **GoTo.com** (http://www.goto.com/), a search engine for which you have to *pay* to get listed. You actually place a bid for placements on search pages. For instance, if you are selling CDs, you might offer to pay, say, 13 cents for every time your site is displayed in a response to a search for various keywords: *music, rock, van halen*, and so on. Ray Owens, owner of **Joke of the Day** (http://jokeaday.lyris.com/), reported that he spent $250 on placements at GoTo.com; he bid 13 cents per placement, and because that was higher than anyone else bidding for those keywords he came up first on the lists, and received almost 2,000 new visitors to his site. That's not bad, considering that with banner ads you can easily spend many times that sum. You can try out the system for as little as $25.

MORE ADVERTISING ADVICE

There are a number of sites that will help you in your search for the right advertising. Try a few of these:

Ad-Guide.com

http://www.ad-guide.com/

Ad-Guide is actually a searchable subject index of all things dealing with Internet advertising—banner advertising programs, service providers, e-commerce, etc. At the time of writing they had 99 resources dealing with banner advertising. There are dozens and dozens of banner exchanges and other banner programs online; you can get a great idea of their scope here.

ClickZ Network

http://www.searchz.com/

Another advertising and e-commerce search engine, ClickZ will give you both listings of advertising programs and articles about the way they work. You'll find searchable directories of different types of advertising services, too, from banner design and banner networks to e-mail copywriting services and opt-in e-mail lists.

Internet Advertising Resource Guide: Management

http://www.admedia.org/internet/management.html

This site lists Internet-banner advertising networks, ad-management software, and links to pricing guides and campaign-management services. Browsing through these listings will give you an idea of what other people are doing and what you could do.

Mark Welch's Web Site Banner Advertising

http://www.markwelch.com/bannerad/

This site is an exhaustive overview of all forms of Web site banner advertising, from advertising networks to ad registries to lists of available ad-creation resources and even banner-ad creation programs. You'll also get Mark Welch's down-to-earth commentary about the business and particular companies.

CHAPTER THIRTEEN

Affiliate Programs

The Internet has been the impetus for many a new business. Tens of thousands of entrepreneurs have seen the Internet as a completely new opportunity, and now they're struggling alone trying to build their new enterprises. If this describes your situation, wouldn't it be helpful if you could recruit a sales force? Better still, wouldn't it be helpful if you could recruit a sales force and pay them only if and when they actually sell something?

Of course this would be beneficial to many businesses, and in fact many large businesses have already tried this, by setting up what are known as *affiliate* or *associate* programs (or *revenue sharing* programs, and other similar terms). Amazon.com and CDnow, for instance, both have over 100,000 affiliates working with them—100,000 Web sites selling their wares. Peter likes to compare affiliate systems with Internet malls. The malls are a stupid idea, based in real-world concepts of retailing rather than cyberspace concepts. Malls make sense in the real world, because geography matters out there. But in cyberspace geography is no longer important—or perhaps we could say there's a new geography at work in cyberspace, a geography of interests. When Web pages on different sides of the planet are as close to each other as Web pages on different sides of a street, location is no longer important. What really *is* important are associations between people —and their Web sites—based on mutual interests.

Anyway, enough of the theory. Here's how an affiliate program works. The first step is to find Web-site owners who might want to sell your products on their site. If you sell camping equipment, perhaps you can find Web sites related to camping and other outdoor sports. If you sell CDs, you can find music- and band-related sites. And if you sell books … well, you can recruit sites related to just about any subject, because for just about any subject there's a book.

The next step is to set up special links from your affiliate sites to your site. You need some way to code links so that when someone clicks on a link at an affiliate's site and reaches your site, it's clear where the person came from.

Finally, you need some way to track sales and pay commissions. When someone clicks on a link at an affiliate's site, reaches your site, and buys something, you have to record that sale, calculate the commission (typically between 5 and 20 percent), and pay the commission to the affiliate.

GOOD NEWS AND BAD

Affiliate programs can do wonders for a business, if run properly. Jason Olim, co-founder of CDnow, told Peter that CDnow's affiliate program was essential to their success, that it was as important to them as any of the expensive partnerships they'd bought into with companies such as Yahoo! and *Rolling Stone*. Yet it cost a fraction of the price of those partnerships.

The Good News, then, is that affiliate programs really do work. The bad news is that they can be difficult to set up and a lot of work to run. Ideally an affiliate program has to be completely automated, so that people can sign up as affiliates without any human interaction on your part. A program should take all the details, provide the necessary coded link, and record all visits from people passing through the affiliate's site. There aren't many programs that can do that right now (what you really need is an affiliate program integrated with your shopping-cart system). But there are a few. And in any case, affiliate programs are still worth looking at, because setting them up will become easier as new software tools are released.

Affiliate programs can work well for the companies running them, and, sometimes, for the people signing up for them. Peter makes $100 to $150 a month from a couple of programs (Amazon.com and ComputerLiteracy.com). He sells books at his Web site himself, but also points people to these books stores. He figures that some people would rather buy from a bookstore than from his site, so he signed up as an affiliate at those stores. Most affiliates probably make very little money at all, though. But many site owners are happy to put up an affiliate link to a site selling a product they like, even if they only get enough to buy a beer or two each month.

AFFILIATE DIRECTORIES

There are a number of affiliate directories you may want to look at. These sites can be very useful in a number of ways. First, you can see how other companies are running their affiliate programs; you'll find links to sites with programs, and articles about the different programs. You may find advice on running your program, including information about affiliate software, and discussion groups where you can ask questions. (AssociatePrograms.com has a Web forum, for instance.) These sites also list what they regard as the top affiliate programs, too, so you can get an idea of what it takes to make it work. And if you do decide to set up your own program, you'll probably want to register with these sites as another way for people to find you and sign up. Take a look at these sites:

Affiliate Trade Links Network
http://www.atlnetwork.com/

AssociateCash
http://www.associatecash.com/

AssociatePrograms.com
http://www.AssociatePrograms.com/

Associates Online
http://www.associatesonline.com/

CashPile
http://www.cashpile.com/

ClickQuick
http://www.clickquick.com/

ClicksLink
http://www.clickslink.com/

LinkShare
http://linkshare.com/

Mark Welch's Web Site Banner Advertising
http://www.markwelch.com/bannerad/ba_commission.htm

NetAffiliate
http://www.netaffiliate.com/

Partnerprogramme.com
http://www.partnerprogramme.com/ (in German)
http://www.partnerprogramme.com/english.htm (in English)

Refer-It.com
http://www.refer-it.com/

SiteCash.com
http://www.sitecash.com/

Note that these sites are generally slanted toward site owners wanting to sign up for affiliate programs in order to make money, rather than to site owners wanting to set up their own programs. But nonetheless, you'll find them very useful; who knows, perhaps you could sign up for a program to increase your own site's income.

THE TYPES OF PROGRAMS

There are several forms of affiliate programs, each with its own benefits and drawbacks. If you know anything about the world of advertising, you may recognize that these plans have real-world parallels. The whole concept of the affiliate plan, in fact, is really simply another version of the per-sale advertising programs, in which advertisers pay the media for each sale that is made, rather than paying for the advertising itself.

Per Sale

This is the most common form of program; if an affiliate sends you a visitor who ends up buying a product from you, you pay the affiliate something. It may be a flat fee. For instance, the Computer Literacy bookstore pays a $10 fee for every new customer an affiliate sends over, regardless of how much the customer spends. On the other hand, the payment may be a percentage commission; Amazon.com pays a flat 15 percent on all sales, while CDnow has a sliding scale—the more sales generated by an affiliate, the higher the percentage the affiliate receives. Percentage commissions seem to be more common than flat fees, partly because it just seems to make more sense if your company sells a lot of different products—a customer at Amazon.com may spend $10, or may spend $100, so Amazon.com provides larger payments for larger sales. Computer Literacy, however, feels that finding a new customer is well worth $10, which is far more than the average commission paid by Amazon.com. And perhaps they're right—Peter much prefers sending people to Computer Literacy, so maybe this large fee is really encouraging affiliates to push customers their way.

The advantage of a per-sale payment is that it's performance based. Ultimately what you're trying to do is make a sale, so you're paying for the final result. And it's hard, impossible one might say, for an affiliate to cheat with this kind of program. A sale's a sale, whereas, as we'll see in a moment, an inquiry or a click may not be the real thing.

Per Inquiry

Some companies with affiliate programs are using a per-inquiry program; when someone visits their Web site and requests information, the affiliate gets a commission. For instance, **Web Card** (http://www.printing.com/) will pay affiliates $1 each time a visitor provides address information so that they can send a few sample postcards (they also pay a 10 percent commission on sales). The disadvantage with this type of program is that you're not paying for an end result; you're just paying for the first step in the process, so you'd better be *really sure* you know how many inquiries you can convert into sales! Another disadvantage is that there's some potential for fraud. If an affiliate encourages all his friends and relatives to make an inquiry, you're paying for inquiries that have no value.

Pay-Per-Click Programs

With one of these programs you pay people to send *clicks* to you; you're paying, in effect, for referrals rather than actual sales or even inquiries. Each time someone visits your site thanks to the actions of an affiliate, you owe some money. Note, by the way, that a per-click program is really a form of advertising program; banner advertisers generally pay for each time their banner is seen, but sometimes they pay for each time someone clicks on a banner—so per-click programs are often set up by mainstream banner-advertising companies.

You may already have figured out the major problem with this sort of plan: fraud. All the affiliate has to do is to register a click, and there are many ways to do that in ways that won't benefit you. Affiliates can trick people into visiting your site, perhaps using spam to reach tens of thousands of people and overselling your site in some way; you may get lots of visits, but they may not stay for more than a few seconds. It's even possible for an affiliate to set up a *program* to click through to your Web site. The visitors you see aren't even real visitors.

CREATING YOUR OWN AFFILIATE PROGRAM

Now we come to the tricky part. How do you set up an affiliate program? It's okay for big companies, who can hire programmers to build the necessary programs for them. But if you're a small business, or even a single-person business, how do you set one up for yourself?

It's not necessarily easy, but it will get easier soon. Ideally you need a program that automates every step of affiliate sign-up, visitor tracking, and commission tracking. Better programs will allow affiliates to visit your site at any time and view their stats—see how many people have visited your store after going through their sites, see how many sales were made and how much commission was earned, and so on. The affiliate software you use has to be compatible with your shopping-cart software, too, or built into the software itself. In fact you may find that unless you have the shopping-cart system running on your server, the affiliate system will be unable to work with it. You might find that if you're using one of the shopping-cart services that run on someone else's server (see Chapter 2), you will be unable to use a separate affiliate program. (On the other hand you may be able to find a shopping-cart service with a built-in affiliate-program utility, as you'll see in a moment.)

Affiliate Software

Right now there are relatively few low-cost affiliate systems to choose from. Here are a few places to look.

Affiliate Shop

http://www.affiliateshop.com/

This is a very new system, launched early in 1999. They charge just $19.95 a month to host an affiliate system on their server. Unfortunately their site currently lacks important information, and there's no phone contact provided, so you may have trouble finding the information you need (as we did!).

AffiliateZone.com

http://www.affiliatezone.com/

AffiliateZone.com will install an affiliate program on your server for $350 (sometimes less; they recently had a $250 special promotion running). If you visit their site you'll find a list of the shopping-cart systems they have worked with in the past, and an evaluation-request form to have them check out your system and see if they can work with it. They will also host your site if you wish; you can use their affiliate program and their shopping cart, ClickStore, so you get full integration.

Your Own Associate Program

http://www.palis.com/new/yoap7/

This system costs $199 if you want to install it yourself, or $549 fully installed. (Further customization of your site is $50 an hour.) This system *may* work with your shopping-cart system, but there's a good chance it won't. It has built-in order forms, though, which you may find sufficient. In a moment we'll look at shopping-cart systems with built-in affiliate programs. You could consider Your Own Associate Program to be such a system, but it might also be considered the opposite; an affiliate system with a built-in shopping cart. In other words, you may not find all the shopping-cart features you want or need, as the focus for this product has been affiliate tracking. This system also appears to be highly recommended, though.

Commission Junction

http://www.commission-junction.com/

These guys will actually run your affiliate program for you. Their software costs $495 if you want to set it up yourself, $945 if you want them to do it for you. You put $250 on deposit (money used to pay your affiliates), and then they run the program for you, maintaining the system and paying affiliates. You'll have to pay a 15 percent fee to Commission Junction for the service—for every dollar you pay an affiliate, you'll pay them 15 cents.

LinkShare

http://linkshare.com/

LinkShare not only has the software you need to set up an affiliate program, but they also have a network of Web sites that are signing up as affiliates with LinkShare clients. (Currently 15,000 sites have signed up.) They provide a simple form that affiliates can use to join multiple affiliate programs at the same time.

ClickTrade

http://www.clicktrade.com/

This company has no sign-up fee, but charges a commission of 30 percent on everything you pay to your affiliates; if the payout to the affiliate is $100, you pay ClickTrade $30. They have a clever system for tracking sales. When a visitor clicks through an affiliate to your site, a cookie is saved on his hard disk. (The cookie is a little text file containing information identifying this person as an affiliate visitor.) You have to be able to put a tracking image on the final confirmation page that is created by your shopping-cart system; that tracking image comes from the ClickTrade server. When the server sends out the image, it also checks the user's cookie files to find the one it set when the visitor first clicked through to your site.

Be Free!

http://www.befree.com/

This is the real thing, the affiliate system used by Barnes and Noble, XOOM.com, Network Solutions (the company running InterNIC), and a number of other large Internet retailers. Barnes and Noble picked it, they say, because they believe it's the best system available. As you can imagine, this is not a cheap system. (Here's a hint: when a software publisher doesn't publish its prices on its Web site, you know it's going to cost a lot of money.) If you don't want to spend at least $7,500 for software installation, plus "customization" fees, plus 5 percent of your gross sales, don't bother contacting Be Free!, Inc.

Here are some other systems you may want to look at:

EComWorks (Creates and runs complete affiliate programs)
http://www.ecomworks.com/

RevShare 2000 ($789 including installation)
http://nationsweb.com/affiliates/

WebGenie ($597, 30-day free trial)
http://www.webgenie.com/

WebStationOne ($600 – $6,000)
http://www.webstationone.com/affiliates/

Shopping-Cart Systems

Another method, perhaps a little simpler than trying to integrate an affiliate program with a shopping-cart program, is to work with a shopping-cart program that has built-in affiliate support. We've found a couple, though there may be more (and there most certainly will be more soon).

Yahoo! Store

http://store.yahoo.com/

Yahoo! Store makes it very simple to add affiliates to an affiliate program, although it's not fully automated; you have to physically add a site. You enter the URL of the affiliate site, and Yahoo! Store will generate two more URLs for the affiliate. The first URL is for the affiliate to put into the link to your site, to identify visits as being generated from their site. The other URL is for the affiliate to check out how much traffic has come through their site and how much they have earned. You can also specify how much commission the affiliate earns—either a percentage of the sale or a flat fee for the number of visits sent to the site.

Merchandizer

http://www.merchandizer.com/

The Merchandizer shopping-cart system is one of the best on the Internet, and it includes a built-in affiliate tracking system. This is a fully automated system; affiliates can visit the site and sign up to join your program. The software generates the URL and provides all the information the affiliate requires, tracks sales, figures out commissions, and so on. And this is all included in the shopping-cart price of $79 a month ($229 setup), which is a pretty good deal. This system is a *PC Magazine* Editors choice; the only problem with this system is that it has so many features it will take you a little while to figure it all out!

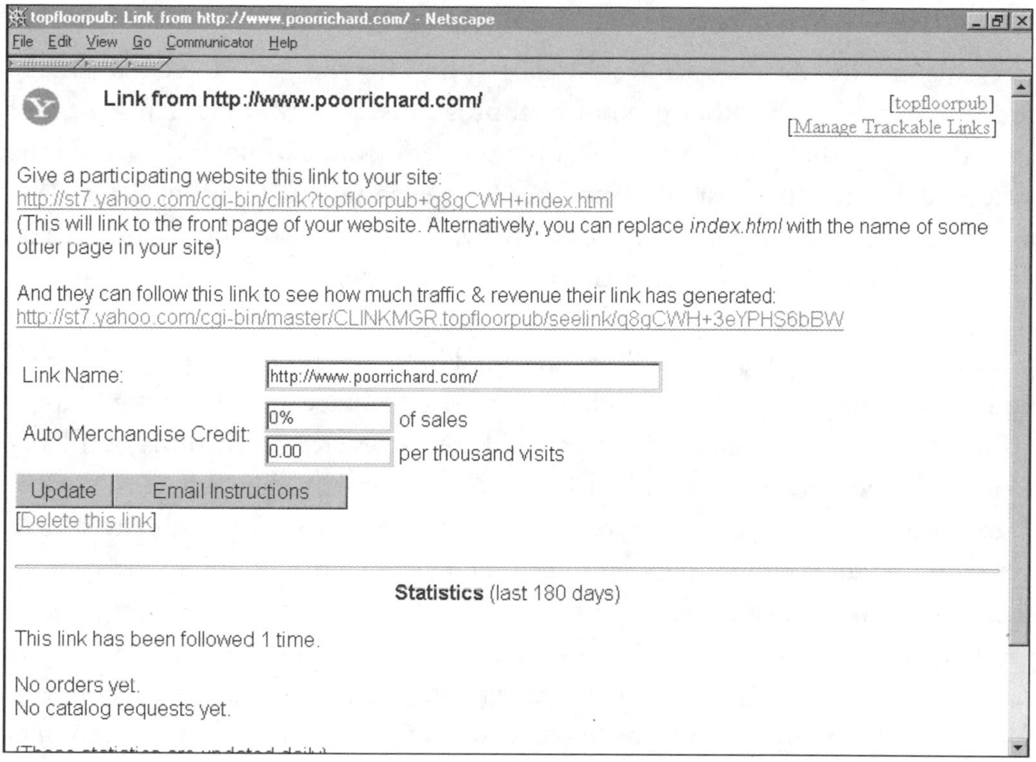

FIGURE 13.1: Yahoo! has a built-in affiliate system.

A Cruder Method

There's a very simple method for setting up affiliates, though it's not automated; you'll have to set up and track each affiliate manually. You simply provide each person with a Web page at your site. For instance, you might create a sales-pitch page—selling the visitor on the features and benefits of your product—and duplicate it, providing each page with a different number or name. You then give the URL to the appropriate page to each affiliate:

> http://www.topfloor.com/orders/0123.htm,
> http://www.topfloor.com/orders/0124.htm,

... and so on.

Some shopping-cart systems can track where someone comes from when they enter the shopping-cart system. (See the information about the Referrer Report in Chapter 14.) The shopping cart looks at the Referrer information—the URL of the page containing the link the user has just clicked on—and saves it with the order. You can then look at the order information to find the name or number of the Web page, and figure out which affiliate sent the visitor.

MAKING THE MOST OF YOUR PLAN

Creating an affiliate plan is all very well, but how do you get it to actually make money? As with most other promotional programs, it works only if *you work at it*. It's unlikely that you can just set it up and let it run, and hope that it will be successful. In fact many small businesses have experimented with affiliate plans and given up, finding that the work involved wasn't worth the payoff. A few companies have so much traffic that an affiliate program is bound to work for them, but most of us need to really push a program.

The affiliate program should be integrated into your promotions, of course. If you have a newsletter, you should use it to encourage people to sign up as affiliates. It's also a good idea to have an affiliates' newsletter to encourage affiliates to actually send people to you. You'll want to register with the affiliate sites we've mentioned in this chapter, of course, and perhaps work with those affiliate sites to get attention for your program; do some kind of special promotion to get yourself mentioned on the first page.

Let's take a look at a really successful affiliate program, CDnow's *Cosmic Credit* program. Of course CDnow is a big company, with a lot more money to play this game than most of this book's readers. But nonetheless, they have had some great ideas that you can apply to your own affiliate program.

CDnow's affiliate program is the oldest on the Web; they began paying people commissions way back in late 1994, almost prehistory in Web terms. But they didn't pay a great deal of attention to the program; it was something that just chugged along almost on its own for a while, with resources applied to it intermittently. But early in 1998 they decided to assign more people and money to the program, and the results were phenomenal. They entered 1998 with around 15,000 affiliates, but doubled that number in around four months. They then more than *tripled* that number by the fall, reaching over 100,000 affiliates. Amazon.com announced that they had 100,000 affiliates a little before CDnow reached that point, though considering CDnow's affiliate growth it's probably the largest program on the Internet today.

What's so special about this program? They work it really hard. They do a lot of things to encourage affiliates to send them customers, and to make the affiliates feel that they are really part of an enterprise in which both sides benefit.

For instance, when a visitor clicks to CDnow through an affiliate site, the affiliate's banner appears at the top of the CDnow page. In effect CDnow's site appears to be incorporated into the affiliate's site, and the customer can quickly return to the affiliate by clicking on the banner.

They also instantly credit an account with the commission earned. Most affiliate programs simply mail a check to an affiliate, though sometimes the affiliate has to reach a minimum before being issued any money. CDnow, however, credits all sales commissions to the affiliates' accounts immediately, and the money in the accounts can be used to purchase items at the CDnow store. This is something most companies seem to have missed—your affiliates can be your customers, too, so why not let

Watch for Spammers

One danger that companies running affiliate programs have to watch out for is spammers. Some spammers sign up for affiliate programs, and then put their affiliate link into an e-mail message and send it to millions of people. This is a great way for you to get a lousy reputation! CDnow avoids this problem by instantly closing spammer accounts, and by making it clear that they do not pay commissions to spammers.

them spend their commissions at your store? CDnow will send a check eventually; if the affiliate doesn't use the money in the account, and if it goes over $100, a check is sent out at the end of the calendar quarter. (Quarterly payments seem to be the norm for affiliate programs.)

CDnow also has bonus programs; it sends money and goods (CDs, T-shirts, and so on) as gifts, over and above the normal commissions, when affiliates reach certain levels. They'll even sometimes give gifts to people simply for sending a certain number of visitors to the site, regardless of whether those people bought anything.

CDnow employs two people full time to go looking for potential affiliates. They don't just wait around, hoping people will sign up as affiliates; they go out looking for music sites, inviting people to join. They'll even go looking for non-music sites when appropriate. For instance, when the Godzilla and Titanic soundtracks came out, CDnow went looking for movie Web sites that might want to sell the soundtracks.

They don't just sit back and let the orders roll in, either—they do all sorts of things, including special promotions. For instance:

- They gave away a Van Halen drumhead to the affiliate who sold the most of a new Van Halen album. (The winner sold $10,000 worth of albums!)
- They automatically submit every affiliate site to the Lycos search engine.

- They provide services such as discounts with Web-promotion companies and banner-swap programs.
- They create banners and RealAudio files that affiliates can use at their Web sites during promotions.
- They ran a contest in which they gave away a computer and two graphics packages, including a digital camera, scanner, and color printer.
- They promoted a new Smashing Pumpkins album and paid the top-earning affiliate a $50 bonus.
- They gave away a signed and illustrated David Lee Roth cowboy hat to the top-earning affiliate during a promotion for a David Lee Roth album.
- They gave an autographed Gibson guitar to the affiliate that sold the most copies of Big Wreck's *In Loving Memory Of...* album.

CDnow is particularly interested in very busy fan sites, which have a lot of traffic, and large e-mail newsletters and discussion groups. These sites can turn into very successful affiliates; the Van Halen winner is a Van Halen fan site, with a great deal of traffic, for instance.

They also held an *Unheard Bands* contest. Sponsored by the *College Music Journal*, Musician's Friend (a music-equipment catalog company), Tripod (a Web-site "community"), and Disc Makers (a CD manufacturing company), CDnow called for music from unpublished bands that were affiliate members. (CDnow had discovered that many of their affiliates were musicians.) They pressed 500 CDs for the winning band, gave 400 to the band, and kept 100 to hand out as promos.

CDnow also sends a regular e-mail bulletin to their affiliates, informing them of what's going on in the store—special promotions, upcoming releases, and so on. We've seen affiliate reports that are very poorly designed. They seem to be huge blocks of dense text. CDnow's report is broken into small blocks, with lots of whitespace, so it's easy to read.

Affiliate programs can really work well, if you are prepared to work hard. They're part of the new direction that Internet commerce is moving in, away from old concepts—like malls—toward using the real power of networking to bring in business. They're not necessarily something to be entered into lightly, because of the work involved in setting them up and running them, but they're certainly worth taking a look at.

CHAPTER FOURTEEN

Tracking Results and Responding

You're spending a lot of time and energy, and perhaps even money, to promote your products and services on the Internet. How do you know if it's all working? How do you know which bits are working and which are not? How can you measure the results of your efforts?

One of the nice things about operating on the Internet is that it's possible to track things much more closely than you could in the real world. There are tools you can use to see when people are talking about you, to see how people are arriving at your site, to see which sites are linking to you, and so on. This information can be very useful if used properly, or a great distraction if not.

In this chapter, we're going to look at a variety of ways that you can measure results:

- Using your hit logs
- Looking at the Referrer Report
- Creating "doorway" pages to receive hits
- Backlink checking
- Searching at search sites
- Using automated search utilities
- Employing Web clipping services
- Monitoring discussion groups
- Checking offline publications
- Analyzing the *real* results

WHAT ARE HITS?

First, what's a hit, and why do we care? There's a lot of nonsense spoken about hits. You'll often see huge hit claims pertaining to particular sites: 10,000 hits a day!, 50,000 hits a day!, 1,000,000 hits a week!, and so on. Some Web-site owners are clearly trying to imply by such claims that they are getting this number of *visitors* each day. (Just seen on CNN … a story about a store selling provisions for a Y2K disaster—that is, when all the computers stop working on the first day of the year 2000 and civilization collapses. They're getting a million visitors a month, according to the journalist. And if you believe that, we've got some land to sell you in Idaho …) But what really is a hit? It's a transfer from the server to a browser. So here's a quick way to double or triple the hits at your site: add more graphics. Each time a browser transfers a text page that has no graphics, that's one hit. But if the page has a graphic inside it, that's two hits— the page itself and the graphic. If it has five graphics, that's six hits. Each transfer is a single hit. Or simply add a lot of errors—links to nonexistent graphics. That's a great way to increase your hit count, because each error will be counted as a hit, yet you won't be transferring much data.

This means, of course, that a site designed to carry lots of small graphics on every page, or a site with lots of broken links, can generate very large hit rates. One major cybermall claims 11 million hits a month. And at least some of that mall's clients believe that the mall means 11 million visitors a month: "Hits are classified as people that actually came to my Web site," one client told me. (Think again, buddy!)

A single visit to your Web site might generate a single hit—or ten hits, perhaps, or several hundred, as the visitor makes his way through a variety of graphic- and error-laden pages. Each page viewed, and each graphic within those pages, is a single hit. A while back Peter saw a Netscape press release that began with this statement:

2.9 MILLION VISITORS PROPEL NETSCAPE INTERNET SITE TO OVER 100 MILLION HITS A DAY.

It also included this:

Nielsen I/PRO undertook an independent audit of the Netscape site, which found that an average of more than 2.9 million visitors accessed the site daily, with an average visit length of 9 minutes. On the average business day, visitors to the site view a total of close to 10 million pages.

Let's consider this: 2.9 million visits, 10 million pages, 100 million hits. In other words, for every 100 hits, Netscape is getting only 2.9 visits, and the average visitor is viewing only 3.5 pages, so an awful lot of those hits are being taken up with in-line images and other bits and pieces.

There are other terms you might hear in addition to hit. There's *request* or *access*, defined by some as a page that is transferred; it doesn't include the in-line graphics or errors. And a visit means that a single browser comes to your site and requests single or multiple pages. You'll also hear the term *unique visits* or *unique hosts*. As people are getting wise to the "lots of hits" nonsense, this unique visits statistic is becoming more commonplace. It means "forget hits, forget pages, we get x visits to our Web site." Of course this is a far more useful statistic, although still open to some abuse, depending on how it's measured. For instance, every time someone visits your site, the server can look at the IP (Internet Protocol) number that identifies the visitor's computer. Suppose that the statistics program regards a visit as pages transferred to a particular IP number over, say, a 30-minute period. A visitor comes to the site, and looks at a few pages. Thirty-one minutes later—after going for coffee—the same visitor looks at another page. That's counted as two visits. In contrast, if the program regarded a visit as activity from an IP number over a two-hour period, then this would be just a single visitor.

IP Numbers Change

You probably get a different IP number each time you log onto the Internet. If you access the Internet through an online service or Internet service provider (other than a cable TV company), an IP number is automatically assigned to you when you log on. That means that if you lose your connection for some reason and log back on and go back to the previous site, the log program will identify you as a different *visitor—your one visit is now identified as two.*

As you can see, statistics can be made to work in many different ways—lies, damn lies, and statistics—but at least the unique visitors statistic is much more useful than some of the others. Using it, you can get a very good idea of how many people are visiting your site each day, each week, or each month.

ACCESS OR "HIT" LOGS

An access log is a record of activity at your Web site. The Web server records information in the log each time someone requests something from your Web site. If your Web site is hosted by a Web-hosting company, you'll probably have access to some kind of log. This is yet another reason to move your Web site from an Internet service provider or online service, which usually *don't* provide access logs.

What sort of information is saved in the log? It varies, depending on the system being used to create the log, but typically it's information such as the following:

Weekly Report—the number of requests for data and amount of data transferred each week

Daily Report—the number of requests and amount of data transferred each day

Hourly Report and Hourly Summary—the number of requests and amount of data transferred each hour of each day, and the amount transferred each hour of an average day

Domain Report—the number of requests and amount of data transferred to different domains … that is, a report showing you the domains of your visitors

Host Report—a list showing the domain names of the top 100 host computers visiting your site (the people who spent the most time at your site)

Directory Report—the number of requests and amount of data transferred from each directory in your Web site

File-type Report—the number of requests and amount of data transferred, broken down by file types (.htm, .gif, .zip, and so on)

Request Report—the number of requests and amount of data transferred, broken down by specific file names

Referrer Report—the number of requests that originated from the top 100 referrers; that is, it shows you who is linking to you

Browser Report—the number of requests broken down by the type of browser sending the request

Status Code Report—the status codes sent to the browser, such as error codes for missing pages

Not all systems provide all this information, and some provide more. The reports listed above come from a program called Analog, from the University of Cambridge Statistical Laboratory, whose programmers claim is the most popular log-file program in the world. Nonetheless, there are many others; Analog may have around 20 percent of the "market" (it's actually a free program). So there's a good chance you'll have these or similar reports available.

You can use this information in a variety of ways. You can see, for instance, which areas of your site visitors find most interesting. Perhaps you should find out why they're so important to people, and perhaps even highlight these areas of your site in promotional efforts.

You can correlate visits with your promotional and advertising efforts and use the correlation to figure out how well you are turning visitors into customers. If you see a lot of visits after a magazine article appears, for instance, then the article has probably helped send visitors to you. But if you notice only a small rise in sales of your products, then you're not taking advantage of those visitors.

You can also get a good feel for the hit-to-visit ratio—that is, how many hits the average visit generates—which indicates how busy each visitor is at your site. Do they mostly come, look around for a moment, and leave? Or do they give your site a thorough viewing? You can also experiment with your content and see how changes cause people to move through your site in different directions. You can see which areas people are interested in; if you've created an area of your site that nobody spends any time in, for instance, perhaps you should dump it and focus on the more popular areas.

GETTING TO YOUR ACCESS LOGS

Most Web-hosting companies provide logs. Some companies even e-mail you a log regularly; with others, you have to go to a specific Web page to view your logs. You can see an example of a log page in Figure 14.1. This particular log shows information about the browsers that requested data from a Web site; each line represents requests from Web browsers in a particular domain. In the right column you can see the host name. In other words, this information won't point back to an actual browser, but rather to the domain in which that browser is operating. You may in some cases find that visitors are coming from a particular small domain—one of your competitors' domains, for instance, or a customer's domain—but more often it will be a domain owned by an ISP or online service. For instance, if you found, say, `ad19-039.compuserve.com` in the report, this would be a domain owned by the online service CompuServe.

However, in some cases, you may be able to follow a visitor through your site using this domain name; it will remain the same throughout the session. For instance, look at this information extracted from a report provided by a different log program:

```
dialup-06-38.netcomuk.co.uk "GET /ipn/techwr/
dialup-06-38.netcomuk.co.uk "GET
/ipn/techwr/guideline.htm HTTP/
dialup-06-38.netcomuk.co.uk "GET
```

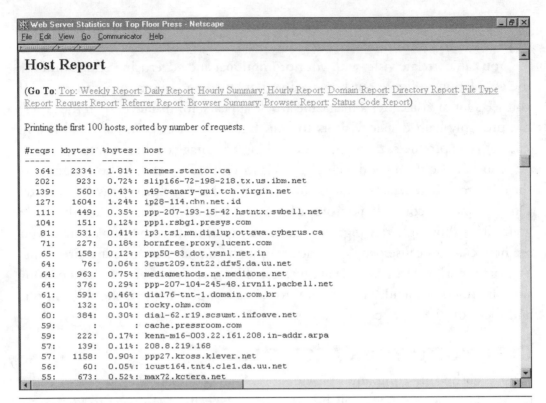

FIGURE 14.1: A log file from Analog, a very popular log program

```
/ipn/images/redarrw.gif HTTP/
dialup-06-38.netcomuk.co.uk "GET
/ipn/techwr/testimon.htm HTTP/
dialup-06-38.netcomuk.co.uk "GET
/ipn/techwr/$100k_frm.htm HTTP/
```

This program provides specific information about particular data transfers. In this case, a single visitor started by requesting `/ipn/techwr/`; in other words, the server sent the default file (index.html) from this directory. But then he clicked on a link to the `guideline.htm` file. You can also see that the `redarrw.gif` file was transferred, but this doesn't mean much, as that's probably an embedded file inside `guideline.htm`. We can see that he then went to `testimon.htm`, and finally to `$100k_frm.htm`.

Some Web-hosting companies also provide simple log summaries showing the hosts that accessed your site, the files that were requested, when all this took place, the total amount of traffic, and so on. These may be daily, weekly, or monthly reports, so you can get a quick overview of what's happening at your site. You can see a sample in Figure 14.2.

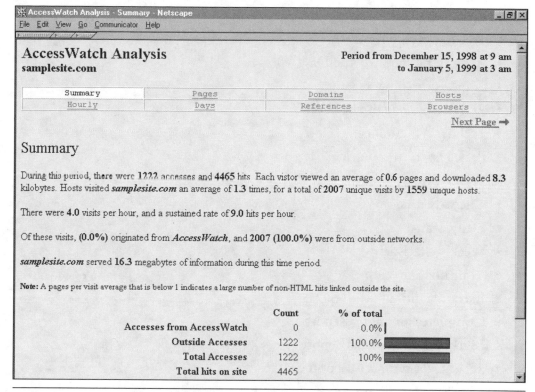

FIGURE 14.2: A summary report from a program called AccessWatch

MANIPULATING ACCESS REPORTS

If you want more statistics than your Web-hosting company provides, you can add your own log programs, from simple single-page counters to sophisticated $10,000 programs. You can also use services provided by other companies, which may be necessary if you want to sell advertising; the third party keeps track of your traffic and provides the report to you and any advertisers you authorize.

What sort of statistics might you expect if you use a good service or logging program? The following list is an example taken from the NetIntellect Web page:

- General Summary
- Visitor Profile by Origin
- Visitors by Continent
- Top Visitor Organizations
- Top Visitor Countries/Zones
- Top Requested Files
- Top Referring URLs/Sites

- Top Requested File Types
- Top Referred Files
- Activity by Hour of the Day
- Top Visitor Browsers
- Activity by Day of the Week
- Technical Summary
- Peak Day of the Week
- Server Errors
- Client Errors
- Daily Statistics
- Weekly Statistics
- Monthly Statistics
- Executive Summary Report
- Complete Summary Report
- Marketing Summary Report
- Technical Summary Report
- BPA Standard Report

Some of these programs don't run on the server at all. Rather, they take the log files created by the server and manipulate them to put the information into a useful form. So while the server may be a UNIX server, the analysis program may be running in Windows NT. Following are some programs to check out:

AccessWatch ($18 per year)
  http://accesswatch.com/

net.Analysis (From $7,900 and up)
  http://www.netgen.com/

NetIntellect and NetIntellect Express ($49 and up)
  http://www.webmanage.com/

Web Page Access Counters and Trackers (A very good list of programs and services)
  http://www.markwelch.com/bannerad/baf_counter.htm

WebTracker ($495)
  http://www.cqminc.com/webtrack/

WebTrends ($299 and up)
  http://www.webtrends.com/

Yahoo!-Log Analysis Tools

http://www.yahoo.com/Business_and_Economy/Companies/
Computers/Software/Internet/World_Wide_Web/Log_Analysis_Tools/

There are also a number of services that provide free site statistics for small sites, sometimes in exchange for your carrying a banner at your site. Most provide very simple statistics, though. The following are low-cost and not-quite-so-low-cost services:

Accrue Insight ($17,000 and up)

http://www.acrue.com/

Audit Bureau of Circulations (Charges big bucks!)

http://www.accessabc.com/

HitWatchers

http://www.hitwatchers.com/

Siteflow ($950 and up)

http://www.siteflow.com/

InternetCount (Free)

http://www.icount.com/

NetCount and AdCount (Price Waterhouse—starts at $98 per month)

http://www.netcount.com/

PageCount (In exchange for a banner)

http://www.pagecount.com/

StatTrax ($5 per month to 10,000 hits)

http://www.stattrax.com/

WebSideStory's HitBox (Free)

http://wss5.websidestory.com/wc/world.html

We're not suggesting that you run out and find a program or service, by the way. Most small businesses have more important things to do than track this sort of stuff, as we'll discuss in a moment (see "*Not Just Hits*" below).

YOU WANT E-MAIL ADDRESSES, RIGHT?

Many new Web-site owners want to be able to grab the e-mail addresses of their visitors from the log files. After all, they've heard people talk about these wonderful log files, and heard that you can track "who" visits your site. Unfortunately—or fortunately from the visitor's point of view—the term "who" has been used very loosely in the Web-tracking business. You cannot grab an e-mail address from a browser unless the user chooses to give it to you.

We know a lot of people won't believe this. After all, they've read in the press that it's possible for Web sites to grab e-mail addresses that have been entered into the browser's mail program settings. This is completely incorrect. While there is a system called identd that works on UNIX servers that can do such a thing, this is rarely used. For identd to work, the Web server and the computer the browser is working on must both be running UNIX and both must be using identd, a situation that is quite rare these days. Relatively few users are working with UNIX. (Most are using some form of Windows or MacOS.)

There's another trick, in which the Web page includes an <IMG> tag that uses FTP to grab the embedded image. If the browser is one that can send the user's e-mail address as a login name to FTP sites, and if the user has told the browser to do so (it's an option in Netscape Navigator), that address is sent to the FTP site and included in the log. In Netscape Navigator this option is turned off by default; that is, the browser won't use the e-mail address unless told to. Apparently some older browsers may launch an FTP program, but then the user can see what's going on. All in all, this method is, to quote one Web administrator who's tried it, "pretty useless."

There is currently no reliable way to grab e-mail addresses from Web browsers visiting your site; the only way to grab addresses is by using one of these unusual exceptions or by exploiting a software bug in some browsers. And as the vast majority of browsers in use don't have any such bugs—at least, bugs that have been discovered—and won't work with identd or the FTP trick, you can forget about grabbing e-mail addresses. Such bugs existed in some earlier browsers, such as Netscape Navigator 2. But the browser companies fix these bugs as soon as they find them, and so the bugs are removed from the Web as people upgrade their browsers. No browser company with the slightest bit of sense would knowingly create a browser from which a Web site could take an e-mail address without the user realizing.

In any case, it would be a trifle rude to steal e-mail addresses even if there were a reliable way to do it, so even if such a system existed—and we'd tell you if it did—we wouldn't explain how to use it.

NOT JUST HITS

People have got a little too wrapped up with hits. Hits don't often mean much. Listen to what Edward Tufte had to say. Tufte writes about information design—about how to present information in a way that people can readily understand it. (He was writing about this for 20 years or more before the Web.) "Look at the phoniness of the statistics," he said, "their hit numbers, 'One million hits to our site!' All those hits are to the home page, and most people never make it to the next screens. The numbers drop almost exponentially; 90 percent never make it to the second page, and 90 percent of those people never make it to the third page."

He's absolutely right. So don't get too wrapped up with simple hit statistics. You have to know what a hit really means. So what does a hit to your site really mean? It means that something was transferred from the Web server to a Web browser. It doesn't mean that the data actually arrived, nor that the person receiving it wanted it or paid any attention to it. It doesn't prove that the person receiving it took action as a result, or plans to return, or will act in any manner that is beneficial to you or your company.

Surely, there has to be a better way! Of course there is. Far more important than a measure of hits is genuine activity at, or related to, your site, such as the following:

- How many people are filling in a form to give you their e-mail address, so you can tell them when the Web site is modified or when you release your next product?

- How many people are signing up for your electronic newsletter?

- How much activity is there in your discussion group or chat group?

- How many hits to your autoresponder are you getting—that is, how many people are looking for more information?

- How many people are adding links to your link pages (if you have an automatic link-adding CGI), or sending you links via e-mail?

- How often is your Web site mentioned in the newsgroups and mailing lists, or in the press?

- How many sites have links to your site?

- How many people are e-mailing you directly with questions?

- How many orders are you taking?

These are all really strong indications of how your Web site is doing, of how useful it is to other Internet users—and to you. So hits can be useful, but don't concentrate on them to the exclusion of more important measures. You can spend an awful lot of time analyzing hits and requests and visits, time that, in many cases, can be better spent in some other way—by setting up some kind of promotion to bring people to your site, for instance.

That's not to say that you should simply ignore these reports. There are a couple of ways in particular that the reports can be very useful.

THE REFERRER REPORT

Most logs will contain a Referrer Report (or something similar). Take a look at this; it can be a great way to find out where people are coming from. For instance, you might see something like this:

```
Referrer Report
Printing the first 100 referring URLs, sorted by
number of requests.
#reqs: URL
———  ——
172: http://webdesign.miningco.com/blnew.htm
93: http://dir.yahoo.com/Business_and_Economy/
Companies/Books/Shopping_and_
Services/Booksellers/Computers/Internet/Titles/
World_Wide_Web/Web_Page_Design/
56: http://www.topfloor.com/cgi-bin/hazel/hazel.cgi
53: http://www.score.org/resourceindex/resource.html
42: http://www.webjump.com/jumppoint/
36: http://www.hostfind.com/info/help/host.feature.
html
29: http://search.yahoo.com/bin/search?p=free+web+
site
[etc....]
```

When a browser sends a message asking for a Web page, it includes a little bit of information saying where it found the link; it sends the URL of the page containing the link on which the visitor clicked. (Of course if the visitor typed the URL into the browser's location box, no referrer information is sent.) This information is saved in the log. As in the above report, only the top 100 referrers may be saved, so if you have a busy site, some of the referrers that brought you few visitors will "drop off the bottom."

You can often find interesting stuff in these logs. You may find sites linking to you that you hadn't found any other way. And even if you use some of the other methods in this chapter for finding out who's linking to you, the referrer report shows you something more important. A link is nice, but much more important is a link that is actually sending visitors to you.

CREATING A DOORWAY PAGE

If you've ever paid any attention to a TV infomercial, or read mail order ads in papers and magazines, you've surely noticed that they often include a department number. Infomercials often ask you to request a particular extension number, and sometimes order forms contain suite or box numbers. These are generally completely unnecessary for you to get your order to the right person. These are, in fact, codes used by the vendor to keep track of responses. Dept. EM05 may mean an ad in the May edition of *Entrepreneur Magazine*, extension 1299 may mean an infomercial running in December of 1999, and so on. Why bother? So that you can see where orders are coming from. If Dept. EM05 gets a huge number of orders, you know your *Entrepreneur Magazine* ad is worthwhile; if it doesn't, there's probably no point running it again.

Well, you can play the same little "coding" game on the Web. You can use a special link for particular ads and promotions, so that you can measure how many people use that link. There are many ways to do this. Affiliate programs (as discussed in Chapter 13) often use a special program. For instance, if you use the following link, the Web server at CDnow will track your movements around the **CDnow** site, and if you actually buy something Peter will earn a commission: http://www.cdnow.com/from=sr-919191.

But there's a much easier way to do this sort of thing. You've already seen how to look at your logs for information. Now you need to know how to create a special page—often known as a doorway page—so that you can use this page as the equivalent of a department or extension. For instance, you put an ad in *The Yak Herder's Info Newsburst* e-mail newsletter. In the ad you include a URL something like this: http://yourdomain.com/visit/yak.htm. You create a page called yak.htm in the visit directory. The ad runs, and you can then look at your hit logs to see how many times the yak.htm file has been viewed.

Don't Always Use This

While you may want to use this technique for all links—in ads and special promotions carried out on the Web—you may not want to use this technique for all your print promotions. It's nice to be able to measure responses to print ads, but it's also nice to be able to give people reading the ads a nice, simple URL, rather than a URL with some kind of coding built in.

Got it? Simple. But there's one catch. You don't necessarily want people to really visit this yak.htm page. You want them to visit your main page. Of course you could create lots of copies of your first page, but then you have to maintain all those pages—if you change one, you'll have to change them all.

An easier system is to forward people from the yak.htm page to your main page ... which is also very easy to do. Here's how it's done. You need to add a META tag right below the <HEAD> tag at the top of the Web page. If you use an HTML authoring program, and never see the HTML tags, look for the command that allows you to view the source of a page, the underlying HTML codes. At the top of the page you'll see this tag: <HEAD>

Put the cursor right after this tag, press Enter, and then type this:

```
<meta http-equiv="REFRESH" content="xxxx; url=yyy">
```

Replace the xxx with a number, the number of seconds delay before the visitor is forwarded to the next page. You may want the page to wait a few seconds, to tell the visitor what's going on; that's useful if you're using a redirection page to tell people that you've moved your site, for instance. But in this case, when you're using the page to measure results from an ad, you'll probably want them to move as quickly as possible, so you can put a 0 there, which means "go to the next page right away."

Next, replace yyy with the full URL of the page to which you are forwarding the visitor—probably your site's main page. You want to end up with something like this:

```
<html>
<head>
<meta http-equiv="REFRESH" content="10;
url=http://www.poorrichard.com/">
```

By the way, you should also include a normal link from this page to the new one too. Not all browsers will forward (most will, but a few older ones won't), so you can create a link telling the visitor to click on it to go to the site's main page.

If you want to see a forwarding page in action, use this link: http://www.poorrichard.com/examples/autofwd2.htm.

This page is set to forward after ten seconds, so you'll have plenty of time to see it. If you'd like to see this page's source code, click on your browser's Stop button as soon as you enter the page; that ensures that it won't forward. Then you can use the View|Source command in your browser.

Now you've got the redirection page—the doorway page—set up. Each time someone uses the URL pointing to this page, the Web server will keep track of it. Periodically you can look in your hit logs and search for that filename (in our Yak example, `yak.htm`) and see how many times it's been used. There's one catch, though. If it hasn't been used very often, then it may not turn up in the logs; your logs may only show you the 100 busiest pages, for instance, so if you have a very large site and a very poorly performing ad, you may not see the page in the logs.

BACKLINK CHECKING

Another way to check your results is to find out how many people are linking to you. The referrer report shows one method—or rather, it shows you the 100 or so links that are sending the most people to you. But there are other ways to discover who's linking to you. We've already covered this in some detail—see Chapter 8.

You can use backlink checking to see who's linking to your site and what they're saying about your site. Maybe they're saying, "This is a great site!" If they are, drop them a note and thank them. If your site is just part of a list, don't worry about it. Just check to make sure everything's spelled right and send a note to the site owner if it's not.

Look for other promotional opportunities. Perhaps a site reviewed one of your products … ask if they'd like to review another. If you have an affiliate program (see Chapter 13), ask if the site would like to sign up. Maybe you can find sites to do drawings (see Chapter 10). There are many ways you can work with sites that have linked to you, so keep an open mind.

WHAT ARE THEY SAYING ABOUT YOU?

You can use the Internet to find out if your company is being talked about in newsgroups and mailing lists or on the Web. You can also check to see if your site is being talked about offline, in newspapers and other publications.

The Internet is a free speech forum of major proportions. There are lots of people talking about lots of stuff, and one of the things they're talking about might be your company. In many cases, that's harmless. They might mention that they bought something at your store, or sent a donation to your organization, or used your company to do some work at their office. It's when someone starts posting negative information about your company that you've got to be concerned.

Every negative statement about your company is an opportunity for you. If you catch it, maybe it's something you can act on. Maybe a customer misunderstood the guarantee policy, or is posting something that's factually incorrect. In either case you can correct them (nicely) and make an impression on the other people on the newsgroup or mailing list. In the case of a Web site, you have to convince the site owner to put up your side of the story, though sometimes you won't be able to do that.

And in the case when your business did do something bad and is in the wrong? In that case, you apologize, you make good if you can, and then you shut up.

There are several different tools you can use to find out what people are saying about you, your company, and your products—from basic work with search engines to paying thousands of dollars for professional online monitoring. We'll take a look at all the levels of your options.

Using Search Engines

Tracking the occurrence of your name on the Web is pretty easy. Throughout this book we've been giving you hints about using search engines. So to search for *your* products and company name, simply enter those words into the search engines. But perhaps your company or product name is pretty generic. Say the name of your company is ACME and it sells electrical supplies. If you enter ACME in AltaVista, you're going to get over 70,000 results. But enter additional keywords appropriate to your

Trademarks and Copyrights

If you have trademarks and copyrights, you might want to monitor the Web in order to protect them. In this case you've got to be careful; you can set yourself up for some bad PR. In the cases where your trademarks are being blatantly misused, or your copyrighted material is being posted online without your permission, you've got a lot of legal leverage to get those problems corrected. But use some common sense. What, for instance, if a 12-year-old is using a trademarked name of yours as a domain name? Heavy-handed legal posturing could backfire, as it did when the Prema Toy Company, owner of the Gumby and Pokey trademarks, discovered a child using pokey.org as a domain name. The negative publicity was so extreme they eventually had to back down.

Colgate-Palmolive, maker of Ajax cleanser and owner of the Ajax trademark, tried to get the owner of the Ajax.org domain to give up his ownership of the domain, and lost big on the public relations side. (They also eventually backed down on their claim.) When you come across what looks like a trademark or copyright violation, first get all the facts you can. Second, try to settle the issue in a positive manner, without threatening letters from lawyers. Turn to legal leverage only as a last result. Your public relations department will thank you!

company—like "electric"—and you'll trim down the results considerably.

You'll get even better results once you've been tracking your company's name for awhile and you get a sense of what keywords the people who talk about you use.

Obviously you don't want to spend every day going over search engines and finding examples of your own company name. There are resources—some online, some software—that will help you automate your search for your company name.

Free Automated Search Utilities

If you're looking for ways to track changes to search engines and Web sites, the Web has a few great resources for you.

TracerLock

> http://www.peacefire.org/ tracerlock/

Beware Case-Sensitive Search Engines

It's popular today to do strange things with the capitalization of product and company names, capitalizing letters within the name for instance, or using a lowercase letter at the beginning: GEnie, CompuServe, eMerge, and so on. Your customers may or may not remember how to capitalize your company name, so when searching for your company's name on case-sensitive search engines, such as AltaVista, use all lowercase letters. In other words, if you are searching for GoodExampleCo using AltaVista, enter it in the search box as `goodexampleco`*. Searching for* `goodexampleco` *will find* `goodexampleco`*,* `GOODEXAMPLECO`*,* `GoodexampleCo`*,* `GoOdExAmPlEcO`*, and so on. Searching for* `GoodExampleCo` *will find only* `GoodExampleCo`*, and will miss all the other results noted above.*

TracerLock is a free service, sponsored by Peacefire, which allows you to monitor AltaVista for the occurrence of up to five sets of keywords. For example, you could monitor for all of the following:

```
acme AND electric
acme AND electrician
"acme electric"
"electrical supply"
acme AND electric AND purchased
```

Each day TracerLock will search AltaVista for pages that match your search term and were indexed exactly three days previously. If there are results, the first ten will be sent to you in an e-mail. TracerLock only searches AltaVista, but

AltaVista has a big database. If you want to track your company, this is an excellent addition to your toolbox.

The Informant

http://informant.dartmouth.edu/

The Informant works a little like TracerLock, but covers a lot more ground. Here's what happens. First you have to register (the service is

Check the Page Source

Did you get a match for a Web page that mentions your company, but you can't find a mention of your company anywhere on the page? Check the page source. You might find that your trademark is being used as a Meta-Tag keyword.

free) and specify how often you'd like to receive search engine updates—once every three, seven, 14, 30, or 60 days. Next, you specify three queries—sets of words where you'd like to find all the words in the set (an AND query) or any word in the set (an OR query). We don't recommend using OR queries unless the keywords are very unusual. For each query, you'll have the choice of searching Excite, AltaVista, Lycos, or Infoseek. (It doesn't appear that you can search all of them; you can only choose one to search.) After that you'll be given the option of monitoring five specific URLs for changes—that is, The Informant will take a look at these pages to see if any of them have changed, and inform you if so.

Now, at the interval you specified, The Informant will find the top 10 Web pages that are most relevant to your keywords. If there is a new page in the top 10, or if any of the pages in the top 10 have changed, you'll get an e-mail. It'll also look at the five pages you specified to see if there are any changes.

Since The Informant checks out only the top 10 pages at each search engine, you won't get the comprehensive results that you'll get with TracerLock, but you have more search engine choices and you can monitor specific URLs. (And hey, they're both free, so there's nothing that says you can't use both engines.)

URL-Minder

http://www.netmind.com/html/url-minder.html

URL-Minder doesn't specifically query search engines; instead, it tracks changes to particular pages. You can use this resource to check on competitor's pages, check on pages important to your industry, and so on. You give it your e-mail address, tell it the URLs to watch, and specify some extra information, such as whether you want URL-Minder to send you a copy of the new page.

Of course you can also use this system to track changes in the search engines for you. Enter a query on a search engine—like AltaVista—and click the Search button. After you get the results, you'll see a very strange-looking URL in the URL location box at the top of your browser. Let's do an example. Say you search for "acme electric" on .com domains. The search query would look like this:

```
+"acme electric" +domain:com
```

The URL in your browser's URL location box would look like this:

```
http://www.altavista.com/cgi-bin/query?pg=q&kl=XX&q=
%2B%22acme+electric%22+%2Bdomain%3Acom
```

All you have to do is cut that URL out of the location box and paste it into the URL-Minder URL registration box. You can do this as many times as you like with as many different search queries as you like. URL-Minder supports an unlimited number of URLs to update. URL-Minder will, in effect, repeat your search for you periodically. It's not a perfect system, though. Since URL-Minder can check only the first page of results, it won't be as thorough as TracerLock. And unless you're very careful and do a very clear and specific search, you may end up with a lot of unimportant notifications. On the other hand, you can check many more query combinations using this method because you won't be restricted to just three.

Web Clipping Services

As you see, each of these above online tools has some drawbacks and limitations. However, if you use all of them and spend a little time searching the search engines occasionally, you'll cover a lot of ground. But perhaps you've got more money than time. In that case, you should check out the for-pay "Web clipping" services, such as these.

CyberAlert

http://www.cyberalert.com/

CyberAlert uses a combination of software and human review to conduct a daily search for "topics" (keyword sets) on "feeder sites" (any searchable Web entity—general search engines, online databases, specialty search engines, and so on). The clippings generated by this service are gathered, sorted, and the duplicates eliminated. They're saved in an "in-box" accessible to you when you log in to the Web site.

As you might imagine, CyberAlert offers comprehensive coverage of the Web, and even of Usenet newsgroups if you include DejaNews as one of your "feeder sites." On the other hand, this service is expensive, starting at $1,995 a month. There are no "per clip" (per item found) fees.

CyberCheck Internet Monitoring

http://www.cycheck.com/

CyberCheck offers two basic services. For the first service, called Forum-Check, they will monitor over 150,000 online forums for the keywords you specify and monitor up to five Web sites for changes. The forums include Web-site discussion groups, e-mail discussion groups, newsletters, and Usenet. They'll send you the results via e-mail or fax and do not have a "per clip" fee. The second service is called WebCheck. With WebCheck, CyberCheck will do a thorough, daily monitoring of selected Web sites, with no "per clip" charges for the materials they deliver to you. CyberCheck also offers several additional "a la carte" services, including human, in-depth monitoring of news groups and mailing lists and daily instead of weekly clipping delivery. CyberCheck does not post its prices on its Web site, but it does offer a free trial of the ForumCheck service.

CyberScan Internet Clipping Service

http://www.clippingservice.com/

CyberScan has a "per clip" fee of $2, but its base rates are much lower than CyberAlert (and you can limit the number of clips per report that you receive). This service searches the Internet for the keywords you specify, and returns clips to you every business day, weekly, or monthly as you prefer: via e-mail, fax, Federal Express, or postal mail. CyberScan's costs start at around $50 and go up depending on the services you want and the frequency with which you want to be sent clippings.

There are a variety of other services that offer online monitoring. Check here:

eWatch
http://www.ewatch.com/

HyperNews
http://www.hyper-news.com/

Webclipping
http://www.webclipping.com/

Yahoo!—Clipping and Monitoring Services
http://dir.yahoo.com/Business_and_Economy/Companies/Corporate_
Services/Public_Relations/Clipping_and_Monitoring_Services/

The services and sites described above can search mostly the Web, but can also search Usenet in certain cases as well. (Many search engines, including AltaVista, Excite, and HotBot, offer searches of Usenet.) But there are tools that are specifically designed to search mailing lists and Usenet newsgroups.

NEWSGROUPS AND MAILING LISTS

Usenet newsgroups are like particularly crowded, noisy, and opinionated public forums. Everybody on the Internet can drop by, sound off, start fights, and occasionally quietly and intelligently express an opinion. There's a lot of spam on Usenet newsgroups, too, which has greatly cut down on their effectiveness as a public forum. That's one of the reasons that mailing-list discussion groups are becoming much more popular than newsgroups—they're easier to control than newsgroups. While there are several places you can go to search Usenet, there are few places that you can search a large number of mailing lists at once. Expect that to change over time, however.

Searching Newsgroups

DejaNews is probably the most famous newsgroup-searching tool, but there are others, such as remarQ and Reference.COM. A number of Web search sites also provide the ability to search newsgroup messages, too. Yahoo!, for instance, allows you to search newsgroup messages ... but in fact they simply link over to DejaNews to actually carry out the search.

DejaNews

http://www.dejanews.com/

DejaNews offers access to over 80,000 newsgroups, with simple searching and advanced searching that allows you to search their archives all the way back to 1995 (when many of you reading this probably weren't even on the Internet). You can even specify a particular newsgroup to search, and search for messages from a particular e-mail address or with a specified subject line. You can register on DejaNews to get free Web-based access to newsgroups, and a free DejaNews e-mail account.

remarQ

http://www.remarq.com/

remarQ archives 30,000 newsgroups. You can search for a particular newsgroup, or search the messages held by all the groups. However, remarQ's search system is way too simple; all you can do is enter a keyword—or several keywords, perhaps—but it currently won't let you do the sort of advanced searching available at DejaNews.

Reference.COM

http://www.reference.com/

Reference.COM has some very useful features, but it's not clear if this service is being maintained. It looks like it was set up to run sometime in 1996, and has been left on its own ever since. It does work—you can search for keywords and find quite recent messages. But it's not clear exactly what the system is archiving, because the background documentation is so out of date. It states that there are 15,000 newsgroups, but it's been a long time since there were that few.

Still, it has one feature that is particularly useful; you can set up queries to run automatically, with the results to be sent to you by e-mail, a great way to find out when someone says something about you, your company, or products in one of the newsgroups archived by Reference.COM (whatever that might be). If you're interested in tracking a particular newsgroup, you could look it up at Reference.COM to see if it's archived there, and then, if it is, set up an automatic query to keep watch on that group for you.

Searching Mailing Lists

It's difficult to find out what's being said about your products in mailing-list discussion groups. If you had the time, you could check with individual groups (see Chapter 9 for more information about finding these groups). Many groups have archives, often stored at a member's Web site. If there are one or two very important mailing-list discussion groups that you track, then you can search those archives now and then.

As for searching thousands of discussion groups at once ... that's more difficult. The only service we're aware of is **Reference.COM** (http://www. reference.com/); not only can you search Usenet newsgroups at Reference. COM, but you can also search mailing-list discussion groups and Web-forums (Web-site-based discussion groups). Reference.COM has an index of over 100,000 mailing lists, but it doesn't archive nearly as many. It's really not clear how many mailing lists it does archive; still, you may want to try a few searches here to see what turns up. It has a simple search interface that allows you to search about 10 days' worth of postings, or a more advanced search that goes back about a year.

CHECKING OFFLINE PUBLICATIONS

The above tools will give you plenty of ways to search discussions going on throughout the Internet. But there are Internet tools that are pretty useful for tracking what's being said in offline publications, too. There are plenty of free and pay resources available, and even the pay resources are pretty reasonably priced. The free ones usually track only a few weeks' worth of news. The pay services, not surprisingly, track much greater collections of news.

Free Tools

Several search engines offer tools for tracking news in offline media. Excite and Northern Light are two of the "biggies."

Excite's NewsTracker

http://nt.excite.com/

Excite's NewsTracker tracks the news from 300 online newspapers and magazines. You can do a search from the NewsTracker site or you can set up a "clipping service" that allows you to track up to 20 different topics (your company name, the name of your industry, competitor names, etc.). Every time you log in to NewsTracker, you'll be able to access your customized clipping file.

NewsTracker has a couple of drawbacks. From Tara's experience searching it, she doesn't think the stories in its database are more than a couple of weeks old. Furthermore, 300 publications isn't that much. (At your local library, yes. At your favorite newsstand, absolutely. But 300 publications only scratches the surface when it comes to Internet-based repositories of information.) The service is free, however, and the clipping service is handy.

Northern Light Current News

http://www.northernlight.com/news.html

Northern Light has a premium search service that allows you to search through publication articles for a fee, but their Current News service is free. The Current News service searches through a two-week archive of news from 77 sources, including newswires and press release wires.

The drawbacks to this service are obvious: only two weeks' worth of information and a fairly low number of sources. However, where Northern Light shines is that you can specify just how recent the stories should be (within the last two hours, within the last day, or within the last two weeks) and you can also search by category. Eleven categories are available, including Business, Sports Articles, and Weather Conditions.

There are several other free places online where you can search through news archives:

HotBot: News Channel
   http://www.newsbot.com/

Newshub
   http://www.newshub.com/

TotalNEWS
   http://www.totalnews.com/

News Hunt (a collection of links to newspaper and other publication archives)
   http://www.newshunt.com/

Pay Services

The drawback of the free services is that they're very limited. Unless you've been tracking your company's appearances in the media since the beginning of your promotional program, the limits to their archives are going to frustrate you. You might also find yourself annoyed by the limited number of publications the free services cover, especially if your product or service is highly technical or otherwise oriented towards a niche. There are some pay services available, however, and some aren't particularly expensive.

The Dow Jones Publications Library

   http://www.wsj.com/Publib/

Free search access to the Dow Jones Publications Library comes with a subscription to the online Wall Street Journal, which costs $59 a year. Accessing news stories from the DJPL costs about $2.95 each—less if you want only a citation.

The DJPL has, in Tara's opinion, the most complete archive of publications this side of a super-expensive resource like **LEXIS-NEXIS** (http://www.LEXIS-NEXIS.com/). There are hundreds of resources here, gathered from all over the world. They run the gamut from mainstream periodicals like *USA Today* to very specialized business and technical publications. Some of the available archives go back decades; most go back at least a few years.

You can get really lost searching here, and you can spend a lot of money, too. Tara's a cheapskate, so she'll use this resource to find media occurrences of a company name, and then try to find the article somewhere else. If you anticipate retrieving a lot of articles here, you'll want to check out subscription options that allow you to pay a certain amount each month and get a certain number of articles free.

Electric Library

http://www.elibrary.com/

The Electric Library has a smaller publications database than the Dow Jones Publications Library, but you get unlimited searching and retrieving for $9.95 a month. (There's no "per article" cost like there is with the Dow Jones Publications Library.) Electric Library indexes the archives of over 150 publications, including a few newswires and press-release wires. The basic search is a little hard to get used to (sometimes the queries you enter don't react like you'd expect them to). However, the power search will give you a way to easily narrow down your search, including by date and publication type. (You can search pictures, television transcripts, and other types of media in addition to publication archives.)

If your company is a mainstream company and wouldn't appear in the more esoteric and specialized media covered by the Dow Jones Publications Library, you could do a lot of your searching via Electric Library. Keep in mind, however, that the Electric Library doesn't carry nearly as many local newspapers as the Dow Jones Publications Library, so if you're getting a lot of mentions in smaller papers, you'll miss them.

Northern Light

http://www.nlsearch.com/

Northern Light is a very interesting Web-search hybrid. When you search Northern Light you search both a database of Web sites and what they call a "special collection." The special collection consists of over 5,000 books, journals, reviews, magazines, and news wires. Searching the special collection is free, but when you find something you have to pay to read it. Accessing content in the special collection will cost you per item (prices range from $1 to $4 depending on the article). The Northern Light special collection has especially strong science and health collections of publications.

Northern Light's collection is far smaller than the Dow Jones Publications Library. However, since it's a "pay as you go" plan, those who access small numbers of articles will find this a much less expensive research option. Furthermore, Northern Light's special collection content offers abstracts that can be reviewed before paying for the content. The abstracts give you a good idea whether the information you're looking at is relevant to the subjects in which you're interested.

Computer Magazine Archive

http://cma.zdnet.com/

This archive contains over 200,000 articles from 200 magazines, journals, and newspapers. It's $7.95 a month, or $69.96 a year, but you can get the first two weeks free. Better still, go to the **ZD Rewards program** (http://cma. zdnet.com/texis/zdrewards/) and get a trial membership; it's just $1. That'll get you 30 free days in the program, which, along with the Computer Magazine Archive, provides lots of other interesting benefits. If you

Point and Clip

Once you've gotten your past press mentions squared away, you might want to try media "clipping" services. Clipping services offer you the chance to track mentions of your company name or news related to your company's industry. **NewsPage**, *at* http://www.newspage.com/, *is a great way to track information and news related to particular industries. Every business day NewsPage will send you a summary of information related to your industry. NewsPage also offers an extensive customized Web page that contains all news relevant to the industries you're tracking. NewsPage offers free services, but the premium services, which offer wider access to more industry news, run about $6.95 a month. If you're interested in tracking news by keyword—like your company name, name of your competitor, etc.—check out* **Inquisit** *at* http://www.inquisit. com/. Inquisit *filters over 300 publications by keyword and sends you the results. You can have an unlimited number of these "Inquisit agents" for only $12.95 a month. Tara thinks that when it comes to pay services, this is one of the most best-kept secrets on the Internet.*

decide to continue after the 30 days, it's just $49.95, which is around $20 less than the full price of the Computer Magazine Archive. (This offer is current at the time of writing; it's not apparent how long it will continue.)

Luce Online

http://www.luceonline.com/

Luce Online is part of **Luce Press Clippings** (http://www.lucepress.com/), a company that's been in business over 110 years. This is a serious press-clipping service; they read 15,000 U.S. newspapers and magazines, and work with affiliates in other countries if you want to go farther

More Clipping Services

There are plenty more clipping services, both online and offline. See **Yahoo!'s Clipping and Monitoring Services** *page:* http://dir.yahoo.com/Business_and_Economy/Companies/Corporate_Services/Public_Relations/Clipping_and_Monitoring_Services/.

afield. This service can be expensive, but if you need a top-of-the-line service, it's hard to beat a long-lived clipping service such as Luce.

THE REAL RESULTS

Ultimately there's only one way to figure out how your promotional campaign is going: by looking at what you are trying to achieve, and seeing to what degree you have achieved it! Trying to sell books? Well, the real feedback you want is book sales. Trying to get donations for your non-profit organization? The real result, then, is whether you are getting donations.

However, these other techniques we've discussed—for measuring visits to your sites and how often and where you are mentioned on the Web and in the media—are still very important. Think of a marketing and promotions campaign as a *flow* of people. You want people to talk about you, your products, and services, so that people will visit your site, so that some of them will do whatever it is you want them to do—buy something, be convinced by your ideas, donate money …

These techniques help you measure that flow. You can see if people are talking about you; if they're not, there's your problem. You can see if people are visiting your site; if they're not, then maybe you have to get far more people talking about you than you realized! And finally, you can see whether people are doing what you want them to do once they reach your site. If they're not—if people are visiting your site, but they're not doing what you want them to do— then perhaps your "sales message" simply isn't very good. But there's another thing to consider. You can't evaluate whether your site is working well until you understand a critical fact about Internet visits.

Many Hits, Few Sales

We've discussed hits, and we've discussed visits. You've learned that a hell of a lot of hits could mean lots and lots of visits … or perhaps not quite so many. But what does it mean if your site is getting a lot of visits? Have you succeeded? And what does "a lot" or "many" mean on the Internet? There's something you need to understand about Internet enterprise. It's not like the real world.

Imagine, for instance, that you own a small store on a small-town main street, or maybe in a mall. Each day you get, oh, let's say, 1,000 people visiting your store. Happy? Probably. Different businesses vary, but in most real-world businesses 1,000 visitors probably translates into significant sales. Perhaps 80 percent of the visitors buy, perhaps just 50 percent. But in most cases 1,000 visits means a lot of sales.

It's different on the Internet. While 1,000 visitors a day may be very exciting, it's much less so when you realize that the numbers work differently on the Internet. An Internet visitor is not worth as much as a real-world visitor, because a visitor on the Internet is far less likely to buy. If you're selling a product at your site, what proportion of your 1,000 visitors are likely to buy? Eighty percent? Very, very unlikely. Fifty percent—not much chance. No, bring the numbers way down. Start thinking in terms of one or two percent.

Of course there are many variables involved—your sales will depend on the type of product you're selling, how well you pitch the product, on the guarantee you offer and your shipping terms, and so on. In some cases it may be possible to "convert"—to get sales from a visitor—for a much higher proportion of the time. But in general Internet commerce, conversion rates are in the single digits. For instance, Jason Olim, writing in *The CDnow Story* (Top Floor Publishing, co-authored with Peter, by the way), says that "conversion rates vary tremendously, depending on where the visitor comes from, for instance, and even from which page they come from at a particular site. Some pages send us visitors that 'convert' at the rate of as low as 0.1 percent … others may send visitors that convert at a rate of 10 percent."

Forrester Research examined Web conversion rates and found that 35 percent of Web sites reported making two or fewer sales for every hundred visitors. Forty-four percent were making no sales, so that leaves just 22 percent making higher sales—though probably in most cases not much higher. And many of the 35 percent are probably getting much lower conversion rates—one per hundred, one per two hundred, one per three hundred …

So if you use the techniques in this chapter and find that you have lots and lots of visitors, yet you're not selling much, reappraise the numbers. Are you converting 10 percent of your visitors? You're way ahead of the pack! Converting just one percent? Well, it's still pretty normal for this type of commerce.

This may come as a disappointment to many, but knowledge is power. We want you to understand the reality, and then work from there. If you have lots of visitors, and convert only one or two percent, there are two things you can do. First, you can work hard to bring *more* people to your site. Sorry, but it's constant work. (There's been enough hype about how the Internet is paved with gold; the reality is that it's not … it takes a lot of effort to succeed on the Internet, just as it does in the real world.)

Catalogs, Not Stores

The second thing you can do is realize that this "problem" of numbers is a double-edged sword. If you are converting a small percentage of visitors, you should realize that if you can convince just one person in one or two hundred to buy from you, you've just increased your business tremendously.

We hear a lot about Web stores. Companies set up shops or stores online, as if these sites are cyberspace versions of the real thing. But a better parallel with the real world may be catalogs. In two very important ways, Web sites that sell things are very similar to real-world, mail-order catalogs. And changing the way you think about your Web site may help you refocus and find new ways to sell products.

The first parallel with catalog companies is that a Web site, as we've seen, needs to reach a large number of people in order to make a sale. It may take 40, 50, 100, perhaps 200 or more visitors to a Web site for every sale. But real-world stores are not like this. You can bet that out of every 100 people that walk into The Gap or Sears, far more than just one will buy. But catalog sales *are* like this. Catalog companies know they need to send out a huge number of catalogs in order to keep the sales coming in. I don't know the actual numbers, but conversion rates are certainly similar to Web sites.

The other major parallel between Web sites and catalogs is that catalog companies spend an awful lot of time, money, and energy "tweaking" things, and testing. Sure, stores do this to some extent, as well. But it's nowhere near as important in the retail-store environment as it is in catalog sales. This is a natural outcome of the conversion ratio. Low conversion rates mean you have to find a lot of people before you can get one to buy, but they also mean that very small changes can make a very big difference. For instance, if you only get one person in a hundred to buy, that means if you can tweak things just very slightly, and convince one more person out of every 200 to buy, you've just increased your sales by 50 percent. The catalog business is a "mature" business; it's been around a long time, and long ago it learned that it had to tweak things, that small changes could produce large increases in sales. So catalog companies constantly experiment with new ways to present products, with special offers, colors, illustration and design, and so on. Already some of the big players on the Web have recognized that they have to constantly experiment, in the same way that the catalogs do. Eventually, Peter believes, people running commercial Web sites will have to learn direct-mail skills, and will gradually come to realize that they're not really running stores at all.

PART IV

E-MAIL PR

CHAPTER FIFTEEN

E-mail Basics

There's much more to the Internet than just the World Wide Web. The Web is just one of several important software systems running on the Internet, yet it's the one that gets the most press and attention. But e-mail is in many ways more important than the Web. We know plenty of people who don't spend much time on the Web but spend plenty of time rummaging through an e-mail box. E-mail provides a direct communication channel, rather than a broadcast channel. The Web is a great place to let visitors and prospects know all about your products and services. It's an excellent place to have press releases, product shots, and technical information available for journalists. But when it comes down to building relationships and staying in touch, you just can't beat e-mail.

This chapter is all about getting the most you can out of e-mail, whether you're sending out press releases or sending out newsletters. We'll be looking at programs that you can use, deadly sins of e-mail (like spam), and how to personalize the e-mail you send to your customers. Let's start with applications. What program are you using to send out your e-mail?

E-MAIL APPLICATIONS

You may be using the e-mail application that came with your Internet setup package. That application might be Eudora Light, or the e-mail programs that come with Netscape Communicator or Microsoft's Internet Explorer.

Those applications might be good enough for what you've been doing. But if you want to take your e-mail to another level, you should investigate other possibilities. There are several great packages out there that can help your online marketing and promotional efforts.

Eudora Pro

http://www.eudora.com/

Eudora Pro is one of the oldest personal-computer e-mail packages on the Internet, and until the last couple of years it was indisputably the most popular. There's a free version called Eudora Light, and that might be the one you're using. (Many ISP's bundle it with their introductory software.) However, upgrading to the pay version has a lot of payoffs:

- Eudora Pro allows you to make filters for your e-mail. (More on that later.)
- Eudora Pro has a built-in spell-checker (always important for making a good impression!).
- Eudora Pro offers *stationery*, great for sending personalized versions of messages you have to send often. (Stationery are boilerplate e-mail messages—you create a message in the normal way, specifying the subject line and body of the message. Then instead of actually sending the e-mail, you save it as stationery. When you want to reply to a message with a "form letter" that you've created as stationery, you can select the Reply With command and select the stationary you want to use.

These are just a few of Eudora Pro's features compared to Eudora Light. As you see, Eudora Pro offers many more options for organization, which you'll need as you accumulate thousands and thousands of e-mail messages. Eudora Pro is available for Windows and the Macintosh.

Pegasus

http://www.pegasus.usa.com/ faqs.asp

You won't see full-page ads for Pegasus in your favorite computer magazine, and you won't get direct mail encouraging you to try the new

Keep Up To Date

It's a good idea to keep up to date with your e-mail software. They all have bugs and serious design flaws, and now and then there are potential security problems discovered related to e-mail programs. To make sure you've got the most recent and secure version, either check the publisher's Web page every couple of months or sign up with the company's mailing list so you're alerted every time a new version of the program comes out. (Upgrades, even for commercial programs, are often free.)

version of Pegasus. That's because Pegasus is completely free. That's right, free; the only thing you have to pay for is a paper version of the documentation if you want one.

Don't assume that Pegasus, just because it's free, is a weak program. It isn't. It has a powerful filtering system, for example, and is quite capable of mailing to several thousand people at a time; it's one of the few personal e-mail programs that are suitable for use as mailing list discussion group programs or for newsletter publishing. (Many of the popular commercial programs are not capable of being used for this purpose.)

It also has a great address book, and works with networked computers. The downside of Pegasus is that because it does so much, it can take a while to learn. Non-technical users who want to just read and send e-mail would be better served to stick with a program like Eudora. If you're a real geek, though, and want all the control you can get, Pegasus is worth playing with. Pegasus is available for Windows, DOS, and Macintosh.

Converting Address Books and Mailboxes

If you're converting from one e-mail program to another, be sure to check to see if there are programs available that convert your old e-mail boxes and address books from your old program to the new program. If such programs are available, the Web site for the e-mail program you choose should mention them. You can learn more about converting **Eudora mailboxes** *at* http://mango.human. cornell.edu/kens/MoreFAQ.html# Convert. *There's an online service for converting address books at* http://www.interguru.com/ mailconv.htm.

Microsoft Outlook

http://www.microsoft.com/outlook/

Of course Microsoft has an e-mail client. What, did you think they would leave it up to everybody else? The core advantage of Microsoft Outlook is that it integrates well with other Microsoft Office applications, including Microsoft Word and Internet Explorer. If you've acquired a Windows-based computer in the last year or so, you probably already have Outlook Express, a simpler version of Outlook that contains the e-mail portion, on your computer. (In earlier incarnations of Outlook there were two separate programs, Internet Mail and Internet News.)

Outlook combines contact management with sending e-mail, allowing you to do scheduling and follow-up via e-mail. Outlook also offers several pre-created forms which allow you to save and forward information in different formats (library card catalogs, "While you were out" messages, and so on). On the other hand, in many ways Outlook is not as powerful as Eudora or Pegasus.

Test, Test, Test

Most of the programs mentioned here have "light" versions and evaluation versions available. Do as much software testing and evaluation as you can stand. You're going to be using your e-mail an awful lot, so be sure that you're comfortable with what you're using!

If you've already got a contact manager, all this is going to be overkill for you. On the other hand, if most of your contact management needs are e-mail based, you might find Outlook is suitable both for sending e-mail and keeping in touch.

Netscape Messenger

http://www.netscape.com/
messenger/start/

Netscape Messenger comes bundled with Netscape Communicator, so it's free. Unfortunately it's not as full-featured as the other e-mail applications we've mentioned. On the plus side, because it's integrated into Netscape Communicator, you can view HTML mail (that is, e-mail messages formatted using HTML) with no problems and without opening a separate browser program (the other programs can also display HTML mail, though not always quite as well). It also allows you to read newsgroup messages, so if you

Can You Get a POP Box?

As we discussed in Chapter 2, you need a POP e-mail account in order to use these programs. (If you are working with a large corporation, you may have an IMAP account which will work, too—but if you are accessing the Internet through a service provider, you'll probably get a POP box.) But some online services provide non-POP e-mail accounts. If you're using such a service, you may not be able to use a POP program such as the ones we've described here. However, check with your service. They may have a POP option. CompuServe, for instance, allows you to convert your e-mail system to POP.

work in newsgroups very often you'll find it convenient to be able to use the same program to read them. On the other hand, Messenger's filtering is not as good as the other programs, so keeping your messages organized might be more of a challenge. Messenger is available for Windows and Macintosh.

Other E-mail Programs

There are dozens of e-mail applications available. These are just a few of the other ones you might want to check out.

Akmail (Windows; a great program, but no longer in development)
http://www.akmail.com/

The Bat (Windows and Windows NT)
http://www.ritlabs.com/the_bat/

Calypso (Windows and Windows NT)
http://www.mcsdallas.com/

DTS Mail (Windows and Windows NT)
http://dtsoftware.simplenet.com/

MailSmith (Macintosh)
http://web.barebones.com/products/msmith/msmith.html

PowerMail (Macintosh)
http://www.ctmdev.com/

TransSoft's Mail Control (Windows and Windows NT)
http://artemis.centrum.is/~bhg/

Choosing an e-mail program isn't something you can do in five minutes. You'll need to work with the different products available, and get a feel for the features you like and use the most. E-mail will be a lifeline of contact between you and your customers, so make sure you're using a program with which you're comfortable!

THE BASICS OF GOOD E-MAIL

We can't give you instructions on how to use every possible e-mail program you might use. So instead of giving you "click here click there" kind of instructions, we're going to give you an overview of how to best use e-mail. For the purposes of this chapter, we're dividing e-mail into three sections: address lines, subject line, and body.

Address Lines

The address lines in an e-mail message are the instructions that you provide to tell the e-mail system where the message should go. Putting someone's e-mail address in the To: line means you want the e-mail to go to that person. Your name and address in the From: line shows that the e-mail came from you. This isn't rocket science. But there are a couple of lines that you might not know about, or might not understand how to use properly—namely, the Cc: and Bcc: lines.

> **To:**—You think you know how to use the To: line. But did you know that you can put multiple e-mail addresses on that line? Quite likely. But did you know you probably shouldn't in most cases? It's *very* rude to put dozens of e-mail addresses in the To: line, particularly if the people don't know each other and have no reason to—because each message on the To: line will be visible to every recipient. For instance, don't put the addresses of 1,000 of your closest friends on the To: line when forwarding a joke a colleague just sent you. (You should use Bcc: for that.)

> **Cc:**—The Cc: line means *Carbon Copy.* Putting e-mail addresses in the Cc: line means that a copy of the e-mail will be sent to those e-mail addresses, in addition to the address on the To: line. In some programs you can use the Cc: line as the sole address line—you don't need to put anything on the To: line. In others, you can only use the Cc: line if you use the To: line as well. In general, you can list as many e-mail addresses in the Cc: line as you like. But again, you probably shouldn't. The Cc: line is visible to everyone getting the message, so don't use it if the people receiving the message don't need to know that others received the message.

> **Bcc:**—Pay attention: the proper use of a Bcc: line is one of the secret weapons of good e-mail. Bcc: stands for *Blind Carbon Copy.* The Bcc: header works like the Cc: line: it sends copies of an e-mail to the e-mail addresses you specify. The difference is that the Bcc: recipients' identities are protected from other recipients. People receiving Bcc: copies can see all the addresses on the To: and Cc: lines, but the To: and Cc: recipients cannot see the Bcc: addresses. In addition, if you have multiple Bcc: recipients, they cannot see the addresses of one another either.

When would you want to use Bcc:? When you're sending e-mail to dozens, perhaps hundreds, of people at a time. Say you wanted to send a product update to 100 e-mail addresses—or perhaps you're running a small newsletter using your e-mail program, mailing out to 1,000 subscribers. If you put the e-mail addresses in the To: header or the Cc: header, then the recipients of the message would have to scroll through 100 (or 1,000) e-mail addresses in order to get to

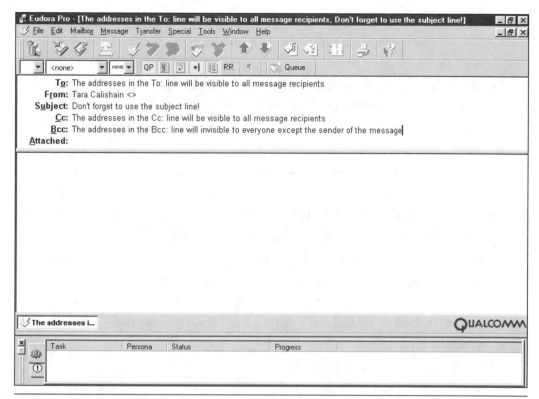

FIGURE 15.1: Be careful how you use your header lines.

the update. That's inconvenient, but it's also going to get you a lot of complaints. People don't want you to give their e-mail addresses to hundreds of other people like that! If you put the addresses in the Bcc: header, however, nobody will see anyone else's address.

If your e-mail program allows you to send a message to just the Bcc: recipients—as, for instance, Eudora Pro 4.0 does—then you can leave the To: line empty. If your program forces you to use the To: line, then put *your* address on the To: line, so you'll get a copy back.

Subject Line

Using the address lines appropriately is important, but so is using the subject line effectively. The better your subject line, the better the chance that your e-mail message will be read. The subject line is like the cover of a book. The impression your readers get from the subject line plays an important role in whether your message gets read. With that in mind, we've got some Dos and Don'ts for you:

DO make your subject line as specific as possible. If you're replying to someone's e-mail, use their subject line with whatever clarification is necessary.

DON'T use generic subject lines like "Your phone call," "The information you requested," or "What we were talking about." Those subject lines used to be okay, but more and more spammers are using them.

DON'T make subject lines to long—generally no longer than about 10 words.

DON'T USE ALL CAPITAL LETTERS OR EXTRA AMOUNTS OF PUNCTUATION IN YOUR SUBJECT LINE!!!!!????????

DON'T use a misleading subject line. If you're sending out a press release, don't use the subject line of "Your phone call." This will damage your credibility and possibly get your e-mail address tossed into somebody's e-mail filter so they never see any more of your e-mail messages.

DON'T leave the subject line blank. That's like having a book with a blank cover. Make sure your subject line says something, even if it's just a basic "My feelings on xyz."

DO learn how to use informal subject lines for business. The real trick to many business relationships is to change them from formal to informal. There are so many stodgy, formal, boring business communications that one that reads smoothly and easily can stand out—but this only works if you can write well!

DO make sure your spelling and grammar are correct.

DO make sure your subject line is compelling, interesting, and screams out, "Open this e-mail!"

Once you've got a subject line that works—one that makes the recipient want to open the message—you want to write an e-mail body—the actual message—that lives up to it.

The Body of Your E-mail

The body of the e-mail is, of course, where you get your message across. For that reason you want to have a "lean and mean" e-mail body, as concise as possible. Do we have some Dos and Don'ts for you? Of course we do.

DO quote. "Quoting" is when you include a portion of a previous e-mail message when you reply to it or forward it to someone else, in order to add context to your current e-mail message. Many people get huge amounts of e-mail, and it's easy to forget what you said in an earlier message, or what a particular correspondence relates to; quoting earlier text makes it easy for recipients to quickly figure out what's going on.

DON'T over-quote. You'll often see messages in which someone quotes an entire 40- or 50-line e-mail message, and then adds two or three words at the end, making it hard to find the response and cluttering up the message. Just quote the piece of the message to which you are replying, or just a snippet to remind the recipient what you were discussing.

DO make sure your e-mail is spell-checked and uses good grammar. Many e-mail programs have spell-checkers, and you can always run important messages through a word processor's grammar checker, or have someone edit it for you.

DO keep your e-mails to about 60–70 columns wide. That way you're assured that most e-mail readers will be able to read them all right. If you make them more than 80 columns wide, then your message might be broken up
into raggedy, short,
and uneven lines like this.

DO make sure that you're sending an e-mail message to the right address. It's really embarrassing to send a private e-mail message to an entire mailing list (and you'll probably do it at least once in your Internet life, so get ready for it).

DO keep the emoticons to a minimum. Emoticons are little symbols that are a substitute for voice tone and facial expressions. This, for example— :-> —is an emoticon of a smiling face. Emoticons are sometimes useful to make the point that you're kidding or that a reader shouldn't take you seriously, but a lot of people find them annoying. Keep the emoticons and other emotional notations— <grin> or <smile> —to a minimum.

DON'T write a message in your word processor and then paste it into the e-mail program. Word processors often add special "typesetting" characters, such as curly quote symbols, em-dashes, ellipsis, and so on. If you place these symbols into an e-mail message, the message *may* go through okay. But many e-mail systems don't like these symbols, and will scramble the message in some way—for instance, the recipient may see each line break in the message preceded by =20.

DO make sure that your e-mail messages are text-only. Some e-mail readers cannot display HTML mail very well, and others can't display it at all. Also, be sure that you don't put attachments to your e-mail. What you think is so cute and something you want to pass on can turn out to be a computer-crashing headache for someone else. (Some programs have plain-text and HTML settings that you can choose.)

As you look over these Dos and Don'ts, you'll see that a lot of them are common sense. There's a reason for that; e-mail is a lot like business communication. As long as you keep that in mind, you'll be fine. As we've stated over and over in this chapter, e-mail is an exceptionally powerful tool. But it's also subject to a lot of abuse.

E-MAIL PROBLEMS

Every time you send regular mail, you spend money. Whether it's a 33-cent stamp or a bulk-mail indicia, it costs something to send mail. On the Internet, however, many people don't have to pay anything beyond their connection costs, removing one of the barriers to communication. This gives rise to a lot of silliness. The two biggest examples of this silliness are spamming and chain mail.

Spamming

Free direct business mail to potential customers all over the world! Send

Attachments

E-mail messages are just plain text. But you can send computer files of various kinds by attaching them to e-mail messages. Theoretically you could send anything as an attachment, but we don't recommend it unless the person you send the attachment to knows about it in advance and agrees to it.

People don't like receiving attachments for various reasons. They can't be sure that the attachments don't contain viruses: executable files, programs, can carry viruses, and programs such as Word and Excel can carry viruses embedded in macros. (By the way, plain-text e-mail messages cannot carry viruses.) If you send attachments, you're telling the recipient, in effect, to spend time opening it to see what's in it, which is a little rude. And in some cases very large attached files can crash e-mail programs. Don't send attachments unless the recipients have a reason to know they'll be receiving it.

thousand and thousands of pieces of mail without spending a dime! Sounds great, doesn't it?

That's the whole problem!

Since discovering the Internet and the ease by which they could contact millions of people, a wide variety of people have started taking advantage of spamming, otherwise known as unsolicited bulk e-mail. Their unsolicited advertisements may be promoting good products, but all too often they're promoting scams, pornography sites, inaccurate information about stocks, and so on. And

What is Spam?

Tara defines spam as "unsolicited bulk e-mail." Peter prefers to be a bit more specific, calling it "unsolicited and indiscriminate bulk e-mail." Unfortunately some people have taken to defining spam as "unsolicited commercial e-mail" (sometimes written as UCE). This definition is a real problem, as we'll explain in a moment.

in any case, whether the products being promoted are legitimate or not, the flood of unwanted e-mail into your inbox is a real nuisance.

Does that mean all spam is for illegitimate companies and causes? Of course not. But much of it is. And if a legitimate company relies on spam to get its message across, it's immediately putting itself in the same class with porn companies and get-rich-quick schemes. Is that a place you want to be?

Some people react to the condemnation of spam with the response, "What's the big deal? Just hit the Delete key." Let's look at that argument for a minute, and examine the possibility of just legitimate companies using e-mail. Let's say there are about 4,500,000 companies in the United States. (We got that number from an economic census at the **U.S. Census Bureau:** http://www.census.gov/epcd/www/ecensus.html.) Since the Internet doesn't have distance restrictions, let's say all of these companies want to send you unsolicited e-mail once a year. Just once.

Just one e-mail a year from each of these companies means you'd be getting over 12,300 messages a day in your mailbox. And that doesn't count companies that send more than one e-mail a year and companies outside the U.S. Right now you might think that unsolicited e-mail isn't that big a deal, because these companies are not on the 'Net. But the Internet population, of citizens and businesses, is only going to get larger, and the problem of unsolicited e-mail, as more and more businesses decide that there "isn't any harm in sending one unsolicited e-mail," is going to grow exponentially.

Furthermore, in many cases—particularly outside the United States—phone costs are calculated by the minute. Having to stay connected to download spam means that these unfortunate users have to pay to download e-mail they don't want.

Please don't let your business add to this problem. Help support responsible use of e-mail by using only "opt-in" e-mail lists (where the addressee has requested to be added to the list), and by protecting the e-mail addresses of your customers and prospects by refusing to rent or sell your lists of e-mail addresses.

We haven't mentioned the really negative repercussions of sending unsolicited bulk e-mail. Things like, oh, lawsuits. Criminal prosecutions. Threats from ticked-off hackers. Mailbombs (attacks by huge numbers of e-mail messages that will overload your mailbox). The complete loss of respect in the online community. Stuff like that. Think twice.

For more information on spamming and what you can do to prevent it—and what can happen to you if you indulge—check out the following Web sites:

Stop Spam FAQ
http://just4u.com/webconsultants/spamfaq.htm

Junkbusters (covers telemarketing and junk mail in addition to spam)
http://www.junkbusters.com/

O'Reilly Stop Spam Center
http://stopspam.oreilly.com/

The Coalition Against Unsolicited Commercial E-mail
http://www.cauce.org/

Junk Email Resource Page
http://www.junkemail.org/

Fight Spam on the Internet!
http://spam.abuse.net/

The Spam-L FAQ
http://oasis.ot.com/~dmuth/spam-l/

These resources should give you some idea of the problems of spam and the problems you face if you get involved with it.

The Spam Overreaction

Many people and anti-spam organizations have taken to defining spam as UCE—*unsolicited commercial e-mail*. Originally the definition was very different, but some anti-spam groups have forced it to evolve toward this definition. If you're doing business on the Internet, especially if you're publishing an e-mail newsletter, you should be very careful about endorsing such a vague and sloppy definition.

For instance, Peter recently received an e-mail that was completely unsolicited—he'd never heard of the person before, let alone given her his e-mail address or asked her to contact him. It was definitely commercial; she contacted him in relation to her job, and asked him to give her something of economic value. It was, according to this absurd definition, spam.

But she was a writer for *PC World,* asking for a review copy of his book, *Poor Richard's Web Site.* He was happy to hear from her, of course, so he didn't regard it as spam. But according to the UCE definition, he could, if he decided he didn't want to hear from her, justly consider it to be spam. And, according to many anti-spam groups, he should then be allowed to sue her or force her ISP to close down her account. With a definition as vague as this, if you don't like what you hear, it's spam; if you do, it's not. So be careful what you ask for; you might just get it.

Consider the opposite of this case, for example. If you contact a journalist who you've never spoken with before, that journalist could, under the UCE definition, regard your message as spam. In most cases journalists won't, but now and then you will run into people who will be very rude, accuse you of spamming, and even contact your ISP to complain. Note that Peter has used the methods in Chapter 16 to contact thousands of journalists very quickly. He's had overwhelmingly good reactions—journalists thanking him for the offer of a review book, for instance, and asking for a copy; journalists thanking him for thinking of them but turning down the offer; journalists turning him down, but suggesting he contact a colleague. He's received a handful of messages asking, quite politely, to be removed from his list. And he's received just one or two rude messages accusing him of being a spammer.

In fact Peter's been accused of spamming far more often in the case of *solicited* e-mail! Thanks to this anti-spam hysteria, newsletter publishers are routinely accused of spamming, by people who have subscribed to the newsletter! They forget they've subscribed, or perhaps share an account with someone who subscribed. For instance, Peter once received a rather rude e-mail message telling him to stop sending his "garbage." He wrote an article in his newsletter (http://PoorRichard.com/newsltr/) about spam, quoting this message. A day or two later someone sent Peter a message apologizing for the behavior of his wife! This gentleman had subscribed to *Poor Richard's Web Site News,* but when his wife found the message in their inbox she just assumed it was spam.

This anti-spam hysteria is a serious problem. Newsletter publishers are continually being accused of spamming, and are sometimes banned from sending mail to particular domains. All it takes is an accusation, and when the definition of spam is this sloppy, it's not hard for people to be convinced that the accusation is correct, regardless of the facts.

Peter prefers to define spam as *unsolicited and indiscriminate bulk e-mail.* It's unsolicited because the recipient has had no contact with the sender and did not request anything. It's indiscriminate in the sense that the sender has no real reason to think you have any interest in his product or service; all you are to him is an anonymous e-mail address. And it's a bulk mailing; it's sent to a large number of people at one time. The bulk mailing is what really wastes the time and resources of the Internet.

There's a real difference between buying millions of e-mail addresses on a CD and sending everyone a message asking them to visit your foot-fetish Web site, and carefully selecting a number of Web-site owners who might want to review your product and mailing them all a polite message suggesting this.

Chain Letters

Just as irritating as spam, but usually done for better intentions, are chain letters. Once you've been on the Internet long enough, you'll get one. The plea to help a child who's dying of cancer. The ominous warning of a new virus. The humorous poem that you're asked to pass along to as many people as possible.

Chain letters are usually sent from one person to dozens or hundreds of people. (If they don't use the Bcc: header, you can see exactly how many people it went to.) They're often sent because someone felt sorry for a little girl dying of cancer, or they wanted to pass on a warning about a virus, or they wanted to warn everyone that the government is about to tax Internet access, or some similar altruistic reason. The problem is that most of these legends, warnings, whatever, are fake. You can help stem the flow of urban legend chain letters by ignoring them, or perhaps e-mailing the sender and letting him know that the messages are false.

For more information about these false messages, see the following Web sites:

antivirus online: hoax alert!
   http://www.av.ibm.com/BreakingNews/HypeAlert/
CIAC Internet Chain Letters
   http://ciac.llnl.gov/ciac/CIACChainLetters.html
CIAC Internet Hoaxes
   http://ciac.llnl.gov/ciac/CIACHoaxes.html
Computer Virus Myths Home Page
   http://www.kumite.com/myths/

Don't Spread that Hoax!
  http://www.nonprofit.net/hoax/hoax.html

The Email Folklore Homepage
  http://www.people.virginia.edu/~ymb5v/

The Urban Legend Combat Kit
  http://www.tourbus.com/archive/tb102998.htm

Urban Legends at the Mining Company
  http://urbanlegends.miningco.com/

HANDLING E-MAIL—FILTERS, BOILERPLATE, & AUTORESPONDERS

Once you've been on the 'Net for a while and you've done a lot to promote your business, you'll find yourself getting a lot of e-mail. Tara gets about 200 e-mail messages a day and she doesn't even want to think about how many messages Peter gets. Eventually you've got to do something that organizes the messages a little bit even before you look at them. That's where filtering comes in.

Filtering

All good e-mail programs allow filtering. (Some "light" versions of e-mail packages don't, however; you may have to pay to get good filtering ... or, paradoxically, get a free program such as Pegasus.) A filtering system takes a look at the information in the incoming mail—what the subject line says, for example, or who the e-mail is from—and acts on the information that's filtered. For example, you could set up a filter in your e-mail to play a sound when you get e-mail from certain people. More importantly, you can create filters to automatically sort all your incoming and outgoing messages into separate folders and boxes. You could set up filters to:

- Automatically delete e-mail from certain people. (Sometimes that's called a killfile.)
- Play an alert when you get e-mail with a certain subject.
- Put e-mail directed to certain e-mail addresses (if you use more than one) in a certain folder in your e-mail box.
- Mark a message from a particular person in some way—with a particular color, for instance.
- Automatically forward a message with a particular word in the subject line, or from a particular person, to someone else.

- Add or remove an e-mail address from an address book. (Few programs can play this trick, though—Pegasus and AKMail can; the big commercial programs currently cannot.)

Filters can be invaluable in your business communications, especially if you're a single-person operation with several different e-mail addresses. You could filter different addresses—support@, marketing@, or owner@, for instance—into different folders, assign them different priorities, or even send automatic responses to them.

Pegasus has the strongest filtering system of any e-mail program we know of that is in current development—as we noted earlier in the book, you can build a mailing list with it. (**AKmail** probably has better filters, but it appears that it won't be developed any further; it's still available, though, at http://www.akmail. com/.) If you want to set up several elaborate filters, check out Pegasus as a potential program. Or look at Eudora Pro 4.0, because its relative simplicity will

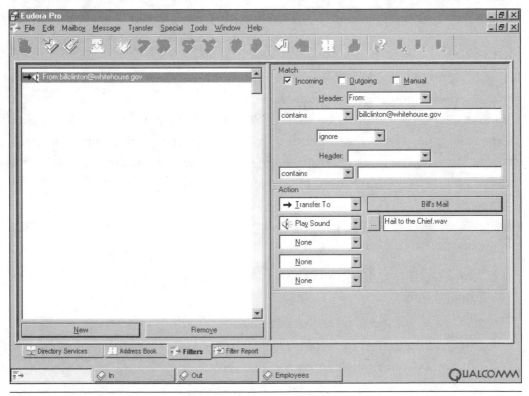

FIGURE 15.2: This filter moves all the mail Peter receives from the President—a considerable quantity, of course—into a particular folder, and plays *Hail to the Chief* when it arrives.

make it more likely that you will create filters. If you don't plan to do much filtering and don't need more than basic filters, a program such as Netscape Messenger or MS Outlook will probably do.

Whatever program you're using, learn to work with the filters. You *cannot* effectively work online if you simply dump all your incoming e-mail messages into one box and all the outgoing ones into another. You *must* find some way to organize them.

Using Stationery or Boilerplate

Some e-mail packages offer some kind of boilerplate feature—the

Filters Must Be Easy

Unfortunately the e-mail software publishers don't seem to understand that powerful filtering features are no good unless they're easy to use. If it takes you five minutes to create a filter, you won't do it very often—so if you get scores of e-mail messages each day, you won't be able to keep it all organized very well.

Currently the program that creates filters the quickest is Eudora Pro 4.0. It's possible to create filters with as few as four mouse clicks—still too many, but a vast improvement over earlier versions and better than most other programs.

ability to save boilerplate message text, and to insert that text into outgoing messages. Eudora, for instance, has "stationery," which means that boilerplate can be turned into e-mail messages that you can customize with a few keystrokes. Pegasus even includes a mail-merge feature, which means that each e-mail can be customized with the recipient's name.

For instance, Peter has a number of messages he has to send repeatedly. When people inquire about advertising in his newsletter, he has to send out a message containing rates and subscription information; when someone's credit-card was declined, he has to inform them; and so on. He uses Eudora's stationery feature to create boilerplate messages, and then uses the Message|Reply With command to pick the appropriate response.

If your e-mail package doesn't offer these kinds of features, you can fake them. Create the text of your message in a text editor. (Make sure that it's in a text editor, and not a word processor. As we noted before, if you use a word processor you'll get weird characters that won't translate into plain-text e-mail.) When you're ready to send out several copies of an e-mail, you can paste the text of the message into a new e-mail and customize it in a few places. (You can mark them with ***, or @@@, or some other way to signify that those blanks need to be filled in. You need to make sure that those blanks get filled in, because you don't want the e-mail to go out that way.) The only problem with this approach is you've got to remember to fill in the subject line. The most lovely e-mail in the world is going to get hurt badly by a blank subject line.

Auto-Responders

Filters can be configured to act as "auto-responders." Auto-responders immediately respond to an e-mail message by sending an e-mail message back. This message contains some kind of information—if someone e-mails to your adinfo@ address, for instance, you could send back information about advertising rates. If you prefer not to work with many different e-mail addresses, you could also set up filters to work on a particular subject line; you might tell people to e-mail you with the words *Newsletter Advertising* in the subject line, for instance.

If you use a lot of auto-responders, you might also create them through your hosting company's auto-responder feature. Any POP e-mail account should come with the ability to set up auto-responders (see Chapter 3). When you get a Web-hosting account for your domain, you'll get a POP account, too, and you should get a number of auto-responders. If you set up the auto-responders at the server, then the mail will never even reach your e-mail program; rather, the POP server will automatically respond for you.

Auto-responders can be very useful in many ways. Peter has used them in association with newspaper articles, for instance, offering free reports to people to e-mail to the auto-responder address. You might also use them for free drawings—you could tell people to e-mail a particular auto-responder to join your newsletter and to be entered into a free drawing for one of your products.

However, there are two problems with auto-responders running on a server. First, they may not be very good. Some are too simple to be particularly useful. A good auto-responder should be able to do the following:

- Quote the incoming message in the auto-response
- Save the incoming message
- Grab the e-mail address from the incoming message and put it in a text file
- Redirect the incoming message somewhere else (to a mailing list server, for instance)

The last two of these are particularly important, as they enable you to build mailing lists from messages sent to your auto-responders. You may have trouble finding an auto-responder with all these features, unfortunately; it may be easier to set up a complicated auto-responder using your e-mail program (which is okay unless the auto-responder is getting hit by vast amounts of e-mail).

The other problem is that many hosting companies make setting up the auto-responders way too complicated. Some companies expect you to understand the intricacies of writing procmail scripts (special scripts that tell procmail—an e-mail system installed on many servers—how to run). The company you choose either should have a simple system that allows you to fill in a form to create your auto-responders, or should offer detailed, step-by-step instructions.

Auto-responders can be very useful when all you want to do is send a piece of boilerplate back to someone. Sometimes, however, although you need to send back something that is 90 percent boilerplate, you may still need to customize a little bit. So you'll probably end up combining auto-responders with stationery features.

Say, for example, that you're selling advertising for your newsletter. Someone could send an e-mail to an address you've set up—maybe your adinfo@ address—and immediately receive your ad rates and terms. Once they've decided to run an ad, they would send another e-mail to you personally with the text of the ad.

When you receive their ad, you will want to return a notice that you'll be running the ad, when it will be running, and how much it will cost. However, you can't use an auto-responder to convey that kind of information. That's where a boilerplate or stationery message comes in. You can use a boilerplate message to provide most of the details—the terms of your advertising, a notice of when your newsletter runs, and legalese. You can then fill in the blanks with custom information, such as the text of the ad, the cost of the ad, and any additional information.

The amount of personalization you can do with your e-mail program varies a lot according to the program. Be sure to check for stationery and mail merge when you're looking for an e-mail application that uses a lot of personalization. (Unfortunately, few currently have mail-merge.) Some programs, like Eudora, also offer different "personalities" or accounts—ways to insert different e-mail addresses and signatures into your e-mail. When you're handling many different kinds of e-mail—technical support, working with vendors, collaborating with different people in your company—it's time-

Major Mail Merge

There's another way to do e-mail merge—using a mail-merge program such as WorldMerge or Campaign. We'll look at that subject in Chapter 16.

saving to use different addresses for different purposes, and then filter the various outgoing messages and responses into different folders.

Now that you know how to create good e-mail, you need to parlay this skill into communicating with editors. E-mail can be your most powerful tool in building relationships with media and making the most of your PR, so check out the next chapter for the basics of online PR.

CHAPTER SIXTEEN

Reaching Journalists Online

Electronic PR isn't that much different from offline PR in its goals. You're trying to get coverage for your product or service—favorable coverage, hopefully. Alternatively, you're trying to tell your story or publicize a cause. Where online PR starts differing from offline PR is in the tools you have at your disposal. You've got many more resources to find journalists, reach journalists, and keep up with journalists online, and doing so doesn't require such an outlay of time or money as do traditional methods.

You've also got the opportunity to make your job and the editor's job a lot easier. Further, you have the opportunity to personalize your content, and doing so is well worthwhile. So few PR people do this that it'll make you really stand out. (Tara's been on both ends of the PR machine, and she knows whereof she speaks.)

The major focus on promotion can be divided into three parts:

1. Finding the journalist
2. Contacting the journalist
3. Staying in touch with the journalist (substitute "editor" or "columnist" or whatever for "journalist")

WHAT ARE YOUR GOALS?

We're going to be talking about how to contact journalists. But *why* are you contacting journalists? What do you want, ultimately, to happen because of this contact? There are a few things you could be going for. Which one you want is up to you.

Special Bonus Tip

If you're really good and you don't mind spending a little money, you can have the journalist come to you—but we'll leave that to the end of the chapter.

Product story—Maybe you want a story written about your product or service, so that more people can learn about it. This is difficult coverage to get unless you have an unusual "hook" you can present to the journalist. A new coffee shop isn't going to attract a product story unless it serves unusual food, the waitresses wear roller skates, it's open between midnight and noon, etc.

Product review—Sometimes when you can't wrangle coverage, you can convince a journalist to review your product. The catch here is that your product has to be useful to a wide range of the journalist's readership. If you write a software program designed to help build pacemakers, your daily newspaper won't review this product. However, a medical-software journal might. You have better chances of getting your product reviewed if you stay aware of editorial calendars and what journalists are looking for at particular times, too. What's the difference between a product review and a product story? The review tends to be more focused on what the product can do for the reader. The story has a wider appeal, and is related to the background of the product rather than the product itself.

Human-interest story—Sometimes you can create a "human-interest" story out of your situation; the journalist gets an interesting or fun story, while you get your product or company mentioned in the press. For instance, in the early days of **CDnow** (http://www.cdnow. com/) they used to pitch the *twib*

What's an Editorial Calendar?

Magazines have to plan out their issues months in advance—they can't throw together a few articles a week before the magazine goes to press. In order to plan their issues effectively, and in order to help advertisers know when their advertising dollars are best spent, they publish editorial calendars. Editorial calendars are overviews of what each issue of a publication will contain. For example, a computer magazine might devote an issue to home networking. The editorial calendar might be as detailed as a list of articles and special features, or as vague as listing that the issue will cover home networking. Monthly magazines, since they have to be put together several months in advance, have the most rigid editorial calendars; they usually don't change. Weekly magazines are more flexible, since they don't need to be completed months in advance and can change their content in reaction to current events. And newspapers, of course, change constantly, though even they have topics that they cover according to a calendar (like holiday topics, tax information, summer vacations, etc.).

story to journalists; *twib* meant "twins in the basement," and referred to the founders, Jason and Matthew Olim, working in their parents' basement. Journalists wrote about how these two "kids" were building an online store on a shoestring, how Matthew brushed his teeth in front of the computer, how Jason spent his guitar fund on the business, and so on.

An interview—If you can get interviewed in the press you can position yourself as an expert in your area. Although the article will not directly focus on your products or services, you can mention them and the journalist may mention them in the introduction to the interview.

A mention in a story—Sometimes if a journalist is doing a story on your industry or something related to your industry, he or she might want to interview you or someone else in your company as an expert. While this doesn't give your company or service a lot of exposure, you can get your company mentioned and sometimes establish yourself or your company as an expert. This often works well when you're a company of one person, an author, or in some other way running a solo operation.

A little mindshare—Occasionally you'll contact a journalist who will immediately want to do a story on you. But more often the journalist will listen to your pitch and let you know that there's no coverage opportunity for you at the moment. In that case, you want to establish yourself in the journalist's mind as an expert, so that when they do plan to do a story that might involve you in some way—either through a quote, coverage, or review—you'll come to mind. That's why establishing a relationship with a journalist is so important.

Ideally you should have some idea of what you want before you contact the journalist. You may contact a journalist hoping for a review, but find they need an interview instead. It's important that you can respond quickly to their needs, and if they don't need anything you should be prepared to work on building a relationship with them if that's possible. (We'll talk more about building relationships later in the chapter.)

FINDING THE JOURNALIST

High-powered PR firms use really expensive means to find out which editors cover their products and services, the kind of stories they're running, and when they're being run. Products from places like MediaMap and Press Access can run hundreds, and sometimes thousands, of dollars. If you're reading this you probably can't immediately afford to do something like that—but there is a way to get information from these big boys for free. We'll explain how in a minute.

Track Media by Specialty

In the first few chapters we instructed you to make a list of the several different kinds of groups who would be interested in your product or service. If you've got that list of groups now, you're going to find looking for editors a much more organized process. Track media by their specialty, using the resources in the earlier chapters, to find editors. If you have a Web site for educational software, for example, you could divide media into resources for parents, teachers, grandparents, and possibly even kids.

Some of you are going to find this easier than others. The inventor of a new onion-cooking machine can look for the food editor, and the writer of a baseball trivia book can give the sports editor a try. But what if you're heading a non-profit organization that encourages pet owners to walk their cats on leashes? What if you've started a Web page devoted to the many uses of the color mauve?

There are a few rules of thumb to find out who's who, and where. When checking out a publication's Web site, look through the Web site for links that say things like "About this site" or "Press Releases." (The most easily navigable newspaper site Tara's ever seen is the **Los Angeles Times**. Check it out at http://www.latimes.com/.)

If you're trying to get the attention of a particular columnist, check his or her column first. A lot of times columnists put contact e-mail addresses at the end of their columns. Try to contact the addresses on a columnists' page before trying to find the columnist in a staff list. Often, though, especially in large publications, these are not personal e-mail addresses but just addresses put there to make it look like they're responsive to their readers; the chance of actually getting to someone through such an e-mail address is slim. (The smaller the publication, and less well-known the writer, the more likely the address will actually go straight to the columnist.) You won't know until you try!

Some newspapers have only a small presence on the Web and a single e-mail address for the entire paper. If you can't find the information you're looking for, you can send e-mail to that address and ask. Other papers list several e-mail addresses. For small papers, try contacting the managing editor when you're unsure of which department you should be seeking out. For larger papers, look for an assistant or associate editor in the department you think is the most appropriate.

As you gather up contact information, you can drop people into your contact-management program or database (see Chapter 2), or put them in a simple addressing program and spit them out on Rolodex cards. Whatever method you use to keep them organized, be sure to note the full name, title, publication name, address, phone and fax number, e-mail address, and Web site.

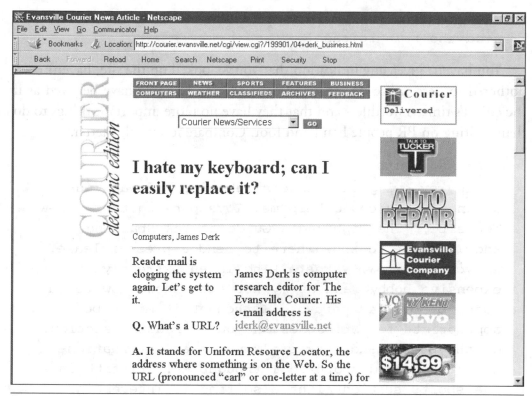

FIGURE 16.1: On some columnists' sites, like this one, you'll see a Web address.

And be sure to denote any keywords that'll make clearer how they might be interested in your product or service. That way, if you're looking for promotional opportunities later, you can search your contacts by keyword. For example, say you add a math homework helper to your line of educational software. You'd want to reach teachers and possibly parents. If you could search by keyword for publications targeted to teachers, you'd find your promotional work a lot easier to do. This information will come in handy later as you track your contacts with editorial people.

You might be a little concerned about e-mailing these people out of nowhere and asking, bold as brass, who should get a press release and how they like receiving it. Most of the times when we've done this people have been pretty nice about it. It all comes across in your presentation. Consider this e-mail:

```
Dear Sir/Madam

I am writing to find out who at your paper might be
interested in my new Web site, "The Tightwad's
Guide to Yak Stalking." I have a news release I
```

```
want to send you so please let me know where to
send the news release.
```

You haven't given any indication that you've looked on the site, haven't even bothered to personalize the query letter at all, and basically have behaved as if the editor's time is worthless and that they have no more important things to do than waiting on PR people hand and foot. Compare it with this letter.

```
Dear Ms. Smith,
I was reviewing The Bugle's Web site and was won-
dering if you could help me. I've put together a new
Web site, "The Tightwad's Guide to Yak Stalking,"
and I'd like to know where to send a press release.
As you may know, yak stalking is an extremely
expensive hobby, and as my Web site shows how to cut
costs by over 40 percent, I thought it might be
appropriate for Mr. Jones in your financial section.
On the other hand, yak stalking is an internation-
ally recognized sport so I thought Ms. Griffith in
the sports section might also find it interesting.
If you could give me some guidance in this matter
(both who should receive the release and in what
form it should be sent), I would much appreciate it.
```

See how different these two letters are? In the second letter you've shown that you've looked at the paper, you've made an effort to find out where your press release belongs, and you've given a bit of additional information on exactly why you want to send a press release. Don't be worried about approaching these people. Most people are nice about it; and if they don't want to get a news release from you the worst they can say is "no."

Actually, the worst they can say is something like, "Get away from me, you stupid PRjerk! How you could possibly get the idea in your pointed head that I would be even remotely interested in your pathetic little press release!?" You're going to get that sort of response now and then; you're now doing for-real promotions. (You've heard of trial by fire? That was your trial by rudeness.)

THE MORE THE MERRIER

Contacting particular media outlets one by one is all very well, but it's a lot of work. There has to be a better, faster way. Luckily there is. There are a number of companies that are in the business of creating lists of media contacts, and keeping the lists up to date. (Writers and editors move around between publications, so these companies track their movements.) Two of the best of these companies are PressAccess and MediaMap.

PressAccess

http://www.pressaccess.com/

If you've got a lot of money, consider one of PressAccess' guides to the media. These are not cheap: PressAccess' materials run between $800 and almost $5,000. If you can't afford that, check out PressAccess' free **Hot News** feature, which gives you the latest moves in the online editorial community. (It's available at http://www.pressaccess.com/main.htm#HotNews.) While you're there, check out their other PR resources, like their PR case studies and links to publications.

MediaMap

http://www.mediamap.com/

Tara has used some of MediaMap's resources, and finds them very useful. Their prices run much the same as PressAccess', but they also have a lot of free materials available at http://www.mediamap.com/free_info/, such as *Alert!*, a weekly column of editorial moves and miscellany, and *Hot off the Press*, a monthly update of media changes.

More Affordable Resources!

So you think $800 to $5,000 is a little much, eh? (And after all, this is *Poor Richard's Internet Marketing and Promotions*.) Well, there are other options. There are a number of directories available at a much lower cost (though, not surprisingly, the quality of the data is not going to be quite the same as these high-priced sources). There are various ways you can get media-contact lists without spending an absolute fortune.

PR Resources Available in Print and Online

Until recently, the many resources offered by the two companies described above were available only in printed format. Now, however, many of them are available on CD-ROM and, of course, some of them are available on the Web. Check out all the different resources and take some time to think about what you'd be most comfortable with before you part with the big money.

Build Your Own Contact List

You can build your own media contact list if you have the time. This may be laborious, but if you work smart, you can cut the time it takes to build a list dramatically. For instance, there are directories of links to newspapers on the Internet. If you use an offline browser (see Chapter 2), you can use the directories as a starting point to download pages at each newspaper, and then find the newspaper's contact information. The following are some useful directories of media contacts:

Editor & Publisher's Newspaper List (Links to thousands of papers, magazines, radio shows, syndication services, and so on)
http://www.mediainfo.com/emedia/

Electronic Newsstand
http://www.enews.com/

FAIR's Media Contact List
http://www.fair.org/media-outlets/media-contact-list.html

Gebbie Press (A great site; includes a free downloadable directory of almost 8,000 papers and TV stations)
http://www.gebbieinc.com/

John Hewitt's Trade Magazine List
http://www.azstarnet.com/~poewar/writer/pg/trade.html

Parrot Media Network (Fantastic directory of newspapers, TV, radio, and more)
http://www.parrotmedia.com/

Peter Gugerell's E-Mail Media list (A huge list of e-mail addresses for media around the world)
http://www.ping.at/gugerell/media/

Peter Gugerell's Media: Index of Indices (A great place to find links to other directories)
http://www.ping.at/gugerell/media/e2indx.htm

Queer Resources Media Directory
http://qrd.tcp.com/qrd/

MediaUK
http://www.mediauk.com/

Yahoo!—News & Media
http://www.yahoo.com/News/

Yahoo!—News and Media Directories
http://dir.yahoo.com/News_and_Media/Web_Directories/

Then there's the library. Yes, that's right, get off your backside—you've probably been staring at the screen too long, anyway—and walk/run/bike/drive to an actual library and look for the following guides:

Bacon's Newspaper-Magazine Directory

Bacon's Radio-TV-Cable Directory

Newsletters in Print

Writer's Market

If you're not in the U.S., you'll find that your country has similar directories; talk with your librarian. However, consider the law of diminishing returns. You can get a huge amount of media-contact information online. You can get contact information for most U.S. papers online, for instance, so trying to fill in the gaps by going to Bacon's directories may not be worthwhile. You'll spend a lot of time—that is, money—for just a few more contacts. On the other hand, you'll be able to find much more detailed information, such as the names of individual editors and writers. And some directories may provide information that's difficult to find online, such as real-world—that is, paper—newsletter addresses.

Buy a List

You can also buy media lists. Some of the most affordable are the U.S. All Media E-Mail Directory from Direct Contact Publishing, Publicity Blitz from Bradley Communications, and the All-In-One Media Directory from Gebbie Press.

The **U.S. All Media E-Mail Directory** from Direct Contact Publishing (http://www.owt.com/dircon/) contains almost 12,000 e-mail addresses. It's $99 in ASCII text (comma delimited format, so you can import it into a database). This is a really cost-effective directory, well worth buying. The Web site also has a page on Ten Commandments for Sending E-Mail to the Media, and other good advice.

Bradley Communication's **Publicity Blitz** database is another huge contact list. For $295 you'll get a database

ImediaFax

ImediaFax (http://www.imediafax. com/), *a service from the same company that produces the U.S. All Media E-Mail Directory, can produce highly customized media-contact lists at a very low price. You can use these lists for e-mail campaigns, as well as fax and snail mail. We'll look at this service in detail in Chapter 18.*

with around 19,600 entries. For $445 you can get a one-year subscription that provides four quarterly updates. You can buy this directly from **Bradley Communications** (no Web site yet: 800-989-1400 or 610-259-1070), or from **Open Horizons**, a publisher of books and databases for the small-publishing business (http://www.bookmarket.com/, 515-472-6130, 800-796-6130).

Gebbie Press (http://www.gebbieinc.com/) publishes the All-In-One Media Directory. For $270 you can get its TV/Radio, Dailies/Weekly Newspapers, and Magazines directories, with a total of around 21,000 entries. Gebbie Press told us that virtually all of the entries have e-mail addresses (in the electronic version of the database—not in the printed version).

For a really massive list, see **MediaFinder** (http://www.mediafinder.com/), which sells a CD containing seven major media directories, including *Samir Husni's Guide To New Consumer Magazines*, *The National Directory of Magazines*, and the *Oxbridge Directory of Newsletters*, with over 100,000 publications, for $1,095

> ## Just a Few Problems
>
> *Unfortunately a number of these low-cost database have some serious formatting problems. Peter has bought and worked with three of these low-cost media databases, including two of the ones we've mentioned here, and* all three *had problems with the way in which data was entered into the database or formatted, making importing the databases into a program difficult, and meaning that they had to be cleaned up before use. So be prepared for a little work before you can use these … and if you're not very technically capable, see if you can find a friendly database geek to help you.*

(North American edition) or $1,500 (World edition). The CD has a lot of detailed information and allows you to build mailing lists by specifying the criteria. There's also a subscription that allows you to use the database online, pulling the data from their Web site, starting at $395 for three months. This may seem to be an expensive database, but when you look at it at a price per entry, it's around the same as the others I've mentioned here.

CONTACTING THE JOURNALIST

Here's rule number one: use the delivery method that each journalist specifies. If he asks you to e-mail your release, e-mail it. If he asks you to fax it, fax it. If he asks you to send it by carrier pigeon … well, at least explain that you can't and apologize. If you find out the delivery preferences and then ignore them, you've got two strikes against you already.

Before you start contacting a journalist you'll need a couple of things:

1. **Group-specific "boilerplate."** Boilerplate is basic promotional information that gives information about what you're promoting. It's different from a press release in that it's very brief, usually just a couple of paragraphs, and is specific to the group you're targeting. For example, you wouldn't send a parent's magazine the same boilerplate you'd send a teacher's magazine, but you might send them the same press release.

2. **The press release.** The press release is the information about your product or service. If you don't know how to write a good one, we'll explain in Chapter 17. Press releases are a lot longer than boilerplate and contain a wider variety of information. You also don't always have to write different ones targeted to different groups. (If you are sending press releases to extremely different groups—to doctors and to lay people, for example—you might want to write two different press releases.)

Distributing Wide-Area Press Releases

You can also send out press releases across the wire services, reaching hundreds, perhaps thousands, of journalists at once; see Chapter 17.

Contacting Radio and TV Media

In this chapter we're focusing mostly on print journalists—editors of magazines and newspapers. There are lots of TV and radio opportunities out there too, but you should go about contacting them a little differently.

For radio, you should concentrate on contacting particular radio shows instead of the station as a whole. Different shows have different producers, and different people looking for different types of talent. A morning show might want something "light," something interesting but not very controversial to talk about. A drive-time radio show, on the other hand, might want to talk politics, or religion, or something else that keeps the audience active and involved. You can get an idea of the various radio shows online at **Yahoo!'s Radio Programs** page: http://dir. yahoo.com/News_and_Media/Radio/Programs/. Check out the **Talk Radio Show Prep Site** at http://users.aol.com/cookeh/prep.html to get an idea of what talk radio DJs are looking for and what they need to get their shows done. (Remember, they need news as much as newspapers, and they've got to fill an hour or two every day.) You can also take a look at **ShowIdeas** at http://www.showideas.com/.

If you've got some money to spare, you can invest in a couple of items designed specifically to help you book radio shows. Bradley Communications offers, among other things, the **Radio-TV Talk Show Report**. This report goes out to producers and other people who book radio and TV talk shows; they turn to the Report when they're looking for show guests. Bradley Communications also offers promotional materials for general PR (like lists of media broken down by category) and materials for specific kinds of PR (like the Book Marketing Update). They don't have a Web site yet, but you can contact them here:

> Bradley Communications
> 135 E. Plumstead Avenue
> P.O. Box 1206
> Lansdowne, PA 19050-8206
> 800-784-4359
> 610-259-1070

You can also check out **RadioTour.Com** at http://www.radiotour.com/. For a fee, they'll make sure that radio talk shows know about you, and help you get booked on radio shows. There's also **GuestFinder.Com** (http://www.guestfinder.com/), a Web-based directory used by the media. (We'll look at this company a little later in this chapter.) And there's a new one, **Great Guests** (http://www.PublicityCity.com/). For $99 you can be included in a newsletter, along with just five other people, that is sent to over 1,500 radio-show hosts.

Television shows, unlike radio and print publications, are more interested in visual things. Do you having a juggling act? Do you use common household items to illustrate principles of science? You might be better on TV than radio. For TV, in addition to the boilerplate we've already described, you should have a tape of previous television appearances and a picture of yourself. You'll need to contact the producer of a particular television show, and you'll need to get guidelines of how they want to be contacted—they have particular deadlines, want to receive materials in a certain way, and so on.

There are a lot of TV talk shows represented online. You can get a good listing at **Yahoo!'s Talk Shows page:** http://dir.yahoo.com/News_and_Media/Television/Shows/Talk_Shows/. You can also get additional information at **TV Talk Shows** at http://www.tvtalkshows.com/, or **The National Talk Show Guest Registry** at http://ourworld.compuserve.com/homepages/ntsgr/. Radio-TV Interview Report and GuestFinder.Com are also read by TV reporters.

Once you've got that together, you're ready to write the journalist. Here you go:

- Write to only one journalist per publication. If a writer in one section turns you down, you can write to another one, but don't e-mail several at once. All you'll do is alienate all of them. Don't make it obvious, at least, that you're contacting several at once.

- If you must write to more than one journalist at once, send each message separately, or use the Bcc: line. (See Chapter 15 for more information about the Bcc: line.) *Don't* send the same e-mail message to two journalists with both names on the To: line or one on the To: line and the other on the Cc: line. If each knows that you've written to someone else, it's too easy for them both to "let the other one handle it."

- Use a subject line that means something. Don't POST IN ALL CAPS, and don't use a misleading subject line (like `Re: Returning your phone call`). We'll talk more about the elements of good e-mail in the next chapter.

- Address the journalist by name if you know it. Tara prefers to address the journalist as "Dear Mr./Ms. So-and-so." She knows some people address editorial contacts by first name, but she finds that too informal. If you don't know the name of the journalist, address it to "Job Title of the Magazine Name"—like Business Editor of the Seattle Times, for example. Try to avoid "To Whom it May Concern;" it looks like mass mail.

- Structure your e-mail like this: personal comments ("I saw your column on such-and-such, and I wanted to suggest the following story idea"), then whatever of your boilerplate is appropriate, and then your press release if it's necessary. (It's useful if you're doing a straight review pitch—in which you want your product or service reviewed—or a coverage pitch—in which you just want coverage for your product or service. It's not so important if you're just letting the journalist know you exist and you're trying to make a connection.)

- Never, never, never, *never* send a press release that's anything other than plain text. Don't make it a Microsoft Word document, don't attach screenshots, and don't send the press release itself as an attachment! If journalists want that material, they can get it from you later. *Never assume that they want it!*

- Be sure to include an e-mail address or some other way they can contact you within the body of the e-mail. Don't assume they can simply reply to your e-mail. You don't know what's going to happen to that e-mail; it might get forwarded, printed out, or any number of things.

- If a journalist e-mails you asking for something—a review copy of your product, a paper copy of the press release, a technical contact from whom he can get some answers—

Yes, They Can Be Rude

Sometimes harried journalists might treat you in a way that you might consider a bit rude. Don't let it rile you; it's probably got less to do with you than with a tight deadline or a really heavy workload. Keep your communications courteous, and don't get into a flame war.

answer him as quickly as you can. Even if you can't get what he may want immediately, let him know you've received the request. Don't leave journalists hanging; they're often working under tight deadlines and time is of the essence.

- If the journalist replies to you asking to be taken off your list, *take him off*. And apologize.

- Don't follow up with a phone call unless the journalist specifically asks for it! You can follow up a few weeks after you send e-mail, but follow up with e-mail. Don't call and ask, "Did you get my e-mail?" You're going to come across as pushy—overly pushy.

- If at first you don't hear from a journalist, try again—but don't send 50 e-mails in the course of a month. Once every couple of weeks will be fine.

When Tara was doing PR for a living, her goal was to be the PR person that journalists were glad to hear from. She wanted to distribute such great stuff, in such an easy-to-use format, that journalists would always be glad to see her name in their in-boxes. She facilitated this by trying to always answer requests for more information promptly and helping in any way she could. She's not sure if she was always successful, but the goal was good.

Try to approach your journalist contacts the same way. A lot of books on publicity make the point over and over again that journalists need PR people; they need them for leads and for help in making the news. And that's true. But it's also true that it's a symbiotic relationship, a two-way thing. You don't inherently deserve coverage; you earn it. And one way you earn it is by distributing high-quality information about high-quality products and services.

One of the best ways to learn how to work with journalists is by listening to what they say about the whole PR process. There are several places on the Web that can give you Dos and Don'ts on contacting journalists via e-mail.

The Care & Feeding of the Press

http://www.netpress.org/careandfeeding.html

This site was written for members of the PR profession by journalists who have a whole bunch of sad stories to tell. Thrill as you get several good ideas for press releases! Chill as you look at some truly bad examples of PR writing! Cringe as you recognize mistakes you might have made had you not known better!

Tips and Tricks for the Public Relations Clueless

http://www.strom.com/awards/27.html

David Strom is a long-time computer journalist who puts together a nice package of PR tips and tricks on this page. Our favorite tip is number seven: "Learn the long-lost art of follow-through."

Press Release Tips for PR People

http://marketing.tenagra.com/releases.html

Andrew Kantor (*not* Andy), senior editor of *Internet World*, gives you eight tips to make his and other editors' lives easier. Take heed.

Hallahan Course Resources: Publicity Primer

http://lamar.colostate.edu/~hallahan/hpubty.htm

If you need a lot of inspiration, or aren't clear on what makes good subject for news, you need to check out this site. It consists of several lists—four keys to success in publicity, a publicity materials checklist, etc.

Internet News Bureau: Tips on Writing and Media Relations

http://www.newsbureau.com/tips/

A clearinghouse of links for PR hints and tips.

DernWeb: The Well-Tempered Press Release

http://www.dern.com/welltemp.html

Daniel Dern is a journalist who's been on the Internet for a looong time. This page provides a bevy of information on reaching journalists online—including a sample press release.

How to Get the Press on Your Side

http://www.frugalfun.com/press.html

Shel Horowitz, author and marketing whiz, provides several ideas for getting publicity. Shel's ideas are oriented toward low-budget marketing and small-business marketers. He also has a free monthly newsletter of marketing tips available.

Copywriting Profit Center

http://www.mrfire.com/Knowledge/Copywriting/

Joe Vitale goes all-out to give you the best possible information on writing press releases, advertising copy, and marketing documents. If you need some encouragement, visit this site; "Mr. Fire" dispenses a lot of enthusiasm.

Your initial series of contacts will take a lot of time. You're going to have to send a lot of e-mail and write a lot of personal notes. There's going to be a lot of research involved. The key to getting it all done is breaking it down into doable chunks.

Your initial promotion, to get everything moving, will take a lot of time, but don't look at it like you're going to have to do that much researching and contacting forever. John Kremer, a renowned expert on book promotion, puts forth the idea of just doing five promotionally oriented things a day (he calls this the "Rule of Five"). Just five things a day will build into a very strong ongoing effort. You'll maintain a lot of momentum and get into the habit of looking for promotional opportunities.

Sooner or later you'll be all done. You'll have done all your research, checked all your resources, and contacted all the editors you want. Does this mean that you just sit back

Track Your Contacts

You can do something as elaborate as working with a customized contact database (see Chapter 2), or something as simple as just keeping copies of all the e-mails you send to a journalist. Just make sure you do something to track when you've contacted a journalist, what you sent, and what the response was. It'll keep you from re-sending information, and help you learn more about what the journalist does and does not want to see.

on your laurels and wait for the reviews to go in? Heck no! Your real work's just begun.

MASS MAILINGS

If you have a large list of journalists' e-mail addresses, such as the U.S. All Media list we mentioned earlier, you may want to consider a mass mailing. Rather than contacting journalists one by one, you can contact a thousand or two at the same time.

You can use this method in a number of ways. You could use it to distribute press releases (see Chapter 17), for instance. Peter uses it to ask journalists if they want review copies of his books. Now, we're not talking about spam. First, you shouldn't send e-mails to everyone on a list—you should only pick appropriate media contacts. If you're trying to distribute review copies of a book about the economics of Yak herding, don't send e-mails to the music and sports magazines.

Secondly, it's possible to use lists of media contacts made up of e-mail addresses of journalists who have asked to be included. The U.S. All Media list, for instance, is checked by its owner, Paul Krupin. Paul has told us that all the people on the list have given their consent to be there.

Now, this means that many of these addresses are going to be e-mail addresses that get a lot of traffic—not so much personal addresses, but addresses set up in order to catch press releases and various other clutter. That doesn't mean that mailing to these addresses won't work, though. Peter generally gets a 10–20 percent favorable response when mailing to a targeted list looking for book reviewers.

How, then, do you mail to all these people? The simplest way is to copy the e-mail addresses and paste them into an e-mail message, but as we've mentioned before, you should *not* paste hundreds of e-mail addresses into the To: or Cc: line! Use the Bcc: line.

But even pasting addresses into the Bcc: line isn't the best way to handle a mass mailing, though. Some e-mail programs won't like you pasting hundreds, perhaps thousands, of addresses into the Bcc: line. And wouldn't it be nice if you could do a simple mail merge, putting the journalists' first names at the top of the messages?

There are a number of mail-merge programs that will help you personalize mass e-mails, and some contact-management programs (see Chapter 2) have e-mail merge utilities built in—ACT! does, for instance.

Peter has worked with three mail-merge programs—**NetMailer** (http://www.alphasoftware.com/), **Campaign** (http://www.arialsoftware.com/), and **World-Merge** (http://www.coloradosoft.com). Both NetMailer and Campaign have significant bugs and user-interface problems. NetMailer may not be available anymore, however, and in fact the last time Peter tried, he was completely unable to get NetMailer to work in Windows 98.

Campaign is unusual in that it can pull data out of a database. Most mail-merge programs require that you import the addresses you want to work with into the program's own database. But Campaign allows you to "point to" a database—for instance, to an Access database—and then tell it which fields to pull data from. It provides a very quick way to create and run a mail-merge campaign, once you understand how to work it … but it may take a little while to learn. It even allows you to modify individually merged messages. For instance, you can generate 1,000 different mail-merged messages, each with the recipient's name at the top of the message. Then, before you send the messages, you can go in and modify some of them individually—add a personal note to a few of the messages, for instance. (Campaign is probably the only program that will let you do this.) It's a great little program, despite the design problems and bugs.

You can try a demo version of Campaign, which you can use as long as you want for free. However, it appends an advertising message to the end of each message, so you probably won't want to use it for real! The full version of Campaign costs $495 from Arial Software. It's also sold by **Direct Contact** (http://www.owt.com/dircon/), the publisher of the **U.S. All Media E-Mail Directory**, and at the time of writing you can buy Campaign from them at a significant discount.

WorldMerge is the easiest of all the programs that Peter's tried, and it will also pull data out of a database. Peter stores his data in an Access database, then points to the database within WorldMerge, and then sets up a "query" (that is, tells WorldMerge how to choose which contacts to send to). It doesn't have some of Campaign's advanced features. On the other hand, it's *much* easier to use, and is only $40. There's a free demo available; though, as with Campaign, it'll print a little advertising blurb at the bottom of each message.

There are other mail-merge programs available:

eMerge (For the Mac—$175)
  http://www.galleon.com/

e-Mail Xpress (For the Mac—$99; at the time of writing this is not
  available, but the publisher is trying to sell it, so it may revive.)
  http://www.iso-ezine.com/emx/

InfoPress Email-On-Demand ($995)
  http://www.castelle.com/

Stealth Mail Bomber ($99.95)

   http://wizardware.com/

WWMail ($39.95)

   http://wizardware.com/

By the way, some of this software—in particular Stealth Mail Bomber—is what may be termed *spam software; it's* designed for use by e-mail spammers. That doesn't mean it can't be put to good (and legitimate) use, though.

THE LONG-TERM VIEW: STAYING IN TOUCH

With some editors and journalists, you don't really click. You send them your information, and they might give you a review, and they might not, and the whole thing's pretty lukewarm.

On the other hand, there are some editors with whom you really hit it off. You have a good time talking product and they seem very interested in your product. They may or may not agree with your views, and they may have some concerns with your product, but they give you good feedback. This sounds like the beginning of a beautiful friendship.

But it's only a beginning. You're going to have to do some work to keep it up.

Read

This sounds like a no-brainer, but if you want to keep up a relationship with journalists, read their writing. You want them to be interested in you? Be interested in them! Read their stuff and drop them a note every now and again when you have a reaction to one of their stories. (Don't pepper them every week with "Hi! Great column!" Give them some feedback.) Let them know what you think about their stuff. You don't have to be a sycophant. If you disagree say so. Sometimes a well-thought-out, articulate disagreement is more engaging than the most ardent fan letter.

Help Them

If you see something you think a journalist would be interested in, send it his way. However, keep a balance—don't send ten resources a day, and don't send knuckleheaded information (like chain letters, scams, and obvious resources. It's a good bet that every

But Don't Fake It ...

Don't think you're interested enough in a journalist to read his stuff? Then don't read it. We're not advocating that you read stories you don't care about. Your apathy will show in your communications, and we're not out to create a nation of phonies.

computer columnist in America knows about Yahoo!). Don't be too pushy when using a referral; don't focus on your own online resources and nothing else. Rather, try to be unbiased, and refer to your own resources only when really appropriate.

Assume Nothing

When building a relationship with journalists, some promoters think they only have to do so much helping, communicating, and relationship building, and then they will have "earned" coverage from the journalist.

Hogwash.

> ## Refer Them to Someone Else
>
> *If you can't provide something that a journalist needs, have an alternative handy. The journalist might want something that's a bit out of your field. If you can, hook him up with someone you know who can answer his question. That way, you've just done something good for two different people.*

This is not a game of basketball. You shouldn't be keeping score of how many resources you've referred to the journalist, how many ideas you've given them, or how much feedback you've offered. Would you track how many movies you've recommended to your friends, or how many favors you've done them, and then demand that they do you a favor before you'd be friends anymore? This is a silly perspective. Your focus should be on helping reporters do their jobs better. If your helping involves the reporter using you in a story or some other coverage, great. If it doesn't, you have still positioned yourself well in the mind of the journalist.

When they need something in your field of expertise, they'll likely think of you. Besides, not everything is within a journalist's control. He may interview you, get several quotes, and then everything in the story that referred to you and your company may get cut out. (This happens all the time. It's happened to both of us now and then. For instance, Peter's e-mail newsletter was just about to be named by a major computer magazine as one of the most useful newsletters on the Internet … when the sidebar containing that piece of praise was cut from the article at the last moment.)

Do you feel that building a relationship with a journalist doesn't provide enough immediate benefit to be worth your time? Fine; consider the fact that you will have participated in a dialogue with a journalist that will have taught you a lot about how to do your public relations better. You'll also get good karma and the Poor Richard Seal of Approval. But don't decide that it's not fair, or unjust, if you don't get editorial coverage after you've been communicating with a journalist for six months and giving him good resources.

Are there times when you should consider investing less time in your relationships with journalists? Sure. When they repeatedly ask for review copies of your product and never seem to review anything. When they take up huge amounts of your time—say, two or three hours at a stretch—getting help on a story, do this several times, and never attribute the information you provide or get a quote from you. There's a difference between a mutually beneficial relationship and getting run over.

You might notice a similarity here between the methods we're discussing for keeping in touch with customers and prospects, and those for keeping in touch with journalists. In both instances you're trying to build credibility and help the person you're contacting. A customer or prospect wants to solve a particular problem. A journalist wants to get a story researched or written. Come at it from that perspective—from what they want and what they need.

Putting together your list of journalists will take the most time initially. Contacting them will also take a lot of time, but since you'll get some immediate feedback you'll find it's a lot more fun. But where you can really get a lot from this chapter, both personally and professionally, is investing some time and effort in building relationships. We recommend you make this an ongoing priority. Take advantage of John Kremer's "Rule of Five" and build some momentum toward your promotion.

SPECIAL BONUS TIP: GETTING JOURNALISTS TO COME TO YOU

Ongoing promotion is very important, but a lot of it is a game of chance. When you send a news release to a journalist, you're hoping that your information will be so compelling and interesting that they'll want to do a story on it right away, or that they're getting ready to do a story on your field and that they can use your information.

Of course, if you're using an editorial-calendar service (a service you can purchase from Media Map, Press Access, or other companies that let you know a publication's schedule of coverage throughout the year) you'll know when the publication is going to cover a certain topic, which can help you decide when you should approach them for coverage. But the editorial calendars change, and daily publications like newspapers are much more flexible in deciding what they're going to cover. One major event may cause their coverage to shift completely from a couple of days to a couple of weeks.

When something like this happens, journalists need to be able to find a source of expertise for the topics they're writing about. They can do that via search engines (and that's one reason to promote your Web page), but they also use their own sources of experts. If you're willing to invest a little money (from about a hundred dollars to several thousand dollars), you can be a part of these online resources.

Online Expert and Guest Resources

The Expertise Center

http://www.expertcenter.com/

The Expertise Center provides a listing of speakers, consultants, and trainers. This site will provide you with three levels of listings. A basic listing (all your contact information except for a Web page) is free. A link that includes a link to a Web page costs $150 per year. A full "business presence" on the Web starts at about $2,000 a year. This site is oriented more towards speakers and those who make public appearances.

Experts Directory

http://www.experts.com/

This site positions itself as the Internet's "Worldwide Directory of Experts." It lists several different types of experts and resources, including breaking them out by "New and Notable," "Political Resources," etc. It's also searchable. A basic listing on this site will cost you $249 for the first year and $195 for every year after that. There are several other options here—you can set up a guest book for your page, include a form on your Web page, get your entire Web site hosted with the Experts Directory, etc.

GuestFinder

http://www.guestfinder.com/

GuestFinder is extremely media-oriented. (Peter's also a member—check out the Web site if you want to see what he looks like!) As you might guess from the name of the site, GuestFinder is oriented towards guests—of radio, television, newspaper, or magazine interviews. GuestFinder is searchable and also lists guests by category. Guests are also mentioned on the front page when current events come up that coincide with the guests' interests. GuestFinder does have certain requirements. Authors must have a book listed in *Books In Print*. Spokespersons must be the official listed contact for the organization listed on their page. Speakers must be experienced professional speakers, and experts must be recognized experts in their fields. These restrictions make for a high-quality guest list. However, if you're kind of unusual and off-beat, but still an expert, consider GuestFinder anyway (their guests include a man who eats bugs, for instance). GuestFinder also offers a category called "Hosts of Notable Web Sites"—but your Web site better be notable or forget about it. GuestFinder contacts the media monthly to alert them to new site and guest information. A page listing for this site costs $199 a year. One thing you need to be aware of is that once you submit the page to be put up, that's it. You can change e-mail, web site links, and phone number information any time during the year for no cost, but changing anything else in your page will cost you.

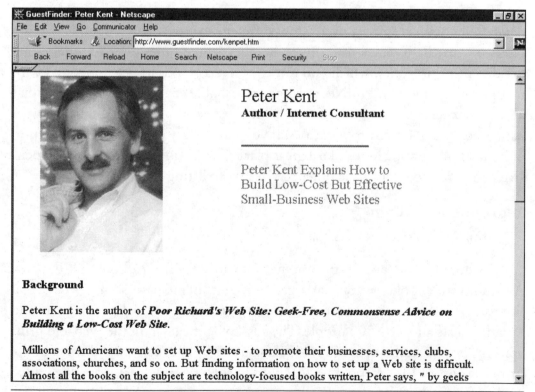

FIGURE 16.2: A GuestFinder page will let a journalist know what you look like, show your credentials, and also give him an idea of the questions he should ask during an interview—everything a journalist needs in an easy-to-read package.

NPC Directory of News Sources

http://npc.press.org/sources/

A service of the National Press Club, this service is a searchable directory of news sources. Obviously the clout of the NPC adds a lot of appeal to this site, and the sources seem to lean more toward news resources and less toward guest resources like GuestFinder. Check out the quotes on the site to get an idea of who's using this directory. With this directory you can do two things: submit a listing or buy an ad. A 100-word listing costs $410. A 100-word listing with a logo is $440. Adding your listing to more than two directory topics costs extra. An ad is a bit more expensive; a full-page ad starts at $995, and a half-page ad starts at $600.

ProfNet

http://www.profnet.com/

ProfNet was designed to help reporters who are researching stories. Its expert database contains leads on over 2,500 different expert sources. ProfNet Search sends out media inquires to ProfNet members three times per day (queries are divided into categories, which you can choose, so you don't get smothered with inappropriate queries). ProfNet also has a searchable experts database, which has a very inexpensive listing: $100 per listing per year for corporations, $50 per listing per year for non-profit entities. If you have a very professional or technical organization, this site looks like a great place for a listing (and $100 is inexpensive compared to a lot of the other services we're listing here).

YearbookNews.Com

http://www.yearbooknews.com/

YearbookNews.Com is the online version of the Yearbook of Experts, Authorities & Spokespersons, a large book you might have seen at your local library. The print version of this resource is entering its eighteenth year, and currently lists almost 1,500 people. The cost to be included in the Web and print versions of the Yearbook is $595. While you might have to wait to be put in the print version of the yearbook (it's only published once a year), you'll be added to the Web site almost immediately.

Other Sources for Experts and Guests

There are plenty of other places online that list guest and expert resources for the media. Check these out and see if you or your Web site is a fit.

Pitsco's Ask an Expert
(Experts from all over the
Web who have volunteered
to answer questions)
http://www.askanexpert.com/

ShowIdeas (An online magazine
for radio and TV producers;
listings start at $125/year)
http://www.showideas.com/

PublicityCity
http://www.publicitycity.com/

BusinessWire (Offers an
"Expert Source" service)
http://www.businesswire.com/

ExpertFind
http://www.expertfind.com/

Will it Work?

These sites are great if you really are an expert or noted person. However, if you're not an expert, don't try to fake your way into the experts-only resources. You could lose your credibility and the money you've invested if you're kicked out of a listing.

And even if you are *an expert, that doesn't mean you'll automatically be flooded with media inquiries. We've heard of people who've done very well from some of these listings, and others that haven't benefited much at all.*

You remember the old saw, "you never get a second chance to make a first impression?" It's just as true when making media contacts as when meeting your next-door neighbors. It's important to spend some time researching media materials, polishing up your materials, and creating a great contact e-mail so you can make the best impression possible.

Once you've made the initial contact, you can make the most out of your promotion campaign by staying in touch with journalists, helping them do their jobs, and positioning yourself in a few online guides so that, when necessary, journalists can find you.

One very important tool of the promoter or publicist is the *press release* (or *news release*, as some say it should be called). There are many tools available for sending out press releases; you can use press-release services, or perhaps your own e-mail program. In the next chapter, we'll take a look at the anatomy of press releases and your options for sending them out.

CHAPTER SEVENTEEN

Electronic Press Releases

Press releases—boring waste of time or powerful PR weapon? From their typewritten beginnings they've been the way to get the company line out on any number of things—new products, new personnel, events, ideas, and other information. And in many cases they're a colossal waste of paper ... or, in cyberspace, an enormous waste of perfectly good electrons. It doesn't have to be that way, though. *You* don't have to produce boring, pointless press releases.

In fact press releases can be a critical part of your promotions. In this chapter we'll take a look at the whys and hows of press releases, give you a crash course on writing a great press release, and let you know how to distribute them.

WHY A PRESS RELEASE?

Thousands of pages and sites are being added to the Web every day. How do you stand out above the crowd? You use a press release and get the information on your new site to news desks all over the world. Whether or not your press release gets coverage is another matter, but getting the information to the press is the first step.

A new Web site isn't the only reason for a press release. You might also want to write a press release to:

- Announce the release of a new product or service
- Kick off a new sales event
- Respond to a national event or announcement by a competitor
- Announce significant personnel changes
- Keep in contact with shareholders

The press release is a great package into which you can put information like this. It's an accepted format and is simple for journalists to read. It's also easy to archive on your Web site so visitors can get an idea of your history.

Are there topics that are inappropriate for a press release? Sure. Don't use a press release to nationally announce the fact that you've painted all your trucks. Don't use a press release to announce your Christmas party. Don't use a national press release to announce the fact that you now deliver to Elm Street in addition to Pine Street.

Remember the power of the Internet—you're reaching a global or national audience, depending on which distribution service you use. You may have news that's appropriate to announce only in your town. In that case, call the business desk of your local newspaper and tell them what's up, or write a letter. Don't waste the money and effort of an Internet-distributed press release on local news. You've heard of the "Boy who cried wolf?" You don't want to be the "Company who cried news;" it's not only that you'll get a reputation for putting out bad press releases, but you'll also waste your time and money.

If you're not sure whether your local news deserves a national push, ask yourself whether you could see it on the AP wire as a unique or interesting happening. If in doubt, don't distribute.

When developing an idea for a news release, try to get a great "hook." Focus on the benefit of what you're offering, not just the offering itself. For example, say you've created an online directory of chess clubs throughout the United States. (You're a company that sells chess strategy books, and you correctly figured it would be a good way to get people interested in chess to your site.) There are two ways you can angle this. The first is simply to announce that you've put up an online directory of chess clubs. Whoopdee do. The second is to promote your great new resource as devoted to bringing

Mail Merge

You can use the mail-merge techniques we talked about in Chapter 16 to send out a press release to a list of journalists.

What's AP? What's a Wire?

AP is short for Associated Press. They send out news all over the world. Pick up your local newspaper and you'll see that a lot of stories come from AP. If you want to see stories from the AP, you can check out an AP, national news wire feed at **WRAL TV:** *http://www.wral-tv.com/news/national/. (WRAL subscribes to AP wire services and passes them on to viewers.) The term* wire *probably comes from long ago when copy was actually "wired" (telegraphed) to newspapers.*

together chess aficionados all over the country and to promoting one of the oldest strategy games in the world.

See the difference?

We've already said this a couple of times, but we want to repeat it until it's stamped on your brain in inch-high letters:

Nobody Cares Like You Do

Nobody cares about your product or service as much as you do. They care only about how it will benefit *them*. Make it easy for everybody by immediately letting them know the benefits through your marketing communications—and that includes your press releases. Press releases should focus on benefit-to-the-user. *Benefit, Benefit, Benefit.* Try this. Go to the **Yahoo! Press Releases** page, and take a look at a few press releases (http://dir.yahoo.com/Business_and_Economy/ Companies/News_and_Media/News_Services/Press_Releases/). This page links to various press-release services, at which you can find many releases. Dig around and you'll find some that are good and some that are bad. And you'll probably discover that what characterizes a bad release is that it doesn't seem to be saying anything to you, nor to anyone else probably. It's written by someone who doesn't understand that a press release has to be written from the standpoint of the reader—*what's in it for me?*—not the company issuing the release.

Could we make it any clearer? Probably not without getting even more annoying. Now that you know what's news and what's not, and now that you know how to slant your news so it's of interest to others besides yourself, you too can put together a great press release.

ANATOMY OF A GREAT PRESS RELEASE

Not all press releases are created equal. Putting a little extra time into making sure you've got an excellent headline and compelling content will mean the difference between having your press release read and having it ignored. And this, of course, affects your chance of coverage. There are three things to focus on when writing the press release: the headline, the body, and the contact information.

Headlines

Before we get into this discussion of headlines, let's look at an example to illustrate how important a good headline is. Figure 17.1 is a screen shot of BusinessWire's list of high-tech news releases.

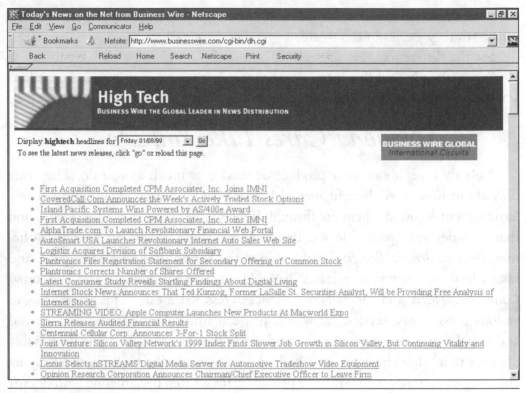

FIGURE 17.1: BusinessWire's High-tech News Releases

As you can see, all this screen contains is a stack of news release headlines. They're all crammed together and they're kind of hard to read. Tara visits this page regularly and usually just skims it, looking for headlines that jump out at her. And she's not the only one who does this.

You need to write a headline that stands out from the pack on a list such as this. Let's take a look at some imaginary scenarios with good and bad headlines.

SCENARIO

You're announcing a new service to sell custom-designed letter openers to large corporations.

BAD HEADLINE: Custom-Designed Letter Openers Now Available

GOOD HEADLINE: New Service Creates Unique, Personalized Desk Tools for Businesses

THE BIG IDEA: The first headline attracts only those who are interested in letter openers. The second headline, on the other hand, attracts anyone who's interested in "desk tools" (ambiguous enough to get people curious), personalized items for business, and so on. Even if they're not specifically interested in letter openers, by making your headline compelling you get them to read the body of the news release. You get two chances to get them interested in who you are and what you're doing.

SCENARIO

You've just hired a former high-level executive to run your company's marketing operations.

BAD HEADLINE: Fred So-and-so named Marketing VP of BadExampleCo

GOOD HEADLINE: Former Fortune 500 COO Named Marketing VP of GoodExampleCo

THE BIG IDEA: Journalists read about hundreds, sometimes thousands, of people per day. You can't expect them to remember who Fred So-and-so is (unless his real name is Ted Turner or Michael Jordan). Instead of naming a name, name an accomplishment. Journalists might not know who Fred is, but they know that a former Fortune 500 COO could be serious news.

SCENARIO

You're a computer company giving away uninterruptible power supplies in the wake of a recent series of lightning storms in your area.

BAD HEADLINE: BadExampleCo Offers New Power Supplies to Storm Victims

GOOD HEADLINE: GoodExampleCo Vows to Give Away 5,000 Power Supplies After Lighting Storms

THE BIG IDEA: In the first headline, it isn't clear that your company is actually giving away power supplies. The extent of your generosity also isn't clear. The words "give away" and "5,000" make a real splash.

Creating a great headline is a balancing act. You want to give a lot of detail without using too many words. You want to create interest without giving away the entire release's contents. And you want to create excitement without appearing to be nothing but hype. The headline should also flow easily into the body of the news release.

The Body of the Release

News releases have a structure that makes them most effective. They're not as elegant as haiku, of course, but by getting each element in its place you can create a very effective release.

Tara's found that the following structure for a news release works well:

How Long is a Good Headline?

You can't judge the impact of a headline by its length. You can get a lot across in just seven or eight words. If you find your headline going beyond a dozen words, consider a subheadline, like this:

HEADLINE: BadExampleCo Vows to Give Away 5,000 Power Supplies

SUBHEADLINE: Company to help community after devastating lightning storms

---

First Paragraph—Overview

This should be a one-paragraph summary of the entire news release, giving editors enough information that they can decide how valuable the release is to them without having to read the whole the whole thing.

> **Example:** Following the lightning storms that took place in North Carolina last week, BadExampleCo pledged to give away 5,000 uninterruptible power supplies to small-business owners who lost data due to power outages.

Second Paragraph—A Few Details

A few details to add to the summary. The details shouldn't be critical, but should help "flesh out" the summary.

> **Example:** GoodExampleCo's giveaway comes in the wake of a week's worth of lightning storms that caused over 100 power outages and destroyed an estimated $4 million worth of unsaved data.

Third Paragraph—A Quote

A quote should support the press release. If you've read a lot of press releases, you know the quotes sound "canned" ("'This is a great day in the history of BadExampleCo,' said CEO John BadExample."). Make the quote relevant to the story, something that journalists can follow up on if they decide to pursue the story. You can add a little descriptive information but try to make the quote the core of the paragraph.

> **Example:** "We feel like we should support the community," said GoodExampleCo CEO John GoodExample. "The data loss caused by this storm was devastating. Since we can do something to prevent this in the future, and help the economy of North Carolina, we will."

The Rest—Information From Most to Least Important

You may have read about an "inverted pyramid" form of news release, where the most important information should appear early in the news release, followed by less and less vital information. From what we've seen, that seems to work well. Tara has had press releases run in a publication practically as-is, which is great when it happens because the publication runs exactly your point of view, with no details removed. Unfortunately, that doesn't happen often. What does happen is that the editor might not have time to read all the way through your press release, so you should make sure all the important stuff is really early on.

Other Body Elements

About the company—*About the company* information is vital when you're a publicly held company (since you may be required to disclose certain information

---

A Little Trick

Here's a little trick we learned from our newsletter-publishing friend, Randy Cassingham (http://ThisIsTrue.com/). When he writes press releases he tries to include the names and stock-market ticker symbols of major companies—Netscape (NSCP), Microsoft (MSFT), and so on. He stumbled across this trick quite accidentally, after he found that one press release in which he'd mentioned a major company seemed to get more attention than the others. It turns out that many people search press-release archives for company names and their ticker symbols.

Of course you should only mention companies that are relevant to the press release—but look for ways to include them if at all possible. Randy has suggested that eventually people will start stacking their press releases with ticker symbols in order to trick searchers, in the same way that people use tricks like font-matching and title packing in order to fool the search engines (see Chapter 5). Randy has even coined a new term for this type of press-release trickery—he calls it over-stocking.

by the Federal Exchange Commission), and helpful if you're a small company or unusual in your structure or product offerings. After the subject of the press release has been covered, a couple of paragraphs outlining your company, services, and products is helpful. Sometimes you'll see a press release with six paragraphs of body information and six paragraphs of "About the company" information. Every product the company has ever released is listed, every office they have around the world is listed, several top executives are mentioned by name, etc. That strikes us as overkill; we don't recommend it.

Disclaimer—If you're a publicly held company and are making statements about your earnings or your future activities, you might have to insert a disclaimer about the contents of the news release being "forward-looking statements" or something like that. Be sure to put this disclaimer after the rest of text, before any trademark statements, and before your contact information.

Trademark statement—Sometimes, especially if you're announcing a partnership, you'll end up scattering a lot of registered trademarks throughout your press release. At the very end of the press release copy—after the body of the information and any disclaimers—your trademark statement makes a good wrap-up paragraph. Some people put the trademark statement at the absolute end of the news release—after the body copy and contact information. We think that if it's at the absolute end like that, it won't get read. On the other hand, it'll be easy to refer to if an editor needs to check the status of a trademark mentioned in your news release.

Contact information—You're going to think this is pretty basic, but contact information is possibly the most vital part of your news release. You write a riveting headline. You write a mind-bending news release body. The editor

---

The Press Release Length

A question we sometimes hear is "How long should a press release be?" The smart-aleck answer to that question is "Long enough to say what needs to be said." A more helpful answer is probably "Not more than two double-spaced, single-sided pages." If your release requires more space, use it, but realize you'll pay distribution services more for sending out longer releases and you probably won't get much more coverage for your release's length.

You don't have to tell every last detail when you distribute a news release. Leave out enough information that the editor has to follow-up, but don't leave out so much that the release isn't clear in what it's announcing.

who reads it is absolutely falling all over himself to run it in his publication. But what if he can't contact you to get additional information or clarify something in the news release? Make sure that you have thorough contact information: name, phone number, address, and *e-mail address!* You'd be amazed at how many press releases available online don't include e-mail addresses. Fax numbers are optional. Try to list two contact people, so if there's a problem with reaching one, an editor can try for another.

Different press-release distribution services include different levels of contact information in their press releases, but when you're distributing news releases yourself, make sure that you have as much contact information as possible. And while we're on the subject of press releases, we might as well mention one of Tara's pet peeves: corporate press release archives without PR contact information. When you add press releases to your corporate archives, make sure that PR contact information remains available in the archives, either from a separate page or on the press releases themselves.

Once you've written the news release, proofread it. Twice. Then have someone else proofread it (preferably a professional editor). And then check to make sure all the contact information works. (Would you be surprised if we told you we've tried to contact companies after reading press releases, only to discover the contact e-mail address provided in the release didn't work?) By the way, this is a good rule of thumb for *all* communications that include cyberspace addresses—e-mail addresses, URLs, FTP site names, Telnet sites, and so on. Always check that what you wrote is correct. It doesn't matter too much if you slightly misspell your street address or

Basic Press Releases

If you're using a press release to announce an event, or provide very basic information, you don't have to create the sort of formal, fully fleshed-out press release that we've described above. Instead, you can merely list the "5 W's" and fill in the blanks that way, like this:

Who:
What:
Where:
When:
Why:

Every W should have an explanation of no more than a paragraph. Bear in mind, though, that this release format doesn't work if you have a lot to say. If you try to use this to fill out a product launch news release and the Why: section takes up about four paragraphs, it's better just to write a regular news release.

city name; we may complain about the post office, but correspondence will probably still get through. But make a mistake with a single character in your e-mail address or URL, and it's as good as useless. Finally, find someone who isn't familiar with your company, and get him to read your press release. Ask whether everything's clear. Ask what he thought the press release was about. Sometimes if you know your company really well, you make assumptions about how much other people know. Make sure that someone outside your company can read your press release and get the gist of what you're trying to say. (The reader doesn't have to know anything about your new super-widget to know your press release is about an upgrade to version 2.0 of the widget.)

DISTRIBUTING PRESS RELEASES

It doesn't matter how good your press release is; it's no good to you unless you can get people to read it. You have to find some way to distribute it to the right people. You can either distribute a press release yourself, or you can hire a service to do it.

If you've got a general press release that would be of interest to a lot of people, a press-release distribution service can help you get your message out to writers and editors you might not even know about. On the other hand, if your news release is of interest to only a very narrow range of people, you might be able to reach all of them yourself without paying for a press-release service.

For example, let's say you represent an organization dedicated to the prevention of infant blindness. Your potential audience is anyone concerned about their kids' health. That's a pretty large audience. You should use a press-release distribution service. On the other hand, you might represent a medical company that makes a device that tests the sensitivity of infant corneas to light. Your potential audience includes health clinics and

Press Releases For Other Purposes

You can use a press release for some of the announcement services like Net-Happenings (see Chapter 8), but you might want to cut it down to the most essential 200-300 words. Don't use a really long press release for announcement services; it won't get read.

hospitals. That's a very narrow audience. You could still use a press-release service, but you'd want to make sure that you could target medical journals and other relevant publications and editors.

Distributing press releases via e-mail is a lot like distributing newsletters. (If you've followed the instructions of the last couple of chapters, you hopefully have a nice list of journalists and publications that are appropriate to your product or service.) Make sure the press release is in plain text, and not some kind of word-processing file. Send the press release in the body of the e-mail, and not as an e-mail attachment. Make sure there are blank lines between paragraphs so the text of the news release is easy to read. Make sure the lines of the press release are not more than about 60-65 characters.

Also, try to personalize the press releases, as we discussed personalizing

---

Finding E-mail Addresses

You can buy or compile directories of journalists' e-mail addresses. Try **MediaUK** *at* http://www.mediauk.com/, **Gebbie Press** *at* http://www.gebbieinc.com/, *and the* **U.S. All Media E-Mail Directory** *at* http://www.owt.com/dircon/. *See Chapter 16 for more information about media-contact sources.*

---

your other communications with journalists. Include some kind of salutation and an informal introduction to the press release—a sentence or two about why the press release is relevant to them.

One more thing: put the headline of the news release in both the subject line and the body of the e-mail message. If the editor copies the body of the e-mail message, you want to make sure the copy includes the headline.

Even if you've gathered a great list of editors together from all your research, consider using a press-release distribution service if you have a general-interest or large audience. Even if you did thousands of hours of research, you probably didn't find every appropriate editor for your news release. Press-release distribution services can help you fill in the holes.

Press-Release Distribution Services

When it comes to press-release distribution services, there are the big two online services—BusinessWire and PR Newswire. M2 PressWIRE is also pretty large but doesn't offer everything the first two do—such as, at the time of writing, the ability to read press releases online. Finally, there are the other services, which offer more customized help, specialized news-release distribution (news releases sent to very specialized lists of editors), and the ability to put your news release on the Internet for free.

The Big Services

BusinessWire

http://www.businesswire.com/

BusinessWire is one of the largest distribution services. BusinessWire offers press-release distribution services worldwide. They distribute to thousands of television stations, radio stations, newspapers, magazines, wire services, and other media. In addition to plain-text releases, they can also distribute photographs, streaming video, streaming audio, spreadsheets, and even PowerPoint presentations. Not only do they offer national and global distribution of press releases, but they can also distribute to particular states and special-interest markets (college newspapers, sports media, legal media, etc.). The cost for distributing a release through BusinessWire depends on what kind of release you send and to what markets you send it. They charge for a certain number of words, with an additional charge for more words (yet another reason that you don't want to write an overly-long news release), though their fax-distribution costs vary depending on what time of day you want to distribute the release. BusinessWire also has a membership that offers you the ability to distribute a corporate profile, a free newsletter, recaps of your news release on headline roundup services, and a certain amount of media monitoring for mention of your news.

BusinessWire offers other services in addition to just distributing news releases. For a fee, you can be added to BusinessWire's "Expert Source" service, which helps connect journalists to experts of the day. If you're continuously generating information that you'd like to send the media—like research, the results of polls, or product information—you'll appreciate the editorial "greenhouse" part of Expert Source. Expert Source allows you to post abstracts of surveys, research, and other story ideas, which are in turn promoted to editors as possible story ideas. If you don't want to keep a press-release archive on the Web, you can keep one on Business Wire with their Electronic Media Kit service. They'll even help you design a Web site.

When Should You Distribute?

You might think the question of when to distribute a press release is kind of an odd question. But when it comes to press releases, not all days are created equal. Mondays seem to have an inordinately high number of press releases, while Fridays are not as busy. Tara doesn't like sending out news releases on Mondays because she doesn't want to get lost in the shuffle of editors catching up on weekend news. She also doesn't like sending releases out on Fridays, because who knows which editors have decided to take a three-day weekend? For the most part she likes to send out press releases in the middle of the week—on Tuesdays, Wednesdays, and Thursdays.

Unless you've got an emergency, don't distribute press releases on the weekend; you'll miss a lot of editors who don't monitor the wire on the weekend.

PR Newswire

http://www.prnewswire.com/

PR Newswire also distributes news releases worldwide, and, like BusinessWire, they offer distribution to specialty media groups and can even create media sites. PR Newswire, like BusinessWire, also offers a variety of fax services, including fax-on-call services and fax distribution. PR Newswire's release headlines are a lot easier to read online, since they're not all stacked up together, as you can see in Figure 17-2.

PR Newswire charges by the number of words in the press release, and of course charges vary depending on how widely you distribute the press release.

BusinessWire and PR Newswire are the two biggest press-release distributors online, and because of this you'll find that you get a lot of "bonus" distribution. Your press release will show up in Northern Light's specialty publications search, Excite's NewsTracker, and the Dow Jones Publications Library. It'll end up on NewsPage and other online newsgathering services. You'll get a lot of extra reach if you use these extremely popular services.

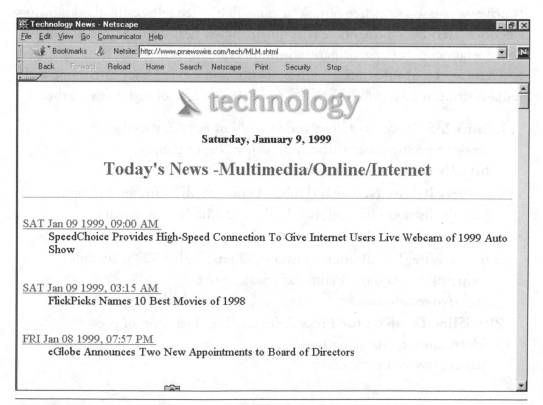

FIGURE 17.2: Reading PR Newswire press releases online

M2 PressWIRE

http://www.presswire.net/

M2 PressWIRE is also a large service, and is distributed on some Web news-gathering services like NewsAlert. However, the news releases they distribute do not appear to be archived on as many Web sites and databases as either BusinessWire or PR Newswire. Unlike PR Newswire and BusinessWire, however, they sell memberships to their newswire. Once you've paid for a membership (currently $160), you can send as many releases using their wire services as you like. You don't pay by the length of release or by to whom you're sending the release. However, the type of data that they will transmit is limited. It seems to be primarily text; they do not offer a photo or logo transmit service, and give no indication that they transmit any other non-text information like audio or video. Further, we also couldn't find a list of where they actually send press releases, and at the time of writing you can't read their press releases on their Web site. They do offer a free service, however—a way to transmit certain kinds of press releases at no cost. If you're launching a new Web site, try this service and see what kind of response you get. You can get the details about the **PressWIRE free service** at http://www.presswire.net/free.htm. You can submit free releases in the following categories: staff appointments, environment news, healthcare or medical news, Web site launches, and participation in shows or conferences.

There are many other press-release distribution services that offer large-scale media distribution. The following list gives you an idea of just a few of them:

Bacon's Info (Bacon's offers a wide variety of publicity tools and services; press-release distribution is just one of them.)
http://www.baconsinfo.com/

The Press Release Network (Dubai, United Arab Emirates. Strengths include distribution to global, India, and Middle East media.)
http://www.pressreleasenetwork.com/

Internet Wire (Distribution to over 6,300 media for $225. Includes archiving for 90 days. Plain-text releases only.)
http://www.gina.com/

PRESSline Database for Press Releases (Free inclusion of press releases in their database.)
http://www.us.pressline.com/

Yahoo!'s Press Release page
http://dir.yahoo.com/Business_
and_Economy/Companies/
News_and_Media/News_
Services/Press_Releases/

"Handmade" Press-Release Distribution

Sometimes, especially with a large potential audience, sending out press releases en masse can be the best way

---

Free Press Releases

Don't feel like spending any money for a press release? Check out http://www.webwire.com/ for free news-release distribution. Note, however, that you'll end up with your news release placed among lots and lots of others. You get what you pay for.

---

of reaching the editors who might be interested in your product or service. But if your audience is smaller, or your product or service very unusual, or you simply want distribution with a more human touch, you might want to check out "Handmade" press-release distributors. These are distributors that specialize in custom delivery of press releases, "opt-in" lists for journalists (that is, e-mail lists that journalists can choose to join, or at least consent to be added to), and specific media targeting.

Xpress Press

http://www.xpresspress.com/

Xpress Press offers an "opt-in" distribution service for journalists who are interested in receiving press releases. Journalists request to be added to the Xpress Press service, and indicate what type of releases they're interested in. When a company wants to distribute a press release via Xpress Press, Xpress Press goes through its database and finds journalists who are appropriate for that news release. In other words, they build a custom list targeted toward the release every time the service is used.

They target pretty well, too. Tara receives research-oriented releases from them, and has been happy with the quality and appropriateness of the materials she has received.

Sending a release via Xpress Press is $225. (They will write the release for you for an additional charge, and there is a $25 charge if they have to type in your release from faxed or mailed copy.) Since they create a custom distribution list for every release that goes out, there's no way to know in advance how many editors will get your release, but Xpress Press does generate a list of the media contacted when the job is done.

If you have an unusual news release or news that defies the typical categories that are available through other distribution services, Xpress Press would be a good resource to investigate.

URLWire

http://www.urlwire.com/

We spoke earlier in this book about building relationships with journalists. It appears that the whole idea behind URLWire is building relationships with journalists full-time. Eric Ward, the guy behind URLWire, will build a distribution list for you from his list of over 6,500 journalist contacts around the world. Like Xpress Press, his is an "opt in" list of journalists who have asked to hear about specific topics.

After building a list, he personalizes between 200-300 press releases, each containing, as his Web page describes it, "content specific for the recipient." This is Cadillac service, and as you might expect comes with a Cadillac price. Ward states on his site that his service runs between $500-$2,000, with an average price for a campaign running about $600. If you really want to go all-out with your promotion, have a very specialized resource, or have an unusual resource that defies categorization, investigate URLWire.

NetPOST

http://www.netpost.com/

Eric Ward also has a service called NetPOST, a similarly detailed and customized service. The difference is that NetPOST is for publicizing your Web site to search engines and subject listings, and isn't for distributing news releases.

Internet Media Fax

http://www.imediafax.com/

Internet Media Fax allows you to select a list of media to whom your press release will be sent by fax. The release will cost you 25 cents per page. For example, if you sent a two-page news release to 50 fax pages, it would cost $25. You have around 30,000 publication listings to choose from, and you can create your own targeted list from several different categories. If you've got a very specialized product or service, which has a minimal number of appropriate publications, you might want to check out this service. Its minimum charge is $25, a lot less than many of the other services listed in this chapter. We'll be looking at this in more detail in Chapter 18.

Targeted Press Releases

Maybe you want to target your releases but you don't need the customization levels of these services. There are some services that target releases without building customized lists. Check out these sites:

BookFlash (Promotes books)
http://www.bookflash.com/

Collegiate Presswire (Distributes to college newspapers)
http://www.cpwire.com/

eworldwire (Can customize by several factors, including category, state, and area code)
http://www.eworldwire.com/

News Bureau (Offers targeted releases in a variety of categories, including food and drink, travel, and sports)
http://www.newsbureau.com/

News Target (Several Internet categories and several vertical-market categories like beverages, farming, and power and energy. They recommend using their service in conjunction with a major wire service.)
http://www.newstarget.com/

Press Flash
http://www.pressflash.com/

PRWeb (Free posting of news releases in dozens of different categories)
http://www.prweb.com/

TechWire (Promotes technology information)
http://www.ezwire.com/

WPRC Press Release Resources (A large directory of press-release and other resources)
http://www.wprc.com/pr/wprcpr.html

Yahoo!—Communications and Media Services
http://dir.yahoo.com/Business_and_Economy/Companies/
Communications_and_Media_Services/

This chapter and the previous two were designed to give you a crash course in media contact: how to find editors, how to contact them, how to make the most of that great power tool e-mail, and finally how to write and distribute press releases.

———————

A lot of the skills you'll gain in the online world will carry over into the offline world as you go about promoting your product and service. In fact, there's a lot of "real world" promotion you can do to give your online concerns—Web sites, newsletters, or what have you—a push. In the next chapter we'll take a look at offline promotion possibilities and why they shouldn't be neglected.

PART V

OUTSIDE THE INTERNET

CHAPTER EIGHTEEN

Real-World Promotions

If you focus too closely on the Internet, you're missing the big picture. Of course everyone assumes that the Internet *is* the big picture. They think that from now on, everything can be done online, so there's no need to worry about the offline world. This attitude doesn't make a lot of sense. The Internet is new, so new that most people aren't using it much, relatively speaking; most people spend far more time reading, watching, or listening to media other than the Internet.

The real world is full of ways to reach millions of people at once—radio, TV, magazines, newspapers. For instance, at the time of writing it looks like one of Peter's books will be mentioned by a business columnist in a syndicated newspaper column going to 50 big cities around the USA. Millions of people read those papers. How many places on the Internet can you reach millions of people at once? Very few, yet there are many such opportunities in the real world.

Experienced Internet marketers know that one of the best ways to get people to visit your Web site is to leave the Internet for a while and go looking for people out in the real world. Surveys of users show that one of the primary ways in which people learn about new Web sites is through the *non*-Internet media. You've noticed the big Internet companies advertising on TV and in national magazines, haven't you? Amazon.com, Excite, CDnow, Goto.com, and a number of others are spending a lot of money to reach people through more traditional media.

The Internet is merely a tool. It has a number of unusual and remarkable characteristics, but these characteristics are not such that the Internet can replace all other tools. So let's consider what you can do *off* the Internet to promote your business enterprise *on* the Internet. Let's start with the simple stuff—your print materials.

DON'T FORGET YOUR PRINT ADS

We've seen dozens of print materials—such as flyers and brochures—from companies that seem ashamed of their Web sites. At least they don't seem to want to tell anyone about the sites. For instance, one small publishing company, selling books and software, has a flyer that explains how to place orders; it provides the full street address, a telephone number, and even a toll-free phone number. But it includes neither an e-mail address nor a Web site URL. Yet the company has both a Web site and an e-mail address. So why isn't that information on the flyer?

One reason might be that the company has a lousy Web site. Perhaps it's a billboard-style Web site—it just sits there in cyberspace, a couple of pages of vague description about the company and its products. It gives no way to order online, and no way even to find much information online. Why isn't the information in the flyer online? Perhaps the Web site isn't mentioned because the company doesn't see how to get any value out of it, and the Web site is there only to catch people who pass by in cyberspace—which it won't, unless people already know where it is. But that doesn't explain why the flyer doesn't at least list the e-mail address.

This sort of thing is still quite common—companies with Web sites and e-mail addresses but no mention of them in their print ads. It's a simple step to include your cyberspace addresses in everything you print—on business cards, in newspaper ads, Yellow Page ads, brochures, flyers, and everything else. If you put your phone number on these things, why not your e-mail address and URL? If your Web site provides value to your customers and prospective clients—if it provides information and customer support, a way to order online, and ancillary services that you've created as a complementary service—then don't hide all this. Let people know about it.

Don't just put your URL in your print ads, though—explain *why* people should visit your site. Mention the services you offer, and give people a reason to come to your site. If you plan to use your Web site as an extension of your business—as a way to reduce order-taking and customer-service costs, for instance—then herd your customers in the right direction. Mention, for example, that your customers can get the latest product information at your site (they can, can't they?). That's important to many people in this instant-gratification world. People want information right away, and your Web site is a way to provide it.

Here's an example of a very simple, yet effective, use of print materials. *Mile High Comics*, a chain of comic stores in Denver, CO, distributes flyers at science fiction conferences. All people need to do is fill in their e-mail addresses and drop the forms in a box; Mile High Comics then adds these people to its mailing list. (Why doesn't Mile High Comics simply provide their e-mail address and tell people to e-mail them to subscribe? Because they know that the more hoops people have to jump through, the less likely they are to do something. It's better to grab someone's e-mail address now on a paper form, than hope that they remember to subscribe when they get home.) This is a very easy thing to do, and something that can be combined with other forms of print advertising, too. For instance, your ads can have a line at the bottom saying: "Sign up for our free e-mail newsletter! E-mail us at signup@yakherding.com."

WEB CARDS

Here's a nice way to promote your Web site in a very visual way; use Web cards. At least two companies on the Internet are selling postcards with pictures of Web sites on them; you provide the URL of the page you want to put on the card, and the text you want to go with it, and these companies will create the cards and mail them to you.

These postcards have a glossy picture of your site on one side, and text on the back—they can look really good, if your Web site is "photogenic" that is. You can get free samples at these sites:

Web Card Press
  http://www.webcardpress.com/
Web Cards
  http://www.printing.com/

You can use these in all sorts of ways. Mail them to people as postcards; insert them in information you are mailing to existing clients, so you can be absolutely sure they know about your Web site; pin them up on billboards; pass them out at tradeshows; and so on. At Web Card Press you can actually design the card online. You get to pick the font, type a message, and specify how the card should be laid out. You'll see a picture of a card online, with your Web site on the card ... at least you will if the system's working properly, though sometimes it's not.

One caveat: if you need a large number of cards printed, you may find it cheaper to work with a full-service printer; there are a number that specialize in creating full-color postcards, and can probably do your job more cheaply. But in smaller quantities you may not be able to beat Web Card Press or Web Cards.

These companies are starting to produce other printed products with Web-site images, too, such as greeting cards and business cards.

PLAIN OLD BUSINESS CARDS

You don't have to spend a lot of money to promote with cards. You can even use plain old business cards. Our friend Randy Cassingham, publisher of **This is True** (http://www.ThisIsTrue.com/), has simple printed cards that he gives away in mass quantities. *This is True* is an e-mail newsletter with around 160,000 subscribers. It contains weird but true stories gleaned from the news wires.

Randy had a few simple business cards printed up at a CopyMax (a print shop inside the larger Office Max stores). These are the thermographic (raised letter) cards, so they look good. He's managed to hand out around 5,000 in the last 18 months or so. They cost $50 for 2,000, so that's still only $125 worth. Just *how* does one get rid of that many so quickly? Well, Randy sells books to his subscribers, compilations of the This Is True stories that many subscribers buy as Christmas and birthday presents. "The cards go out with all the books," he says. "I leave them around, I put them in with the check when I pay bills (THEY give ME bill stuffers!), my family and friends hand them out, etc." The most important distribution method, he says, is sending them out with books: "People who buy books have already said (with their Visa card) that they like the stuff, so I give them something to help spread the word!"

MAIL AND FAX PRESS RELEASES

Most publications are "online" to some degree. Most journalists have e-mail addresses these days. But the problem with e-mail is *e-mail overload*. We're reaching the stage where people ignore a huge proportion of their e-mail, because they simply don't have time to deal with it all. That doesn't mean trying to contact someone by e-mail is a waste of time, but it does mean that you may want to supplement e-mail contact with mail and fax. Also, as all good marketers know, hitting someone with your story from multiple directions can often help push your story to the front.

In Chapters 16 and 17 we discussed how to send out press releases across the Internet. You can also find help on the Internet for sending out real-world press releases. Peter recently sent out a release about one of his company's books (*The CDnow Story: Rags to Riches on the Internet*) to 344 journalists via fax, for a total cost of $86; that included the cost of the list of fax numbers and the faxing process. Within a few hours of transmission, he got his first response. *Board-watch Magazine*, a well-known and well-respected magazine devoted to the online world, planned to run a story about the book.

One of the most convenient methods for sending out fax press releases is **ImediaFax** (http://www.imediafax.com/). This is a great little system. You begin by picking the type of media you want to fax to—newspapers, magazines, and broadcast media—and how you want to select the contacts: by industry, editor, classification, media name, state, metro market, or circulation. For instance, you might choose to contact magazine editors. You would first choose which types of magazines you're interested in (Advertising, Banking, Jewelry, Law, and so on). Then you'd select the type of editors you want to contact at each magazine—the Book Review editors, the Feature editors, the New Product Review editors, and so on. You can even see a list of the magazines that ImediaFax has found for you, and omit certain magazines from the list.

In this manner you can drill down the list until you've made your selections according to various criteria, and omitted the contacts you're not interested in, until you end up with your final list. You can now choose to send a press release by fax, or you can get all the names in a text file so you can import them into a database and send a press release by mail. This really is a great way to build a contact list very quickly and get the press releases sent out in a matter of hours. And at 25 cents a page it can be very affordable. You could also set up your own fax system, of course, using your computer or a broadcast fax machine. At around a minute per page, you could probably fax out the releases for nine cents each, perhaps less.

You might also want to send press releases by snail mail (that's Internet jargon for the post office), though this can get a little expensive and time consuming—around 45 cents per press release, plus plenty of folding and stuffing. Many of the directories and listings we mentioned in Chapters 16 and 17 also include snail-mail addresses. In particular, the **U.S. All Media E-Mail Directory** from Direct Contact Publishing (the same people who own ImediaFax—http://www.owt.com/dircon/) contains street addresses as well as e-mail addresses; Bradley Communication's Publicity Blitz contains almost 20,000 street addresses at a very good price; and the **Gebbie Press** directories (http://www.gebbieinc.com/) are also a good value. **Para Publishing** (http://www.parapublishing.com/) sells mailing-label-formatted lists of a wide variety of different media contacts: 7 trucking magazines, 67 travel writers, 1,857 newspapers, and so on.

ARE FOLLOW-UPS ESSENTIAL?

Many PR people will tell you that follow-ups are essential; in other words, after mailing something out, you should call. There's no doubt that follow-ups can make your marketing campaign much more effective. Calling journalists and trying to keep your products and services in their minds can make a big difference. But it's still possible to carry out an effective PR campaign with a pretty low level of follow-up. PR guru Marcia Yudkin believes that follow-up calls are not necessary, that it's quite possible to market your products without follow-up calls, though "if you're especially effective on the phone and have the time, follow-up calls might be worth a try." The problem for many small-business people is finding the time, and you may find it a more effective use of your time and money—which, you'll remember, are much the same thing—to send out a follow-up press release, or the same press release to another couple of thousand contacts, than to call and talk with people. You should probably limit calls to just high-profile publications, the sort of places that will give you a large payback if they do run your story.

ANOTHER FORM OF CYBERSPACE—RADIO

Cyberspace really began around 150 years ago with Samuel Morse's first telegraph transmission in 1844. After all, that was the beginning of electronic communications, crude as it may have been. Since then we've seen the development of a variety of electronic forms of communication—systems that create "an imaginary space where electronic communications take place," as cyberspace is sometimes defined. These include telephones, television, radio, computer bulletin board systems, the online services, and the Internet.

There's one area of cyberspace with a truly enormous number of "users," an area that's very cheap and easy to use for the marketing of products: radio. There are almost 12,000 radio stations in the U.S., and hundreds of different talk shows playing on these stations or syndicated to multiple stations.

One way to promote your site is to promote yourself as a talk-show guest. If you've got something worth saying, you can easily get on a radio talk show. As Joe Sabah, author of *How to Get on Radio Talk Shows All Across America*, points out, radio talk shows need guests. As an example, his book discusses a radio station in Pittsburgh, PA, which has five hosts, each with an average of about 65 guests a month—or almost 4,000 guests a year.

People buy products they hear mentioned on talk radio; Joe Sabah has been on well over 600 talk shows and has sold more than $330,000 worth of the books he promotes on those shows. TV shows are even more productive; popular TV talk shows can launch best-sellers and celebrity careers.

Radio is a relatively efficient way to get the word out about your Web site. You generally don't have to go anywhere; you do the show at home or your office using the telephone. And you can track down the talk shows through a variety of radio-show databases. You may be able to build your own using the Web sites I mentioned earlier, or you can buy one. Joe Sabah (talkshows@aol.com, 303-

722-8288) sells a database of 700 talk shows, along with his book, for around $99. Bradley Communication's Publicity Blitz database includes thousands of radio stations and talk shows, as do the Gebbie Press directories. Peter used some of these directories and e-mailed hundreds of radio stations asking for an invitation, and indeed did scores of radio shows, some big, some small.

You could also use some of the media-interview services discussed in Chapter 16: **GuestFinder** (http://www.guestfinder.com/), **Radio Tour** (http://www.radiotour.com/), **Great Guests** (http://www.PublicityCity.com/), and **Radio-TV Interview Report**. And here's yet another of these services: **HotTopics** (http://www.bookpromotions.com/hottopic.htm).

ADVERTORIALS

Do you know the term *advertorial*? It refers to a newspaper ad that is camouflaged as an article. Many papers carry advertorials—it's a way for a newspaper to fill space, with what appears to be editorial content, at a very low cost. Free, actually. Here's how this all works.

Companies pushing their products pay an advertorial company to carry an article for them. The company may provide the text, or it may pay more and have the advertorial company write the article for it. Either way, the text has to read like a newspaper article rather than an ad. The advertorial company then lays out the article to look just like a newspaper article, and prints it along with scores of other advertorials in a large newspaper-like publication, which they send to thousands of newspapers.

The newspapers receive this for free, and can run the articles for free; the advertorial companies make their money from the companies providing the articles. Now, there's a bit of a gamble involved here. If you create an article that newspapers are interested in, it may be run in many newspapers across North America. If you don't … then it won't. On the other hand, advertorial companies often have guarantees. Metro Creative Graphics, for instance, will re-run your article, perhaps even with changes, if it doesn't appear in at least 100 papers. (Note, however, that they assume that for every newspaper clipping they find, they've missed three, so they are actually guaranteeing to send you 25 newspaper clippings of your article.) These services are not cheap, though—you can easily spend $2,000 or $3,000 or more.

Will advertorials work for you? That's hard to say. It depends on the product you're writing about, the quality of the article, whether the article is suitable for the time of year, and so on. Peter's experience was mixed; he created an advertorial for *Poor Richard's Web Site*, and although it did appear in dozens of small papers around the country, he's not really sure how much business he received from it. On the other hand, there are a number of companies that swear by advertorials—a publisher of books about antiques, and another publisher selling books about real estate, use advertorials very effectively.

If you'd like to look into this form of publicity, contact these companies:

Metro Creative Graphics
   http://metrocreativegraphics.com/

News USA
   http://newsusa.com/

Family Features Editorial Services (specializes in the food and
   lifestyle sections of newspapers)
   http://www.culinary.net/

MORE THAN WE CAN COVER

Of course there's far more to learn about real-world marketing and promotions than we can cover here. There have been tens of millions of words written about real-world, low-cost marketing, so we suggest you get out and read a few good marketing books, and then consider how to use the ideas online, and how to use the ideas offline to promote your products online.

Here are a few books to get you started:

- *Guerrilla Marketing,* by Jay Conrad Levinson, who has written about a zillion Guerrilla Marketing books: Guerrilla Marketing, Guerrilla Marketing Attack, Guerrilla Marketing Excellence, Guerrilla Marketing Online, and so on. They're well known and well respected.

- *Six Steps to Free Publicity*, by Marcia Yudkin, Plume/Penguin. From a well-known publicity guru.

- *1001 Ways To Market Your Books*, by John Kremer, Open Horizons (http://www.bookmarket.com/). You may not be publishing books, but nonetheless this is a great primer on marketing. Kremer comes up with many ideas that can be applied to all sorts of products. Flick through this book at a bookstore and see if you can apply any suggestions to your situation … then buy the book.

- *Marketing Without Megabucks*, by Shel Horowitz. The subtitle is *How to Sell Anything on a Shoestring*, and the book explains just that.

CHAPTER NINETEEN

Sales Basics—Not *All* the Rules Have Changed

The Internet has provided a remarkable impetus to new businesses. Thanks to media hype, and the fact that in many ways the Internet really does provide a new sales channel that makes it easier to reach customers, a lot of people with little or no business experience (and even less sales and marketing experience) have started new enterprises.

Under the misapprehension that "the rules have changed," and that the Internet means "nothing will be the same again," these people are attempting to sell products online without understanding the first thing about sales. There's a slight arrogance here, too. Many people with more technical skills than business skills think that their time has come, that "sales" skills are no longer necessary, that technology is now king.

Technology is just a tool, though. Human nature remains the same as it was before 1994, so although the manner in which you can reach people has changed, all the basic principles of sales remain the same. What are those principles? That's what we're going to touch on in this chapter.

Peter learned these sales techniques the hard way—selling encyclopedias door to door (back in the days when encyclopedias were books rather than plastic disks). He also sold telecommunications equipment, photographic business cards, and burglar alarms. Later he sold his technical-writing services. And today, as publisher of Top Floor Publishing, he's back selling books again (though not door to door).

So to save you some time (and some shoe leather), here's a primer in sales, the basic techniques you need to understand if you want to succeed in selling your products and services.

IT'S A NUMBERS GAME

Marketing and sales are not easy; the work just never ends. Inexperienced marketers don't realize how much work it takes to promote a product. Furthermore, they often equate sales leads with sales. (A *lead*, in sales terminology, is a contact with a *prospect*, someone you believe may become a customer.) They get excited when they make contact with prospects, and excited when they feel that they are close to making a sale. Having made a contact, they often slack off a little; they take a rest while they wait for the inevitable sale. What they don't realize is that there's "many a slip twixt cup and lip." Most leads will not turn into sales, however close the sale may appear. You need many, many leads.

This is a double-edged sword. Understand the numbers and you can see the road to success. As sales people in training are told many times, the real secret to success in the sales business is not sneakiness or smooth talking; it's hard work. You must make contact with prospects over and over again. Sales really is a numbers game, and once you know the numbers you can plan what it takes to meet your goals.

On the Internet, making contact is relatively easy. But the ratio of contacts to sales is even worse than in the real world. You may have to make contact with 100 people in order to make a sale, and may need to get your message in front of 10,000 people in order to find those 100.

Salespeople "don't get no respect" among the general public. Most people have the idea that the truly successful salesperson is somehow too slick for his own good. In fact, many of the really top sales people are not like this at all; their secret is that they are very persistent and work very hard. Sales is quite simple— the more leads you get, the more prospective clients you contact, the more sales you'll make! You may have heard Woody Allen's claim that "80 percent of success is turning up." Eighty percent of sales success is turning up ... again, and again, and again.

BELIEVE IN YOUR PRODUCT

If you don't believe in your product, how can you sell it? You can't; at least, you can't do so very well. If you sell a product that you know is not very good, you'll do so only halfheartedly. You'll never really be able to push the product hard, because in the back of your mind there'll be a little voice saying, "well, that's not *quite* true, now, is it?"

It sometimes seems that the Internet has turned into a vast get-rich-quick seminar. We receive scores of get-rich-schemes in our e-mail inboxes every day. Most of these schemes are based on this basic principle: "Here's this great product you can buy from us; you can then sell it to other people, and you'll make a fortune." Of course in most cases the touted product is not very good (if it even exists at all). Nonetheless, thousands of people are signing up to sell these products, and most will ultimately fail. One major reason for their failure is that it's hard to sell bad products. It's hard because people don't *want* bad products, and it's hard because you won't be able to put all your energy into a product you don't believe in.

If you know your product is good, you'll feel comfortable trying to convince people to buy it. And you'll be able to handle the rejection that's an occupational hazard of any sales or marketing job.

LEARN TO HANDLE REJECTION

If sales is a numbers game, with far more losses than wins, then it follows that you're going to experience a lot of rejection. Most people who go into sales cannot handle this, and eventually leave the profession. A salesperson spending all day on the phone, or all day knocking on doors, experiences a huge number of rejections. Until you've done this sort of job you can't imagine the effect it has on you—being told *No*, over and over, scores or hundreds of times a day.

Luckily for you, selling products on the Web is not the same. You're not going to experience the same type of personal rejection. But your product will be rejected, far more often than it's accepted. And that can be depressing. You'll see from your logs, for instance, that 300 people arrived at your site today ... yet you only sold three or four products. *What's wrong*, you want to know; *why did all those people turn you down?*

Successful salespeople understand that rejection is all part of the numbers game, so they don't let it get them down. They know that if, on average, 99 people out of 100 are going to reject their product, then all they have to do is find 100 people in order to make a sale. The cup isn't half empty; it's half full (or, perhaps more accurately, the cup isn't 99 percent empty, it's one percent full). Rejection is no longer something to be feared, but something to be accepted as a normal part of the sales and marketing process.

TELL PROSPECTS WHAT YOU WANT THEM TO DO

Here's another principle that sales trainers drum into their students over and over again—you've got to *ask for the sale!* This principle was put into verse by Elizabethan poet Robert Herrick over 300 years ago:

> *To get thine ends, lay bashfulness aside*
> *Who fears to ask, doth teach to be denied*

Herrick was actually talking about seduction, but the principle is the same. Herrick knew that in order to be successful in sexual conquests, one has to—at the right moment—make a move and ask the "prospect" to buy in to what one is "selling." If you're too bashful to ask, what will happen? The prospect may be unsure, though ready to be swayed—but if you don't ask, the prospect isn't going to buy. Worse, someone else may ask the prospect first.

You have to tell prospects what you want them to do. Don't simply provide information and hope that people at your Web site will make the "obvious" choice. Don't write ads that present your products and then just hope that people will know what to do. You have to *tell them*. Tell them to click here, tell them to visit right away to find out about the special offer, tell them to order right now!

GIVE A GUARANTEE

Don't be afraid to give a guarantee, and a good one at that. Remember that it's very easy to set up store on the Web, and many people are understandably nervous about doing businesses with companies they've never heard of before; if anyone can set up a Web store with minimal expense, how can one be sure they're "for real?"

How can you convince prospects that doing business with you is safe? Even if they're fairly sure that you will ship what you're selling, they may not be sure that what you're selling is worth having. How can you convince them that it's safe to order from you?

Web-site owners should look at the way direct-marketing companies—mail-order companies—have handled this issue. (These companies have been dealing with similar problems for a hundred years, after all.) They clearly state their guarantee, often several times. And the guarantee is usually a more than generous one, typically a 100 percent guarantee for a year. To inexperienced marketers this type of guarantee is somewhat frightening. They envision their products flooding back to them 11 months after they've sold them. But the secret is that if you have a good product, and you're selling at a fair price, very few of your products will ever be returned to you, probably a small fraction of one percent. (Less than 0.3 percent of the books Peter's sold across his Web site have been returned.)

The guarantee can be a real encouragement to buy. You're saying, in effect, "go ahead, even if you're not sure you want this product ... you can always return it." Once the product is in their hands, another sales technique takes over, something known in the sales business as the "puppy dog close." Once a buyer has a product in his possession, he's unlikely to return it. Imagine a family with children, shopping for a puppy. They find a small dog the kids seem to like ...

but they're not quite sure they want to buy. "Take the puppy home tonight," says the store owner. "If you change your mind you can always bring the puppy back tomorrow." Will the dog ever be returned? Not likely. And the same is true of your products. Despite the guarantee, buyers will almost never return a product. (On the other hand, if your products are garbage ... then that's another story.)

THE SALES MESSAGE—IT'S AN ART

Writing sales messages presents two problems to most people. They often can't write very well to begin with. And writing a sales message is more difficult than writing, say, a simple business letter. You're trying to persuade someone to do something for you, and that's not easy. Writing a sales message is an art. In order to learn this art, you have to change your mindset a little. It's worth reading a few books on this subject. You might look at *Cash Copy*, for instance, by Dr. Jeffrey Lant (ISBN: 0940374234). This book is sold mainly by mail order, and though bookstores can order it for you, it may take a while to get. (If you search for the words *cash copy* at http://www.AltaVista.com/, though, you'll find a number of places selling it so you can get it more quickly.) This is an excellent introduction to writing sales pieces. In the meantime, consider the following points.

Benefits, Not Features

"Nobody wants a quarter-inch drill," the sales maxim goes, "they want a quarter-inch hole." A subtle, yet important difference. When you're selling a product, think about what benefit the buyer will gain. You'll often see Internet companies blaring various technical details about their products—in particular, it seems, companies selling computer products, hardware and software, seem to have no idea of this concept. They focus on all the little intricacies of their products, forgetting that nobody cares ... they want to know what the product actually does for them.

When you're writing sales pieces—e-mail ads, sales information at your Web site, even banner ads in which you have only a few words worth of space to work with—you must remember this concept. Try to forget about the technical details, and focus on what your product actually *does*.

Forget Your Own Concerns—Consider the Client's

Here's another mistake often made by inexperienced marketers. They are unable to put themselves in their clients' shoes. They always look at the product from their own point of view, from the point of view of their own company. This, of course, is similar to focusing on features rather than benefits. We discussed this concept earlier, when explaining that your Web site must serve your visitors in some way. Step into your prospects' shoes, and think about what they want. Forget what *you* want to achieve, and think instead about how you can help your clients achieve what *they* want. If you can't do this, you can't write effective sales pieces.

Cut the Jargon—Write Simply

Yet another problem for many people on the Internet: they often find it difficult to write simply and directly. They're too wrapped up in the jargon of their business and the jargon of the Internet. Sometimes that's okay. If you're sure the people you're selling to are as fully conversant with the jargon as you are, then you might get away with it. But why risk it? Why write using jargon when it's quite possible to write in plain English and be understood by far more people?

Do not overestimate the knowledge of your prospects, especially Internet and computer knowledge. The personal computer may have been around 25 years, and if you believe the media then everyone and his dog uses the Internet day in and day out. But the fact is that most people are fumbling around with technology they don't really understand. If you throw too much computer and Internet jargon into your sales messages, you'll just confuse most people.

Bring Objections into the Open

An important technique taught to salespeople—and one that can be used, very carefully, when writing sales pieces—is to bring objections into the open. (By *objections* we mean reasons that a prospective client may have for not wanting to buy from you.)

Let's say that your product has an inherent problem, one that prospects are likely to be concerned about and see quite clearly. You could ignore the problem, of course, and hope the prospect doesn't think too much about it. But he will. On the other hand, you can bring the objection out into the open, deal with it, and move on.

For instance, let's say you're selling kites. And let's say that it's clear that your kites are a little on the expensive side, and that you often hear objections from people about the price. It's clear that price is holding people back from buying. You could write a sales piece that doesn't mention price until the end, when you ask for the sale. Or you can start talking about the price early on. You point out that this kite isn't for everyone, that this isn't some toy store kite selling for five bucks. No, the customer's paying for quality here, one of the world's best kites, a real work of art … and that doesn't come cheap.

Don't try to hide problems and avoid objections that you know are going to arise anyway. Deal with them head on and early on, and perhaps even turn them into advantages.

Everything's a Sales Piece

Don't forget that when you're selling, everything's a sales piece. Every bit of business communication, everything that carries a message from you to prospective clients, can carry information that may help sell your products. That's not to say that you have to turn every communication into a long sales pitch, that you have to beat people over the head with your sales message. But think of little ways in which you can reach people. The signature block in your e-mail message can be used to carry a sales message, a sidebar or a copyright footer in your Web pages, your business cards, your search-engine listings … all these can be little sales messages.

FIND A WAY TO STAY IN TOUCH

Finding prospects and getting sales is a lot of hard work. But you can make it a little easier by finding a way to stay in touch. Just because you can't convert a prospect to a buyer today, doesn't mean you can't do so next week or next month. And if someone buys from you today, he might do so again later if you present him with something else he'd be interested in.

The Internet provides an easy way to keep in touch with people—e-mail. Try to persuade visitors to give you their e-mail addresses. Sign them up for new-product bulletins and newsletters, for instance. Keeping in touch with them costs a fraction of the price of real-world mailings, so it's a big mistake not to tap into this potential market.

READ A FEW SALES BOOKS

What are most new Internet marketers reading? They're reading mostly geek stuff. Sure, they read a few books about Internet marketing like this one. But they also read books on setting up Web sites, on creating Web pages, on HTML and Web design, on Internet basics. All of this reading is okay, but it's like an auto mechanic spending all his time learning about how to use his tools, and little or no time learning about how to fix cars.

Read a few books about selling. Take a trip to your local bookstore, or browse through the categories in an online bookstore and see what you can find. There's no lack of books on the subject, so pick one or two best-sellers and read them. Learn a little about the mail-order business, too—about the methods used to convert catalog recipients to buyers, for instance. As we've mentioned elsewhere in this book, Web sites have a lot in common with mail-order catalogs. In many ways they are closer to catalogs than to stores, in fact.

Yes, yes, you may find the idea of all this rather distasteful. Salespeople are regarded as the lowest of the low, barely a notch or two above politicians. But if you're reading this book, then we can be fairly sure you're trying to sell something. It may be your products and services, or perhaps your ideas and beliefs. Whatever you're up to on the Internet, if you're trying to convince people to take some kind of action, then you're *in the sales business!* Learn about the business, not just the tools. When you fully understand the principles, you'll be able to use the tools to put the principles into action.

Index

THE CDNOW STORY: RAGS TO RICHES ON THE INTERNET

How Twin Brothers in a Basement Built an Internet Success

Early in 1994 twin brothers Jason and Matthew Olim began creating CDnow, an Internet music store. Working in their parent's basement, on a shoe-string budget, they competed against Fortune 500 companies with tens of millions of dollars to spend ... and won. In 1997 CDnow earned almost three times as much as its nearest rival, and owned one third of the online music business. From first-month revenues of $387 in August of 1994, the company grew to sales of $16.4 million in 1997, and industry analysts predict 1998 revenues of $60 million.

How did two kids barely out of college, with no business or retail experience, build one of the world's largest Internet stores? By focusing on a single purpose—building a better music store. *The CDnow Story* explains how they did it: what they did right and what they did wrong. Jason Olim describes how he and his brother began by creating a store that had no shelves and no stock—customers buy CDs online and the Olims pass the orders on to a distributor. He explains how they brought people to their Web site and compares their strategies with their competitors, explaining why they came out on top.

With Internet commerce growing at a tremendous pace, many companies are floundering in cyberspace. Millions of dollars have been lost on ill-conceived and poorly executed online projects. Unlimited budgets are no guarantee of success, but CDnow has shown that shoe-string operations *can* succeed. Let the Olims, founders of one of the most successful companies in cyberspace, teach you how to compete online.

Twin brothers Jason and Matthew Olim are the founders of CDnow, the world's largest online music store. Peter Kent is the author of 36 computer and business books, including *Poor Richard's Web Site* (also from Top Floor Publishing), and the best selling *Complete Idiot's Guide to the Internet* (Que).

**The CDnow Story:
Rags to Riches on the Internet**
is available in bookstores both online and offline, and at http://TopFloor.com/
by Jason Olim, with Matthew Olim and Peter Kent   ISBN: 0-9661032-6-2

MP3 AND THE DIGITAL MUSIC REVOLUTION:

Turn Your PC into a CD-Quality Digital Jukebox!

Hundreds of thousands of computer users around the world are discovering new ways to play and manage music—through their computers. Music is software, and computers are being used to play and manipulate it. Using the new MP3 format, computers can store CD-quality music in 1MB/minute files. Along with the music, the computer files can also store album art, recording-artist bios, notes, and even the songs' lyrics.

With the tools on the included disk, PC users can play music on their computers—if they have good sound cards and speakers, it will sound as good as a CD. They can copy music from their CDs—or tapes and vinyl—and save it on their computers. With a low-cost cable they can connect their computers to their audio systems, integrating the two systems. They can create playlists, selecting tracks from different CDs. Having a party? Create an 8-hour playlist, start playing at the beginning of the party, and the computer will handle the rest.

Digital music is portable, too. Users will learn how to create customized tapes—cassettes and DAT—from their music collection, and even how to cut their own music CDs. And they'll hear about the new MP3 players, products with no moving parts that allow you to carry your music with you wherever you go. This book explains the entire process, from installing the enclosed software to cutting CDs. Readers will learn how to shift their music from one media to another with ease, and even how to find public domain and "freeware" music on the Internet. Band members will learn how to use the new music formats to promote their bands by releasing music on the Internet.

POOR RICHARD'S EMAIL PUBLISHING

Creating Newsletters, Bulletins, Discussion Groups and Other Powerful Communications Tools

E-mail publishing is booming—it's growing faster than the World Wide Web. Publishing newsletters, bulletins, and announcements, and running mailing-list discussion groups is a powerful way to promote a product or service ... it's also a cheap and relatively low-tech tool.

E-mail publishing can also be a simple one-person business. Newsletters such as *This is True* and *Joke of the Day* have subscription lists well over 100,000 people, in over a hundred countries around the world, yet are run by individuals working on their own or even part time. These entrepreneurs are using their e-mail newsletters to generate a comfortable income in advertising sales and ancillary product sales.

You can learn everything you need to know about e-mail publishing the way these people did: the hard way, by trial and error. Or you can read *Poor Richard's Email Publishing* for geek-free commonsense advice on how to publish using e-mail. Written by a successful e-mail newsletter publisher, *Poor Richard's Email Publishing* will explain how to host a simple newsletter or mailing list using a free or low-cost e-mail program; how to find people to sign up for your service; how to write an e-mail message so that it won't get messed up enroute to the subscribers; how

to find articles and information; how to find an e-mail publishing service when your list grows too large; and plenty more.

You'll even find out how to sell advertising, in both newsletters and discussion groups. You'll also learn how to host a mailing list discussion group. Hundreds of thousands of discussion groups are run through the Internet's e-mail system. You'll find out how to moderate a list; how to encourage people to join; how to use the list to promote a product without alienating members of discussion groups; how to find advertisers; how to price your ads, the different types of ads; etc.

If you want to get in on the fastest growing area of Internet communications ... you need *Poor Richard's Email Publishing!*

Poor Richard's Email Publishing
is available in bookstores both online and offline, and at http://TopFloor.com/
AVAILABLE JUNE 1999
by Chris Pirillo   ISBN: 0-9661032-5-4

POOR RICHARD'S WEB SITE:

Geek-Free, Commonsense Advice on Building a Low-Cost Web Site

Poor Richard's Web Site is the *only* book that explains the entire process of creating a Web site, from deciding whether you really need a site—and what you can do with it—through picking a place to put the site, creating the site, and bringing people to the site. It is full of commensense advice that Amazon.com called an "antidote to this swirl of confusion" and "straightforward information." Praised by *BYTE magazine, Publisher's Weekly,* and *USA Today, Poor Richard's Web Site* can save you thousands of dollars and hundreds of hours.

❝**Poor Richard's Good Advice.** With all great new things comes a proliferation of hucksters and snake-oil salesmen, and the Internet is no exception. The antidote to this swirl of confusion lies in Peter Kent's *Poor Richard's Web Site.* The analogy to Ben Franklin's volume is appropriate: the book is filled with the kind of straightforward information the Founding Father himself would have appreciated."

—Jennifer Buckendorff

⌂ **amazon**.com

❝We highly recommend this book."
—Peter Cook & Scott Manning
Philadelphia Inquirer

❝We highly recommend that you get a copy."
—*Marketing Technology*

❝Very well written."
—*Library Journal*

❝Buy This Book! … The lessons of just the first three chapters, alone, saved us thousands of dollars and many hours of work."
—David Garvey
The New England Nonprofit Quarterly

❝I've found a great book that explains it all—Poor Richard's Web Site. This is a practical, no-nonsense guide that lucidly covers topics like how to set up a domain with the InterNIC, how to promote your Web site and how to actually use all those features that hosting services provide."
—David Methvin

Poor Richard's Web Site
is available in bookstores both online and offline, and at http://PoorRichard.com/

Poor Richard's Web Site:
Geek-Free, Commonsense Advice on Building a Low-Cost Web Site
by Peter Kent   ISBN: 0-9661032-8-9

FREE INFORMATION ABOUT SETTING UP A WEB SITE

http://PoorRichard.com/

If you are setting up a Web site, or just thinking about doing so, visit http://PoorRichard.com/, the site associated with *Poor Richard's Web Site: Geek-Free, Commonsense Advice on Building a Low-Cost Web Site*. You'll find free information of all kinds: special reports on various subjects—such as a directory of over 75 shopping-cart programs and services, and a list of places to register e-mail newsletters—links to hundreds of Web sites with services that will help you set up and promote your site, several chapters from the book, and more.

Also, sign up for the free e-mail newsletter, *Poor Richard's Web Site News*. With 12,000 subscribers in over 80 countries, this is one of the most respected newsletters on the subject.

You can read back issues and subscribe to the newsletter at http://PoorRichard.com/newsltr/, or to subscribe by e-mail, send an e-mail message to subpr@PoorRichard.com.

The Main Page: http://PoorRichard.com/

The Newsletter: http://PoorRichard.com/newsltr/

E-mail Subscriptions: send a blank e-mail message to subpr@PoorRichard.com

☞ *(continued from the back cover) ...*

There's plenty of advice floating around these days about how to set up business and carry out promotions online. Unfortunately, much of it is just plain wrong. For example, you may have heard that setting up in an Internet mall is a good idea. In general it's not. You may have been told that banner advertising is a great way to bring people to your site. It may be, but it probably isn't. (In Chapter 12 you'll learn a simple rule of thumb to figure out if it's likely to work for you).

Poor Richard's Internet Marketing and Promotions provides techniques that really do work—techniques the authors have actually *used* successfully. For instance, Peter Kent has used low-cost e-mail newsletter advertising (no, not spam!), to attract people to his site, affordably and effectively. (You'll learn how to do it yourself in Chapter 12.) Tara Calishain has used press releases "over the wires" very successfully—a $75 press release, if written well and properly targeted, can buy the equivalent of tens of thousands of dollars of advertising. (Check out Chapter 17 to try it for yourself.)

In *Poor Richard's Internet Marketing and Promotions* you'll learn:

- How to prepare your Web pages to make sure they're properly registered in the search sites
- Where else you should be registering your site, and why search sites probably *won't* send a flood of traffic your way
- Why banner advertising is a good way to lose money, and how to test it without spending too much
- How to create an e-mail newsletter, using your own e-mail program, a free service, or a high-powered newsletter server
- Why affiliate programs are a great way to promote your products, and how to set up a low-cost affiliate system

These are not expensive systems that only large companies can use. The techniques in this book can be used by anyone, including individuals and small companies on tight budgets. Many of the techniques are free grassroots techniques that take time, not money. Others are very low-cost procedures that are well within the budget of most people.

More importantly, these techniques have been used in the real world. Top Floor Publishing, publisher of this book, is a small company founded by best-selling author Peter Kent. Without the clout and budget of a large publisher, Peter Kent was able to use these techniques to push *Poor Richard's Web Site*, the first book in this series, onto the Internet Business